Time out of Time

TIME OUT OF TIME
Essays on the Festival

Edited by Alessandro Falassi

University of New Mexico Press
Albuquerque

"Pamplona in July" from *By-Line: Ernest Hem-ingway* edited by William White is reprinted by permission of Charles Scribner's Sons. Copyright © 1967 Mary Hemingway. (Originally appeared in The Toronto Star.)

Library of Congress Cataloging-in-Publication Data

Time out of time.

  1. Festivals. I. Falassi, Alessandro.
GT3930.T56 1987   394.2'6   86-30804
ISBN 0-8263-0932-1
ISBN 0-8263-0933-X (pbk.)

Contents

Preface

Time out of Time is a collection of essays on festivals chosen from different historical periods and geographical areas and examined by authors applying different methodologies and various theoretical perspectives.

Presenting a series of articles that adequately covered the festivities of all continents would have required several volumes. Although the festivals included here take place in Europe, North and South America, Africa, Asia, and Oceania, the criterion of selection was not geographic. I have included some festivals on the basis of their established fame among social scientists and laymen, such as the Carnival of Rio de Janeiro, the Palio of Siena, the Fiesta of Pamplona, and the North American rodeo. Others were included on the basis of their representativity, because they present social patterns (i.e., religious devotion, social protest) or structural features (i.e., symbolic inversion) particularly relevant for the theoretical discussion and study of festivals that have been renewed during the last decade. A group of articles is focused on such theoretical issues instead of specific festivals, covering terminology, definition, classification, symbology, structural patterns, and semiotic features. The interested reader will also be able to take good advantage of the bibliographic notes at the end of each contribution, which provide useful insights into the specific issues and festivals discussed. Similarly, the extended bibliographic notes to the introduction should provide adequate leads into all current trends in the study of festivals.

The book includes mainly original materials, provided by recognized area and genre specialists. I have limited the reprints to a very few articles, usually overlooked by specialists, which I believe are especially worthy of renewed attention. They are three classic literary accounts (Goethe's, Hemingway's, and Huxley's), plus two articles (Thiers's and Eberhard's) not easily available. As for the four translations of articles not available in English, two are little-known pieces by seminal authors, Arnold van Gennep and Vladimir Propp; the other two, by Maurice Coyaud and Marianne Mesnil, are considered standard reference points by European specialists.

The first section of the book deals with the literary versus the scientific approach to festive events and presents portraits by outstanding literary figures and social scientists on the festivals they visited. Their different training and outlook result in different styles of writing: brilliant and emotional, intrigued and baffled, detached and matter-of-fact. The posthumous piece by Victor Turner is exemplary. Both rigorously scientific and enthusiastically participatory, it shows how theoretical concerns may give the spectator not only understanding, but also enjoyment of a festival.

The second section deals with continuity and change, and discusses the series of theoretical and practical issues that arise when centuries-old festivals encounter emerging cultures, ethnic groups, or ruling powers—or when new festivals get established in opposition to, or against the backdrop of, older and established historical contexts.

The third section presents theoretical articles particularly significant for the poststructuralist trends in the social sciences of the last decade. Poetics, rhetoric, semantics, and semiotics are applied to the study of festival. These pieces are pioneering attempts at clarifying the nomenclature of festive events, the historical meaning of their spatial and temporal frames, or the classification of all festivals of a given culture. Some are in-depth studies of a single distinctive feature of festival, such as the mask or the pageant. This section shows innovative approaches—their outlook, theoretical possibilities, and difficulties—that already have yielded important preliminary results.

The fourth section presents a substantial group of what could be termed classic ethnographic reports. Festivals are presented against their ethnographic background and with detailed accounts of their constitutive events, to show how they treat themes central in their culture. Analytical comments and interpretive conclusions are provided, but the data remain valid and available for further investigation or different interpretation.

The book is intended primarily, even if not exclusively, for students and scholars in the fields of folklore and anthropology. Among them, I wish to acknowledge the precious suggestions and help of a few, based on their teaching and researching festivals: Roger Abrahams, Richard Bauman, Alan Dundes, Paolo Fabbri, Louis Marin, Mari Lyn Salvador, Beverly Stoeltje, Victor Turner, Rosemary Levy Zumwalt. At the University of New Mexico Press in Albuquerque, Emmy Ezzell, Beth Hadas, Barbara Jellow, and Luther Wilson turned the inevitable complexities of publishing a book like this into a pleasant experience.

University of California, Los Angeles
January 1987

1 / Festival: Definition and Morphology

Alessandro Falassi

I

Festival is an event, a social phenomenon, encountered in virtually all human cultures. The colorful variety and dramatic intensity of its dynamic choreographic and aesthetic aspects, the signs of deep meaning underlying them, its historical roots and the involvement of the "natives" have always attracted the attention of casual visitors, have consumed travelers and men of letters alike. Since the last century, scholars from disciplines such as comparative religion, anthropology, sociology, and folklore have concerned themselves with the description, the analysis, and, more recently, the interpretation of festivities. Yet little explicit theoretical effort has been devoted to the nomenclature of festive events or to the definition of the term *festival*. As a result, the meaning of *festival* in the social sciences is simply taken from common language, where the term covers a constellation of very different events, sacred and profane, private and public, sanctioning tradition and introducing innovation, proposing nostalgic revivals, providing the expressive means for the survival of the most archaic folk customs, and celebrating the highly speculative and experimental avant-gardes of the elite fine arts.

Etymologically the term *festival* derives ultimately from the Latin *festum*. But originally Latin had two terms for festive events: *festum*, for "public joy, merriment, revelry," and *feria*, meaning "abstinence from work in honor of the gods." Both terms were used in the plural, *festa* and *feriae*, which indicates that at that time festivals already lasted many days and included many events. In classical Latin, the two terms tended to become synonyms, as the two types of events tended to merge.[1]

From *festa* derived the Italian *festa* (pl. *feste*), the French *fête* (pl. *fêtes*) and *festival* (adj.), the Spanish *fiesta* (pl. *fiestas*), the Portuguese *festa*, the Middle English *feste, feste dai, festial* then *festival*, at first an adjective connoting events and then a noun denoting them.

Feria (pl. *feriae*) had a semantic implication of lack, intermission, and absence that remained in the original meaning of the Italian *feria* (abstinence from work in honor of a saint), *ferie* (time away from work), and *giorni feriali* (days of absence of religious ceremonies) as well as in the medieval *feriae* (truce), *feriae matricularum* (festive vacation for University students), and the Spanish *ferias* (day of rest in honor of a saint). The meaning of "empty" (which could be taken to indicate that festival is the resounding cage of culture) was later joined and overshadowed by the festive events that progressively filled such days of "rest from." Thus *feria* became the term for market and exposition of commercial produce, such as in the Portuguese *feira*, the Spanish *feria*, the Italian *fiera*, the Old French *feire*, then *foire*, and the Old English *faire*, then *fair*.

Other secondary meanings of these two basic terms indicate in different languages forms of festive behavior or segments of festivals, such as *feast* and *festine* for an abundant formal meal, the Spanish *fiesta* for public combat of knights to show their ability and valor, the Latin *festa* for sacred offerings, the Rumanian *festa* for "prank," or the Italian *festa* and the French *fête* for "birthday celebration" or simply "warm welcome."[2]

In contemporary English, festival means (a) a sacred or profane time of celebration, marked by special observances; (b) the annual celebration of a notable person or event, or the harvest of an important product; (c) a cultural event consisting of a series of performances of works in the fine arts, often devoted to a single artist or genre; (d) a fair; (e) generic gaiety, conviviality, cheerfulness.[3] Similar common-language uses are to be found in all Romance languages.

As for the social sciences, the definition that can be inferred from the works of scholars who have dealt with festival while studying social and ritual events from the viewpoint of various disciplines such as comparative religion, anthropology, social psychology, folklore, and sociology indicates that festival commonly means *a periodically recurrent, social occasion in which, through a multiplicity of forms and a series of coordinated events, participate directly or indirectly and to various degrees, all members of a whole community, united by ethnic, linguistic, religious, historical bonds, and sharing a worldview.* Both the social function and the symbolic meaning of the festival are closely related to a series of overt values that the community recognizes as essential to its ideology and worldview, to its social identity, its historical continuity, and to its physical survival, which is ultimately what festival celebrates.[4]

II

Scholars have defined various types of festival, relying mainly on the sacred/ secular dichotomy first discussed by Durkheim. This is more a theoretical than a practical distinction, since each type usually includes elements of the other, even if secondary and subordinate. Religious festivals have evident secular implications, and secular ones almost invariably resort to metaphysics to gain solemnity and sanction for their events or for their sponsors. Another basic typological distinction that is often made draws upon the setting of the festival, opposing rural to urban festivals. Rural festivals are supposedly older, agrarian, centered on fertility rites and cosmogony myths, while the more recent, urban festivals celebrate prosperity in less archaic forms and may be tied to foundation legends and historical events and feats. Another typology can be based on power, class structure, and social roles, distinguishing among festivals given by the people for the people, those given by the establishment for itself, and those held by the people for the establishment, by the establishment for the people, and by the people against the establishment.[5]

Festive behavior has also been studied as a whole complex with one basic symbolic characteristic. While some scholars have indicated as most important the symbolic inversion, the topsy-turvy aspect apparent in festivals such as the Roman Saturnalia or the Feast of Fools, others have insisted on the similarities between daily and festive behavior, stressing that the latter parallels the former but with a more stylized form and with greatly increased semantic meaning.

The two approaches are not mutually exclusive. If we consider that the primary and most general function of the festival is to renounce and then to announce culture, to renew periodically the lifestream of a community by creating new energy, and to give sanction to its institutions, the symbolic means to achieve it is to represent the primordial chaos before creation, or a historical disorder before the establishment of the culture, society, or regime where the festival happens to take place.

Such representation cannot be properly accomplished by reversal behavior or by rites of intensification alone, but only by the simultaneous presence in the same festival of all the basic behavioral modalities of daily social life, all modified—by distortion, inversion, stylization, or disguise—in such a way that they take on an especially meaningful symbolic character. Consequently, both symbolic inversion and intensification must be present in the festival, and in addition there will be the element of symbolic abstinence—for instance from work, from play, from study, from religious observances. In sum, festival presents a complete range of behavioral modalities, each one related to the modalities of normal daily life. At festival times, people do something they normally do not; they abstain from something they normally do; they carry to the extreme behaviors that are usually regulated by measure; they invert patterns of daily social life. Reversal, intensification, trespassing, and abstinence are the four cardinal points of festive behavior.[6]

III

A morphology of festivals must indicate their minimal units and their possible sequences. Such a theoretical operation, analogous to what Vladimir Propp did for the constituent parts of the folktale, may aim at an archetype accounting for all festivals, or more accurately at "oicotypes" accounting for a class of festivals of the same kind or from the same cultural area.[7] Studies have indicated that several constituent parts seem to be quantitatively ever-recurrent and qualitatively important in festive events. These units, building blocks of festivals, can all be considered ritual acts, "rites," since they happen within an exceptional frame of time and space, and their meaning is considered to go beyond their literal and explicit aspects.

The framing ritual that opens the festival is one of *valorization* (which for religious events has been called sacralization) that modifies the usual and daily function and meaning of time and space. To serve as the theater of the festive events an area is reclaimed, cleared, delimited, blessed, adorned, forbidden to normal activities.[8]

Similarly, daily time is modified by a gradual or sudden interruption that introduces "time out of time," a special temporal dimension devoted to special activities. Festival time imposes itself as an autonomous duration, not so much to be perceived and measured in days or hours, but to be divided internally by what happens within it from its beginning to its end, as in the "movements" of mythical narratives or musical scores.[9] The opening rite is followed by a number of events that belong to a limited group of general ritual types. There are *rites of purification* and cleansing by means of fire, water, or air, or centered around the solemn expulsion of some sort of scapegoat carrying the "evil" and "negative" out of the community. If the rationale of these rites is to expel the evil that is already within, as in exorcisms, other complementary rites aim at keeping away the evil perceived as a threat coming from outside. These rites of safeguard include various forms of benediction and procession of sacred objects around and through significant points of the festival space setting, in order to renew the magical defenses of the community against natural and supernatural enemies.[10]

Rites of passage, in the form described by van Gennep, mark the transition from one life stage to the next. They may be given special relevance by being part of a festive event. These may include forms of initiation into age groups, such as childhood, youth, adulthood, and even public execution of criminals, or initiation into occupational, military, or religious groups.[11]

Rites of reversal through symbolic inversion drastically represent the mutability of people, culture, and life itself. Significant terms which are in binary opposition in the "normal" life of a culture are inverted. Sex roles are inverted in masquerade with males dressing as females and females dressing as males, social roles with masters serving their serfs. Sacred and profane spaces are also used in reverse.[12]

Rites of conspicuous display permit the most important symbolic elements of the community to be seen, touched, adored, or worshipped; their communicative function is "phatic," of contact. Sacred shrines, relics, magic objects are solemnly displayed and become the destination of visitations from within the immediate boundaries of the festival, or of pilgrimages from faraway places. In sacred processions and secular parades, the icons and symbolic elements are instead moved through space specifically adorned with ephemeral festive decorations such as festoons, flower arrangements, hangings, lights, and flags. In such perambulatory events, along with the community icons, the ruling groups typically display themselves as their guardians and keepers, and as depositories of religious or secular power, authority, and military might.[13]

Rites of conspicuous consumption usually involve food and drink. These are prepared in abundance and even excess, made generously available, and solemnly consumed in various forms of feasts, banquets, or symposia (lit. "drinking together at the end of a banquet"). Traditional meals or blessed foods are one of the most frequent and typical features of festival, since they are a very eloquent way to represent and enjoy abundance, fertility, and prosperity. Ritual food is also a means to communicate with gods and ancestors, as in the Christian belief in the presence of Christ in the sacred meal of Communion, the Greek tradition that Zeus is invisibly present at the ritual banquets of the Olympic Games, or the practice of the Tsembanga Maring people of New Guinea, who raise, slaughter, and eat pigs for and with the ancestors. In far less frequent cases, as in the potlatch, objects with special material and symbolic value are ritually consumed, wasted, or destroyed.[14]

Ritual dramas are usually staged at festival sites, as rites have a strong tie to myths. Their subject matter is often a creation myth, a foundation or migratory legend, or a military success particularly relevant in the mythical or historical memory of the community staging the festival. By means of the drama, the community members are reminded of their Golden Age, the trials and tribulations of their founding fathers in reaching the present location of the community, the miracles of a saint, or the periodic visit of a deity to whom the festival is dedicated. When the sacred story is not directly staged, it is very often hinted at or referred to in some segments or events of the festival.[15]

Rites of exchange express the abstract equality of the community members, their theoretical status as equally relevant members of a *"communitas,"* a community of equals under certain shared laws of reciprocity. At the *fair,* money and goods are exchanged at an economic level. At more abstract and symbolic levels, information, ritual gifts, or visits may be exchanged; public acts of pacification, symbolic *remissio debitum,* or thanksgiving for a grace received may take place in various forms of redistribution, sponsored by the community or a privileged individual, who thus repays the community or the gods for what he has received in excess.[16]

Festival typically includes *rites of competition,* which often constitute its cathartic moment in the form of games. Even if games are commonly defined as competitions regulated by special rules and with uncertain outcome (as opposed to ritual, the outcome of which is known in advance), the logic of festival is concerned with the competition and the awards for the winner; the rules of the game are canonic, and its paradigm is ritual. The parts or roles are assigned at the beginning to the personae as equals and undifferentiated "contestants," "hopefuls," "candidates." Then the development and the result of the game create among them a "final" hierarchical order— either binary (winners and losers) or by rank (from first to last). Games show how equality may be turned into hierarchy.[17] Besides games in the strict sense, festival competitions include various forms of contest and prize giving, from the election of the beauty queen to the selection of the best musician, player, singer, or dancer, individual or group, to awards to a new improvised narrative or work of art of any kind or to the best festive decorations. By singling out its outstanding members and giving them prizes, the group implicitly reaffirms some of its most important values.

Athletic or competitive sporting events include individual or collective games of luck, strength, or ability. These have been considered a "corruption" of older plays of ritual combats with fixed routine and obligatory ending, such as the fight between Light and Darkness representing cosmogony, then progressively historicized and territorialized into combats between, for example, the Christians and the Moors, or representative individuals, the champions (literally "the sample") carrying the colors of the whole group.[18]

In their functional aspects, such games may be seen as display and encouragement of skills such as strength, endurance, and precision, required in daily work and military occupations; such was for instance the rationale of medieval mock battles.[19]

In their symbolic aspect, festival competitions may be seen as a metaphor for the emergence and establishment of power, as when the "winner takes all," or when the winning faction symbolically takes over the arena, or the city in triumph.

At the end of the festival, a *rite of devalorization,* symmetrical to the opening one, marks the end of the festive activities and the return to the normal spatial and temporal dimensions of daily life. [20]

IV

Admittedly, a complete or even an extensive morphology of festivals will correspond to very few—if any—actual events. Real-life festivals will not present all the ritual components listed, not even in "de-semanticized,"that is, secondary and scarcely meaningful, forms. A complete festival morphology will correspond to the complete festive cycle, and several of its parts will form the configuration of each of the actual festive events. [21] This fragmentation of the festive complex into events distributed all along the calendrical cycle follows the course of history and its trends of centralization and decentralization in social life, as well as the interplay of religious and secular powers and their division in the running of social and symbolic life and its "collective rituals." Furthermore, in today's western and westernized cultures, larger, often more abstract and distant entities try to substitute themselves for the older, smaller, tightly woven communities as reference groups and centers of the symbolic life of the people. [22] Today we try to bring the audience close to the event by means of the mass media, or to bring the event close to the audience by delegating smaller entities such as the family, to administer it everywhere at the same time, or to fragment the older festivals into simpler festive events centered on one highly significant ritual. Such fragmentation is seen in the United States, where the ritual meal is the focus of Thanksgiving, the exchange of gifts the focus of Christmas, excess of New Year's, military might and victories and civic pride are the themes underlying the parade on the Fourth of July and the Rose Parade. Carnivalesque aspects underlie Mardi Gras and Halloween. And symbolic reversal is nowhere more evident than in the demolition derby. Even the tradition of dynastic anniversaries is present, modified though it may be, in Washington's and Lincoln's birthdays; competitions are perfectly typified by the Indianapolis 500, the Superbowl, and the Kentucky Derby. Even the archaic tendency to consider the ritual games of the festival as cosmic events may be surfacing in the term *world championship,* obstinately used for events that in the strict sense are encounters of local teams playing a culture-bound and territorially limited game, such as American football or baseball. Festive rites of passage take place on Valentine's Day, at debutantes' balls, drinking celebrations of the eighteenth birthday and fraternity and sorority rushes. Rites of deference and confirmation of status include presidential inaugurations, Father's Day, and Mother's Day. The archaic Kings and Queens of the May have their functional equivalents in the yearly beauty pageants of Miss, Mister, and Mrs. America. Plays have been grouped in various yearly festivals of the arts that range from Shakespeare festivals to the Oscars ceremonies in Los Angeles, through symphonies, jazz festivals, and fiddling contests. And the modern *ferias,* the county fairs, are numerous and ever-present. [23]

If not festival proper, such events are part of a festive cycle, a series of events that in other times and cultures would fall within tighter boundaries of time, space, and action. This festive complex is everchanging and evolving. But with all its modifications, festival has retained its primary importance in all cultures, for the human social animal still does not have a more significant way to feel in tune with his world than to partake in the special reality of the Festival, and celebrate life in its "time out of time."

NOTES

1. For the meaning of *festival* in Latin see *The Oxford Latin Dictionary*, ed. P. G. Glare (Oxford: Clarendon Press, 1982), pp. 686, 694–95; *Lexicon Totius Latinitatis*, ed. Egidio Forcellini (Padua: Typis Seminarii, 1940), 2:452–53, 468; Charles Du Cange, *Glossarium Mediae et Infimae Latinitatis* (Niort: Favre, 1884), 3:436–38, 462–63.

2. For the meaning of *festival* in the Romance languages, see the *Vocabolario degli Accademici della Crusca*, 5th ed. (Florence: Tipografia Galileiana, 1886), 5:757–58, 814–20; *Dictionnaire de l'Académie Française*, 8th ed. (Paris: Hachette, 1932), 1:537, 554; *Real Academia Española, Diccionario de la Lengua Española*, 19th ed. (Madrid: Espasa-Calpe, 1970); José Pedro Machado, *Dicionario Etimológico da Lingua Portuguesa*, 3d ed. (Lisbon: Horizonte, 1977), 3:38, 40.

3. For the meaning of *festival* in English, see for instance the *Middle English Dictionary*, ed. H. Kurath and S. M. Kuhn (Ann Arbor: University of Michigan Press and London: Oxford University Press, 1952), 3:451, 529; *The Shorter English Dictionary*, ed. C. T. Onions, 3d ed. (Oxford: Clarendon Press, 1973), pp. 742–43; *Webster's Third New International Dictionary*, ed. P. Babcock Gove (Springfield, Mass.: Merriam Co., 1976), pp. 815, 841.

4. For the meaning of *festival* in the social sciences, see *Dictionary of Folklore, Mythology and Legend*, ed. Maria Leach (New York: Funk and Wagnalls, 1949), 1:376; *Dictionary of Mythology Folklore and Symbols*, ed. Gertrude Jobes (New York: Scarecrow Press, 1961), 1:563; *The Encyclopaedia of Social Sciences*, ed. Edwin R. A. Seligman (New York: Macmillan, 1937), 6:198–201; *Encyclopaedia of Religion and Ethics* (New York: Scribner's, 1961), 5:835–94. For general discussions of festive events, see Victor Turner, ed., *Celebration: Studies in Festivity and Rit-*

ual (Washington: Smithsonian Institution Press, 1982), especially pp. 11–30, and also his "Liminal to Liminoid, in Play, Flow and Ritual," *Rice University Studies* 60 (1974), pp. 53–92; Robert J. Smith, "Festivals and Celebrations," in Richard Dorson, ed., *Folklore and Folklife* (Chicago and London: University of Chicago Press, 1972), pp. 159–72, and his *The Art of the Festival* (Lawrence: University of Kansas Press, 1975); Carla Bianco and Maurizio del Ninno, eds., *Festa. Antropologia e Semiotica*, Acts of the International Congress of 1978 in Montecatini (Florence: Nuova Guaraldi, 1981); Roger Caillois, "Theorie de la Fête," *Nouvelle Revue Française* 27 (1939): 863–82; 28 (1940): 49–59; Beverly Stoeltje, "Festival in America," in Richard Dorson, ed., *Handbook of American Folklore* (Bloomington: Indiana University Press, 1983), pp. 239–46; John J. MacAloon, "Cultural Performances, Culture Theory" in his (ed.) *Rite, Drama, Festival, Spectacle* (Philadelphia: ISHI Press, 1984), pp. 1–15; Jean Duvignaud, *Fêtes et Civilizations* (Paris and Geneva: Weber, 1973); Marianne Mesnil, "The Masked Festival: Disguise or Affirmation?" *Cultures* 3 (1976) no. 2:11–29. For festive events as symbolic representations of worldview, see Alan Dundes and Alessandro Falassi, *La Terra in Piazza: An Interpretation of the Palio of Siena* (Berkeley and Los Angeles: University of California Press, 1975). Compare Clifford Geertz, "Deep Play: Notes on Balinese Cockfight," *Daedalus* 101 (1972): 1–37.

5. For the sacred/profane dichotomy and semantic pair, see Emile Durkheim, *The Elementary Forms of the Religious Life* (London: Allen and Unwin/New York: Macmillan, 1915); Mircea Eliade, *The Sacred and the Profane* (New York: Harper Torchbooks, 1961). Compare Sally F. Moore and Barbara G. Myerhoff, eds., *Secular Ritual* (Amsterdam: Van Gor-*

cum, 1977). For the contemporary situation, see Robert Bellah *Beyond Belief: Essays on Religion in a Post-Traditional World* (New York: Harper and Row, 1970). For an application to contemporary festivals, see Bruce Guiliano, *Sacro o Profano? A Consideration of Four Italian-Canadian Religious Festivals* (Ottawa: National Museum of Canada, 1976); Jean Duvignaud, "Festivals: A Sociological Approach," *Cultures* 3 (1976) no. 1: 13–28; Frank Manning, *The Celebration of Society: Perspective on Contemporary Cultural Performances* (Bowling Green, Ohio: Bowling Green University Popular Press, 1983).

6. For festive inversion, see Barbara Babcock, ed., *The Reversible World: Symbolic Inversion in Art and Society* (Ithaca: Cornell University Press, 1978). Excess, affirmation, and juxtaposition are discussed in Harvey Cox, *The Feast of Fools: A Theological Essay on Festivity and Fantasy* (Cambridge, Mass.: Harvard University Press, 1969). Joseph Pieper, *In Tune with the World: A Theory of Festivity* (New York: Harcourt, 1965) discusses festive behavior as a form of assent to the world as a whole. See also his *Uber Das Phänomen Des Festes* (Cologne: Westdeutscher Verlag, 1963). Contrast Yves-Marie Berce, *Fête et Revolte* (Paris: Hachette, 1976), Mikhail Bakhtin, *Rabelais and His World* (Cambridge: MIT Press, 1968), and Miguel de Ferdinandy, *Carnaval y Revolucion y diecinueve ensayos mas* (Rio Piedras, Puerto Rico: Editorial Universitaria, 1977). Analogies between daily and festive behavior are stressed in Roger Abrahams and Richard Bauman, "Ranges of Festival Behavior," in Babcock, *The Reversible World*, pp. 193–208. Roger Caillois, *Man and the Sacred* (Glencoe: Free Press, 1959) sees festival as periodical excess and chaos. On transgression see, for instance, Robert J. Smith, "Licentious Behavior in Hispanic Festivals," *Western Folklore* 31 (1972): 290–98; Sherry Roxanne Turkle: "Symbol and Festival in the French Students Uprising" (May–June 1968) in Sally Moore and Barbara Myerhoff, *Symbols and Politics in Communal Ideology* (Ithaca: Cornell University Press, 1975), pp. 68–100.

7. Vladimir Propp, *Morphology of the Folktale* (Austin: University of Texas Press, 1968). For the concept of Oicotype see C. W. Von Sydow, "Geography and Folktale Oico-types," in *Selected Papers on Folklore* (Copenhagen: Rosenkilde and Bagger, 1948), pp. 44–59.

8. For rites of sacralization see, for instance, Mircea Eliade, *Patterns in Comparative Religion* (New York: Sheed and Ward, 1958), pp. 367–87 and *The Sacred and the Profane*, pp. 20–65.

9. This concept of time appears in Claude Lévi-Strauss, *The Raw and the Cooked* (New York: Harper and Row, 1969), pp. 15–16. Compare Edmund Leach, "Cronus and Chronos" and "Time and False Noses" in his *Rethinking Anthropology* (London: Athlone Press, 1961), pp. 124–36; Mircea Eliade, *The Sacred and the Profane*, pp. 85–95.

10. For rites of purification and safeguard see, for instance, Peter Rigby, "Some Gogo Rituals of 'Purification': An Essay on Social and Moral Categories," in E. R. Leach, ed., *Dialectic in Practical Religion* (Cambridge: Cambridge University Press, 1968), pp. 153–78; Mary Douglas, *Purity and Danger* (London: Routledge and Kegan Paul, 1966).

11. For rites of passage, see the classic Arnold van Gennep, *The Rites of Passage* (Chicago: University of Chicago Press, 1960); Barbara Myerhoff, "Rites of Passage: Process and Paradox," in Victor Turner, *Celebration*, pp. 109–35; Max Gluckman, "Les Rites de Passage," in his (ed.) *Essays on the Ritual of Social Relations* (Manchester: Manchester University Press, 1962), pp. 1–52. For discussion of extensive ethnographic comparative data, see Frank Young, *Initiation Ceremonies: A Cross-Cultural Study of Status Dramatization* (New York: Bobbs-Merrill, 1965) and Martha N. Fried and H. Morton, *Transition: Four Rituals in Eight Cultures* (New York: Norton, 1980); Judith Brown, "A Cross-Cultural Study of Female Initiation Rites," *American Anthropologist* 65 (1963): 837–53.

12. For rites of reversal see Barbara Babcock's discussion in *The Reversible World*, pp. 13–36. Rich comparative materials and iconography from Europe appear in Giuseppe Cocchiara, *Il Mondo alla Rovescia* (Turin: Einaudi, 1963). A theoretical discussion of the concept is in Rodney Needham, "Reversals," in his *Against the Tranquility of Axioms* (Berkeley and Los Angeles: University of California Press, 1983), pp. 93–120.

13. On pilgrimages see Surinder Mohan

Bhardway, *Hindu Places of Pilgrimage in India* (Berkeley and Los Angeles: University of California Press, 1973); Victor Turner and Edith Turner, *Image and Pilgrimage in Christian Culture: Anthropological Perspectives* (New York: Columbia University Press, 1978); and Victor Turner, *Process, Performance and Pilgrimage: A Study in Comparative Symbology* (New Delhi: Concept, 1979). For parades and processions, see, for instance, Sydney Anglo, *Spectacle, Pageantry, and Early Tudor Policy* (Oxford: Clarendon Press, 1969); Albert D. Mackie, *Scottish Pageantry* (London: Hutchinson, 1967); Leroy F. Vaughn, *Parade and Float Guide* (Minneapolis: Denison, 1956); David Colin Dunlop, *Processions: A Dissertation, Together With Practical Suggestions* (London: Oxford University Press, 1932).

14. For classic rites of conspicuous consumption and ritual offerings, see H. G. Barnette, "The Nature of the Potlatch," *American Anthropologist* 40 (1983): 349–58. For an interpretive essay, see Alan Dundes, "Heads or Tails: A Psychoanalytic Study of Potlatch," *Journal of Psychological Anthropology* 2 (1979): 395–424; Roy A. Rappaport, *Pigs for the Ancestors: Ritual in the Ecology of a New Guinea People* (New Haven: Yale University Press, 1968); Evon Z. Vogt, *Tortillas for the Gods: A Symbolic Analysis of Zinacanteco Rituals* (Cambridge: Harvard University Press, 1976); Henri Hubert and Marcel Mauss, *Sacrifice: Its Nature and Function* (Chicago: University of Chicago Press, 1964); E. S. Drower, "The Ritual Meal," *Folk-Lore* 48 (1937): 226–44; Sula Benet, *Festival Menus 'round the World* (New York: Abelard-Schuman, 1957).

15. On the relationship between ritual drama and festival see, for instance, Tristram P. Coffin and Hennig Cohen, "Folk Drama and Folk Festival," in their *Folklore in America* (New York: Doubleday, 1966), pp. 195–225; Victor Turner, "Social Dramas and Ritual Metaphors" in his (ed.) *Dramas, Fields, and Metaphors. Symbolic Action in Human Society* (Ithaca: Cornell University Press, 1974), pp. 23–59; Abner Cohen, "Drama and Politics in the Development of a London Carnaval," *Man* 15 (1980): 65–87; Alfonso Ortiz, "Ritual Drama and Pueblo Worldview" in his (ed.) *New Perspectives on the Pueblos* (Albuquerque: University of New Mexico Press,

1972), pp. 135–62; Richard Schechner, "Ramlila of Ramnagar and America's Oberammergau: Two Celebratory Ritual Dramas," in Victor Turner, *Celebration*, pp. 89–106; Paul Radin, "The Ritual Drama" in his *Primitive Religion* (New York: Dover, 1957), pp. 289–306.

16. On ritual exchange see the classic Marcel Mauss, *The Gift* (New York: Norton, 1967). On pp. 40–41 Mauss discusses the three obligations to give, to receive, and to reciprocate. See also Raymond Firth, "Symbolism in Giving and Getting," in his *Symbols Public and Private* (Ithaca: Cornell University Press, 1973), pp. 368–402. For ethnographic data, see for instance G. A. M. Bus, "The 'Te' Festival or Gift Exchange in Enga (Central Highlands of New Guinea)," *Anthropos* 46 (1951): 813–24. On economic aspects see Roger Abrahams, "The Language of Festivals: Celebrating the Economy," in Victor Turner, *Celebration*, pp. 161–77.

17. On games, play, and ludic elements in festival see the seminal Johann Huizinga, *Homo Ludens: A Study of the Play Element in Culture* (Boston: Beacon Press, 1955) and Roger Caillois, *Man, Play and Games* (Glencoe: Free Press, 1961). Context is discussed in John M. Roberts, Malcom J. Arth, and Robert R. Bush, "Games in Culture," *American Anthropologist* 61 (1959): 587–605. *Communitas* and *hierarchy* are terms of a semantic pair introduced and discussed by Victor Turner in *The Ritual Process. Structure and Anti-structure* (Chicago: Aldine, 1969), pp. 94–204.

18. These concepts are discussed in Mircea Eliade, *Patterns in Comparative Religion*, pp. 319–21, 431–34. See also Herbert Jennings Rose, "Suggested Explanation of Ritual Combats," *Folk-Lore* 36 (1925): 322–31.

19. For medieval mimic battles see, for instance, William Heywood, *Palio and Ponte* (London: Methuen, 1904).

20. See notes 8 and 9.

21. A classic extensive study of a complete festival cycle in Arnold van Gennep, *Manuel de Folklore Français Contemporain*, 9 vols. (Paris: Picard, 1938–58). Comparative data are in E. O. James, *Seasonal Feasts and Festivals* (New York: Barnes and Noble, 1963). For the festive cycle of a single religious group, see, for instance, M. M. Un-

derhill, *The Hindu Religious Year* (Oxford: Oxford University Press, 1921), and Sangendi Mahalinga Natesa Sastri, *Hindu Feasts, Fasts, and Ceremonies* (Madras: M. E. Publishing House, 1903).

22. A discussion of contemporary history, politics, and festivals is in George Mosse, *The Nationalization of the Masses* (New York: Fertig, 1975). For historical evolution and change of meaning in festival, see Marianne Mesnil, *Trois Essais sur la Fête* (Brussels: Editions de l'Université, 1974). For a specific case study see Victor Barnouw: "The Changing Character of a Hindu Festival," *American Anthropologist* 56 (1954): 74–86.

23. For festivals in the United States see the thorough introduction in Beverly Stoeltje, "Festival in America." For a general study see W. Lloyd Warner, *The Living and the Dead: A Study of the Symbolic Life of the Americans* (New Haven: Yale University Press, 1959). For the festive cycle see Jane M. Hatch, *The American Book of Days*, 3d. ed. (New York: Wilson, 1978). For festivals of ethnic groups, see for instance, Melwin Wade, "'Shining in Borrowed Plumage': Affirmation of Community in the Black Coronation Festivals of New England (c. 1750–c. 1850)," *Western Folklore* 40 (1981), no. 3: 211–31; Evon Z. Vogt, "A Study of the Southwestern Fiesta System as Exemplified by the Laguna Fiesta," *American Anthropologist* 57 (1955): 820–39. For individual events, see, for instance, Jack Barry Ludwig, *The Great American Spectaculars: The Kentucky Derby, Mardi Gras, and Other Days of Celebration* (Garden City: Doubleday, 1976); Ron Dorson, *The Indy 500: An American Institution Under Fire* (Newport Beach: Bond-Parkjurst Books, 1974). For individual festivities, see, for instance, John E. Baur, *Christmas on the American Frontier 1800–1900* (Caldwell, Idaho: Caxton, 1961); Howard Sickel, *Thanksgiving: Its Source, Philosophy and History* (Philadelphia: International Printing Company, 1940); William H. Cohn, "A National Celebration: The Fourth of July in American History," *Cultures* 3 (1976), no. 2: 141–56; Ralph Linton and Adelin Linton, *Halloween Through Twenty Centuries* (New York: Shuman, 1950); Jack Santino, "Halloween in America: Contemporary Customs and Performances," *Western Folklore* 42 (1983): 1–20. General notes are in Ian Brunvand, "Customs and Festivals" in *The Study of American Folklore* (New York: Norton, 1968), pp. 197–210; John A. Gutowski, "The Protofestival: Local Guide to American Folk Behavior," *Journal of the Folklore Institute* 15 (1978): 113–30; Mary T. Douglas, ed., *Food in the Social Order: Studies of Food and Festivities in Three American Communities* (New York: Russell Sage Foundation, 1984); W. Lloyd Warner, "An American Sacred Ceremony" (Memorial Day) in his *American Life: Dream and Reality* (Chicago: University of Chicago Press, 1953), pp. 1–26. For the actual organization of festivals, see Joe Wilson and Lee Udall, *Folk Festivals. A Handbook for Organization and Management* (Knoxville: University of Tennessee Press, 1982).

PART I

Men of Letters and Social Scientists Reporting from the Scene of the Festival

2 / The Roman Carnival

Johann Wolfgang von Goethe

Goethe began planning his Italian journey in the summer of 1786, on his thirty-seventh birthday. The trip was to be a pilgrimage to the archaeological remains and social survivals of the classical antiquities, which had great importance in his literary and poetic works. He left Karlsbad on September 3, 1786, and arrived in Rome on October 29. On February 22, 1787, he left for southern Italy, and returned to Rome on June 7, 1787. On April 23, 1788, he left for northern Italy and Germany, reaching Weimar on June 18, 1788. Goethe was in Rome for the Carnivals of 1787 and 1788, wrote this description after the latter in 1788, and published it in 1789 as an illustrated booklet. It was intended as a kind of souvenir book and literary Baedeker, a guidebook for prospective visitors, to whom it "may provide a pleasing perspective of an over-thronged and tumultuous merry-making . . . which may in future be visited with our book in hand."

Goethe presented the Roman Carnival as the modern derivation of the pre-Christian pagan Saturnalia. The streets were transformed by decorations of flowers, tapestries, and lights into salons and galleries. The noise was incredible: yells, blasts of mortars, trumpets made of sea shells such as in ancient Rome. The streets were overflowing with crowds of people wearing masks derived from their Roman past, such as the two-faced ones similar to the image of Janus. Others came from the comic opera, or Commedia dell'Arte, or from uniforms or folk costume. The Corso, Rome's main street, was jammed with long lines of decorated carriages, reminiscent of ancient mythological floats, with beautiful women on display. Commoners, noblemen, soldiers, prelates, dignitaries: the whole city came to see and to be seen.

Crowds were animated by improvised dramas: furious battles with comfits and sugar-coated almonds; farces of giving birth, of a brawl, of seeking asylum after a murder; puppet theaters; rope-dancing booths. Inside the theaters balls, pantomimes, and living mythological tableaux took place. Each day was closed by the parade and race of the "barberi" horses, which took place along the narrow path left by the separating of the crowd—a dramatic race with many falls and accidents. Festivities ended with a banquet of red meats, suggesting the most accepted etymology of Carnival (Carnem, vale! Farewell, meat! Farewell, flesh!). Contemporary scholars will find in Goethe's account, written with the punctiliousness of a philologist, many instances of symbolic inversion, such as the curious universal greeting "sia ammazzato!" (to death!), which reverses daily polite addresses such as "salute!" (to your health!) or "viva!" (long life!); women bothering and attacking men; and masks crossing boundaries of geography, social class, status, or sex—men masked as women, women as men, hermaphrodite Pulcinellas. Occasionally the tumultuous crowd parted, opening up, as in the Piazza del Popolo before the horse race, affording "perhaps one of the finest sights in the present world."

Yet, on the whole, Goethe judged the Roman Carnival not simply as a pleasant spectacle, a joyful amusement, an aesthetic experience bringing exhilaration to the spirit. He saw it as unmistakably authentic, not given to the people but by the people to themselves, and because of that a mirror of culture and a metaphor of life itself. The crowded streets suggested to the great poet the ways of the world, where "freedom and equality can only be enjoyed in the tumult of folly," and where pleasures are as fleeting as the Palio horses.

The Roman Carnival.*

Johann Wolfgang von Goethe

In undertaking a description of the Roman Carnival, we cannot but fear the objection being raised that such a festival is a subject not properly admitting of description. So vast a throng of sensible objects would, it may be represented, require to pass in review immediately before the eye—would require to be personally seen and comprehended in his own way by each person wishing to obtain any idea of it.

This objection becomes all the more serious when we have ourselves to confess, that to the stranger viewing it for the first time, especially if he is disposed and qualified only to *see* it with his bodily eyes, the Roman Carnival affords neither an

*Reprinted from *Goethe's Travels in Italy* (London: George Bell & Sons, 1883), pp. 485–515. Published originally as *Das Römischer Karneval* in 1789, with twenty drawings by Georg Schütz and Georg Melchior Kraus. A new critical edition of *Das Römische Carneval* was published in 1984 (Frankfurt: Inselverlag).

integral nor a joyous impression—is neither a particular gratification to the eye nor an exhilaration to the spirits.

The long and narrow street in which innumerable people lurch hither and thither, it is impossible to survey; it is scarcely possible to distinguish anything within the limits of the tumult which your eye can grasp. The movement is monotonous, the noise stupefying, the days of the festival close with no sense of satisfaction. These misgivings, however, are soon dissipated when we enter into a more minute explanation, and indeed the reader will have to decide for himself at the end, whether our description justifies our attempt.

The Roman Carnival is a festival which, in point of fact, is not given to the people, but which the people give themselves.

The state makes little preparations, and but a small contribution to it. The merry round revolves of itself, and the police regulate the spontaneous movement with but a slack hand.

Here is no festival to dazzle the eyes of the spectator, like the many Church festivals of Rome; here are no fireworks affording the on-looker from St. Angelo a single overwhelming spectacle; here is no illumination of St. Peter's Church and dome, attracting and delighting a great concourse of strangers from all lands; here is no brilliant procession on whose approach the people are required to worship with awe. On the contrary, all that is here given is rather a simple sign that each man is at liberty to go fooling to the top of his bent, and that all licence is permissible short of blows and stabs.

The difference between high and low seems for the time being abolished, every one makes up to every one, every one treats with levity whatever he meets, and the mutual licence and wantonness is kept in balance only by the universal good humour.

In these holidays the Roman exults, down to our times, that the birth of Christ, though able indeed to postpone for some weeks, was not adequate to abolishing the feast of the Saturnalia and its privileges.

It shall be our endeavour to bring the riot and merriment of these days clearly before the imagination of our readers. We flatter ourselves we shall be of service to such persons as have once been present at the Roman Carnival, and would like to entertain themselves with a vivid remembrance of it, as also to those who still contemplate a journey thither, and whom these few leaves may provide a pleasing perspective of an over-thronged and tumultuous merry-making.

The Corso.

The Roman Carnival collects in the Corso. This street limits and determines the public celebration of these days. Anywhere else it would be a different sort of festival, and we have therefore first of all to describe the Corso.

Like several long streets of Italian towns, it derives its name from the horse-races which conclude the entertainment of each Carnival evening, and with which too, in other places, other festivals, such as that of the patron saint or the consecration of a church, are ended.

The street runs in a straight line from the Piazza del Popolo to the Piazza di Venezia; about three thousand five hundred paces long and enclosed by high, mostly splendid buildings. Its breadth is not proportionate to its length, nor to the height of its edifices. The pavements for foot passengers take up on both sides from six to eight feet. The space in the middle for carriages is at most places from twelve to fourteen feet wide, and therefore, as will be readily calculated, allows but three vehicles at the most to drive abreast.

The obelisk on the Piazza del Popolo is, during the Carnival, the extreme limit of this street at the lower end, the Venetian Palace at the upper.

Driving in the Corso.

On all Sundays and festival days of the year the Roman Corso is a scene of animation. The Romans of wealth and distinction take their drives here an hour or an hour and a half before nightfall in a long continuous line. The carriages start from the Venetian Palace, keeping the left side, and in fine weather they pass the obelisk, drive through the gate, on to the Flaminian way, sometimes as far as Ponte Molle.

On returning at an earlier or later hour, they keep the other side, so that the two lines of carriages pass each other in opposite directions in the best order.

Ambassadors have the right of driving up and down between the rows; this distinction was also allowed the Pretender, who stayed in Rome under the name of Duke of Albania.

The moment, however, the bells have sounded night this order is interrupted. Each one turns the way it pleases him, seeking his nearest road home, often to the inconvenience of many other equipages, which get impeded and stopped in the narrow space.

The evening drive, which is a brilliant affair in all great Italian towns, and is imitated in each small town, if only with a few coaches, attracts many foot passengers into the Corso; each one coming to see or to be seen.

The Carnival, as we may soon more particularly observe, is, in fact, but a continuation or rather the climax of the usual Sunday and festival-day recreations; it is nothing eccentric, nothing foreign, nothing unique, but attaches itself quite naturally to the general Roman style of living.

Climate, Clerical Dress.

Just as little strange will appear to us a multitude of masks in the open air, seeing we are accustomed the whole year through to so many striking scenes of life under the bright glad heaven.

On the occasion of every festival the outspread tapestries, the scattered flowers, the painted cloths stretched above your head, transform the streets into great salons and galleries.

No corpse is brought to the grave without the accompaniment of the masked fraternities. The many monks' dresses habituate the eye to strange and peculiar figures. It indeed looks like Carnival the whole year round, the abbots in their black dress appearing among the other clerical masks to represent the more noble *tabarros* (cloaks).

Commencement.

With the beginning of the new year the playhouses are opened, and the Carnival has taken its start. Here and there in the boxes you notice a beauty, in the character of an officer, displaying to the people her epaulettes with the greatest self-complacency. The driving in the Corso becomes more thronged. The general expectancy, however, is directed to the last eight days.

Preparations for the Concluding Days.

Many preparations announce to the public the approach of the paradisiacal hours.

The Corso, one of the few streets in Rome which are kept clean the whole year, gets now more carefully swept and tidied up. People are busy seeing that the small basalt blocks, square-hewn, pretty and uniform, of which the beautiful pavement consists, are in proper trim, any which are in any degree worn being removed and replaced by new basalt-wedges.

Besides this you observe living indications of the near approaching event. Each Carnival evening, as we have noticed, closes with a horse-race. The horses kept for racing are mostly little, and, on account of the foreign extraction of the best of them, are called "Barberi."

A racing horse, in a covering of white linen, closely fitted to the head, neck and body, and adorned with bright ribbons at the seams, is brought in front of the obelisk to the spot whence later on he is to start. He is trained to stand still for some time with his head directed to the Corso. He is next led gently along the street, and at the Venetian Palace is treated to some oats, to make him feel the greater inducement to speed swiftly to that place.

As this practice is repeated with most of the horses, to the number often of from fifteen to twenty, and this performance is always attended by a number of merry noisy boys, a foretaste is thus given to the inhabitants of the greater uproar and jubilee shortly to follow.

Formerly the first Roman houses kept race-horses in their mews, and it was deemed an honour to a house for one of its horses to have carried off a prize. Bets were laid, and the victory celebrated by a feast. Latterly, however, this fancy has much declined, and the desire to acquire reputation by horses has percolated down into the middle, nay into the lowest class of the people.

From those earlier times, probably, has been handed down the custom that a troop of riders, accompanied by trumpeters, go about through the whole of Rome exhibiting the prizes, and riding into the grounds of distinguished houses, where, after discoursing some trumpet air, they receive a gratuity.

The prize consists of a piece of gold or silver brocade, about three and a half ells long by not quite an ell broad, which, being attached to a piebald pole, is made to wave in the air. On its lower end is worked cross-wise the picture of some running horses.

This prize is called *Palio*, and as many days as the Carnival lasts so many of these quasi-standards are displayed by the procession just mentioned along the streets of Rome.

Meanwhile the Corso begins to alter its appearance. The obelisk now becomes the limit of the street. In front of it a grand stand is erected, with many rows of seats ranged above each other, and looking right into the Corso. Before this scaffold the lists are set up between which the horses must be brought out to run.

On both sides, moreover, great scaffolds are built, attached to the first houses of the Corso, the street in this way being continued into the square. On both sides of the lists stand small, raised and covered boxes for the persons who are to regulate the running of the horses.

Up the Corso you see further scaffolds raised in front of many houses. The squares of St. Carlo and of the Antoninus Column are separated by palings from the street, and everything sufficiently betokens that the whole celebration shall and will be confined within the long and narrow Corso.

Lastly the middle of the street is strewn with *puzzolane*, that the competing horses may not so easily slip on the smooth hard street.

Signal for the Complete Carnival Licence.

In this way expectation is every day fed and kept on the strain till at last a bell from the Capitol, shortly after noon, announces that people are now at full liberty to go fooling under the bright heaven.

Immediately on hearing it the serious Roman, who has been watchful the whole year round against falling into any slip, doffs his earnestness and gravity.

The bricklayers, who have been thumping away up to the last minute, pack up their tools and make merry over the end of their labour. All balconies, all windows are gradually hung with tapestries; on the raised pavements on both sides chairs are set out; the tenants of smaller houses and all children are in the street, which now ceases to be a street, and resembles rather a large festive salon, a vast adorned gallery.

Superintendence.

While the Corso grows ever more animated, and among the many persons walking in their usual dresses a Punchinello here and there shows himself, the military have mustered in front of the Porta del Popolo. Led by the general on horseback, in good order and new uniform, with clanging music, they march up the Corso, and at once occupy all the entrances to it, appoint a couple of guards to the principal places, and assume the oversight of the whole festivity.

The lenders of chairs and scaffolds now call diligently to the passers-by, "Luoghi! Luoghi, Padroni! Luoghi!" ("Places, gentlemen, places!")

Masks.

The masks now begin to multiply. Young men, dressed in the holiday attire of the women of the lowest class, exposing an open breast and displaying an impudent self-complacency, are mostly the first to be seen. They caress the men they meet, allow themselves all familiarities with the women they encounter, as being persons the same as themselves, and for the rest do whatever humour, wit or wantonness suggest.

Among other things, we remember a young man, who played excellently the part of a passionate, brawling, untameable shrew, who went scolding the whole way along the Corso, railing at every one she came across, while those accompanying her took all manner of pains to reduce her to quietness.

Here comes a Punchinello, running with a large horn attached to bright cords dangling about his haunches. By a slight motion, while entertaining himself with the women, he contrives to assume the impudent shape of the old god of the gardens in holy Rome, and his insolence excites more mirth than indignation. Here comes another of like kidney, but more modest and placid, bringing his fair half along with him.

The women having just as much a mind to don the breeches as the men the petticoats, the fairer sex show no contempt for the favourite costume of Punchinello; and in this hermaphrodite figure, it must be allowed, they often show themselves in the highest degree charming.

With rapid steps, declaiming as before a Court of justice, an advocate pushes through the crowd. He bawls up at the windows, lays hold of passers-by masked or unmasked, threatens every person with a process, impeaches this man in a long narration with ridiculous crimes, and specifies to another the list of his debts. He rates the women for their coquetries, the girls for the number of their lovers. He appeals by way of proof to a book he carries about with him, producing documents as well, and setting everything forth with a shrill voice and fluent tongue. It is his aim to expose and confound every one. When you fancy he is at an end he is only beginning, when you think he is leaving he turns back. He flies at one without addressing him, he seizes hold of the other who is already past. Should he come across a brother of his profession, the folly rises to its height.

However, they cannot attract the attention of the public for a long time at once. The maddest impression is swallowed up in repetition and multiplicity.

The quakers make if not so much noise, yet at least as great a sensation as the advocates. The quaker masks appear to have grown so general, on account of the easiness with which old-fashioned pieces of dress can be procured at the second-hand goods' stalls.

The main requirements in reference to these quaker masks is that the dress be old fashioned, yet in good preservation and of fine stuff. You seldom see one in other dress than velvet or silk, his vest being brocaded or laced, and, like the original, he must be of full body. His face is in a full mask with puffed cheeks and small eyes; his wig has odd pig-tails dangling to it; his hat is small and mostly bordered.

This figure, plainly, comes very near the *Buffo caricato* of the comic operas, and as the latter mostly represents a silly, enamoured gull, the quakers show themselves in the character of tasteless dandies. They hop about on their toes with great agility, and carry about large black rings without glass to serve them in the way of opera glasses, and with which they peer into every carriage, and gaze up at all windows. Usually they make a stiff deep bow, and, especially on meeting each other, express their joy by hopping several times straight up in the air, uttering at the same time a shrill, piercing, inarticulate cry, in which the consonants "brr" prevail.

You may often hear this note of salutation sounded by a quaker, and taken up by those of his persuasion next him, till in a short time the whole Corso is rent by their screams.

Wanton boys, again, blow into large twisted shells, assailing the ear with intolerable sounds.

What with the narrowness of the space and the similarity of the masks—for at all hours of the day there may be some hundreds of Punchinellos and about a hundred quakers running up and down the Corso—you soon perceive that few can have the intention of exciting a sensation or attracting attention to themselves. Any bent on that object would have to appear at an early hour in the Corso. Each one is much more intent on amusing himself, on giving free vent to his follies, and enjoying to the full the licence of these days.

The girls and women, in particular, devise methods of their own for merry-making. Every one of them hates above everything to stay indoors, and, having but little money to expend on a mask, they are inventive enough to devise all sorts of ways for disguising rather than adorning themselves.

The masks of beggars, male and female, are very easy to assume; beautiful hair is the first requirement, then a perfectly white mask, an earthen pipkin held by a coloured cord, a staff and a hat in the hand. With humble demeanour they step under the windows, bow before each person, receiving for alms sweets, nuts or other like dainty.

Others take it still easier, and, wrapping themselves up in cloaks, or appearing in a nice house-dress, their faces alone being masked, they go about for the most part without male attendants, carrying as their offensive and defensive weapon a small besom composed of cane-branches in blossom, which they in part use to ward off pestilent fellows, in part to flourish wantonly in the faces of acquaintances and strangers whom they meet without masks.

When four or five girls have once caught a man on whom they have designs, there is no deliverance for him. The throng prevents his escape, and let him turn how he will the besom is under his nose. To defend himself in earnest against such provocations would be a very dangerous experiment, seeing the masks are inviolate and under the special protection of the watch.

In the same way the usual dresses of all classes are made to serve as masks. Grooms with their big brushes fall to rubbing down any back they take a fancy to. Drivers offer their services with their usual importunity. Pretty, on the other hand, are the masks of the country girls, the Frascati maidens, fishers, Neapolitan watermen, Neapolitan bailiffs and Greeks.

Occasionally a theatrical mask is imitated. Some people again take little trouble about a mask, folding themselves up in tapestry or linen cloths, which they tie over the head.

A white figure is in the habit of stepping in the road of others, and hopping before them, by way of representing a ghost. Others distinguish themselves by odd combinations. The tabarro, however, as being the least distinctive, is deemed the noblest mask.

Witty and satirical masks are very rare, for these have a particular purpose in view, and aim at being particularly noticed. Yet I once saw a Punchinello in the character of a cuckold. The horns were moveable, the wearer being able to draw them out and in like those of a snail. When he stopped before the window of a newly married couple, and slipped out only the faint tip of one horn, or stepping up to another window shot out both horns to their utmost length, vigorously ringing the bells attached to their ends, the public in a moment gave merry attention and often laughed loudly.

A wizard mingles among the crowd, shows the people a book with numbers, and reminds them of their passion for lotteries.

One stands in the throng with two faces, so that you are at a loss to distinguish the front from the back of him, whether he is coming towards you or going from you.

Nor must the stranger feel any ill-humour, should he in these days find himself made the subject of jest. The long clothes of the native of the North, his large buttons, his curious round hat strike the fancy of the Romans, who therefore take the foreigner for a mask.

The foreign painters, particularly those given to the study of landscapes and buildings, and who are to be found sitting everywhere in public places in Rome drawing, are studiously caricatured and show themselves very busy with large portfolios, long surtouts, and colossal pencils.

The German journeymen-bakers in Rome, who are often found drunk, are represented in their own or in a somewhat ornamental costume, staggering about with a bottle of wine.

We remember but one satirical mask. It had been proposed to raise an obelisk in front of the Church of Trinità dei Mouti. The proposal, however, was not popular, partly because the place for its erection was very confined and partly because, for the sake of raising it to a certain height, it would be necessary to build a very high pedestal. It therefore occurred to one satirical wit to carry, by way of head-piece, an enormous white pedestal, crowned by an extremely small reddish obelisk. On the pedestal were large characters, the sense of which was guessed perhaps by only a few people.

Carriages.

While the masks are multiplying, the coaches gradually drive into the Corso in the order we have above described when speaking of the driving on Sundays and other holidays, with the difference only that the carriages coming from the Venetian Palace along the left-hand side of the street stop short at the point where the street now terminates, and then turning drive up on the other side.

We have already pointed out that, deducting the space appropriated for the foot pavements, the ground left in the middle of the Corso is at most places hardly more than the breadth of three carriages.

The foot pavements on each side are all blocked with scaffolds, or occupied with chairs, where many spectators are already seated. Alongside of the scaffolds and chairs there is a never-failing stream of carriages moving up or drifting down. The foot-passengers are therefore restricted to the interval between the carriage lines, of eight feet at most. Each one pushes and elbows his way about as best he can, and from all the windows and balconies a thronged populace looks down on a thronged populace.

In the first days of the Carnival only the ordinary carriages are to be seen, each person reserving for the following days anything ornamental or magnificent he has to bring out. Towards the end of the Carnival the more open carriages make their appearance, seating some six persons. Two ladies sit on raised seats opposite each other, displaying their whole figures; four gentlemen occupy the remaining four seats. Coachmen and servants are all in masks, the horses, too, being arrayed in gauze and flowers.

You often see a beautiful white poodle dog decked in rosy ribbons between the coachman's feet, while bells jingle from the horses' trappings; and the display rivets the attention of the public for a few moments.

As may be readily supposed, only beautiful women will mount a seat where they are so much in the eyes of the whole world, and only the fairest of the fair will there appear with unmasked face. When such a queen of beauty takes the Corso, crowning the slow-paced carriage, she becomes the cynosure of all eyes, and from many sides she may hear the words of admiration addressed to her, "O quanto è bella!"

In earlier times, these equipages are said to have been more numerous and more costly, being also rendered more interesting by mythological and allegorical representations. Lately, however, for whatever reason, the more distinguished folk appear to be lost in the mass, being more intent on enjoyment than on showing themselves better than others.

The more the Carnival advances towards its termination, the more splendid do the equipages become.

Even seriously disposed people, who sit themselves without masks in their carriages, permit their coachman and servants to wear them. The coachmen usually select a female dress, and in the last days of the Carnival women alone appear to drive the horses. They are often prettily, nay charmingly dressed. A squat ugly fellow, on the other hand, in the tip-top of fashion, with high frisure and feathers, makes a striking caricature, and as the beauties above referred to have to hear their praises sounded, so must he swallow the affront, when some one steps up to him and shouts, "O fratello mio, che brutta puttana sei!" (Oh, my brother, what an ugly drab you are!)

It is a common thing for the coachman if he comes across one or two of his female friends in the crowd, to lift them up on to the box. They sit beside him, generally in men's clothes, and then the neat little punchinello-legs, with small feet and high heels, often play antics with the heads of the passers-by.

The servants act in a similar style, taking up their male and female friends at the back of the carriage, and all that is left now is a place on the boot, as is the fashion in the case of English country coaches.

The masters and mistresses seem well pleased to see their carriages thoroughly packed; everything is permitted: everything is proper in these days.

Crowds.

Let us now glance at the long, narrow street, where from all balconies and windows thronged on-lookers, standing above long dependent bright cloths, gaze down on scaffolds packed with spectators, and on long lines of chairs on both sides of the street. Between the two lines of chairs crawl two lines of carriages. Between the two carriage lines, again, is a space capable of accommodating a third line of carriages, but which is now wholly occupied by people not walking but elbowing and jostling hither and thither. All precautions are taken to keep the coaches a little apart from each other, to prevent collision in case of a block. Many of the passengers, however, for the sake of a little air, venture to slip out of the throng into the narrow spaces between the wheels of the preceding and the horses of the succeeding carriages, and the greater the danger and difficulty to the walkers, the more do their wantonness and boldness seem to increase.

Most of the foot-passengers moving between the two carriage lines, to avoid danger to limbs and dress, carefully leave an interval between themselves and the wheels and axles of the coaches. Whoever, then, is tired of dragging along with the slow dense mass, and has the courage to do so, may slip into the vacant line between the wheels and the foot-passengers—between the danger and the avoider of it—and may thus in a short time trip over a long stretch of road, till he stumbles against some new obstacle.

Our narrative seems already to trespass the bounds of credibility, and we should scarcely venture any farther were it not for the many people who have been present at the Carnival, and who can vouch for the perfect accuracy of our statements; and were the Carnival not a yearly festival which may in future be visited with our book in hand.

For what will our readers now say, when we assure them that all we have above related is but, as it were, the first stage of the throng, tumult, uproar, and riot?

Procession of the Governor and Senator.

While the coaches push slowly forwards, and at every block come to a standstill, the foot-passengers have no few inconveniences to put up with.

The Pope's guard ride up and down individually among the throng to clear the occasional disorders and interruptions, and in endeavouring to get out of the way of the coach-horses, the foot-passenger only bobs up against the head of a saddle-horse. That, however, is not the worst of it.

The Governor drives in a large state-carriage with a retinue of several coaches along the interval between the two rows of other coaches. The Pope's guard and the servants who go in front warn the people to clear out of the way, this procession taking up for the moment the whole space shortly before occupied by the foot-passengers. The people jam themselves as best they can between the other carriages, and by hook or crook contrive to get to one side or the other. And as water when a ship cuts through it is parted only for a moment, at once commingling again behind the rudder, so the mass of masked and other foot-passengers at once re-unites behind the procession. Soon again, however, the straitened crowd is disturbed by some new movement.

The Senator advances with a similar procession. His great state-carriage and the carriages of his retinue swim as on the heads of the compressed crowd, and while every man, be he native or foreigner, is captivated and enchanted by the amiability of the present Senator, Prince Rezzonico, the Carnival is perhaps the only occasion when people wish him well out of their sight.

While these two processions of the heads of justice and police in Rome penetrated only the first day through the Corso for the sake of formally opening the Carnival, the Duke of Albania drove daily along the same route to the great inconvenience of the crowd; reminding Rome, the old ruler of kings, during a time of universal mummery, of the farce of his kingly pretensions.

The ambassadors, who had the same privilege of driving as he, used it sparingly and with humane discretion.

The Beau Monde at the Ruspoli Palace.

The free circulation of the Corso is, however, liable to interruptions and blocks other than those caused by these processions. At the Ruspoli Palace and its neighbourhood, where the street is not wider but the foot-pavements stand higher than elsewhere, the *beau monde* have taken possession of all the chairs. The fairest ladies of the middle-class charmingly masked, and waited upon by their friends, display their graces to the inquisitive eye of the passers-by. Whoever comes near them lingers to contemplate the fair rows, and each one endeavours, among the many male figures arrayed there, to single out the female ones, and in a pretty officer, perhaps, to discover the object of his longing. At this spot the movement first comes to a stand; the coaches stay as long as possible in this neighbourhood, and as one must come to a standstill at last, one prefers to remain in this pleasant society.

Comfits.

Hitherto our description has conveyed the idea of but a straitened or distressed situation. Now, however, we must relate how the compressed merriment is set in liveliest agitation by a petty warfare, carried on mostly in the way of jest, but often assuming an all-too-serious aspect.

Probably some time or other a fair one, to attract the notice of her passing friend amid all the hubbub and mummery, threw at him some sugared caraways, when, of course, nothing was more natural than that he should turn round and recognise his roguish fair one. This, at all events, has now grown a universal habit, and after a volley one often sees two friendly faces salute each other. Yet partly from economy, and partly from the abuse of the practice, genuine sweets are less used, and a cheaper and more plentiful stuff is demanded.

It has come to be a trade to carry about, among the crowd, for sale in large baskets gypsum trochisks, made by means of a funnel, and having the appearance of sugar-plums.

No man is safe from an attack; every one is, therefore, in a state of defence; and so, in wantonness or otherwise, there arises, now here, now there, a species of duel, skirmish, or battle. Foot-passengers, coach-drivers, spectators at windows, in stands, and on chairs, join in, reciprocally charging and defending.

The ladies have gilded and silver-plated little baskets full of these comfits, and their attendants stand sturdily to defend the fair ones. With their coach-windows dropped down the inmates await an onset. People jest with their friends, and defend themselves obstinately against strangers.

Nowhere, however, is this combat more earnest and general than in the neighbourhood of the Ruspoli Palace. All maskers who have places there are provided with baskets, bags, or handkerchiefs held by the four corners. They attack more than they are attacked. No coach passes with impunity, without suffering at the hands of some or other maskers. No foot-passenger is secure from them. An abbot in black dress becomes a target for missiles on all hands; and seeing that gypsum and chalk always leave their mark wherever they alight, the abbot soon gets spotted all over with white and grey. Often these affrays grow serious and general, and with astonishment you see how envy and personal hatred vent themselves in this way.

All unobserved a masked figure slips up, and with a handful of comfits pelts one of the first beauties so violently and unerringly that the masked face rattles, and the fair neck is marked. Her attendants on both sides are kindled into fury; with the contents of their baskets and bags they storm impetuously on the assailant. He is, however, too well masked and harnessed to suffer from the repeated discharges. The more invulnerable he is, the bolder he plies his onslaught. The defenders protect the lady with their tabarros. The assailant in the brunt of the battle assaults the neighbours too, and what with rudeness and violence generally offends every one, so that the surrounding people join issue and do not spare their comfits or the heavier ammunition, chiefly sugar almonds, that they have in reserve for such cases. At last, overpowered on all sides and with his shot all spent, the assailant is obliged to beat a retreat.

Usually, one does not commit himself to such an adventure without a second to reinforce him with ammunition. The men, too, who drive a trade with gypsum comfits, generally hasten to the scene of such an engagement, ready to weigh out shot from their baskets to any number of pounds.

We have ourselves witnessed a battle of this kind, when the combatants, from want of other ammunition, threw their gilt baskets at each other's heads, and could not be prevailed on by the watch, who suffered from the discharges, to desist from further warfare.

Assuredly, many of these frays would end in stabbings, did not the wound-up *corde*, the well-known instrument of Italian police, at several corners, remind people at all moments in the midst of their frolics how dangerous it would be for them to have recourse to dangerous weapons.

Innumerable are these frays, and generally more in the way of jest than earnest.

Here comes, for example, an open carriage, full of Punchinellos, towards Ruspoli. They intend while passing by the onlookers to hit them all one after the other. Unfortunately, however, the throng is too great, and the carriage is brought to a halt in the middle. All the surrounding people are at once animated by one purpose, and from all sides hail-showers descend on the coach. The Punchinellos in the carriage spend all their ammunition, and for a long time are exposed to a crossfire from all sides, till in the end the coach looks all covered over with snow and hail, in which state, amid universal ridicule and cries of indignation, it slowly moves off.

Dialogue at the Upper End of the Corso.

While in the middle of the Corso these lively and violent games occupy a large part of the fair sex, another part of the public finds at the upper end of the Corso another species of entertainment.

Not far from the French Academy appears, unexpectedly issuing from among the onlooking maskers on a scaffold, a so-called Capitano of the Italian Theatre, in Spanish dress, with feathered hat and large gloves, and begins in emphatic tones to relate his great deeds by land and water. He does not proceed far in his narrative till another Punchinello takes up a position over against him, suggests doubts and objections in reference to his statements, and while appearing to take all in good faith by the puns and platitudes he interjects he brings the great achievements of the hero into ridicule.

Here, too, each passer-by stands still to listen to the lively altercation.

King of the Punchinellos.

A new procession often increases the throng. A dozen Punchinellos choose a king, crown him, put a sceptre in his hand, attend him with music, and, in an ornamental little carriage, lead him up the Corso amid loud cries. All Punchinellos spring up to it as the procession advances, increase the train, and with shouting and brandishing of hats make room for it.

You then observe for the first time how each one endeavours to diversify these universal masks. One wears a wig, the other a woman's hood over his black face, the third for a cap has a cage stuck on his head with a pair of birds in it, dressed as abbot and dame, hopping about on the perches.

Side Streets.

The frightful crush we have endeavoured to the best of our ability to bring before the eyes of the readers drives, of course, a crowd of maskers out of the Corso into the neighbouring streets. There lovers walk more quietly and confidentially together, while madcaps find more scope there for their escapades.

A body of men, in the Sunday dress of the common people, in short doublets with gold-laced vests under them, the hair gathered up in a long descending net, walk up and down with young men disguised as women. One of the women appears to be far advanced in the family way; they walk quietly up and down. All at once the men begin to quarrel; a lively exchange of words arises; the women thrust themselves into the affair; the brawl grows from bad to worse. At last the combatants draw large knives of silvered pasteboard and fall foul of each other. The women, with dreadful cries, rush in to keep them apart, one being pulled in this direction, another in that. The onlookers join in the affair as though it were all in earnest, and try to bring each party to reason.

Meanwhile, the woman who is far gone in the family way falls ill from the shock. A chair is brought. The other women run to her assistance. Her appearance is pitiable, and before you are aware of it, she brings to the world some unshapely brat, to the great merriment of the spectators. The play is over, and the troop move on to some other place to repeat the same, or produce another like farce.

The Roman, who is continually hearing stories of murder, is disposed on every occasion to play with ideas of murder. The very children have a game they call *chiesa*, corresponding with our "Frischauf in allen Ecken." Properly, however, it represents a murderer who seeks refuge on the step of a church. The others represent the constables who in all ways endeavour to catch him without, however, daring to touch the place of refuge.

In the side streets, especially the Strada Babuina, and the Spanish Place, the mirth goes on with equal liveliness.

The quakers, too, come in flocks, the more freely to display their finery. They have a manœuvre which makes every one laugh. They come marching, twelve at a time, perfectly straight on tip-toe, in short and rapid steps, forming an entirely even front. When they come to a square, wheeling to right or left, they all at once form a column and now trip away behind each other. All at once, again, with a right turn they are restored to their former order; then, before you know where you are, again left turn. The column is shoved as if on a spit into a doorway, and the fools have disappeared.

Evening.

Now, evening approaches and everything that has life presses ever more into the Corso. The coaches have already been long at a standstill, nay, sometimes two hours before nightfall no carriage can any longer move from the spot.

The Pope's guard and the watchmen are now busy getting all carriages as far as possible away from the middle, and into a perfectly straight row, and with all the multitudinous crowding no little disorder and irritation are occasioned. Everywhere there is kicking, pushing, and pulling. A horse kicking, those behind necessarily back out of the way, and a carriage with its horses is fairly squeezed into the middle. Straightway descend on the carriage the opprobrium of the guard, the curses and threatenings of the watch.

No use for the unlucky coachman to accomplish apparent impossibilities; imprecations and threats assail him. If he cannot fall in again he must without any fault of his own away into the nearest side street. Ordinarily, the side streets are themselves chokeful of carriages which have arrived too late, and could no longer get into the line, because the circulation was already stopped.

Preparations for the Race.

The moment of the horse-race is drawing ever nearer, a moment on which the minds of so many thousands of men are strained.

The lenders of chairs, the erectors of scaffolds are now more importunate than ever with their cries "Luoghi! Luoghi avanti! Luoghi nobili! Luoghi Padroni!" It is their pressing interest that in the last moments the places they have to dispose of be all taken even though at a less charge.

And fortunate it is that there is still a vacant chair here and there. For the General, with a part of the guard, now rides down the Corso between the two rows of coaches, sweeping away the foot passengers from the only space that yet remained to them. Each one then looks out for a chair, a place on a scaffold, on a coach, between the carriages, or at a friend's window, every one of which is now running over with spectators.

Meanwhile, the place in front of the obelisk is entirely cleared of the people, and affords perhaps one of the finest sights in the present world.

The three façades, hung with carpets, of the above-described grand stands enclose the place. Many thousands of heads look forth, ranged in row above row, giving the picture of an ancient amphitheatre or circus. Above the central scaffold towers up in the air the whole height of the obelisk, the scaffold covering but the pedestal. Here you first become aware of its prodigious height, serving as it does by way of measure of the vast human mass. The open space gives the eye a refreshing sense of rest, and you look all expectation on the empty lists fronted by a rope.

The General now comes down the Corso, as a sign that the place is all cleared, and behind him the guard allow no man to step out of the row of the coaches. He takes a place in one of the boxes.

The Race.

The order of the horses having been determined by lot, they are led by dressed-out grooms into the lists behind the rope. They have no covering of any kind on the body. Here and there spiked balls are attached to them by cords, and the place where they will be spurred is protected by leather till the moment of starting. Large sheets of tinsel are stuck over them. When brought into the lists they are, mostly, wild and impatient, and it needs all the grooms' strength and tact to keep them in.

Their eagerness for the race makes them intractable; the presence of so many people makes them shy. They often toss their heads over into the neighbouring list and over the rope, and this movement and disorder intensify every moment the eager expectancy of the spectators.

The grooms are on the alert to the utmost degree, because at the moment of the start the skill of the man letting off the horse, as also accidental circumstances, tell greatly to the advantage of one horse or the other.

At last the rope falls, and the horses are off.

On the open square they endeavour to get ahead of each other, but when once they come into the narrow space between the two rows of coaches nearly all competition is useless.

One pair are generally in front, straining every muscle. Notwithstanding the scattered gravel fire strikes from the ground, the manes fly, the tinsel rustles, and you hardly catch a glance of them, when they are again out of sight. The rest of the horses impede each other, pushing and driving; and sometimes one clears the cavalcade and away, though late, after the other two, the riven pieces of tinsel fluttering over the forsaken track. Soon the horses are all vanished, the people reunite from both sides and again fill up the race-ground.

Other grooms await the arrival of the horses at the Venetian Palace. They contrive to catch and hold them fast in an enclosed place. The prize is awarded to the victor.

The holiday thus ends with an overpowering momentary sensation, swift as lightning; on which thousands of people have been strained for a considerable time, though most of them would be at a loss to explain the ground either of their expectation or of their gratification.

From the above description it may easily be inferred that this sport is apt to become dangerous both for animals and men. We will cite only a few instances. With the narrow passage between the carriages a backwheel may readily project a little outwards, leaving, perhaps, a somewhat wider space behind it. In this case a horse racing past, and sore pressed by the other horses, will in all likelihood take advantage of the piece of ground left vacant, when almost inevitably he will stumble on the projecting wheel.

We have ourselves seen a case in which a horse in such a plight fell from the shock, the next three horses chasing up behind tumbled over the first, while the last horses happily cleared those that were fallen and continued their career.

A horse falling in this way is often killed on the spot, and not seldom spectators also receive mortal injuries. A great mischief may also arise when the horses suddenly turn about.

It has sometimes happened that malignant, envious people, on seeing a horse a long way ahead of his competitors, have shaken their cloaks in his eyes, and by this action have caused him to turn about and run to one side. Still worse is it when the grooms at the Venetian Square have not succeeded in catching the horses. They, then, irresistibly face round, and, the race-course being wholly refilled with the crowd, many accidents are occasioned that are either not heard of or unheeded.

An End of Order.

The horses generally do not leave the ground till the night has set in. As soon as they have reached the Venetian Palace, little mortars are let off. This signal is repeated in the middle of the Corso, and given for the last time in the neighbourhood of the obelisk.

At this moment the watch leave their posts, the order of the coaches is no longer kept, and assuredly even for the spectator who looks down tranquilly on all from his window, this is an anxious and vexatious moment, and a few remarks regarding it will not be out of place.

We have already observed above that the fall of night, which is decisive of so much in Italy, breaks up the usual drives on Sundays and festival days. There are no watch and no guards, but it is an old custom, an universal convention, that people drive up and down in the order we have described. So soon, however, as Ave Maria is rung, no one will give up his right of turning about at any time and in any way he pleases. The driving during Carnival on the Corso being subject to the same laws, though the crowding and other circumstances make a great difference, no one will give up his right to abandon the established order.

When we look to the prodigious throng, and see the race-course, which had been cleared but for a moment, again inundated in a trice with people, it would seem only reasonable that each equipage should seek in due order the nearest side street and hasten home.

But as soon as the signal has been given, some carriages press into the middle of the street, jamming and confusing the foot-passengers; and as the one coach fancies a drive-up, the other a drive-down, in the narrow space, the two block up each other's way, and often prevent the more reasonable people who have kept the rank from making the least progress.

Let a returning horse now come upon such a complication, and danger, mischief, and vexation increase on all sides.

Night.

And yet, later on, all this muddle and confusion are for the most part happily cleared up. Night has fallen, and each one wishes himself the happiness of a little rest.

Theatres.

All face-masks are from this moment removed, and a great part of the public hasten to the theatre. Only in the boxes you may still see tabarros and ladies in mask-dresses. The whole pit appears again in ordinary costume.

The Aliberti and Argentina theatres give grave operas, with intercalated ballets; Valle and Capranica comedies and tragedies, with comic operas for interlude. Pace imitates them, though imperfectly; and so down to puppet-shows and rope-dancing booths there is a wide range of subordinate theatres.

The great Tordenone theatre, which was once burnt down and on being re-built immediately fell in, unfortunately no longer entertains the people with its blood-and-thunder tragedies and other wondrous representations.

The passion of the Romans for the theatre is great, and was formerly in the Carnival time still more ardent, because only at that season could it be gratified. At present there is at least one play-house open in summer and autumn as well as winter, and the public can in some measure satisfy its desires in this respect the greater part of the year.

It would lead us too far away from the purpose on hand were we to give a circumstantial description of the theatres and their idiosyncracies. Our readers will remember our treatment of this subject at another place.

Festine.

We shall, likewise, have little to relate about the so-called "Festine." They are great mask-balls occasionally given in the beautifully illuminated Aliberti theatre.

Here, too, tabarros have the reputation of being the most becoming mask both for gentlemen and ladies, and the whole salon is filled with black figures, a few character-masks being sprinkled among them.

All the greater curiosity, therefore, is excited when a few noble figures appear displaying, what is a rather rare sight, masks taken from various art-epochs and imitating in a masterly way various statues preserved in Rome. In this manner are shown Egyptian Gods, Priestesses, Bacchus and Ariadne, the Tragic Muse, the Historical Muse, a Town, Vestals, a Consul; all being in accordance with the costume more or less happily carried out.

Dances.

The dances during these holidays are generally in long rows according to English fashion. The only difference is that in their few rounds they mostly express pantomimically some characteristic action or other. For example, two lovers have a fall out, then a reconciliation; they part, and meet again.

The Romans, through these pantomimic ballets, are accustomed to strongly marked gesticulation. In their social dances, too, they love an expression which would appear to us exaggerated and affected. No one will readily engage in dancing who has not learned it artistically. The minuet, in particular, is looked upon as a work of art, and represented, so to say, by but few couples. A couple doing a performance of this kind is quite enclosed by the rest of the company, who watch their movements with admiration, and at the end shower their applauses on them.

Morning.

If the fashionable world amuses itself in this fashion till morning, in the Corso people are busy at break of day cleaning and sorting it. Particular attention is paid to the equal and clean dispersion of the puzzolane in the middle of the street.

It is not long before the grooms bring the race-horse, which yesterday showed the worst behavior, before the obelisk. A little boy is mounted on it and another rider with a whip lashes it from behind, making it speed to the goal at its swiftest pace.

About two o'clock in the afternoon, after the bell has rung out the signal, there begins anew each day the round of the festival as already described. The walkers direct their steps to the Corso; the watch march up; balconies, windows, scaffolds are again hung with tapestries; the maskers multiply and give vent to their follies; the coaches drive up and down; the street is more or less thronged, according as weather or other circumstances are favourable or unfavourable. Towards the end, the Carnival naturally increases in spectators, masks, carriages, dresses, and noise. Nothing, however, which precedes comes at all near to the throng and excesses of the last day and evening.

Last Day.

Generally by two hours before night-fall the rows of coaches are entirely at a standstill. No carriage can any longer move from the spot, nor can any in the side streets squeeze in. The scaffolds and chairs are filled at an earlier hour, although the places are let out dearer. Every one seeks to secure a place at the earliest moment and people await the running of the horses with more intense longing than ever.

At last this moment also flies by. The signal is given that the festival is at an end. Neither carriage, nor masker, nor spectator, however, shifts ground.

All is quiet, all hushed, while the dusk gently deepens.

Moccoli.

Hardly have the shades of night crept over the narrow and lofty street when lights are seen shining forth here and there, at the windows, and on the scaffolds; in a short time the circulation of light has proceeded so far that the whole street is luminous with burning wax-tapers.

The balconies are adorned with transparent paper-lanterns. Each person holds his taper out of the window; all scaffolds are illuminated. The inside of the coaches, from whose roofs hang down small crystal chandeliers shedding light on the company, are very pretty, while in other carriages ladies, with bright tapers in their hands, seem to invite outsiders to contemplate their beauty.

The servants stick little tapers on the edges of the coach-roof. Open carriages appear with bright paper-lanterns. Many of the foot-passengers display high light-pyramids on their heads; others have their lights stuck on reeds fastened together, which often attain, with the rod, to a height of two or three stories.

It is now incumbent on every one to carry a taper in his hand, and the favourite imprecation of the Romans, "Sia ammazzato!" (Be murdered!) is heard from all ends and corners. "Sia ammazzato chi non porta moccolo!" (Murder to him who does not carry a taper!) you hear one calling out to the other, while at the same time trying to blow out his neighbour's taper. What with kindling and blowing out lights and the uncontrollable cry, "Sia ammazzato!" life and bustle and mutual interest pervade the prodigious crowd.

No matter whether the person next you is an acquaintance or a stranger, you equally try to blow out his light, and on his rekindling it to blow it out again. And the stronger the bellowing, "Sia ammazzato!" reverberates from all sides, the more does the expression lose its dreadful meaning, the more you forget you are in Rome, in a place where for a trifle such an imprecation might speedily be given effect to.

In time the expression loses all trace of horror. And as in other languages curses and disparaging phrases are often used as interjections of admiration and joy, so in Italian you often hear this evening "Sia ammazzato!" employed as watch-word, as cry of joy, as refrain for all jests, banterings, and compliments.

Thus we hear jestingly, "Sia ammazzato il Signore Abbate che fa l'amore!" (Be murdered the abbot who is making love!) Or one calls to his intimate friend passing by, "Sia ammazzato il Signore Filippo!" Or, in the way of flattery and compliment, "Sia ammazzata la bella Principessa!" "Sia ammazzata la Signora Angelica, la prima pittrice del secolo!" (Be murdered Signora Angelica, the first painter of the age!)

All these phrases are sung out swiftly and impetuously, with a long drawl on the penultimate or antepenultimate. Amid all this never-ceasing cry the blowing-out and kindling of tapers go on constantly. Whomsoever you meet in the house, on the stairs, whether you are in a room with company, or see your neighbour when looking out from your window, you everywhere endeavour to get the advantage of him in blowing out his light.

All ages and classes contend furiously with each other. They jump on the steps of each other's coaches. No pendant light, hardly a lantern is safe. The boy blows out his father's flame and never ceases crying, "Sia ammazzato il Signore Padre!" All in vain for the father to scold him for his impudence; the boy asserts the freedom of the evening, and only the more savagely murders his father. The tumult, while growing fainter on both ends of the Corso, becomes the more uncontrollable in the centre, so that at last there arises a crush past all conception; past the power of the liveliest memory to realise again.

No one dares move from the place where he stands or sits. The heat of such a throng of people, of so many lights, the smoke of tapers ever blown out and ever rekindled, the infinitude of cries from so many men who bellow the more the less they can move a limb—all this, at last, makes the most robust senses giddy. It appears impossible that many accidents should not happen; that the coach-horses should not get wild; that many persons should not get crushed, squeezed, or otherwise hurt.

And yet, as each one ultimately longs more or less to get away, striking into the nearest lane he can reach, or seeking free air and relief in the nearest square, the mass of people is gradually broken up, dissolving from the ends of the street towards the middle, and this festival of general unrestrained licence, these modern Saturnalia close with a universal stupefaction.

The common people now hasten to feast till midnight on a well-prepared banquet of meat soon to be forbidden, while the more elegant world betakes itself to the playhouses to bid farewell to greatly curtailed pieces. At last the stroke of midnight puts an end to these pleasures also.

Ash-Wednesday.

And so vanishes the extravagant festival like a dream, like a tale—leaving, perhaps, less trace in the soul of the actors than remains in the minds of our readers to whom we have presented the whole in its connection.

If during the course of these follies the rude Punchinello has reminded us, though unbecomingly, of the joys of love to which we owe our existence, if a Baubo on the open square has desecrated the secrets of woman in childbearing, if so many kindled tapers have put us in mind of the end of the holiday, we may in the midst of so much nonsense have had our attention drawn by means of these symbols to the most important scenes in our life.

Still more does the narrow, long, densely-packed street suggest to us the ways of the world, where each spectator and actor, with natural face or under mask, from balcony or scaffold, sees but a short distance before and around him, makes progress in coach or on foot only step by step, is rather pushed than walks, is detained more perforce than of free will, endeavours with all zeal to attain a better and less confined position only to find himself in new embarrassments, till at last he is crushed out of the way.

Might we continue a more serious style of speech than the subject seems to allow, we should remark that the intensest and highest pleasures appear to us like the fleeting coursers but for a moment, rustling past us and leaving hardly any trace on our mind; that freedom and equality can only be enjoyed in the tumult of folly; and that the greatest pleasure only powerfully allures when it trenches upon danger, and tempts us by the offer of bitter-sweet gratifications in its vicinity.

In this way, without premeditation, we should have concluded our Carnival, too, with Ash-Wednesday reflections. Not that we would cast any shade of sadness on our readers. On the contrary, seeing that life as a whole, like the Roman Carnival, stretches far beyond our ken, and is full of troubles and vexations, we would desire that every one should with us be reminded by this careless crowd of maskers of the importance of every momentary, and often apparently trivial enjoyment of life.

Editor's Note

Goethe's essay on the Roman Carnival was included in the two-volume travel journal published as *Italiänische Reise* (Stuttgart and Tübingen: Zweiter Theil, 1816–17). A recent edition, translated and edited by W. H. Auden, is *Italian Journey* (New York: Pantheon Books, 1962). A bibliography on the journey and this essay is in the Hamburg edition of Goethe's *Werke* (Hamburg: Wegner, 1949–62), 14 vols., 2: 679–83, 683–85.

On this journey and its importance for Goethe's work see P. Hume Brown, *Life of Goethe* (London: Murray, 1920), 2 vols., 1: 328–35, 339–45; 2: 629, 636, 725; Albert Bielschowsky, *The Life of Goethe* (New York: AMS Press, 1970; reprint of the 1905–8 edition), 3 vols., 2: 381–95, 402–7.

For his correspondence, see Goethe's *Letters from Switzerland. Letters from Italy* (Boston: Niccols and Company, 1902), pp. 221–87.

Many famous writers visited Rome and left accounts of its Carnival. For example, Michel de Montaigne saw it in 1581. See *The Complete Works of Montaigne*, Donald M. Frame, trans. and ed. (Stanford: Stanford University Press, 1958), pp. 946–47. Adventurer Giacomo Casanova saw it in 1760 and left a brief description of it. See *The Memoirs of Jacques Casanova* (Garden City, N.Y.: Garden City Publishing Company, 1929), p. 217. Madame de Staël witnessed the 1805 Carnival. See her *Corinne ou l'Italie* (New York: Appleton, 1876), pp. 167–75. Commenting on Goethe's account, she wrote (p. 171), "Il faut lire sur ce carnival de Rome une charmante description de Goethe, qui en est un tableau aussi fidèle qu'animé" (On this Roman Carnival one must read a charming description by Goethe, which is a picture of it as faithful as it is animated).

For the origins of the Roman Carnival in

ancient Rome, see for instance Ambrosius Aurelius Theodosius Macrobius, *The Saturnalia*, trans. and ed. Percival Vaughan Davis (New York: Columbia University Press, 1969); A. W. J. Holleman, "Ovid and the Lupercalia," *Historia* 22 (1973): 260–68; *Pope Gelasius I and the Lupercalia* (Amsterdam: Hakkert, 1974); W. M. Green, "The Lupercalia in the Fifth Century," *Classical Philology* 26 (1931): 60–69; A. Michels and A. Kirsopp, "The Topography and Interpretation of the Lupercalia," *Transactions of the American Philological Association* 84 (1953): 35–59. On ancient Roman festivals, see William Warde Fowler, *The Roman Festivals of the Period of the Republic* (London–New York: Macmillan, 1899); H. H. Scullard, *Festivals and Ceremonies of the Roman Republic* (London: Thames and Hudson, 1981); Georges Dumézil, *Fêtes Romaines d'été et d'automne* (Paris: Gallimard, 1975).

For Carnival theater and its relationship with the development of Italian comic theater, see Paolo Toschi, *Le Origini del Teatro Italiano* (Turin: Boringhieri, 1976), pp. 122–412.

For Roman Carnivals from the beginnings through the Renaissance, see Filippo Clementi, *Il carnevale Romano nelle Cronache Contemporanee*, vol. 1 (Rome: F. Setth, 1899).

For Roman festivals of the Middle Ages and the Renaissance, see Fileno Antigoneo, *Feste e Spettacoli di Roma dal sec. X a tutto il XVI, particolarmente nel carnevale e nel Maggio* (Rome: Tipografia Forense, 1861); Josef Bayer, *Aus Italien. Kultur und Kunstgeschichtliche* (Leipzig: Glischer, 1885) (Roman and Florentine carnival festivities from the fifteenth and sixteenth centuries are discussed on pp. 149–224).

For carnivals in the 1600s and 1700s, see Maurizio Fagiolo dell'Arco and Silvia Carandini, *L'effimero barocco: strutture della Festa nella Roma del '600*, 2 vols. (Rome: Bulzoni, 1977–78); Martine Boiteaux, "Carnaval Annexé: essai de lecture d'une fête romaine," *Annales Economies Societés Civilisations* 32 (1977), no. 2: 356–80; Per Bjurstrom, *Feast and Theater in Queen Christina's Rome*, Nationalmusei skriftserie, no. 14 (Stockholm: 1966); Luigi Fiorani, G. Mantovano, P. Pecchiai, A. Martini, G. Oriali, *Riti, cerimonie, feste e vita di popolo nella Roma dei Papi* (Bologna: Cappelli, 1970); Alessandro Ademollo, *Il Carnevale a Roma nei secoli XVII e XVIII* (Rome: Sommaruga, 1883) (Goethe's visit is discussed on pp. 122–27, 131–36, 161–68). For the eighteenth and nineteenth centuries, see Filippo Clementi, *Il Carnevale Romano nelle Cronache Contemporanee*, vol. 2 (Città di Castello: RORE-NIRUF, 1938) (for the period of Goethe's visit, see pp. 165–221).

For descriptions of Roman carnivals and festivities of the period following Goethe's visit, see, for instance, Ugo Pesci, "I moccoletti e il Carnevale a Roma," *Illustrazione Italiana* 7 (1880), no. 7: pp. 99–102; Ignazio Cantù, *Il Carnevale Italiano* (Milan: Vallardi, 1885) (especially chapters IX, X, XI, and XII); Frances Elliot, *Diary of an Idle Woman in Italy* (Leipzig: Tauchnitz, 1872), 2 vols., 2: 67–91.

3 / The Palio at Siena

Aldous Huxley

Not all men of letters who visited festivals had the stamina, objectivity, and systematic outlook of Goethe. Most of them were easily seduced by the picturesque and aesthetic aspects of the celebrations.

In 1925, after his third visit to the Palio of Siena, Aldous Huxley wrote this elegant report for the cultivated elite who read the refined, slightly snobbish Cornhill Magazine *of London. The article is as much a document of their taste and Huxley's brilliant literary style, intelligence, and finesse as it is an account of the festival, since it proceeds by aesthetic notations, digressions, and comparisons rather than by description, analysis, and interpretation.*

Observing the punctilious weeding of the festival grounds, Huxley embarks on a subtle digression on modernity, urban landscape, and Fascist Italy. Looking at the crowded square before the pageant and the race, he recalls the gatherings at the Derby or Wembley sporting events. Admiring the silks, furs, brocades and velvets of the Palio costumes, cut and coordinated with the "faultless taste of the early Renaissance," he compares them to the work of the most famous designers of Paris high fashion—Mrs. Paquin, Jeanne Lanvin, and Isadora Duncan's friend Paul Poiret, whose controversial fashion show in the London residence of Prime Minister Asquith a few years earlier had almost provoked the fall of his cabinet.

The sophisticated name dropping continues throughout the article. While speaking of shrubs and weeds, Huxley mentions Giambattista Piranesi (1720–78), architect and etcher, author of a monumental pictorial work on Roman antiquities. The Palio flags, with their incredibly "modern" patterns, could be "futuristic" or "jazz" (Huxley's wife later defined them as "psychedelic"), or easily part of Picasso's sensational 1917 Parisian stage design for the Ballets Russes of Sergei Diaghilev. The pages in their Renaissance liveries seem freshly out of a Pinturicchio fresco, and Huxley and his readers had certainly admired Pinturicchio's Return of Ulysses at the National Gallery in London. In fact, the Contrada costumes that Huxley saw were inspired by and, in a few instances, faithfully reproduced from the paintings of the Perugian-born Pinturicchio (Bernardino di Betto, 1454–1513), who also painted part of the Sistine Chapel, lived and worked in Siena, and was buried in one of the Contrada churches.

Huxley even has a fitting reference for the dashing cavalcade of Italian carabineri, who clear the race track in their Napoleonic attire: Carle Vernet (1758–1836), the painter who followed Napoleon on his Italian campaign and who painted, on location, his most famous battles as well as the social life of the elegant society of the day.

Not that Huxley was patronizing or condescending. On the contrary, he takes amiable exception to the ideas of John Ruskin (1819–1900), Slade Professor of Art at Oxford and inspiration of the pre-Raphaelite artists largely responsible for the excesses of British neo-Gothic painting in the late nineteenth century. Ruskin also wrote The Stones of Venice, as well as several prefaces to ladies' travel journals and dainty sketchbooks of picturesque city and country life in Italy.

Another personage sarcastically mentioned is the irrepressible Louis Napoleon Parker (1852–1944). Parker was the inventor, organizer, master of ceremonies, and above all the official poet of a score of British pageants (including events at York, Dover, Sherborne, and Claremont for the royal fête of 1907) commemorating anything from the thousandth anniversary of the conquest of Mercia by Queen Ethelfelda or the twelve hundredth anniversary of the town of Sherborne, to the activities of Disraeli and Sir Francis Drake. Compared to these "dead-born English affairs" with all their blank verse, choruses, flannelette costumes and artificially lofty sentiments, the Palio was unmistakably authentic. But Huxley does not pursue this thought. The antiquity and continuity of the Palio are seen as the cause (and not effect, which in fact they are) of its authenticity.

Similarly, Huxley perceived that the Palio is somehow related for the Sienese to gambling and local patriotism, but again the thought is not elaborated. The furious fights after the race are explained and dismissed by the fact that all Sienese want their Contrada to win.

Not even a passing reference is made to the seventeen Contrada wards, the cities-within-the-city which vie for the Palio ten at a time. Nor to their year-round, centuries-old social life and ceremonies involving a population, formal membership, elected officials, territory, club, museum, and church. No mention is made of the choice and drawing of the horses, of the six trial races, or of the banquets the evening before the Palio. Nor is mention made of the complicated system of fierce rivalries and unstable alliances between Contrade. With all the name dropping, not even one Contrada name is mentioned. However, Huxley was not a superficial visitor. He knew the city and its *traditions well. He simply thought that these cold facts were not as effective, suggestive, or aesthetically pleasing as the dashing pages tossing their Picasso flags high into the air with centuries-old grace and nonchalance. Huxley preferred to recreate an enchanted atmosphere: "Was it a fable? . . . or was it true?" Caught between dream and reality, he preferred to postpone speculation indefinitely and invite his readers to enjoy with him the living Pinturicchio frescoes, the flags moving like the painted wings of enormous butterflies, and the swallows flying higher and higher above the tiled roofs and Gothic towers of Siena to catch the last rays of sunset.*

The Palio at Siena*

Aldous Huxley

Our rooms were in a tower. From the windows one looked across the brown tiled roofs to where, on its hill, stood the cathedral. A hundred feet below was the street, a narrow canyon between high walls, perennially sunless; the voices of the passers-by came up, reverberating, as out of a chasm. Down there they walked always in shadow; but in our tower we were the last to lose the sunlight. On the hot days it was cooler, no doubt, down in the street; but we at least had the winds. The waves of the air broke against our tower and flowed past it on either side. And at evening, when only the belfries and the domes and the highest roofs were still flushed by the declining sun, our windows were level with the flight of the swifts and swallows. Sunset after sunset all through the long summer, they wheeled and darted round our tower. There was always a swarm of them intricately manoeuvring just outside the window. They swerved this way and that, they dipped and rose, they checked their headlong flight with a flutter of their long pointed wings and turned about within their own length. Compact, smooth and tapering, they seemed the incarnation of airy speed. And their thin, sharp, arrowy cry was speed made audible. I have sat at my window watching them tracing their intricate arabesques until I grew dizzy; till their shrill crying sounded as though from within my ears and their flying seemed a motion, incessant, swift and bewilderingly multitudinous, behind my eyes. And all the while the sun declined, the shadows climbed higher up the houses and towers, and the light with which they were tipped became more rosy. And at last the shadow had climbed to the very top and the city lay in a grey and violet twilight beneath the pale sky.

One evening, towards the end of June, as I was sitting at the window looking at the wheeling birds, I heard through the crying of the swifts the sound of a drum. I looked down into the shadowy street, but could see nothing. Rub-a-dub, dub, dub, dub—the sound grew louder and louder, and suddenly there appeared round the corner where our street bent out of sight, three personages out of a Pinturicchio fresco. They were dressed in liveries of green and yellow—yellow doublets slashed and tagged with green, parti-coloured hose and shoes, with feathered caps of the same colours. Their leader played the drum. The two who followed carried green and yellow banners. Immediately below our tower the street opens out a little into a tiny piazza. In this clear space the three Pinturicchio figures came to a halt and the crowd of little boys and loafers who followed at their heels grouped themselves round to watch. The drummer quickened his beat and the two banner-bearers stepped forward into the middle of the little square. They stood there for a moment quite still, the right foot a little in advance of the other, the left fist on the hip and the lowered banners drooping from the right. Then, together, they lifted the banners and began to wave them round their heads. In the wind of their motion the flags opened out. They were the same size and both of them green and yellow, but the colours were arranged in a different pattern on each. And what patterns! Nothing more "modern" was ever seen. They might have been designed by Picasso for the Russian Ballet. Had they been by Picasso, the graver critics would have called them futuristic, the sprightlier (I must apologize for both these expressions) jazz. But the flags were not Picasso's; they were designed some four hundred years ago by the nameless genius who dressed the Sienese for their yearly pageant. This being the case, the critics can only take off their hats. The flags are classical, they are High Art; there is nothing more to be said.

The drum beat on. The bannermen waved their flags, so artfully that the whole expanse of patterned stuff was always unfurled and tremulously stretched along the air. They passed the flags from one hand to the other, behind their backs, under a lifted leg. Then, at last, drawing themselves together to make a supreme effort, they tossed their banners into the air. High they rose, turning slowly, over and over, hung for an instant at the height of their trajectory, then dropped back, the weighted stave foremost, towards their throwers, who caught them as they fell. A final wave, then the drum returned to its march rhythm, the bannermen shouldered their flags, and followed by the anachronistic children and idlers from the twentieth century, Pinturicchio's three young bravos swaggered off up the dark street out of sight and at length, the drum taps coming faintlier and ever faintlier, out of hearing.

Every evening after that, while the swallows were in full cry and flight about the tower, we heard the beating of the drum. Every evening, in the little piazza below us, a fragment of Pinturicchio came to life. Sometimes it was our friends in green and yellow who returned to wave their flags beneath our windows. Sometimes it was men from the other *contrade* or districts of the town, in blue and white, red and white, black, white and orange, white, green and red, yellow and scarlet. Their bright pied doublets and parti-coloured hose shone out from among the drabs and funereal blacks of the twentieth-century crowd that surrounded them. Their spread flags waved in the street below, like the painted wings of enormous butterflies. The drummer quickened his beat, and to the accompaniment of a long-drawn rattle, the banner leapt up, furled and fluttering, into the air.

To the stranger who has never seen a Palio these little dress rehearsals are richly promising and exciting. Charmed by these present hints, he looks forward eagerly to what the day itself holds in store. Even the Sienese are excited. The pageant, however familiar, does not pall on them. And all the gambler in them, all the local patriot looks forward to the result of the race. Those last days of June before the first Palio, that middle week of August before the second, are days of growing excitement and tension in Siena. One enjoys the Palio the more for having lived through them.

Even the mayor and corporation are infected by the pervading excitement. They are so far carried away that, in the last days of June, they send a small army of men down in the great square before the Palazzo Comunale to eradicate every blade of grass or tuft of moss that can be found growing in the crannies between the flagstones. It amounts almost to a national characteristic, this hatred of growing things among the works of men. I have often, in old Italian towns, seen workmen laboriously weeding the less frequented streets and squares. The Colosseum, mantled till thirty or forty years ago with a romantic, Piranesian growth of shrubs, grasses and flowers, was officially weeded with such extraordinary energy that its ruinousness was sensibly increased. More stones were brought down in those few months of weeding than had fallen of their own accord in the previous thousand years. But the Italians were pleased; which is, after all, the chief thing that matters. Their hatred of weeds is fostered by their national pride; a great country, and one which specially piques itself on being modern, cannot allow weeds to grow even among its ruins. I entirely understand and sympathise with the Italian point of view. If Mr. Ruskin and his disciples had talked about my house and me as they talked about Italy and the Italians, I too should pique myself on being up-to-date; I should put in bathrooms, central heating and a lift, I should have all the moss scratched off the walls, I should lay cork lino on the marble floors. Indeed, I think that I should probably, in my irritation, pull down the whole house and build a new one. Considering the provocation they have received, it seems to me that the Italians have been remarkably moderate in the matter of weeding, destroying and rebuilding. Their moderation is due in part, no doubt, to their comparative poverty. Their ancestors built with such prodigious solidity that it would cost as much to pull down one of their old houses as to build a new one. Imagine, for example, demolishing the Palazzo Strozzi in Florence. It would be about as easy to demolish the Matterhorn. In Rome, which is predominantly a baroque, seventeenth-century city, the houses are made of flimsier stuff. Consequently, modernisation progresses there much more rapidly than in most other Italian towns. In wealthier England very little antiquity has been permitted to stand. Thus, most of the great country houses of England were rebuilt during the eighteenth century. If Italy had preserved her independence and her prosperity during the seventeenth, eighteenth and nineteenth centuries, there would probably be very much less mediaeval or Renaissance work now surviving than is actually the case. Money is lacking to modernize completely. Weeding has the merit of being cheap and, at the same time, richly symbolic. When you say of a town that the grass grows in its streets, you mean that it is utterly dead. Conversely, if there is no grass in its streets, it must be alive. No doubt the mayor and corporation of Siena did not put the argument quite so explicitly. But that the argument was put somehow, obscurely and below the surface of the mind, I do not doubt. The weeding was symbolic of modernity.

With the weeders came other workmen who built up round the curving flanks of the great piazza a series of wooden stands, six tiers high, for the spectators. The piazza which is shaped, whether by accident or design I do not know, like an ancient theatre, became for the time being indeed a theatre. Between the seats and the central area of the place, a track was railed off and the slippery flags covered parsimoniously with sand. Expectation rose higher than ever.

And at last the day came. The swallows and swifts wove their arabesques as usual in the bright golden light above the town. But their shrill crying was utterly inaudible, through the deep, continuous, formless murmur of the crowd that thronged the streets and the great piazza. Under its canopy of stone the great bell of the Mangia tower swung incessantly backwards and forwards; it too seemed dumb. The talking, the laughter, the shouting of forty thousand people rose up from the piazza in a column of solid sound, impenetrable to any ordinary noise.

It was after six. We took our places in one of the stands opposite the Palazzo Comunale. Our side of the piazza was already in the shade; but the sun still shone on the palace and its tall slender tower, making their rosy brickwork glow as though by inward fire. An immense concourse of people filled the square and all the tiers of seats round it. There were people in every window, even on the roofs. At the Derby, on boat-race days, at Wembley I have seen larger crowds; but never, I think, so many people confined within so small a space.

The sound of a gunshot broke through the noise of voices; and at the signal a company of mounted carabiniers rode into the piazza, driving the loungers who still thronged the track before them. They were in full dress uniform, black and red, with silver trimmings; cocked hats on their heads and swords in their hands. On their handsome little horses, they looked like a squadron of smart Napoleonic cavalry. The idlers retreated before them, squeezing their way through every convenient opening in the rails into the central area, which was soon densely packed. The track was cleared at a walk and, cleared, was rounded again at the trot, dashingly, in the best Carle Vernet style. The carabiniers got their applause and retired. The crowd waited expectantly. For a moment there was almost a silence. The bell on the tower ceased to be dumb. Some one in the crowd let loose a couple of balloons. They mounted perpendicularly into the still air, a red sphere and a purple. They passed out of the shadow into the sunlight; and the red became a ruby, the purple a glowing amethyst. When they had risen above the level of the roofs, a little breeze caught them and carried them away, still mounting all the time, over our heads, out of sight.

There was another gunshot and Vernet was exchanged for Pinturicchio. The noise of the crowd grew louder as they appeared, the bell swung, but gave no sound, and across the square the trumpets of the procession were all but inaudible. Slowly they marched round, the representatives of all the seventeen *contrade* of the city. Besides its drummer and its two bannermen, each *contrada* had a man-at-arms on horseback, three or four halbardiers and young pages and, if it happened to be one of the ten competing in the race, a jockey, all of them wearing the Pinturicchian livery in its own particular colours. Their progress was slow; for at every fifty paces they stopped, to allow the bannermen to give an exhibition of their skill with the flags. They must have taken the best part of an hour to get round. But the time seemed only too short. The Palio is a spectacle of which one does not grow tired. I have seen it three times now and was as much delighted on the last occasion as on the first.

English tourists are often sceptical about the Palio. They remember those terrible "pageants" which were all the rage some fifteen years ago in their own country, and they imagine that the Palio will turn out to be something of the same sort. But let me reassure them; it is not. There is no poetry by Louis Napoleon Parker at Siena. There are no choruses of young ladies voicing high moral sentiments in low voices. There are no flabby actor-managers imperfectly disguised as Hengist and Horsa, no crowd of gesticulating supernumeraries dressed in the worst of taste and the cheapest of bunting. Nor finally does one often meet at Siena with that almost invariable accompaniment of the English pageant—rain. No, the Palio is just a show; having no "meaning" in particular, but by the mere fact of being traditional and still alive, signifying infinitely more than the dead-born English affairs for all their Parkerian blank verse and their dramatic re-evocations. For these pages and men-at-arms and bannermen come straight out of the Pinturicchian past. Their clothes are those designed for their ancestors, copied faithfully, once in a generation, in the same colours and the same rich materials. They walk, not in cotton or flannelette, but in silks and furs and velvets. And the colours were matched, the clothes originally cut by men whose taste was the faultless taste of the early Renaissance. To be sure there are costumiers with as good a taste in these days. But it was not Paquin, not Lanvin or Poiret who dressed the actors of the English pageants; it was professional wig-makers and lady amateurs. I have already spoken of the beauty of the flags—the bold, fantastic, "modern" design of them. Everything else at the Palio is in keeping with the flags, daring, brilliant and yet always right, always irreproachably refined. The one false note is always the *Palio* itself—the painted banner which is given to the *contrada* whose horse wins the race. This banner is specially painted every year for the occasion. Look at it, where it comes along, proudly exposed on the great mediæval war chariot which closes the procession—look at it, or preferably don't look at it. It is a typical property from the wardrobe of an English pageant committee. It is a lady amateur's masterpiece. Shuddering, one averts the eyes.

Preceded by a line of *quattrocento* pages carrying festoons of laurel leaves and escorted by a company of mounted knights, the war chariot rolled slowly and ponderously past, bearing aloft the unworthy trophy. And by now the trumpets at the head of the procession sounded, almost inaudibly for us, from the further side of the piazza. And at last the whole procession had made its round and was lined up in close order in front of the Palazzo Comunale. Over the heads of the spectators standing in the central area, we could see all the thirty-four banners waving and waving in a last concerted display and at last, together, all leaping high into the air, hesitating at the top of their leap, falling back, out of sight. There was a burst of applause. The pageant was over. Another gunshot. And in the midst of more applause, the racehorses were ridden to the starting place.

The course is three times round the piazza, whose shape, as I have said, is something like that of an ancient theatre. Consequently, there are two sharp turns, where the ends of the semicircle meet the straight diameter. One of these, owing to the irregularity of the plan, is sharper than the other. The outside wall of the track is padded with mattresses at this point, to prevent impetuous jockeys who take the corner too fast from dashing themselves to pieces. The jockeys ride bareback; the horses run on a thin layer of sand spread over the flagstones of the piazza. The Palio is probably the most dangerous flat-race in the world. And it is made the more dangerous by the excessive patriotism of the rival *contrade*. For the winner of the race as he reins in his horse after passing the post, is set upon by the supporters of the other *contrade* (who all think that *their* horse should have won), with so real and earnest a fury that the carabiniers must always intervene to protect man and beast from lynching. Our places were at a point some two or three hundred yards beyond the post, so that we had an excellent view of the battle waged round the winning horse, as he slackened speed. Scarcely was the post passed when the crowd broke its ranks and rushed out into the course. Still cantering, the horse came up the track. A gang of young men ran in pursuit, waving sticks and shouting. And with them, their Napoleonic coat tails streaming in the wind of their own speed, their cocked hats bobbing, and brandishing their swords in their white-gloved hands, ran the rescuing carabiniers. There was a brief struggle round the now stationary horse, the young men were repulsed, and surrounded by cocked hats, followed by a crowd of supporters from its native *contrada*, the beast was led off in triumph. We climbed down from our places. The piazza was now entirely shaded. It was only on the upper part of the tower and the battlements of the great Palazzo that the sun still shone. Rosily against the pale blue sky, they glowed. The swifts still turned and turned overhead in the light. It is said that at evening and at dawn these light-loving birds mount on their strong wings into the sky to bid a last farewell or earliest good-morrow to the sinking or the rising sun. While we lie sleeping or have resigned ourselves to darkness the swifts are looking down from their watchtower in the height of heaven over the edge of the turning planet towards the light. Was it a fable, I wondered, looking up at the wheeling birds? Or was it true? Meanwhile, some one was swearing at me for not looking where I was going. I postponed the speculation.

Editor's Note

Aldous Huxley witnessed several Palii in the early 1920s and spent several months in Siena. His second wife, Laura, actually met him for the first time in California, trying to persuade him to write a script on the Palio for an MGM film (it was never made). She also knew all too well the intricacies of the Palio, and on at least one occasion provided "chemical inspiration" for the horses. See Laura Archera Huxley, *This Timeless Moment: A Personal View of Aldous Huxley* (New York: Farrar, Straus and Giroux, 1968), pp. 1–5. Many distinguished men of letters visited Siena and the Palio. See, for instance, Henry James, "Siena Early and Late," in *Italian Hours* (New York: Grove Press, 1959), pp. 246–68; Nathaniel Hawthorne, "Siena," in *Passages from the French and Italian Note-Books*, vol. 10, *The Complete Works of Nathaniel Hawthorne* (Boston and New York: Houghton Mifflin, 1899), pp. 432–58; Algernon C. Swinburne, "Siena," *Lippincott's Magazine* 1 (1868): 622–29. Ernest Hemingway, after a visit to Siena in his last years, allegedly left the typescript of an article on the Palio. It was never published; its present whereabouts are unknown. Among the poets, see Ezra Pound, *The Fifth Decad of Cantos* (New York: Farrar & Rinehart, 1937), pp. 10–11; idem, *The Pisan Cantos* (New York: New Directions, 1948), pp. 74–75, 107; Eugenio Montale, "Palio," in *Le Occasioni*, 5th ed. (Turin: Einaudi, 1945), pp. 96–98. Mario Luzi, "Ritorno a Siena," *Ausonia* 8 (1953): 127–29. For the famous

anecdote of Dante's impassivity in the face of Sienese festivities, see Giovanni Boccaccio, "The Life of Dante," in Philip H. Wicksteed, ed. and trans., *The Early Lives of Dante* (London: Chatto and Windus/Boston: Luce, 1907), pp. 56–57.

For general historical background on Siena, see Langton Douglas, *A History of Siena* (London: John Murray, 1902); Ferdinand Schevill, *Siena: The History of a Medieval Commune* (New York: Harper and Row, 1964); William M. Bowski, *The Finance of the Commune of Siena* (Oxford: Clarendon Press, 1970), and his *A Medieval Italian Commune: Siena Under the Nine 1287–1355* (Berkeley and Los Angeles: University of California Press, 1981). On the medieval origins of the Palio, and the mid-August festivities in honor of the Assumption of the Madonna, see William Heywood, *Our Lady of August and the Palio of Siena* (Siena: Torrini, 1899). See also his *Palio and Ponte* (London: Methuen, 1904), where he discusses ritual games of central Italy from the age of Dante to the end of the nineteenth century, including the Ponte of Pisa, the Calcio of Florence, the Sassi battle of Perugia, and the Palii of different Italian cities.

For a contemporary description and interpretation of the complex Palio symbolic system as a metaphor for the Sienese world view, see Alan Dundes and Alessandro Falassi, *La Terra in Piazza: An Interpretation of the Palio of Siena* (Berkeley and Los Angeles: University of California Press, 1975). For Clifford

Geertz's concept of deep play applied to the Palio, see Alice Pomponio Logan, "The Palio of Siena: Performance and Process," in *Urban Anthropology* 7 (1978): 45–65. For a typical misunderstanding of the Palio, see Timothy Beaumont, "Barbarians of Siena," *The Spectator* 225 (1970): 528. For Sienese writers' and scholars' own accounts of the Palio, see Duccio Balestracci, Roberto Barzanti, and Gabriella Piccinni, *Il Palio: una Festa nella Storia* (Siena: Nuovo Corriere Senese, 1978). Giulio Pepi, *Le Contrade e il Palio* (Siena: La Diana, 1967), and his *Siena: Il Palio* (with English translation) (Siena: Azienda Autonoma di Turismo, 1984) discusses the fascinating if admittedly speculative hypothesis of an Etruscan origin of the Palio. See also Alberto Tailetti, *Aneddoti Contradaioli* (Rome: Olimpia, 1967); Paolo Cesarini, *Il Palio* (Florence: Editoriale Olimpia, 1960); Ranuccio Bianchi Bandinelli, "Il Palio," in *Siena* (Rome: Società Editrice di Novissima, 1934), pp. 16–17; Giovanni Cecchini and Dario Neri, *The Palio of Siena* (Milan: Electa, 1958); Virgilio Grassi, *Le Contrade di Siena e le Loro Feste. Il Palio Attuale*, 2 vols. (Siena: Periccioli, 1972); Alessandro Falassi and Giuliano Catoni, *Palio* (Milan: Electa, 1983) (this last is in English, with extensive bibliography); Aldo Cairola, *Siena: Le Contrade* (Siena: Il Leccio, 1986). For Palio seen through Sienese folksong, see Alessandro Falassi, *Per Forza e per amore: I canti popolari del Palio di Siena* (Milan: Bompiani, 1980).

The Palio has been used as a backdrop for all sorts of fiction in literature, theater, and the mass media, from Flash Gordon and Walt Disney comic strips to Diana Dors films. For an anthology of facsimile strips see Sergio Micheli, ed., *Il Palio per Immagini* (Florence: Nerbini, 1979). One play featuring the Palio is Christopher Fry, *A Yard of Sun* (Chicago: Dramatic Publishing Co., 1970). It also appears in Herman Wouk's *The Winds of War* (Boston: Little Brown, 1971), pp. 56–65, and in the television serial film by the same title, based on the novel, released by the ABC network in 1983.

4 / World Series of Bull Fighting: A Mad Whirling Carnival

Ernest Hemingway

Writer Gertrude Stein claimed the credit for introducing Hemingway to the corridas. On her suggestion, he went to Pamplona in July 1922, saw bullfights that summer, and returned for the bullfights the following two years. In 1924 he took to Pamplona his wife, Hadley (the "Herself" of this article), and a group of friends including John Dos Passos and Donald Ogden Stewart, who was gored by a running bull. When Hemingway rushed to help him, he was also slightly wounded. In Pamplona, he met bullfighter Maera, whose death is described in In Our Time. *Following the circuit of the bullfights, he visited San Sebastian, Zaragoza, Valencia, and Madrid, and met other prominent bullfighters such as Villalta, Lalanda, and Belmonte, who inspired the Belmonte of* The Sun Also Rises. *That winter* The Little Review *announced, "Hemingway is living in Paris, teaching his one-year-old son to bull-fight." In 1925 Hemingway returned to Pamplona for the San-fermines. He met Cayetano Ordoñez and followed him to Valencia, where on his birthday he began to write* The Sun Also Rises. *Pedro Romero, the bullfighter of the novel, was allegedly inspired by Ordoñez. Hemingway continued the novel while watching corridas in Madrid, San Sebastian, and Hendaya, and finished the first draft in Paris in September. The novel appeared in the winter.*

In 1926 Hemingway attended the corrida season in Spain and gathered materials for Death in the Afternoon. *He returned the following year with his second wife, Pauline Pfeiffer, and in Valencia met bullfighters Belmonte and Lalanda. Other visits took place in 1929 and 1930, when he met Manolo Bienvenida, Cagancho, Gitanillo de Triana, and other bullfighters. In 1931 he spent May, June, and July at the corridas, met Felix Rodriguez and Chicuelo, witnessed the debut of Domingo Ortega and the death of Gitanillo de Triana. He finished the manuscript that appeared in its final form in 1932 as* Death in the Afternoon, *a treatise on bullfighting. While working on it, Hemingway had allegedly been present at more than 1,500 corridas. This was to remain Hemingway's only incursion into the social sciences. As a note to the reprint of a few pages of it, he wrote with some irony: "This story was published in a rather technical book called* Death in the Afternoon, *which sold or rather was offered for sale, at $3.50. It is reprinted here in case anyone not caring to spend that appreciable sum for a rather technical book should care to read it."*

Hemingway visited Spain five times during the Civil War. His concern then was not the bullfights but the war, and his efforts were in favor of the Republicans. After 1938, disappointed with the new regime, he did not return to Spain for many years, and in the decade after the war he published only one brief fable about bulls.

He went back to the bullfights only in 1953, after fifteen years of absence, with Mary, his fourth wife. In Pamplona he met and made friends with Antonio Ordoñez, the new star of the arenas. The following year they met for the corrida of San Isidro in Madrid.

A celebrated Nobel Prize winner, Hemingway returned to the Spanish arenas in the fall of 1956 and saw Ordoñez and Curro Gizón. In 1959 Hemingway had his last great summer in Spain. With renewed enthusiasm, he began to work on The Dangerous Summer, *a new book on bullfighting based on the rivalry between Miguel Dominguín, the idol of the crowds of the early 1950s who had returned to the arenas after a few years of inactivity, and Antonio Ordoñez, the new star. Hemingway sided with the latter, and followed him and his clan to the corridas in Madrid, Seville, Zaragoza, Burgos, Barcelona, Victoria, Bilbao. Then he went to Pamplona for the Sanfermines and to the other fiestas of summer. He returned to Cuba in November and was back in Spain in August of 1960 to continue his work on* The Dangerous Summer *in Malaga and in Madrid.*

Hemingway left Spain for the last time at the beginning of October. He had doubts about having been unjust to Dominguín, and from Idaho on October 21 he sent to Life *a telegram praising Dominguín's efforts to rehabilitate himself.*

Hemingway's passion for bullfighting was immediate and lasted all his life. He stepped resolutely into the fiestas and lived them with the crowds and from the street, not from a prudent distance. Even if he refused to consider himself a social scientist, he became a participant observer and a competent aficionado. He made friends and foes among the matadors, got to run the bulls, and felt the horns on his body. The fiestas and the corrida became an important inspiration and setting for some of his masterpieces, and an immediate and effective way to understand a culture and a country that was to become a second home for him.

Here Hemingway describes directly the fiesta's setting with his immediate prose and vigorous style: the city in the sun is overflowing with crowds from all over Spain; in their colorful attire people walk and dance in the streets to the music of the marching bands. The story of his arrival in Pamplona sets the stage, and more direct "authentic" information comes to the reader from the local people's answers to the questions he and his wife ask.

Then come the bulls, who run through the crowds with their deadly horns like the bulls in pre-Christian Mediterranean antiquities. Both the chaotic runs of the mornings in which the bulls trample and gore the men, and the stylized, baroque rituals of the afternoons in which the matadors kill the bulls are shown in their full drama of pride, bravery, and deadly risk.

For those who believe that "the bull doesn't have a chance," these pages also show that indeed the bulls are given one, and more often than not they take full advantage of it. And if in the corridas may remain traces of the ancient sacrificial killing of the bulls, in the runs of the morning one may see equally ancient traces of the ritual offerings of humans to the bulls. Before they enter the arena and meet their destiny in the afternoon, as Hemingway plainly states, it is the Pamplona tradition to give the bulls "a final shot at everyone in town."

World Series of Bull Fighting: A Mad Whirling Carnival*

Ernest Hemingway

In Pamplona, a white-walled, sun-baked town high up in the hills of Navarre, is held in the first two weeks of July each year the World's Series of bull fighting.

Bull fight fans from all Spain jam into the little town. Hotels double their prices and fill every room. The cafes under the wide arcades that run around the Plaza de la Constitucion have every table crowded, the tall Pilgrim Father sombreros of Andalusia sitting over the same table with straw hats from Madrid and the flat blue Basque caps of Navarre and the Basque country.

Really beautiful girls, gorgeous, bright shawls over their shoulders, dark, dark-eyed, black-lace mantillas over their hair, walk with their escorts in the crowds that pass from morning until night along the narrow walk that runs between inner and outer belts of cafe tables under the shade of the arcade out of the white glare of the Plaza de la Constitucion. All day and all night there is dancing in the streets. Bands of blue-shirted peasants whirl and lift and swing behind a drum, fife and reed instruments in the ancient Basque Riau-Riau dances. And at night there is the throb of the big drums and the military band as the whole town dances in the great open square of the Plaza.

We landed at Pamplona at night. The streets were solid with people dancing. Music was pounding and throbbing. Fireworks were being set off from the big public square. All the carnivals I had ever seen paled down in comparison. A rocket exploded over our heads with a blinding burst and the stick came swirling and whishing down. Dancers, snapping their fingers and whirling in perfect time through the crowd, bumped into us before we could get our bags down from the top of the station bus. Finally I got the bags through the crowd to the hotel.

Reprinted in *By-Line: Ernest Hemingway* as "Pamplona in July." See page iv.

We had wired and written for rooms two weeks ahead. Nothing had been saved. We were offered a single room with a single bed opening on to the kitchen ventilator shaft for seven dollars a day apiece. There was a big row with the landlady, who stood in front of her desk with her hands on her hips, and her broad Indian face perfectly placid, and told us in a few words of French and much Basque Spanish that she had to make all her money for the whole year in the next ten days. That people would come and that people would have to pay what she asked. She could show us a better room for ten dollars apiece. We said it would be preferable to sleep in the streets with the pigs. The landlady agreed that might be possible. We said we preferred it to such a hotel. All perfectly amicable. The landlady considered. We stood our ground. Mrs. Hemingway sat down on our rucksacks.

"I can get you a room in a house in the town. You can eat here," said the landlady.

"How much?"

"Five dollars."

We started off through the dark, narrow, carnival-mad streets with a boy carrying our rucksacks. It was a lovely big room in an old Spanish house with walls thick as a fortress. A cool, pleasant room, with a red tile floor and two big, comfortable beds set back in an alcove. A window opened on to an iron grilled porch out over the street. We were very comfortable.

All night long the wild music kept up in the street below. Several times in the night there was a wild roll of drumming, and I got out of bed and across the tiled floor to the balcony. But it was always the same. Men, blue-shirted, bareheaded, whirling and floating in a wild fantastic dance down the street behind the rolling drums and shrill fifes.

Just at daylight there was a crash of music in the street below. Real military music. Herself was up, dressed, at the window.

"Come on," she said. "They're all going somewhere." Down below the street was full of people. It was five o'clock in the morning. They were all going in one direction. I dressed in a hurry and we started after them.

The crowd was all going toward the great public square. People were pouring into it from every street and moving out of it toward the open country we could see through the narrow gaps in the high walls.

"Let's get some coffee," said Herself.

"Do you think we've got time? Hey, what's going to happen?" I asked a newsboy.

"Encierro," he said scornfully. "The encierro commences at six o'clock."

"What's the encierro?" I asked him.

"Oh, ask me to-morrow," he said, and started to run. The entire crowd was running now.

"I've got to have my coffee. No matter what it is," Herself said.

The waiter poured two streams of coffee and milk into the glass out of his big kettles. The crowd was still running, coming from all the streets that fed into the Plaza.

"What is this encierro anyway?" Herself asked, gulping the coffee.

"All I know is that they let the bulls out into the streets."

We started out after the crowd. Out of a narrow gate into a great yellow open space of country with the new concrete bull ring standing high and white and black with people. The yellow and red Spanish flag blowing in the early morning breeze. Across the open and once inside the bull ring, we mounted to the top looking toward the town. It cost a peseta to go up to the top. All the other levels were free. There were easily twenty thousand people there. Everyone jammed on the outside of the big concrete amphitheatre, looking toward the yellow town with the bright red roofs, where a long wooden pen ran from the entrance of the city gate across the open, bare ground to the bull ring.

It was really a double wooden fence, making a long entryway from the main street of the town into the bull ring itself. It made a runway about two hundred and fifty yards long. People were jammed solid on each side of it. Looking up it toward the main street.

Then far away there was a dull report.

"They're off," everybody shouted.

"What is it?" I asked a man next to me who was leaning far out over the concrete rail.

"The bulls! They have released them from the corrals on the far side of the city. They are racing through the city."

"Whew," said Herself. "What do they do that for?"

Then down the narrow fenced-in runway came a crowd of men and boys running. Running as hard as they could go. The gate feeding into the bull ring was opened and they all ran pell-mell under the entrance levels into the ring. Then there came another crowd. Running even harder. Straight up the long pen from the town.

"Where are the bulls?" asked Herself.

Then they came in sight. Eight bulls galloping along, full tilt, heavy set, black, glistening, sinister, their horns bare, tossing their heads. And running with them three steers with bells on their necks. They ran in a solid mass, and ahead of them sprinted, tore, ran and bolted the rear guard of the men and boys of Pamplona who had allowed themselves to be chased through the streets for a morning's pleasure.

A boy in his blue shirt, red sash, white canvas shoes with the inevitable leather wine bottle hung from his shoulders, stumbled as he sprinted down the straightaway. The first bull lowered his head and made a jerky, sideways toss. The boy crashed up against the fence and lay there limp, the herd running solidly together passed him up. The crowd roared.

Everybody made a dash for the inside of the ring, and we got into a box just in time to see the bulls come into the ring filled with men. The men ran in a panic to each side. The bulls, still bunched solidly together, ran straight with the trained steers across the ring and into the entrance that led to the pens.

That was the entry. Every morning during the bull fighting festival of San Fermin at Pamplona the bulls that are to fight in the afternoon are released from their corrals at six o'clock in the morning and race through the main street of the town for a mile and a half to the pen. The men who run ahead of them do it for the fun of the thing. It has been going on each year since a couple of hundred years before Columbus had his historic interview with Queen Isabella in the camp outside of Granada.

There are two things in favor of there being no accidents. First, that fighting bulls are not aroused and vicious when they are together. Second, that the steers are relied upon to keep them moving.

Sometimes things go wrong, a bull will be detached from the herd as they pile through into the pen and with his crest up, a ton of speed and viciousness, his needle-sharp horns lowered, will charge again and again into the packed mass of men and boys in the bull ring. There is no place for the men to get out of the ring. It is too jammed for them to climb over the barrera or red fence that rims the field. They have to stay in and take it. Eventually the steers get the bull out of the ring and into the pen. He may wound or kill thirty men before they can get him out. No armed men are allowed to oppose him. That is the chance the Pamplona bull fight fans take every morning during the Feria. It is the Pamplona tradition of giving the bulls a final shot at everyone in town before they enter the pens. They will not leave until they come out into the glare of the arena to die in the afternoon.

Consequently Pamplona is the toughest bull fight town in the world. The amateur fight that comes immediately after the bulls have entered the pens proves that. Every seat in the great amphitheatre is packed. About three hundred men, with capes, odd pieces of cloth, old shirts, anything that will imitate a bull fighter's cape, are singing and dancing in the arena. There is a shout, and the bull pen opens. Out comes a young bull just as fast as he can come. On his horns are leather knobs to prevent his goring anyone. He charges and hits a man. Tosses him high in the air, and the crowd roars. The man comes down on the ground, and the bull goes for him, bumping him with his head. Worrying him with his horns. Several amateur bull fighters are flopping their capes in his face to make the bull charge and leave the man on the ground. Then the bull charges and bags another man. The crowd roars with delight.

Then the bull will turn like a cat and get somebody who has been acting very brave about ten feet behind him. Then he will toss a man over the fence. Then he picks out one man and follows him in a wild twisting charge through the entire crowd until he bags him. The barrera is packed with men and boys sitting along the top, and the bull decides to clear them all off. He goes along, hooking carefully with his horn and dropping them off with a toss of his horns like a man pitching hay.

Each time the bull bags someone the crowd roars with joy. Most of it is home talent stuff. The braver the man has been or the more elegant pass he has attempted with his cape before the bull gets him the more the crowd roars. No one is armed. No one hurts or plagues the bull in any way. A man who grabbed the bull by the tail and tried to hang on was hissed and booed by the crowd and the next time he tried it was knocked down by another man in the bull ring. No one enjoys it all more than the bull.

As soon as he shows signs of tiring from his charges, the two old steers, one brown and the other looking like a big Holstein, come trotting in and alongside the young bull who falls in behind them like a dog and follows them meekly on a tour of the arena and then out.

Another comes right in, and the charging and tossing, the ineffectual cape waving, and wonderful music are repeated right over again. But always different. Some of the animals in this morning amateur fight are steers. Fighting bulls from the best strain who had some imperfection or other in build so they could never command the high prices paid for combat animals, $2,000 to $3,000 apiece. But there is nothing lacking in their fighting spirit.

The show comes off every morning. Everybody in town turns out at five-thirty when the military bands go through the streets. Many of them stay up all night for it. We didn't miss one, and it is quelque sporting event that will get us both up at five-thirty o'clock in the morning for six days running.

As far as I know we were the only English-speaking people in Pamplona during the Feria of last year [July].

There were three minor earthquakes while we were there. Terrific cloud bursts in the mountains and the Ebro River flooded out Zaragossa. For two days the bull ring was under water and the Corrida had to be suspended for the first time in over a hundred years. That was during the middle of the fair. Everyone was desperate. On the third day it looked gloomier than ever, poured rain all morning, and then at noon the clouds rolled away up across the valley, the sun came out bright and hot and baking and that afternoon there was the greatest bull fight I will perhaps ever see.

There were rockets going up into the air and the arena was nearly full when we got into our regular seats. The sun was hot and baking. Over on the other side we could see the bull fighters standing ready to come in. All wearing their oldest clothes because of the heavy, muddy going in the arena. We picked out the three matadors of the afternoon with our glasses. Only one of them was new. Olmos, a chubby faced, jolly looking man, something like Tris Speaker. The others we had seen often before. Maera, dark, spare and deadly looking, one of the very greatest toreros of all time. The third, young Algabeno, the son of a famous bull fighter, a slim young Andalusian with a charming Indian looking face. All were wearing the suits they had probably started bull fighting with, too tight, old fashioned, outmoded.

There was the procession of entrance, the wild bull fight music played, the preliminaries were quickly over, the picadors retired along the red fence with their horses, the heralds sounded their trumpets and the door of the bull pen swung open. The bull came out in a rush, saw a man standing near the barrera and charged him. The man vaulted over the fence and the bull charged the barrera. He crashed into the fence in full charge and ripped a two by eight plank solidly out in a splintering smash. He broke his horn doing it and the crowd called for a new bull. The trained steers trotted in, the bull fell in meekly behind them, and the three of them trotted out of the arena.

The next bull came in with the same rush. He was Maera's bull and after perfect cape play Maera planted the banderillos. Maera is Herself's favorite bull fighter. And if you want to keep any conception of yourself as a brave, hard, perfectly balanced, thoroughly competent man in your wife's mind never take her to a real bull fight. I used to go into the amateur fights in the morning to try and win back a small amount of her esteem but the more I discovered that bull fighting required a very great quantity of a certain type of courage of which I had an almost complete lack the more it became apparent that any admiration she might ever redevelop for me would have to be simply an antidote to the real admiration for Maera and Villalta. You cannot compete with bull fighters on their own ground. If anywhere. The only way most husbands are able to keep any drag with their wives at all is that, first there are only a limited number of bull fighters, second there are only a limited number of wives who have ever seen bull fights.

Maera planted his first pair of banderillos sitting down on the edge of the little step-up that runs around the barrera. He snarled at the bull and as the animal charged leaned back tight against the fence and as the horns struck on either side of him, swung forward over the brute's head and planted the two darts in his hump. He planted the next pair the same way, so near to us we could have leaned over and touched him. Then he went out to kill the bull and after he had made absolutely unbelievable passes with the little red cloth of the muleta drew up his sword and as the bull charged Maera thrust. The sword shot out of his hand and the bull caught him. He went up in the air on the horns of the bull and then came down. Young Algabeno flopped his cape in the bull's face. The bull charged him and Maera staggered to his feet. But his wrist was sprained.

With his wrist sprained, so that every time he raised it to sight for a thrust it brought beads of sweat out on his face, Maera tried again and again to make his death thrust. He lost his sword again and again, picked it up with his left hand from the mud floor of the arena and transferred it to the right for the thrust. Finally he made it and the bull went over. The bull nearly got him twenty times. As he came in to stand up under us at the barrera side his wrist was swollen to twice normal size. I thought of prize fighters I had seen quit because they had hurt their hands.

There was almost no pause while the mules galloped in and hitched on to the first bull and dragged him out and the second came in with a rush. The picadors took the first shock of him with their bull lances. There was the snort and charge, the shock and the mass against the sky, the wonderful defense by the picador with his lance that held off the bull, and then Rosario Olmos stepped out with his cape.

Once he flopped the cape at the bull and floated it around in an easy graceful swing. Then he tried the same swing, the classic "Veronica," and the bull caught him at the end of it. Instead of stopping at the finish the bull charged on in. He caught Olmos squarely with his horn, hoisted him high in the air. He fell heavily and the bull was on top of him, driving his horns again and again into him. Olmos lay on the sand, his head on his arms. One of his teammates was flopping his cape madly in the bull's face. The bull lifted his head for an instant and charged and got his man. Just one terrific toss. Then he whirled and chased a man just in back of him toward the barrera. The man was running full tilt and as he put his hand on the fence to vault it the bull had him and caught him with his horn, shooting him way up into the crowd. He rushed toward the fallen man he had tossed who was getting to his feet and all alone—Algabeno grabbed him by the tail. He hung on until I thought he or the bull would break. The wounded man got to his feet and started away.

The bull turned like a cat and charged Algabeno and Algabeno met him with the cape. Once, twice, three times he made the perfect, floating, slow swing with the cape, perfectly, graceful, debonair, back on his heels, baffling the bull. And he had command of the situation. There never was such a scene at any world's series game.

There are no substitute matadors allowed. Maera was finished. His wrist could not lift a sword for weeks. Olmos had been gored badly through the body. It was Algabeno's bull. This one and the next five [actually, four, *ed.*].

He handled them all. Did it all. Cape play easy, graceful, confident. Beautiful work with the muleta. And serious, deadly killing. Five bulls he killed, one after the other, and each one was a separate problem to be worked out with death. At the end there was nothing debonair about him. It was only a question if he would last through or if the bulls would get him. They were all very wonderful bulls.

"He is a very great kid," said Herself. "He is only twenty."

"I wish we knew him," I said.

"Maybe we will some day," she said. Then considered a moment. "He will probably be spoiled by then."

They make twenty thousand a year.

That was just three months ago. It seems in a different century now, working in an office. It is a very long way from the sun baked town of Pamplona, where the men race through the streets in the mornings ahead of the bulls to the morning ride to work on a Bay-Caledonia car. But it is only fourteen days by water to Spain and there is no need for a castle. There is always that room at 5 Calle de Eslava, and a son, if he is to redeem the family reputation as a bull fighter, must start very early.

Editor's Note

This article is the continuation of Hemingway's first writing on the bulls, "Bull Fighting is not a Sport. It is a Tragedy," in the *Toronto Star Weekly*, October 20, 1923. Both articles were reprinted in *The Wild Years* (New York: Dell, 1962), pp. 229–38 and 221–28 respectively.

Hemingway wrote extensively on the bulls throughout his career. The *Little Review* 9 (1923) no. 3: 3–5 printed three fragments under the title of Hemingway's book in progress, *In Our Time*. "Pamplona Letter," *Transatlantic Review* 2 (1924) no. 3: 300–302 followed. *In Our Time* first appeared in Paris (Three Mountain Press/Shakespeare and Company) (only 170 copies on rives paper). The "chapters" (fragments) regarding bullfights are: ch. 2, page 10; ch. 12, page 22; ch. 13, page 23; ch. 14, page 24; ch. 15, pp. 25–26; ch. 16, page 27. See also "The Undefeated," *This Quarter* 1 (1925–26) no. 2: 203–32 and *The Sun Also Rises* (New York: Scribner's, 1926) (especially pp. 152–224). The book was reprinted in many foreign editions and in England was known as *Fiesta*. See *Fiesta* (London: Cape, 1927); "Bullfighting, Sport and Industry," *Fortune*, March 1930, pp. 83–88, 139–46, 150; *Death in the Afternoon* (New York: Scribner's, 1932). "The Mother of a Queen," in *Winner Take Nothing* (New York: Scribner's, 1933), pp. 89–96, is a short story on an inept Mexican matador. On pp. 137–53 of *Winner Take Nothing* is reprinted "A Natural History of the Dead," originally in *Death in the Afternoon*, with a note by Hemingway. "The Horns of the Bull"

first appeared in *Esquire*, June 1936, pp. 31, 190–93; retitled "The Capital of the World" it was in *The Fifth Column and the First Forty-Nine Stories* (New York: Scribner's, 1938), pp. 137–49. "The Faithful Bull," *Holiday*, 9 March 1951, is a brief fable about a brave and monogamous corrida bull, illustrated by Adriana Ivancich.

On the Ordoñez-Dominguín rivalry, from the corrida circuit, Hemingway wrote "A Matter of Wind," *Sports Illustrated*, August 17, 1959, p. 43. See also Mary Hemingway, "Holiday for a Wounded Torero," ibid., pp. 44, 47–49, 51, and John Blashill, "Ordoñez vs. Dominguín," ibid., pp. 42–43. See also the trilogy "The Dangerous Summer" (Part 1), *Life*, September 5, 1960, pp. 78–109, "The Pride of the Devil" (Part 2), *Life*, September 12, 1960, pp. 60–82, "An Appointment with Disaster" (Part 3), *Life*, September 19, 1960, pp. 74–96. On Antonio Ordoñez, see Shay Oag, *In the Presence of Death: Antonio Ordoñez* (New York: Coward-McCann, 1969). As for Luis Miguel Dominguín, see the text that he wrote for Pablo Picasso, *Toros y Toreros* (New York: Alpine Fine Arts, 1980), pp. 7–18 (text in Spanish with English translation). On other matadors see, for instance, Carmelo Lisón-Tolosana, *Belmonte de los Caballeros* (Oxford: Clarendon Press, 1966); Manuel Chaves Nogales, *Juan Belmonte: Killer of Bulls* (New York: Doubleday, 1937); José Alfonso, *De Antonio Fuentes al Cordobés* (Valencia: Prometeo, 1969); Winslow Hunt, "On Bullfighter," *American Imago* 12 (1955):343–53.

At his death, Hemingway left a great many typescript and manuscript materials on the world of bullfights and matadors, still largely unpublished. See Philip Young and Charles W. Mann, *The Hemingway Manuscripts. An Inventory* (University Park and London: Pennsylvania State University Press, 1969). Materials on *The Dangerous Summer* are listed on p. 7; on *Death in the Afternoon*, pp. 8–10; on *The Sun Also Rises*, pp. 25–28. See also the sections on short fiction, pp. 37, 45, 54, 56; journalism and other nonfiction, pp. 62, 65, 66; fragments, pp. 90, 99, 103; miscellaneous notes, pp. 115, 118. *The Dangerous Summer* was published posthumously (New York: Scribner's, 1985).

As a bibliographic note at the end of *Death in the Afternoon*, Hemingway referred his readers to the 2,077 (actually 2,045) books and pamphlets listed in Graciano Díaz Arquer, *Libros y folletos de Toros: Bibliografía Taurina, Compuesta con vista de la Biblioteca Tauromaca de Don José Luis de Ybarra y López de Calle* (Madrid: Pedro Vindel, 1931). See also John Hugo E. P. Marks, *To the Bullfight* (New York: Knopf, 1953). A revised and enlarged edition appeared as *To the Bullfights Again* (New York: Knopf, 1967). On Hemingway in Pamplona, see José Maria Iribarren, *Hemingway y los sanferminos* (Pamplona: Editorial Gómez, 1970). On Hemingway in Spain, José Luis Castillo-Puche, *Hemingway in Spain: A Personal Reminiscence of Hemingway's Years in Spain by His Friend* (Garden City, N.Y.: Doubleday, 1974).

On Pamplona and its bullfights, see Luis del Campo, *Pamplona y sus plazas de toros* (Pamplona: Diputación Foral de Navarra, 1971); *Pamplona y Toros, siglo XVII* (Pamplona: Editorial Graficas, 1975); *Toros en Pamplona, siglo XVIII* (Pamplona: Editorial La Acción Social, 1972); J. Jimeno Jurio, *Historia de Pamplona* (Pamplona: Aranzadi, 1974); Gines Serran-Pagan, *Pamplona-Gra-zalema: From the Public Square to the Bullring* (New York: Enquire Printing and Publishing, 1980). Compare Homer Casteel, *Running of the Bulls* (New York: Dodd and Mead, 1953). On bullfights, the best introduction remains the classic José Maria de Cossio, *Los Toros, tratado técnico e histórico*, 4 vols. (Madrid: Espasa-Calpe, 1943–1961). See also Barnaby Conrad, *La Fiesta Brava* (Cambridge, Mass.: Riverside Press, 1950); Kenneth Tynan, *Bull Fever* (New York: Harper, 1955); Angel Alvarez Miranda, *Ritos y jeugos del toro* (Madrid: Taurus, 1962); Carlos Orellana, ed., *Los Toros en España* (Madrid: Editorial Orel, 1969); Antonio Abad Ojuel and Emilio L. Oliva, *Los Toros* (Barcelona: Librería Editorial Argos, 1966); Rex Smith, ed., *Biography of the Bulls: An Anthology of Spanish Bullfighting* (New York and Toronto: Rinehart & Co., 1957); P. Buckley, *Bullfight* (New York: Simon and Schuster, 1958). For the religious, symbolic, and psychological aspects of bullfighting, see Juan Fernández Figueroa, ed., *Los Toros: Bullfighting* (Madrid: Indice, 1964); Andrés Holguín and Carlos Holguín, *Cultos Religiosos y corrida de toros* (Bogotá: Editorial Revista Colombiana, 1966); Alfonso Alvarez Villar, "Psicología de la Tauromaquia," *Arbor* 61 (May–August 1965): 193–205; Jack R. Conrad, *The Horn and The Sword: The History of the Bull as a Symbol of Power and Fertility* (New York: Dutton, 1957); John Ingham, "The Bullfighter: A Study in Sexual Dialectics," *American Imago* 21–22 (1964): 95–102; William H. Desmond, "The Bull Fight as a Religious Ritual," *American Imago* 9 (1952): 173–95; Louis A. Zurcher and Arnold Meadow, "On Bullfights and Baseball: An Example of Interaction of Social Institutions," *International Journal of Comparative Sociology* 8 (March 1967) no. 1: 99–117; Carrie B. Douglass, "Toro muerto, vaca es: An Interpretation of the Spanish Bullfight," *American Ethnologist* 11 (1984): 242–85.

5 / The Pilgrimage of the Rabb

Arnold van Gennep

This article by Arnold van Gennep (1873–1957), the author of The Rites of Passage *and one of the foremost folklorists of this century, shows very clearly the attitude and outlook of the social scientist, even if his visit is not intended as fieldwork and this article is a notebook of impressions rather than a scientific essay.*

He is observing the centuries-old yearly festivities for the Rabb, Ephraim Angaoua, a "Spanish Jew Saint" of the fourteenth century who is the object of pilgrimages and prayers of Jews, Arabs, Berbers, and Christians. To all, the Rabb grants in his goodness graces and favors of different kinds: faithfulness of a fiancé, healing from diseases, prosperity for a business activity, but above all, male children—a highly prized blessing for the male-oriented patriarchal families of his faithful worshippers.

Van Gennep maintains a scientific outlook, learns from the people he meets, transforms every conversation into an interview on the different folk beliefs, oral histories, and religious practices. Any fieldworker will recognize a familiar situation, as the author narrates his responses to questions on his competence, motivation, and honest curiosity. Van Gennep speaks to the natives and to the readers with contagious sympathy and amiability, which win their trust and confidence. Yet he is always pursuing patterns of behavior and the significance of the festival; his respect for what he is witnessing and for his occasional precious acquaintances never leaves him, even when he is faced with the odd, the amusing, or the three classic forbidden topics: sex, religion, and personal cleanliness.

He inquires delicately about menstrual taboos and alleged orgiastic behavior; no irony or skepticism is shown toward the traditional devotional practice, which Europeans and Muslims make fun of, of drinking some consecrated anisette, or toward the episode in which one believer comes from Oran to place on the Rabb's stone a sampler of his cloth and lace in order to gain, by contagious magic, prosperity for his business.

Van Gennep, in his chatty, easy-to-read style, touches nevertheless on types of magic and stages in rites of passage, and gives an accurate account of the context of the festivities and of their central focus—the propitiatory practices used when asking the Rabb for favors. These are described with all their details, acts to perform, types of prayers to recite, form of the request, even the criteria of validity (the faithful must be "pure," the vow must be kept secret). Van Gennep's gratitude for what he has learned from his informants, and his desire to understand as much as possible make him submit patiently and in good spirits to the local ritual routine of the native participants. The female informant tells him goodbye with the promise that he will obtain what he has asked for and will be convinced of the goodness of the Rabb. Van Gennep has no final comment to that. Nor does he tell us his last vow. Yet his devout Tlemcen informants would have found perfectly logical, and not coincidental at all, the fact he told one vow and never had the son he wished for.

The Pilgrimage of the Rabb*

Arnold van Gennep

Tlemcen is invaded by Jews who come from Algiers, from Constantine, from Oran in particular, but also from Fez and from Tangiers: it is the time of the great pilgrimage of the Rabb. For centuries people have come there, and if this year the crowd is smaller, it is because of the municipal elections. The Jews are French citizens, while the Arabs and the Berbers are not. The religion of Jaweh does not require the conservation of personal status to which Islam adheres absolutely.

In the streets are many Jewish women in costume. The men, in contrast, are all dressed in the European fashion, and this produces a bizarre effect: straw hats, jackets, and narrow trousers in ordinary neutral tones next to the enormous skirts like crinolines in black brocade, in sky-blue brocade, or golden yellow, with straight pleats upon which fall great cashmeres whose edges trace tracks in the dust, surmounted by pale faces, milky, barred by eyebrows with kohl, encircled by bright silk scarves trimmed with golden or silver fringes.

In their yellow shoes with rubber heels, which leave cross-shaped marks on the ground, the husbands, the brothers, the uncles, the fathers walk stiffly; and their

*Reprinted from "En Algérie," *Mercure de France* 103 (1913) no. 384: 742–66. Translation by Elizabeth Hadas.

wives, their feet barely stuck into velvet and embroidered slippers, drag their legs, ungainly and fat.

The Jewish women of Oran, attired in our fashion of two years ago, even though they are natives, seem annoyed: do they feel diminished? Or, on the contrary, do they scorn these laggards?

On the square, in outlandish carts, broken char-à-bancs, dusty landaus, painted British carts, gangs of adults and kids are gathering. The Rabb is good to children, and for the few drops of anisette and the few pieces of sugar that it costs, they may as well sanctify the whole family at once. People bring provisions to eat in the new cemetery or, if space is lacking there, in the old cemetery that stretches out along the side of the road. At the gate of the new cemetery, tables are set for the foreigners; the citizens of Tlemcen prefer to picnic on the ground. Introductions go back and forth.

—Schmoul, and the anisette, you have it, the anisette, eh?

—The anisette, I have it in the bottle.

So I, too, would have liked to see the Rabb. Disdaining the overloaded carts, I fled by the dusty road up to the old cemetery, and there I began by wandering from tomb to tomb, under the twisted olive trees, pushing the grass aside from the inscriptions, and amazed—as always in this African land—that here the cemetery is a thoroughfare, a Bois de Boulogne for picnics with pastries, sweets, and idle talk. The large flattened greens, the broken flagstones, the yellowing papers hurt me. And yet, what did I care for these dead of another religion, another race, another land?

I accepted the invitation of the coffee-house keepers and I stayed drinking the eternal carbonated lemonade, to see the troops of Jews in their Sunday attire entering the new cemetery. There, one cannot wander around at will, except at the very back: fences take you straight to the sanctuary, which is surrounded by a round trellis where some climbing plants twist around. In the center, under a rustic roof supported by stakes, is the large slab of white stone under which the Rabb reposes.

By name Ephraim Angaoua, he was a Spanish Jew who, around the end of the fourteenth century, fled to avoid persecution, to Morocco, then to Tlemcen, which he entered riding on a lion that he guided with a snake as a halter. He stopped at first near the grotto whence comes the spring, nowadays sacred, that is dedicated to him; and the Muslims respected this unknown thaumaturge. He was allowed to stay in the city. There he continued his study of the Talmud. He was also a skilled physician. As a reward for healing the daughter of the Sultan he was permitted to summon to Tlemcen his coreligionists from Spain and Agadir and to build them a synagogue. Thus was founded the Jewish community of Tlemcen.

Such a great Saint could not stop making miracles after his death. A month after Easter, the Jews of the surrounding regions come to express their vows to him, just as the Muslims go to say theirs to Sidi Bou Mediene, the great Saint of El Eubbad. And since there are no male or female Catholic saints buried around there, the fervent Catholics, and even some Spaniards, address themselves to the Jewish saint, and to the Muslim saint as well, in order to obtain male children.

I had followed the little path between barriers in the cemetery and had arrived next to the sacred apse. Located there is a sort of small passage, a kind of antechamber: there people make the gestures of the "liminal stage." A rustic roof provides shelter; on each side is a bench and on the ground are some mats. One sits down and takes off his shoes, which some kids remove and take into another, similar antechamber, which one passes through on the way out of the apse.

I had sat down on a bench and was resisting the solicitations of the kids when a young lady sitting next to me, dressed in the European fashion, addressed me.

—Monsieur is doubtless a Frenchman from France?

—In fact, I am.

—And Monsieur is maybe Jewish?

—Upon my faith, I am not.

—Then Monsieur has come for the Rabb? There is nothing as beautiful and as good in this world as the Rabb.

—The fact is, I replied, that I have seen some Jewish ceremonies in Poland; there too there are many Jews, and it is to see if those in Tlemcen say their prayers like those in Poland and in Russia that I have come here. Do you want to tell me how people pray to the Rabb?

Some other ladies and young girls, some in indigenous costume, were taking off their shoes. They raised their heads and, looking at me, began to talk among themselves and with my neighbor. The latter then spoke in the name of all:

—The first thing that one must do is take a bath and purify oneself completely; for women, this sometimes delays the date of their pilgrimage, because there are times when even a bath does not purify enough. . . .

There was a silence. I said:

—Exactly—every month for some days, or else when a woman has just become a mother.

The ladies and girls seemed reassured. Clearly they did not need to insist on some details about which one does not speak except among women. I was well informed about these things.

—Yes, yes, that's it. The hard thing is that, since one must always make the pilgrimage three times—the first one to inform the Rabb that one has come to ask him something, the second to ask him this something, and the third to thank him and take leave—a long time may pass before one does it properly. So I have come from Oran, I have made my first pilgrimage entirely purified, and I thought I would have the time to make the second and the third. But because of the heat or of the journey, it has come early, and today I am impure; I do not have the right to go in there. I will keep you company and we will talk.

I assured the young lady that I blessed, for my part, this unexpected early arrival. In the meantime, her companions had taken off their shoes. I pointed out that one of them had stockings that looked dirty to me.

—The fact is that today is her third pilgrimage; when one has taken the first bath, one must put on clean linen, but one keeps wearing it until everything is over.

Having taken off one's shoes, one goes next to the tombstone and touches it with bare hands, then squats down beside it and kisses the stone a great many times, while inwardly formulating one's vow. Then one puts on the stone a piece of sugar on which is poured some anisette, pure or diluted with water from the source of the Rabb, of which an old woman, who is nearby, keeps a supply in a bucket, or which one has brought along oneself. One eats the piece of sugar while continually repeating the vow. The old woman also sells wax candles, which one burns on the tombstone, and which she puts out as quickly as possible as soon as the one who prays stands up—

as all the good women of our churches do. These candles are white; those of the Muslims are most often green, the symbolic color of the Prophet.

Some men read in a nasal voice passages from the Talmud or some other ritual book, and some entire families install themselves around the tomb, swallowing quite a few pieces of sugar soaked in anisette; people give some even to small children two years old, making them tipsy; some adults also get tipsy, and very rapidly. Muslims and Europeans in Tlemcen delight in making fun of the rite that consists of drinking consecrated anisette. I was not tempted to laugh: the fervor of those honest people was not simulated at all.

But what made me laugh was a terrified exclamation from the woman next to me.

—Not on your knees, Rachel, not on your knees!

In fact, one of the young girls of Oran was on her knees devoutly kissing the white stone. She turned around:

—It is my bodice. How am I to do it?

—However you want; but not on your knees . . .

And turning to me

—It is her fashionable bodice; but it is a sacrilege to kneel in front of the Rabb; it is you people who go down on your knees to pray; but us, we must squat upon the ground.

To squat down! That would have cut the legs of that young girl; she ended up by lying on her stomach, supporting herself on her elbows.

—No, not like that either! Come on, come back, you have done enough!

Blushing, confused, the young girl came back:

—Bah, she told me, I am sure of my fiancé: he is with the Zouaves; he will not leave me; and the Rabb could not do anything about it, after all.

—Don't listen to her, Sir, the Rabb can do anything. Thus, after five years of marriage, I did not yet have a child. I came to pray to the Rabb, and nine months later I had a boy. You can ask him anything: cures, wealth, and to succeed in your business. You see that gentleman; he has put a package on the stone of the Rabb and now he drinks the anisette. I know him well, he sells cloth and lace in Oran. In his package he has samples of all his merchandise, and in this way the Rabb will bless his business.

—Then it is enough to put something on the tombstone or to eat something that has touched that stone in order to make what one wishes take place?

—Yes, it is by the power and by the force of the Rabb, the *baraka* as they say; one can also have the *baraka* at El Eubbad by touching the cloths that are on the tomb of Bou Mediene.

—But prayer counts for something there? And what does one say?

—Here, men know the prayers; we women do not know them, or very few. I, to have my child, said only, the second time: "O Rabb, who came on the lion and who was a great scholar and a great saint, let me have a child, because after being married five years I do not have any and my husband and the other men and women despise me."

—And the inscription?

—I do not know exactly what it means. It seems that there is his name and then "Great maker of miracles, help us." Surely he makes miracles! He has cured many people of hopeless diseases. . . . It is really a pity that you have not taken a bath: then you would have taken off your shoes and you would have accompanied my cousins.

—But I'm not a Jew!

—That does not matter. The Rabb is very good. If you asked him something, having faith, surely he would grant it to you. You must want something, isn't that true?

—Yes, yes, and quite a few things, actually. But since I could not have asked the Rabb for everything at the same time, I would have had first of all to make a choice. And since I had not thought of it. . . .

—Yes, it is a pity; and then, you are not pure enough. But I shall prove to you anyway the goodness of the Rabb.

I looked at the lady, a little surprised. She was refined, delicate, not common at all, blonde with grey eyes (which is fairly frequent among the Jews of Western Algeria) and all taken by an idea that I had not succeeded in guessing.

—Let's see! Well, do you have children?

—Yes, two daughters.

—That's it. Then you will be convinced. You will see!

Leaving to the future the task of gathering information, I returned to the rites of the Rabb. When one is finished with the large slab, one squats upon the ground in front, successively, of thirty-two smaller stones, whitened by chalk, scattered irregularly in the enclosure, and which represent the thirty-two relatives and descendants of the Rabb; people kiss them devoutly; there certain people consecrate still more pieces of sugar with anisette or are satisfied to touch them with the palm of the hand, or with the fingertips, and to kiss the fingers.

In spite of everything, I wanted to laugh when I saw all those stockings, white, yellow, black, green, of all shades and of all qualities imaginable, zigzagging along the small enclosure without worrying about dust or mud. After which, the visitor takes himself to the exit passage, puts his shoes on, and goes with the family to a corner of the cemetery to eat the provisions that one has also taken care to consecrate by contact.

While I was observing, the people of Oran had come out of the enclosure. I stood up in turn and thanked the young lady. But she stopped me and told me:

—It is my turn, now, to ask you for a service. Here is the path that leads to the spring of the Rabb. Go ahead; I will join you afterward.

Naturally, I obeyed. The spring is fairly far. There are no more barriers there, and I saw several families picnicking. The meals on the grass take place most often in the evenings. Venetian lanterns are lit around the sacred place; everywhere people play the accordion, the instrument preferred by the Jews. And people have assured me that many children are conceived on those nights.

When the young lady joined me on the empty path, I repeated to her what the evil tongues of Tlemcen had told me: that the fêtes of the Rabb degenerate at night into orgies. She blushed a little, smiled, and told me:

—The goodness of the Rabb is great, and if people have asked him for a boy, it will be a boy.

We reached the spring. It is hidden in a grotto, not deep, then pours into a basin. The young lady held a bottle in her hand. She bent down to fill it in the basin;

but the level of the water was at least a half-meter lower. She spread her handkerchief and knelt down, without success. When she got up, she looked at me.

—I could reach to get some holy water for you, I told her, but in order to do that it is necessary that I lie flat on my stomach. There is so much mud around the basin that I do not have the courage to do it.

She thought about it, then, without saying a word, undid her skirt, turned it around and spread it on the mud. I was very annoyed, because I was not pure, I, and yet I respect the beliefs of others too much to deliberately perform, before their eyes, acts that would seem sacrilegious to them. This is what I pointed out to the young lady. She was very embarrassed and looked at her skirt with regret; it was indeed not worth it to have spread it in that slimy mud! But she found the solution.

—There, if you want to, lie down on my skirt; first wash your hands well in the water of the basin. Afterward, I will pass you the bottle. This way the water that you take will be pure.

I did as she ordered. I filled the bottle and presented it to her. But she refused it, saying:

—Drink and make your vow.

I looked at her, stunned. Really, she was overdoing it. But she smiled gently. It was silly to give her pain; she had given me information; I had already gone so far. . . . In short, I drank from the bottle, and I said:

—If my next child is not a boy, I will have no more confidence in your Rabb.

—Oh! but you should not have told me! Your vow is not worth anything anymore. Drink again; make another vow, but do not tell me!

I drank a mouthful and gave her back the bottle. Then I took my leave.

She picked up her skirt and went to spread it in the sunshine. And since I was getting away down the empty path, she yelled at me:

—You shall see, you will obtain what you have asked for; and you will be convinced of the goodness of the Rabb.

Editor's Note

Before the publication of this article, Arnold van Gennep was in Algeria in July and August 1911 and again in April through June 1912. His first ethnographic notes and impressions were published as "Alger-Tlémcen-Alger-Tizi-Ouzou," *Mercure de France* 92 (1911) no. 340: 834–87.

His "Études d'ethnographie algérienne" appeared in the *Revue d'Ethnographie et de Sociologie* 2 (1911): 265–346 and 3 (1912): 1–21. Before the latter part appeared, both parts were reprinted as a book with the same title (Paris: Leroux, 1911). A longer essay appeared two years later, divided in three sections. See "En Algérie," *Mercure de France* 103 (1913), no. 384: 742–66. "The Pilgrim-age of the Rabb" was reprinted in van Gennep's book *En Algérie* (Paris: Éditions Mercure de France, 1914), pp. 41–58. The other essays were published as "En Algérie" (part 2), *Mercure de France* 104 (1913) no. 388: 707–38 and "La mentalité indigène en Algérie," *Mercure de France* 106 (1913) no. 396: 673–99.

See also van Gennep's "Recherches sur les poteries peintes de l'Afrique du Nord (Tunisie, Algérie, Maroc)," *Harvard African Studies* 2 (1918): 235–97 and his "Jewish Arts and Crafts in North Africa," *The Menorah Journal* 12 (1926): 43–48.

On the folklore of the area, see also Alphonse Certeux, *L'Algérie Traditionelle. Leg-*

endes, contes, chansons, musique, moeurs, coutumes, fêtes, croyances, superstitions, etc. (Paris: Maisonneuve et Leclerc, 1884). For general background information on the Algerian Jews, see Ernest Mainz, "Mourning Customs of the Algerian Jews," *Proceedings of the American Academy for Jewish Research* 21 (1952): 63–73 and, by the same author, "Les juifs d'Alger sous la domination Turque," *Journal Asiatique* 240 (1952): 197–217. Also see Georges Meynié, *Les Juifs en Algérie* (Paris: Savine, 1887) and Eugene Blum (with the pseudonym Louis Durien), *Le proletariat Juif en Algérie* (Paris: Librairie de la Revue Socialiste, 1899). For the decades following van Gennep's visit, see Michel Ansky, *Les Juifs d'Algérie du decret Cremieux à la liberation* (Paris: Éditions du Centre de Documentation Juive Contemporaine, 1950).

On the Jews of Tlemcen and the setting described by van Gennep see Moise Weil, *Le cimetière israélite de Tlemcen* (Avignon: Se-guin Frères, 1881); Jean Joseph Leandre Bargès, *Tlemcen, ancienne capitale du royaume de ce nom* (Paris: Dupret, 1859), 4; and especially Abraham Meyer, *Études des moeurs actuelles des Israélites de Tlemcen, précédés d'une notice sur Rabbenou Ephraim Aln'Caoua, accompagnés de tableaux généalogiques et chronologiques. XIVe et XVe siècle* (Algiers: Franck & Solal, 1902).

For van Gennep's contribution to the field of folklore studies, see *Les Rites de Passage* (Paris: Nourry, 1907), English trans.: *The Rites of Passage* (Chicago: University of Chicago Press, 1960). See also his monumental *Manuel de Folklore Français Contemporain*, 6 vols. (Paris: Picard, 1937–51). On van Gennep, see Nicole Belmont, *Arnold van Gennep. The Creator of French Ethnography* (Chicago: University of Chicago Press, 1979); Rosemary Zumwalt, "Arnold van Gennep: The Hermit of Bourg-la-Reine," *American Anthropologist* 84 (1982): 299–313.

6 / The Olojo Festival at Ife, 1937

William Bascom

The Yoruba are considered one of the most important ethnic groups of West Africa. Their population amounts to some 10 million, and has constituted the dominant group of Nigeria. Their tradition of urban life and their economy, art, and religion place them at the highest level of cultural achievement among sub-Saharan peoples. Furthermore, specialists affirm that Yoruba slaves and their descendants had the greatest influence on the New World cultures of the Caribbean, Cuba, and Brazil.

In this essay William Bascom, a foremost scholar in anthropology and folklore and a recognized authority on the Yoruba, describes the festivities at the city of Ife, as he witnessed them starting September 28, 1937, less than a month after he began his fieldwork there.

The article has the style of the precise, step-by-step, eyewitness fieldnotes which were its sources. It is written in the tradition of classic, "objective" ethnography. The article has a theme and not a thesis, and aims at providing a scrupulously detailed account of all the public activities of the festival. Analysis and interpretation are not included, since Bascom considered that they belong to a subsequent stage of the research, and to works of larger breadth and length, such as his "The Yoruba of Western Nigeria."

Descriptive articles of the present kind, although they may appear cut-and-dried at first glance, nevertheless contain rich and reliable data for analytical, comparative, and interpretive studies. For instance, scholars interested in body adornment and color symbolism will find valuable information in the description of the Oloko, the messengers who wear the gods' insignia as colors painted on their bodies (half red like Ogun and half white like Odua). The variation of the colors is also recorded, along with the Yorubas' rationale for it. Readers interested in symbolic inversion will notice that the festival is held in honor of Ogun and Oranmiyan, both gods of war, who are worshipped together to ensure peace for Ife. Swords and clubs, traditional weapons and symbols of war, are used in reverse for rituals of peace: a pile of swords serves as altar; swords are struck together and bound in sign of friendship; clubs and knives serve in the killing of sacrificial animals, which are offered to obtain peace.

Students of ritual will also find data which are normally edited out, consciously or not, from most ethnographic reports. A most important set of such data is in the thorough description of the yearly dog sacrifices, which have replaced human sacrifice. Bascom chose neither to sensationalize nor to gloss over such customs. Not that he was indifferent to what he saw, but he mentions without indulgence the heat, the swarms of flies, the crowd, the blood, and the fact that he almost fainted at the scene. Mistakes in ritual routines are also often edited out of studies. Not in this case. The readers may participate in the mistakes of the newly appointed chiefs who do not know the ritual formulas and etiquette, and in the anger, then the amusement, of the king and the audience.

Ethnomusicologists also will find relevant data in the description of the musical instruments, such as the kakaki, the brass trumpets, and the ipe, the ivory trumpets. As both blare and "speak" praises of the king, their "words" are reported verbatim. Readers interested in syncretism will find references to new elements as they are—or are not—integrated into the old rituals, be they shorts, automobiles, drills of policemen in Western attire, or, above all, elements of Christianity. These include "Christian girls" dancing to their drummers—presumably with more modest virginal poise than is to be found in the king's royal swirls. The chief Ejio, who is Christian, while present at the ritual sacrifices, abstains from taking active part in them and resolves for the moment the conflict between tribal religion and Christianity by delegating a representative to participate in the ritual for him. Finally, the Christian calendar (and consequent objections to drumming on Sunday) displaces the date of the festival out of the traditional lunar calendar.

Finally, students of symbolic behavior will have especially important data from the sequence of the royal processions. Before the Olojo festival, the king has made three ritual trips from the palace to the sacred shrines, but no one was permitted to look at him—people had to stay inside their homes, windows and doors were locked, people put cloths on their heads; those caught outside were whipped. Only for the Olojo festival is he visible, and he then receives enthusiastic cheers and praises from his subjects. After the "forbidden" processions, the "permitted" ones become surcharged with meaning, as in the ritual alternating movement between semantic pairs such as fast/feast or abstinence/indulgence.

The Olojo Festival at Ife, 1937

William Bascom

The festival in honor of Ogun, the Yoruba god of iron and war,[1] is celebrated annually at Ife, Nigeria. It is known as Olojo, which means "one who has day" or "owner of the day." It is so called because in earlier times it was the only occasion on which the Oni, king of Ife, appeared in public. In 1937 it was still one of only three occasions on which he left his palace to participate in a traditional religious ceremony. During the Edi festival in honor of Moremi, a wife of Oranmiyan who saved Ife from the Igbo, the Oni sat at the gate to the palace grounds. During the Itapa festival he made three trips from the palace to the shrine of Orisala but on these occasions no one was permitted to see him; in 1937 he went only once but all the townspeople had to stay inside their houses with the doors and windows closed or lie down with cloths over their heads as the Oni passed through the streets with his attendants, who whipped anyone who was tardy in complying. During Olojo, which precedes both of these festivals in the ceremonial year, the Oni left his palace to receive the cheers and praises of his people.[2] It was an occasion of great importance and excitement for the people of Ife.

On two occasions during Olojo young men with their bodies painted half-red and half-white run back and forth between the Oni's palace and the hill of Ogun until they are tired. These men are young messengers or pages (Emese) of the Oni who in this context are known as Oloko. The right halves of their bodies are painted red with camwood (osun) and the left halves white with lime (efun) made by burning snail shells. This is done in honor of Oranmiyan, a deity known as a famous warrior and the founder of the city of Oyo.

According to a myth Oranmiyan had two fathers, Ogun and Odua, the deity who created the earth. While Odua was still ruling as the first king of Ife, there was a war at the town of Ogotun. Odua sent his warrior, Ogun, there to fight for him. Ogun captured some slaves among whom there was a very beautiful woman named Lakange. She was menstruating at the time, but before they returned to Ife, Ogun had intercourse with her. When Odua saw Lakange he was enchanted by her beauty and wanted to take her as his wife, offering Ogun the other captives as his reward. Ogun objected, saying, "But, my master, I have already had connection with her." Odua refused to believe him and took Lakange as his wife in spite of Ogun's protest. She conceived and gave birth to a son who was half-red like Ogun and half-white like Odua. Ogun said to Odua, "Did my words come true or not come true?" (*Oro mi yan tabi ko yan?*) and from then on the boy was known as Oranmiyan.

Actually it is believed that Ogun is very black, but the red side of the messengers' bodies represents him. In 1951 Akogun, a war chief and the town chief responsible for the worship of Oranmiyan, said that Oranmiyan was really black on one side and white on the other. He explained that the Oloko should be painted with charcoal and lime, but that no one wants to put on charcoal so they are colored red and white.

Verger has recorded three versions of the myth in which Ogun[3] is said to be half-black and half-white. He also says that during the festival for Ogun the Oni's messengers are painted half-black and half-white, and he has published an undated photograph showing them with the left sides of their bodies painted black and the right sides painted white.[4] Could this be the result of my 1951 conversation with

Akogun? I cannot otherwise explain the discrepancy. When Mrs. Bascom and I saw the Oloko in 1950 they were red and white. Mr. F. Niyi Akinnaso, lecturer in linguistics at the University of Ife, says that in 1976 they were also red and white, and that he saw women preparing the camwood for their use.

The Olojo festival is considered to be in honor of both Ogun and Oranmiyan. Osogun, the priest of Ogun, Eredumi, the priest of Oranmiyan, and Akogun participate in it. Odua has his own festival, Idio; but Ogun and Oranmiyan are both gods of war and are worshipped together. The festival is performed so that Ife may have peace.

Here I describe only the major parts of the public festival. Private rituals are performed simultaneously for Oranmiyan by Eredumi, and for Ogun by Osogun, by the blacksmiths at their smithies, and perhaps by others. Before the festival begins, everyone buys food for the days ahead because all the markets in Ife are closed on the second, third, and fourth days of Olojo.

The First Day

This day is known as Ijo Ilagun, which was interpreted as meaning "the day to worship Ogun." In the morning young palm fronds (mariwo), which Ogun is said to "own," were hung over the door of Osogun's house and over Ogun's shrine inside the house. Osogun stayed home that day to give food and drink to the chiefs and priests who came to visit him. When I visited him in the morning only Obadio, the priest of Odua, was there, but others might have come later.

Chief Akogun said that he sacrificed to Ogun in front of his house and when he finished he called out, *"Ogun, yeee. Tata, yeee," Tata* being a praise name of Ogun. When this cry was heard in the palace, which must be about a mile away, the Oni sent a messenger to Osogun to say that he was ready, and Osogun left for the hill of Ogun. However, Osogun denied that Akogun begins the festival in this way.

About nine o'clock in the evening I went to Okemogun, the hill of Ogun. It is a small hill facing the main gate of the Oni's palace, with the large Ife market between them. On the hill stand two monoliths sacred to Ogun. The larger one, some six feet tall, is said to be Ogun's staff.[5] Soon the messenger returned from informing Osogun that the Oni was ready, and about 9:15 Osogun started for Okemogun. He cannot come by the direct route from his home, but must come by the road in front of the palace. Further, he must never sit down in the market or in the palace.

Osogun arrived with a crowd of people who carried kerosene lanterns, large torches, and a gasoline lamp. One of the men called out repeatedly during the evening, "Who is the owner of its head?" *(Yesi lo lori re?)* and the group responded, "Ogun is the owner of its head" *(Ogun lo lori re).* These shouts, reminiscent of a college football cheer, referred to the head of the sacrificial dog. Another man in the group had a sideblown trumpet of orange ivory that "spoke" by varying the tones of the Yoruba language in the manner of talking drums.

Osogun directed the completion of clearing the grass around Ogun's staff and the removal of a crosspole and the remnants of the dog that had been sacrificed the year before. Upright bamboo poles were placed around the staff and horizontal poles were placed on top of them, with the new main crosspole facing the market and the palace. Two dogs were brought with their necks tied to sticks, their hind legs around the sticks, and their forelegs tied behind their backs. It was explained that formerly human sacrifices, which were not common in Ife, were bound in the same way.[6] One of the dogs lay quietly near Ogun's staff and the other howled at the bottom of the hill. The dogs and the other sacrificial materials were provided by the Oni.

Obadio and Obalubo, both priests of Odua, arrived, followed by Ejio, an important town chief. Ejio worships Oramfe, the Ife god of thunder and counterpart of Sango. After the festival, he said that he has no association with either Ogun or Oranmiyan that would explain his important role in the Olojo festival, although there must be a reason why he should be the one who kills the dogs for Ogun.

A bundle of fresh palm fronds that had just sprouted was brought and laid on the ground. Osogun cut the binding of the bundle and called to Ejio, "*Olorin, Olorin, Olorin*"; Ejio answered "*Arefe,*" and came forward. "*Olorin*" was interpreted as meaning, "one who beats something heavy" or "one who has something heavy" (i.e., a responsible position) and "*Arefe*" as "something so sharp that it can cut with a single stroke." Throughout the ceremony Osogun called to Ejio, and Ejio responded in this way. Osogun and Ejio each took a palm frond and at the same time picked out the stiff rib (owo), of the kind that are used to make *besoms*, a kind of broom, from one of the leaves. Their helpers removed the ribs from the other palm leaves and from the leaves of the other fronds, allowing the rest of the leaves to hang loosely from the main stems.

Osogun again called to Ejio, who answered and came out of the crowd. Each took an end of one palm frond and bound it to the main crosspole, with Osogun on the right side and Ejio on the left. Their helpers bound the other palm fronds around the staff. It was discovered that one palm frond had been overlooked, and Osogun, apparently angry, ordered his assistants to remove the ribs and bind it to the framework. The ribs were picked up and laid in a pile inside the framework of palm fronds. It was said that the Oni must not step on them, but a few were left on the ground at the approach to the shrine. Attention was called to the skull of the dog sacrificed the previous year, which was in the pathway, but it was left there. Someone said, "The Oni will have to pay for an atonement (etutu) if he stumbles." Notice was sent to the Oni that all was ready, and the palm oil sent by him arrived. During the waiting period a few of the hunters sang about Osogun, about their own lineage, and about their clan taboo against eating peanuts.

The firing of the hunters' Dane guns announced that the Oni was coming. He was preceded by a great band of pressure drums (*dundun, gangan*), iron cymbals (*aro*), large calabashes netted with cowry shells that are shaken like a rattle and beaten like a drum (*sekere*), and two seven-foot-long brass trumpets (*kakaki*). The brass trumpets and the ivory trumpet (*ipe*) blared praises of the Oni. The ivory trumpet spoke: "One who equalled a king before, father of Waleade" (*Atobatele, baba Waleade*)[7] and "One who saw rain, took title, father of Waleade" (*A rojo joye, baba Waleade*).[8] The long brass trumpets spoke partially in Hausa.[9]

This crowd moved through the dark market, its path marked by the light of torches, lanterns, and gasoline lamps. The headlights of the Oni's Buick touring car emerged from the palace, followed by the headlights of the automobile of Lowa, the top-ranking palace chief. The Oni, dressed in a simple white gown, dismounted in the market and the crowd of people approached the hill of Ogun. It was a large crowd but nothing like the one on the second day, when the general public assembled to greet the Oni. Moving through the crowd in a circle of light from a gasoline lamp, the Oni took his place near the left end of the main crosspole.

Osogun entered the framework of palm fronds, which may represent Ogun's house in the forest. He cast a kola nut in divination, invoked Ogun's blessing, and presented a white chicken, a dried hind leg of a bush goat, a dried rat, and a dried fish to Ogun, laying small pieces of the dried meat and fish on a stone near Ogun's staff. Osogun came out and called to Ejio, who answered; but instead of coming himself, Ejio sent a young man who carried a large club of green wood about three feet long and three inches in diameter. The dog, still tied, was brought before the shrine, and the young man raised his club and gave the dog a terrific blow on the head, and another, and another. Had Ejio not been a Christian, he should have done this himself.

As the dog lay bleeding at the mouth, Osogun cut through its throat with a small knife, leaving the head attached to the body by skin at the back of the neck, and then let the dog lie on the ground until it stopped bleeding. Osogun undid a bundle of vines and called to Ejio, who answered and came forward. With Osogun on the right side and Ejio on the left, they tied the dog's hind legs to the crosspole, with the feet far apart and the abdomen facing the market. Osogun cut open the abdomen on both sides, starting from below, and pulled out the entrails so that they hung down. He took the white chicken by the feet and killed it by striking its head against the ground. He called to Ejio who answered and came forward. Taking the same positions they tied the chicken's feet to the hind feet of the dog, with the chicken's abdomen facing the market. Osogun cut open the chicken's abdomen, as he had cut that of the dog, and pulled out its entrails. Then he poured a bowl of orange palm oil over both animals.

I have seen many animal sacrifices since then, but this was my first. Swarms of flies were attracted by the lights and the blood and could hardly be brushed away from my face. It was hot and humid, and I nearly fainted.

Osogun touched the ground with his sword and then touched the dog and chicken. Then, with a young man carrying a lantern leading the way, he started counterclockwise around Ogun's staff. Some of the priests and chiefs present (Obawara, Obadio, Lowa, Aguro, Ejio, Arode, and Ladin) followed him after touching their swords to the ground and then to the sacrificial animals. They circled the staff seven times, stopping each time to touch the ground and the dog and chicken with their swords, as they did again when the last round was completed. Being a Christian, the Oni stood aside as this procession took place.

Osogun took his place at the right side of the crosspole, and the Oni stood opposite him at the left. They spoke to each other, wishing each other well and expressing the hope that they would meet there again next year. They struck their swords together and Osogun turned to Lowa, who substituted for the Oni, and they locked the little fingers of their left hands together and spoke to each other.

The crowd left Ogun's hill, flowing down to the level of the market, and the shouting, drumming, and blaring of the trumpets swelled again. A space was cleared around the second dog at the bottom of the hill. This spot was said to be the place where Ogun "went into the ground" and became a deity. A chair was brought for the Oni, who sat some thirty yards away in the light of a gasoline lamp, talking pleasantly with those near him.

The chiefs and priests laid their swords in a pile on the ground. The iron swords represented Ogun and served as the altar for the second sacrifice. Osogun cut off small pieces from the dried hind leg of the bush goat, the dried rat, and the dried fish and placed them on the swords, invoking a blessing for the whole town, especially for everyone present. He knocked off the tips of two snail shells and poured their liquid onto the outstretched hands of the chiefs and priests who rubbed it over their heads and faces. This was done as a propitiation (*ero*) so that they would live to make the festival again next year. Some of the liquid was poured on the pile of swords. Osogun split and cast a kola nut in divination, rubbing his hands together to indicate that it had come out good again.

Osogun poured palm oil over the dried meat and fish and the swords. He called to Ejio, who answered and again sent the young man as his substitute. The young man killed the second dog with three blows of his club to its head, and Osogun cut its throat as before. Lifting the dog, Osogun let its blood flow over the sacrifice and the swords. He washed the pieces of dried meat and fish, to be taken home, along with the dog, and eaten. The first dog and the white chicken were left hanging until the next festival.[10] Lowa handed seven pence to Osogun, the traditional gift from the Oni. The drums and trumpets began again, and the crowd with its lights moved off through the market, followed by the automobiles of the Oni and Lowa. As the Oni entered the palace gate, the crowd dispersed into the night.

The Second Day

The next day is called Ijo Okemogun, "the day of Ogun's hill." By five o'clock in the afternoon Enuwa square between the palace and the market was crowded, despite a slight rain. People were everywhere, following groups of drummers, singing and dancing. It was festival!

At the center of one of the groups was Akogun, representing Oranmiyan, making his first appearance. His drummers played a special drum (*aluja* or *igunmo*), shaped like a *bembe* drum but with only one head. Akogun carried his wooden Oranmiyan staff, surmounted by a carved male figure. In another group was Gbonka, another war chief descended from an ally of Oranmiyan. Nearby was his leather banner, about eighteen by twenty-four inches, on top of a twenty-foot-long pole. The pole was made of porcupine quills bound together with leather thongs and had an iron tip at the bottom so that it could be stuck in the ground. Arode, a palace chief descended from another ally of Oranmiyan, was present in his finery.

Inside the palace other groups of people were crowded around drummers and dancers. The group of herbalists was distinguished by young men carrying two branches of green leaves. Drums of many kinds were present, as well as iron cymbals, iron gongs (*agogo*) beaten with sticks, and a large sideblown ivory trumpet. Two men with *kakaki* trumpets and many hunters with their Dane guns pointed at the sky awaited the appearance of the Oni. The police stood at attention near the council hall, and the Oni's automobile was waiting. Groups of drummers and men and women were dancing everywhere.

A shout arose as the Oloko, messengers, came running out. They were dressed only in white or leather shorts with their bodies painted red and white in honor of Oranmiyan and his fathers, Ogun and Odua. They gathered in front of the council hall and put on their headpieces. These shallow calabashes, in which were mud images decked with feathers, had been made by the head herbalist. The images, called *oloko*, from which the young men took their title, represent Osanyin, the god of medicine. They are also known as *sigidi*, which all messengers of the Oni use as protection.[11] The Oloko ran or made their way as rapidly as possible through the crowd, back and forth between the palace, where they worship Odua, and Okemogun, where they worship Ogun, striking at anyone in the way with long supple stems of a shrub that served as whips.

Another period of waiting, with more drumming and dancing, was interrupted by a shout that rose through the palace grounds. The Oni had come out. Dane guns were fired off in profusion, with flames flashing from the barrels and smoke rising above the hunters. The *kakaki* trumpets blared salutations to the Oni. The drums, gongs, and cymbals began with a new enthusiasm, and the *sekere* calabashes were shaken above the heads of the players.

The Oni was dressed in his regal robes and wore a beaded crown.[12] Smiling broadly as he recognized friends, he entered his automobile and rode slowly through the palace grounds. Before the Oni was the band of musicians: the two *kakaki* trumpeters, the row of *sekere* calabashes raised on high, and the many drummers, cymbal players, and gong beaters. The hunters followed alongside, firing their guns periodically.

As the band passed under the low roof of the palace gate, the sound seemed to double in volume. By now the crowd outside filled the square and the market. As the Oni's car passed through the palace gate a deafening shout spread from the palace to the hill of Ogun. Besides the musicians, the hunters, the chiefs in full dress, and the mass of people, there were men dressed in their finest, riding prancing horses through the immense crowd. The large state umbrellas could be seen above the heads of the people. It seemed as if all the people of Ife were there to see their king for the first time that year!

On Ogun's hill, near the sacrifice of the night before, stood Osogun, who had again come by the indirect route from his home. He had a long wait as the Oni's automobile passed very slowly through the singing and dancing crowd. One group of dancers after another broke off from the crowd and ran to the hill, but at other times a chief and his followers left the hill to dance out to meet another chief, and their two dancing groups merged. A large crowd gathered around Ogun's staff, and the police struck the gathered people with their rods to clear a path to the two monoliths. Two young men near Osogun kept up a rhythm with two small bells, but it was soon drowned out by the sound of the iron gongs. The Oni's car came part way up the hill and he got out. He took his place to the left of Ogun's staff while the crowd pushed and shoved on all sides.

Osogun gathered the swords of the chiefs and priests and took them inside the palm frond structure. There he marked them with two stripes of red camwood with a stripe of white lime in between. He returned the swords, and the Oni and Osogun struck their swords together, wishing each other well and praying that they might meet there again next year. They then hooked their swords together momentarily. Lowa, again substituting for the Oni, and Osogun locked the little fingers of their left hands together.

As the party moved down the hill, the shouting arose again, and when it reached the bottom the Dane guns were fired. The crowd moved toward the left, dancing down the road that led to the produce market. About a block away, at the side of the road, two flat stones about an inch in diameter had been placed on top of each other. Lowa, acting for the Oni, and Eredumi, the priest of Oranmiyan, rather inconspicuously placed their feet on the stones with Lowa's foot on top of Eredumi's. According to Osogun this was in honor of Aje, the god of money. However, Eredumi said that at that time he received a ram that he was to sacrifice to the dead kings that same day. Symbolically he "took the Oni's feet" to go to Igbodi where the early Oni were buried, because the Oni himself cannot go there.

The Oni entered his automobile and started back to the palace. A crowd of men fell in behind him and, with a lurching dance step, followed singing, "[The time] outside is sufficient, oh" (Leader: *Ode to-o eee*. Chorus: *Ode to-o mm, ode to-o eee*). Slowly the Oni's car made its way through the tremendous crowd, with Lowa's car following. There was still a full festival mood with drumming, dancing, singing, shouting, gong beating, and the blare of the trumpets.

Osogun must not stay to watch or join in the dancing. Each time he goes to Ogun's hill during Olojo he must return home immediately by his indirect route. Even after the Oni entered the palace, the other principals stayed with the crowd near the palace gate and continued their dancing. Gradually groups of people went home to eat and drink, with more drumming and dancing, and the horsemen rode off through the crowd. The third day is a day of rest (Ijo Isinmi).

The Fourth Day

This day is known as Ijo Okemogun Keji, the "second day of Ogun's hill." By four o'clock in the afternoon some of the chiefs were dancing through the streets, each accompanied by their drummers and relatives, visiting the homes of friends. By five o'clock small boys were playing in front of the palace and the crowd began to arrive, many dancing. The gong beaters came through the marketplace to the palace. Inside there were a number of people, some of whom were dancing inside the council hall. A group of Christian girls with their drummers came dancing into the palace grounds. The hunters and the police were waiting, and the police went through a few drills.

The crowd began to gather in front of the Oni's private house. The police cleared an open space for him to come out, but there was still a long wait. The chiefs and priests were still arriving, dancing, and some of them performed in the open space. At one side, behind the crowd, Lowa's sons danced to *sekere* calabashes. The herbalists danced forward, their leafy branches no longer fresh. Some important but unofficial men danced to gongs and calabashes; one wore a black gown that resembled a graduation gown. The police pushed the crowd back to make room for the Oni's automobile, and the large state umbrellas took their places at the doorway to cover him until he entered it.

The Oni came out and the Dane guns fired, the *kakaki* trumpets blared, and the drums and gongs were beaten. This time he was dressed in an orange gown and wore a leather hat instead of his crown. He paused while he was saluted by his chiefs, by the Muslims, by the herbalists, and by visitors from Ila, the capital of another Yoruba kingdom. He entered his automobile, which proceeded slowly through the palace grounds following three *kakaki* trumpets, a row of *sekere* calabashes that could occasionally be seen raised over the players' heads in rhythm, and the other musicians. Far ahead an elder brother of the Oni rode on his prancing horse. The crowd broke and ran for the palace gate in order to be outside in time to cheer the Oni when he came out.[13]

The automobile proceeded slowly through the dancing crowd in the marketplace; the crowd was again immense. New banners, new staffs, and large fans were to be seen. About halfway to Ogun's hill the car stopped and the Oni got out. He trotted counterclockwise in a small circle around a stone located between two market stalls, followed by two of his senior messengers.[14] As he reentered the car, the Oni was met by the Oloko, again painted red and white, returning from Ogun's hill. The car drove slowly part way up the hill, and the police fought back the crowd to let the Oni through and to make a space for the ritual in front of Ogun's staff. Only a few priests and chiefs were there when the Oni arrived. Osogun, who should have been there, was notably absent, having been detained by guests he was entertaining. The sacrificed animal smelled and was swarming with flies.

Osogun appeared in the market dancing with abandon, very wildly compared with the dignified dances of the other priests and the chiefs. He danced rapidly up the hill through a lane opened through the crowd for him. Osogun took his place at the right side of the crosspole and the Oni stood at the left. They struck their swords together, wished each other well, and locked their swords together momentarily. Osogun and Lowa locked the little fingers of their left hands together, and the crowd flowed down the hill amid renewed drumming, trumpeting, and volleys from the Dane guns.

This time the crowd turned to the right and stopped some fifty yards from the place where the second dog had been sacrificed. A triangular space was cleared in front of the Oni, and alternately the town and palace chiefs danced in turn from him to the other two apexes of the triangle. At the third apex they faced Oketase, the hill sacred to Ifa, the god of divination, and saluted him. The visitors from Ila saluted the Oni, all prostrating themselves before him except the representative of Orangun, the king of Ila, who carried a beaded staff topped by a bird. Finally it was the Oni's turn to dance, but he merely waved his fly whisk in rhythm a few times and turned away to his car, which was driven slowly back to the palace. The market was jammed with women who cheered as the Oni passed, and he nodded in recognition or waved his fly whisk at them. Someone ran up to the car and presented him with kola nuts and two bottles of schnapps, which he gave to the musicians. At the palace gate a great cheer went up from his wives, who had waited there to greet him.

Mats and carpets had been spread and two chairs and a beaded cushion had been placed in the veranda at the palace gate. When the Oni had been seated four palace chiefs knelt on his left and saluted him, holding their swords by the blades and touching the handles to the ground, each time saying, *"Wori, wori, wori."* This was repeated with their fly whisks, touching the handles to the ground, again symbolizing submission and loyalty. Together all four took hold of a bundle (*oparù*) of bare twigs bound together with leather and touched it three times to the ground, symbolizing unity, and they repeated this salutation with a staff (ida Oranmiyan) with a thin piece of brass at the top.

The town chiefs on the Oni's right repeated these salutations. However, some of them, who were recently installed in office and did not know the routine, started to get up at the end of every greeting. One touched the ground with the blade of his sword and had to be corrected, and another had to borrow a besom to use in place of a fly whisk. The Oni's annoyance at this ignorance disappeared as he saw the humor of the situation and everyone laughed at them. The town chiefs took their places on the mats at the feet of the Oni and behind him every space was filled, mainly by his wives.

A space was cleared in front of the Oni with drummers at the far end. One by one the town and palace chiefs danced alternately, ending with the more customary salutation. Facing the Oni each knelt, clasped his hands together with arms extended toward the ground, and repeated three times, "*Wori, wori, wori,*" emphasizing each word with a slight but intense motion of the clasped hands. Each touched the mid-fingers of both hands to the ground and to his cheeks, and then stretched out face down in full prostration. The visitors from Ila entered, repeated their salutation, danced briefly, and again repeated their salutation. Finally it was the Oni's turn to dance, and he swirled off through the gate into the palace.

Somewhat later the Oloko came running back to the palace. They had run back and forth between the palace and Ogun's hill earlier,[15] and were running from house to house in search of tips as a reward for their performance. The crowd outside the palace watched the groups of dancers and went home slowly. The chiefs and priests with their followers danced all the way home, where some continued feasting and dancing.

During the fourth day Eredumi sacrificed a ram to Oranmiyan in a private ritual performed in Oranmiyan's grove behind the eighteen-foot-tall monolith known as Oranmiyan's staff near the house of Akogun.[16] The fifth and sixth days of the festival are days of rest, and the markets are open again.

The Seventh Day

The last day of Olojo is called Ijo Etutu, the "Day of Atonement." In 1937, it fell on October 4. I did not witness what happened but Osogun and his followers went to the palace where the Oni gave them money, kola nuts, and palm wine or gin. They left dancing, and the Olojo festival was ended.

Scheduling the Festival

The new moon should always appear on the fourth day of Olojo (Ijo Okemogun Keji). The date of Olojo is announced on the second day of the Luwo festival, on which a full moon appears, as forty days away.[17] These forty days, plus the second and third days of Olojo (Ijo Okemogun and Ijo Isinmi), give forty-two days, the time between the full moon at the Luwo festival and the new moon on the fourth day of the Olojo festival. The announcement is made on the day of Oja Ife market and, starting with the following market day (Iremo), this makes the first day of Olojo (Ijo Ilagun) fall on the day of Oja Ife market. The fourth day with the new moon falls on the day of Ikogun market. In 1937, however, the fourth day would have fallen on Sunday, October 1, and because the Christians objected to drumming on Sunday, the festival was begun four days early, also on the day of Oja Ife market and with the fourth day also on the day of Ikogun market but without a new moon.

NOTES

1. For a general introduction to the Yoruba and their religion, see William Bascom, *The Yoruba of Southwestern Nigeria* (New York: Holt, Rinehart and Winston, 1969); also his "Yoruba Food" and "Yoruba Cooking," *Africa* 21 (1951): 41–53, 125–27; "Urbanization Among the Yoruba," *The American Journal of Sociology* 60 (1955): 446–54; *Ifa Divination: Communication Between Gods and Men in West Africa* (Bloomington: Indiana University Press, 1969). See also E. Bolaji Idowu, *Olodumare. God in Yoruba Belief* (London: Longmans,

Green & Co., 1961); J. F. Ade Ajayi, *Christian Missions in Nigeria, 1841–1891* (London: Longmans Green, 1965); Samuel Johnson, *The History of the Yorubas* (London: George Routledge and Sons, 1921); Jean Herskovitz Kopytoff, *A Preface to Modern Nigeria* (Madison: University of Wisconsin Press, 1965); James S. Coleman, *Nigeria, Background to Nationalism* (Berkeley: University of California Press, 1958); Kevin Carroll, *Yoruba Religious Carving* (London: Chapman, 1967); Isaac O. Delano, *Owe l'Esin Oro. Yoruba Proverbs* (New York: Oxford University Press, 1966); Abayomi Fuja, *Fourteen Hundred Cowries* (New York: Oxford University Press, 1962); G. J. Afolabi, *Yoruba Palaces* (London: University of London Press, 1966); G. J. Afolabi, *Yoruba Culture* (London: University of London Press, 1967); Frank Willett, *Ife in the History of West African Sculpture* (London: Thames and Hudson, 1967) [ed. note].

2. I was told that in earlier times the Oni was concealed behind cloths held by his messengers so that only his crown and its white egret feather could be seen.

3. Johnson and others spell this name *Oduduwa*, but the Oni said that this is wrong. See Johnson, *History of the Yorubas*.

4. Pierre Verger, *Dieux d'Afrique* (Paris: Paul Hartmann, 1954), p. 179 and photo 76. A sixth version of this myth describes Oranmiyan as half-brown and half-white.

5. Philip Allison, *African Stone Sculpture* (London: Lund Humphries, 1968). Allison says that it is probable that the cylindrical stone fragments once formed a tall pillar (see plate 5).

6. Humans were sacrificed at only two festivals in Ife: Idio for Odua and Itapa for Orisala. Only male criminals were sacrificed, and never people of Ife or their slaves.

7. The Oni's praise name, Atobatele, which was inscribed on the front of his new private house on the palace grounds, refers to the fact that while young he spoke of becoming Oni some day, even though he would have to compete for the title. Waleade (Come to the house of crown) is the name of one of his daughters.

8. This refers to the fact that he became Oni during the rainy season.

9. *Baba asiki silangaba, baba Waleade, asiki silangaba, oko Segilola*. The Oni is again called "father of Waleade" and, at the end, "husband of Segilola" (Segi [valuable beads] are honor), the name of one of his wives.

10. See Verger, photo 77. Note the dog's head hanging from its body. Two parts of Ogun's staff can be seen through the surprisingly sparse palm fronds.

11. Johnson (p. 62) calls them sugudu.

12. I was told that he should have worn his oldest, largest crown with beaded fringes, but my photographs show that he did not.

13. I was told that if the Oni had not been a Christian he should have spent the day at the house of his father and gone from there to the hill of Ogun, but I had no confirmation. Confirmation seems to be provided by Pemberton's account of the Ogun festival at Ila-Orangun. Instead, the Oni stayed in the palace and went from there directly to Okemogun. No one can become Oni while his father is still alive.

14. I did not learn the significance of this. I had not observed it on the second day but I was told that it had taken place.

15. See Verger, photo 76. In their haste some of the Oloko, returning from Okemogun, carry their headpieces in their hands. Even assuming that this undated photograph was taken on the fourth, rather than the second day of Olojo, why is the crowd so small? In 1937 I unfortunately missed the opportunity to photograph the Oloko inside the palace ground, and the crowd was too dense to do so once they were outside.

16. See Allison, plate 5.

17. Ten Yoruba four-day weeks. The Yoruba speak of a five-day week, but the fifth day is the first day of the following week. Thus in Ife, the "five-day" week consists of Oja Ife, Iremo, Aiyegbaju, Ikogun, and Oja Ife again. There are only four days in the week as we count them, and only four markets after which the days are named. Similarly Eredumi, who makes the announcement during the Luwo festival, said that he normally announces the first day of Olojo to be "forty-one" days away, but that in 1937 he announced it as "thirty-seven" days away.

7 / Carnival, Ritual, and Play in Rio de Janeiro

Victor Turner

If Carnival is celebrated worldwide, nowhere has it become more locally characterized than in Rio de Janeiro. And if "play" is more revealing of a culture than work, nowhere do people play harder than in the Rio Carnival.

For Victor Turner, a visit to the Rio Carnival as an honored guest becomes the occasion for enjoyment as well as reflection and revisitation of the theory of play, referred and compared to his own ground-breaking studies on ritual. Turner argues that cultural performances are closely related to social structures, social history, and social processes, with their underlying rhetorics. Furthermore, in contemporary mainstream societies, play has inherited functions from religious ritual. In play, whether games, sports, or festivals, people have increasingly become "morally reflexive," relating their lives to traditional values. Turner discusses the definition of "play" offered by two leading European scholars, Dutch Medievalist Johann Huizinga (author of the fundamental Homo Ludens) and French essayist Roger Caillois (author of works on play and games and Festival). Caillois's classification of play into subtypes is explained and retained as valuable. However, his argument appears intrinsically evolutionary and positivist, since it seems to praise the progressive "rationality" of Western elitist societies over what

Turner terms "the nonelitist societies, who now have perhaps most to give to the general stream of human culture." Turner prefers his own dialectical model, in which social phenomena are seen as alternating between "hierarchy" and "communitas," rational organization and creative inventiveness.

Turner experiences an enthusiastic adhesion to the carnival, and explicitly chooses to avoid puritanical "Northern" seriousness in discussing a festival which has "Southern" sensuality, lightness, deftness, and the "butterfly-wing color" of childlike wonders. To do so, he introduces and defines the Rio Carnival in the words of a samba lyric, and carries out his description and analysis with the help of the works by his Brazilian hosts, Rio's own leading anthropologists and students of Carnival, Roberto da Matta and Maria Goldwasser, who, incidentally, rely consistently on Turner's theoretical work.

The article makes brief references to the Rio masks and costumes, to the music and splendid parades where "the whole city worships Aphrodite on the half shell," especially impersonated in the ambiguous beauty of the mulata, which cuts across ethnic and racial divisions and aesthetic categories. The essay also sketches the historical evolution of the carnival music as well as the development of the carnival competitions, from the rude battles of Portuguese entrudos to the relatively recent competitions based on aesthetics with a system of evaluation including nine judges giving points and penalties to parading samba schools' groups.

More space is devoted to the carnival's immediate social context, the samba schools, which organize the parading groups and have a year-to-year social life, extended organization, and status system. This system is in constant evolution. Samba schools are organized in three leagues, with demotion of the schools coming last in the first and second leagues, and advancement of the two schools winning the second and third league to replace them. And below the leagues, there are hundreds of grass-root blocos—less structured and more volatile groups which may eventually become samba schools. Goldwasser's study shows how such intricately complex structure is paradoxically aimed at creating a chaotic antistructure, and what an "awful lot of order" is needed to produce such an elaborate disorder. Da Matta's studies are quoted to relate Carnival to the larger context of Brazilian society in general, and to the famous Brazilian passion for soccer and soccer clubs in particular. Even the politicking around the awards committee, the violence which bursts out when the rankings of the schools are made public, and the underworld characters running the illegal lottery, the old jogo do bicho, are discussed.

Lastly Turner mentions the criticisms of the Rio Carnival by Marxists, who accuse it of being the opiate of the masses, by the bourgeois, who see it as vulgar and violent, and by the high clergy, who consider it immoral and pagan.

On the whole, the Rio Carnival is seen as the creative antistructure of mechanized modernity, its aesthetic Golden Age where all kinds of playful festive behavior are inextricably spun together. From Turner's discussion, the patterns of the festival emerge with all their ritual and symbolic aspects. The structure of the festival and its social and historical context reveal their meanings. For the author, theoretical insights add to, not subtract from, enjoyment of the festival. For the readers, two centuries after Goethe's report, the carnivals, and Festival in general, finally begin to fully disclose their mysteries, their "theorems hidden in the poems."

Carnival, Ritual, and Play in Rio de Janeiro*

Victor Turner

Medieval European carnival had deep roots in the pagan past, having affinities with the Roman Saturnalia and Lupercalia.[1] But it found a place in the calendar of the church year and was normally performed during the four days before Lent. Folk etymology connected it with the medieval Latin phrase *carne vale* (flesh farewell), since it marked a period of fasting and revelry just before Lent, when meat eating fell under interdict. Being connected with a movable fast, carnival, notably, Mardi Gras (Fat Tuesday), its climax, just before Ash Wednesday, became a movable feast. Unlike such civic celebrations as Independence Day (July Fourth), Cinco de Mayo,[2] and others, carnival is set in a cosmological calendar, severed from ordinary historical time, even the time of extraordinary secular events. Truly carnival is the denizen of a place that is no place, and a time that is no time, even where that place is a city's main plazas, and that time can be found on an ecclesiastical calendar. For the squares, avenues, and streets of the city become, in carnival, the reverse of their daily selves. Instead of being the sites of offices and the conduits of purposive traffic, they are sealed off, during carnival, from traffic, and the millions who throng them on foot, drift idly wherever they please, no longer propelled by the urges of "getting and spending" in particular places. What we are seeing is society in its subjunctive mood— to borrow a term from grammar—its mood of feeling, willing, and desiring, its mood of fantasizing, its playful mood: not its indicative mood, where it tries to apply reason to human action and systematize the relationship between ends and means in industry and bureaucracy. The distinguished French scholar Jean-Richard Bloch lamented in the very title of his book, written in 1920, *Carnaval est mort. Premiers essais pour mieux comprendre mon temps*,[3] and the Spanish ethnologist Julio Caro Baroja, approvingly echoed him in 1965, *"el Carnaval ha muerto."* "Carnival is dead," indeed![4] They said as much of pilgrimage when my wife, Edie, and I set out to study this great mass phenomenon in 1970.[5] We found literally millions and millions of people still on the pilgrimage trail in all the world's major religions, and indeed that many so-called tourists were really closet pilgrims. Certainly, carnaval is by no means dead in Brazil, and rumors of its decease elsewhere are greatly exaggerated—one thinks immediately of Trinidad, New Orleans, and *Fastnacht* in many a German town.[6]

But carnaval, though a phenomenon of worldwide distribution—and I am thinking of Japanese and Indian festivals such as the Gion *matsuri* in Kyoto, or the *Holi* festival in northern India[7]—has become in Brazil something fundamentally and richly Brazilian. I say this despite Brazilian criticism by certain middle-class elements that it is vulgar, by Marxists that it diverts the energies of the workers from political activity and blurs class lines, and by those in the higher clergy who look on it as pagan and scandalous. The way people *play* perhaps is more profoundly revealing of a culture than how they work—giving access to their heart-values—I use this term instead of

---

*Also published as "Carnaval in Rio: Dionysian Drama in Industrializing Society," in *The Celebration of Society*, Frank E. Manning, ed. (Bowling Green, Ohio: Bowling Green University Popular Press, 1983), pp. 103–24. The new title and bracketed notes were added by the author shortly before his death. All other notes are the editor's.

key-values for reasons that will become clear, for the heart *has* its values, as well as its reasons.

I am going to throw in a *soupçon* of theory into this *bouillabaisse* of carnavalesque impressions, since one of my recent concerns is the constant cross-looping of social history with the numerous genres of cultural performance—ranging from ritual, through theater, the novel, folk drama, art exhibitions, ballet, modern dance, poetry readings, to film and television. Underpinning each type of performance are the social structures and processes of the time; underlying the social drama or "dramas of living," the Dreyfus Cases and Watergates, are the rhetorics and insights of contemporary kinds of performance, popular, mainstream, and avant-garde. Each feeds and draws on the other: in this way people try to assign meaning to their "behavior," turning it into "conduct." They become reflexive, at once their own subject and object. One of the modes in which they do this is play—including games and sports, as well as festivals. Play paradoxically has become a more serious matter with the decline of ritual and the contraction of the religious sphere—in which people used to become morally reflexive, relating their lives to the values handed down in sacred traditions. The play frame, where events are scrutinized in the leisure time of the social process, has to some extent inherited the function of the ritual frame. The messages it delivers are often serious beneath the outward trappings of absurdity, fantasy, and ribaldry. Stage plays, some movies, and some TV segments do this today. Clearly carnival is a form of play. Let me give you, very briefly, some current theories of play formulated by anthropologists and others, which may give us some clues as to what carnival is about.

The main pioneer in this field is the Dutch medieval historian Jan Huizinga, rector of the University of Leyden in 1933, and author of the celebrated book, *Homo Ludens* (Man at Play, or Man the Player). In it he defined *play* as follows:

> Summing up the formal characteristics of play we might call it a free activity standing quite consciously outside "ordinary life" as being "not serious," but at the same time absorbing the player intensely and utterly. It is an activity connected with no material interest, and no profit can be gained by it. It proceeds within its own proper boundaries of time and space according to fixed rules and in an orderly manner. It promotes the formation of social groupings which tend to surround themselves with secrecy and to stress their difference from the common world by disguise or other means.[8]

Play, then, according to Huizinga, is a "free activity," which nevertheless imposes order on itself, from within, and in accordance with its own rules. He grasps the connection between play and the secret and mysterious, but cannot account for the fact that play is often spectacular, even ostentatious, as in parades, processions, Rose Bowls, Superbowls, and Olympics. One might even say that the masks, disguises, and other fictions of some kinds of play are devices to make visible what has been hidden, even unconscious, for example, the Demon Masks of Sri Lankan and Tibetan exorcism rituals, to let the mysteries revel in the streets, to invert the everyday order in such a way that it is the unconscious and primary processes that are visible, while the conscious ego is restricted to creating rules to keep their insurgence within bounds, to frame them or channel them, so to speak. Huizinga is also surely wrong when he sees play as divested of all *material* interest. He forgets the important role of betting and games of chance—for example, gambling houses, casinos, racetracks, and lotteries. These may have important economic effects, even though playing for money remains completely unproductive, since the sum of the winnings at best only equals the losses of the other players, and the entrepreneur, the bank, is the only ultimate winner; ironically he is perhaps the only one who takes no pleasure in gambling.

A later, more complex, theory of play has been developed by the French scholar Roger Caillois. He uses some exotic terms, but defines them clearly. For example, he says that play has two axes or "poles," which he calls *paidia* and *ludus*. *Paidia*, from a Greek word meaning "child," stands for "an almost indivisible principle, common to diversion, turbulence, free improvisation, and carefree gaiety . . . uncontrolled fantasy."[9] This anarchic and capricious propensity characteristic of children, is countered by *ludus*, from a Latin word meaning "a play, a game," and which Caillois sees as binding *paidia* "with arbitrary, imperative, and purposely tedious conventions, [opposing it] still more by ceaselessly practising the most embarrassing chicanery upon it, in order to make it more uncertain of attaining its desired effects."[10] *Ludus*, in fact, represents how, in the space-time of the subjunctive mood of cultural action, human beings love to set up arbitrary obstacles to be overcome, as in mazes, crossword puzzles, or the rules of chess, which are both a general training for coping with obstacles in the day-to-day world and also a means of totally engrossing the player in a world of play framed and enclosed by its intricate rules.

Caillois has four further concepts for understanding play. These are *agôn*, Greek for "context" or "competition"; *alea*, a Greek word for a dice game, extended to chance, randomness, and gambling in general; mimicry, from the Greek *mimos*, an imitator or actor; and *ilinx*, the Greek term for "whirlpool"—it "consists of an attempt momentarily to destroy stability of perception and inflict a kind of voluptuous panic upon an otherwise lucid mind."[11] Caillois uses these categories to explain the structure of games of strength, chance, or skill, and of play-acting—all these being in the world of "make-believe" (whereas ritual is in the world of "we do believe"). Each category contains games and sports that move from the pole of *paidia*, childhood play (in which he includes "tumult, agitation, and immoderate laughter") to the pole of *ludus* ("purposive innovation"). For example, the category *agôn*, or competition, describes a whole group of games as like a combat "in which an equality of chances is artificially created in order that the adversaries should confront each other under ideal conditions, susceptible of giving precise and incontestible value to the winner's triumph . . . rivalry (usually) hinges on a single quality (such as speed, endurance, strength, memory, skill, ingenuity, and the like) exercised, within defined limits and without outside assistance, in such a way that the winner appears to be better than the loser in a certain category of exploits."[12] Agonistic games range from unregulated racing and wrestling, at the *paidia* (childhood play) end, to organized sport (boxing, billiards, baseball, fencing, chess, Olympic Games, and so on), at the *ludus* end. *Alea* or "chance" presides over "games that are based on a decision independent of the player, an outcome over which he has no control, and in which winning is the result of fate or destiny rather than triumphing over an adversary."[13] For this reason, games of chance have often played an important role in ritual contexts as indicative of the will of the gods, as in the great Indian epic, the *Mahabharata*, where Yudishthira, the oldest of the *Pandava* hero-brethren, gambles away rights of all the brothers to the

Classification of Games

	Agôn (competition)	Alea (chance)	Mimicry (simulation)	Ilinx (vertigo)
◄ PAIDIA ► Tumult Agitation Immoderate laughter	Racing, wrestling, etc. (not regulated) Athletic	Counting out rhymes Heads or tails	Children's initiations Games of illusion Tag, arms Masks, disguises	Children "whirling" Horseback riding Swinging Waltzing
Kite-flying Solitaire Patience Crossword puzzles ◄ LUDUS ►	Boxing, billiards, fencing, checkers, football, chess Contests, sports in general	Betting Roulette Simple, complex, and continuing lotteries*	 Theater Spectacles in general	Volador Traveling carnivals Skiing Mountain climbing Tightrope walking

N.B. In each column games are classified in such an order that the *paidia* element is constantly decreasing while the *ludus* element is ever increasing.

*A simple lottery consists of the one basic drawing. In a complex lottery there are many possible combinations. A continuing lottery (e.g., Irish Sweepstakes) is one consisting of two or more stages, the winner of the first stage being granted the opportunity to participate in a second lottery. [From correspondence with Caillois—*Meyer Barash*]

throne, and their joint wife Draupadi; and they pay the penalty of exile for thirteen years. In our culture, *alea*, chance, ranges from counting out rhymes (*eeny meeny miney mo*), and spinning a coin, at the *paidia* pole, through betting and roulette to simple, complex, and continuing lotteries. *Mimicry* or simulation involves the acceptance if not of an illusion (the very word is derived from Latin *in-lusio*, "the beginning of a game"), at least of a "closed, conventional and, in certain respects, imaginary universe."[14] Through mimicry one can become an imaginary character oneself, a subject who makes believe or makes others believe that he/she is someone other than him/herself. At the *paidia* pole, we have children playing at being parents or other adult roles, or cowboys and Indians, or spacemen and aliens. We progress through charades to various kinds of masking and costuming and disguises until at the *ludus* pole we are fully into theater, masquerade, and in the popular sphere pageants, processions, parades, and other types of spectacle. Even the audience at great sports events, such as Superbowls, is under the spell of *mimicry*. The athletes who perform for them are dominated by *agôn*, competition, but for the audience, as Caillois writes (p. 22): "A physical contagion leads them to assume the position of the contestants in order to help them, just as the bowler is known to unconsciously incline his body in the direction that he would like the bowling ball to take at the end of its course. Under these conditions, paralleling the spectacle, a competitive *mimicry* is born in the public, which doubles the *agôn* of the field or track." This is easily observed among a crowd at a football or baseball game. Anticipating somewhat, we will see how the two-by-four samba beat sweeps up all who watch the Rio Carnaval into mimicry of the *sambistas*, the members of the samba schools, as the schools compete with one another for the first prize in each year's glowing Carnaval. The concept *ilinx* or vertigo involves all games which try to create disequilibrium, imbalance, or otherwise to alter perception or consciousness by inducing giddiness or dizziness often by a whirling or gyrating motion. These range from such children's games as "Ring around the rosy" (Ashes, Ashes, we all fall down!) and musical chairs, through waltzing to horseriding to the intoxication of high speed on skis, water-skis, motor cycles, sports cars, to riding on roller coasters, carousels, or other vertigo-inducing contraptions. Dancing comes under the sign of *ilinx*, as Caillois says, "from the common but insidious giddiness of the waltz to the many mad, tremendous, and convulsive movements of other dances"[16]—I would add, not least the samba! *Ilinx* shows that there is not only cosmos but chaos in the scheme of things.

Caillois sees an evolutionary development, in terms of his scheme, as civilization advances in rationality (he clearly is an optimist who believes in progress), from what he considers the unholy combination of *mimicry* and *ilinx* (vertigo)—which for him characterizes the games and other cultural performances of societies he is pleased to call "primitive" or "Dionysian," ruled, he writes, "by masks and possession"—to the rational sweetness and light of *agôn* plus *alea*, competition and chance, represented by such "civilized" societies as the Incas, Assyrians, Chinese, and Romans,[17] "orderly societies with offices, careers, codes, and ready-reckoners, with fixed and hierarchical privileges, in which *agôn* and *alea*, that is, merit and heredity (which is a kind of chance), seem to be the chief complementary elements of the game of living. In contrast to the primitive societies, these are 'rational,'" he concludes. This is to see society solely from the positivist perspective of social structure, and fails entirely to take into account its dialectical nature, which moves from structure to antistructure and back again to transformed structure, from hierarchy to equality, from indicative mood to subjunctive mood, from unity to multiplicity, from the person to the individual, from systems of status-roles to communitas, the I-Thou relationship, Buber's "essential We" as against society regarded as "It." Antonin Artaud understood at least this: that without a theater of Mask and Trance, of Simulation and Vertigo, the people perish[18]—and this is as true of the most complex and large-scale society as the most obscure aboriginal band. We would do well to value Caillois's analysis of play into concepts, but avoid his evolutionist argument, for it disprizes the nonelitist societies, who now have perhaps most to give to the general stream of human culture—"rationality" having ruined many of our natural resources in the name of procuring material comfort.

However it may be, great industrial nations like Brazil and Japan have not despised their public festivals but elevated them to the scale of their secular achievements—all this without destroying the vertigo and theatricality at their liminal heart. Perhaps the best way of communicating to you how Brazilians, particularly Cariocas, the true inhabitants of Rio de Janeiro, themselves describe Carnaval is to show you the first part of the lyric of a samba composed by the major *sambista* of the renowned samba school Estação Primeira de Mangueira for the Carnaval of 1967:

Quando uma luz divinal	When a light divine
Iluminava a imaginação	Illuminated the imagination
De um escritor genial	Of a writer of genius
Tudo era maravilha	All was miracle
Tudo era sedução	All was seduction
Quanta alegria	How much happiness
E fascinaçao	And fascination
Relembro. . . .	I remember. . . .

Aquele mundo encantado	That enchanted world
Fantasiado de doirado	Clad in the golden dress of fantasy
Oh! Doce ilusão	Oh! Sweet illusion [remember that illusion means "entry into play"]
Sublime relicário de criança	Sublime shrine of childhood
Que ainda guardo como herança	Which I still keep as my heritage
No meu coração	In my heart.

To savor this simple lyric one has to imagine it sung by a *puxador*, which means, surprisingly, a "puller" and may even be applied to a handle or knob on a drawer. In Carnaval it refers to a singer who rides ahead of an entire samba school on a float with a voice amplifier, "pulling" the school behind him, as it were, and some schools consist of many thousands of *sambeiros*, who dance, mime, leap, gyrate, and sing choruses in his coruscating wake. He manages somehow to be at once stentorian and tender, tremendous and nostalgic, epic and romantic. His huge brazen voice is charged with *saudade*, an untranslatable Portuguese term, which is more, far more, than the sum of such parts as "longing, yearning, ardent wish or desire, homesickness, affectionate greetings to absent persons, hankering for a lover or a homeland"—as various Portuguese-English dictionaries inform me.

The last few lines give the clue to a basic feature of Carnaval. It is propelled by *paidia*, childhood play. Freud once said that each of us is at once and successively a man, a woman, and a child. The child is the player in us, and we are at times homesick for childhood's golden land, "sublime shrine of childhood, which I still keep as my heritage." Even the evident sexuality, the visible *libido*, of Carnaval has an infantile quality, like Baudelaire's *"paradis parfumé."* If one wished one could use, I suppose, such barbarous, infelicitous neologisms as "narcissistic display" and "polymorphous perversion," "fantasies about the primal scene," and so on, but this would be to endow the hummingbird lightness, deftness, and butterfly-wing color of Carnaval play with a heavy Northern seriousness, a puritanical spirit of gravity—"denaturing" it, some would say, heaven help them.

The child is the epitome of antistructure, and perhaps this is why Jesus said, "Except ye become as little children, ye shall not enter the kingdom of heaven," the un-kingdom beyond social structure. One of the favorite types of *entitades*, as the invisible beings who incorporate themselves with mediums in such Brazilian cults as Candomblé and Umbanda are called, is the line (*linha*) or legion of *crianças*, children. A medium possessed by a child-guide takes a diminutive name, Pedrinho, Joãozinho, and the like, speaks in a childish treble, and receives little treats, such as candies, from the congregation. The child-image is one link between Afro-Brazilian religious rituals which involve what Caillois would call *ilinx*, "vertigo," and "trance," and Carnaval which involves mimicry, costuming, and the enactment of a libretto or plot (*enredo*)—each samba school has its own, now drawn by governmental edict from Brazil's patriotic past, a rule which makes it difficult but not impossible to slip in some sly digs at the Generals' political performance. All this would make of Carnaval a "primitive" performance in Caillois's terms.

But lo and behold! Wonder of Wonders! We also find within the carnavalesque frame, lots and lots of *ludus* (complicated rules and regulations), *agôn* (competition), and *alea* (chance and gambling). We see that the seemingly and really childlike is impregnated with a vast irony, the vertigo is tinctured by sophistication. *All* Caillois's components are sparking away furiously at once, like the plugs in a racing car, or the wheels of Ezekiel's chariot. We find that everything human is being raised to a higher power, the cognitive along with the emotional and volitional. For the spontaneity and freedom of Carnaval can *only* reach their uninhibited height in the four great days before Lent, *if* there has been a full year of organizing and plotting and planning behind the scenes and a set of rules to channel the extravagant tide of song, dance, and generalized Eros.

Let me tell you about the growth of the samba schools in Rio and how they have been the response of an ever-young ancient cultural genre to modernity. Carnaval has always been a many-leveled, as well as a many-splendored, thing. Today there is not only the centrally organized street carnival of the samba schools competing in leagues in downtown Rio and the internal carnival of the club balls on Mardi Gras itself, but there are also the locally organized processions of groups known as *blocos*, with their own songs and sambas, often subversive of the regime and not at all respecters of its persons, while countless people dressed in their "private fantasies" stroll, flirt, get drunk, and make love in streets and squares from which business and commerce and motorized traffic have been summarily banished. During Carnaval, those centers of Brazilian hierarchy, the house, the office, and the factory, are emptied and closed. The whole city becomes a symbol of Brazilianity, of a single multicolored family brought into the open, which is now transformed into a home. Carnaval may, indeed, invade the sacred homestead itself, as masked revellers swarm through it and out again. Women, no longer under the *patria potestas* of fathers or the *manus* of husbands, as in ancient Rome, become the very soul of the samba in street and club. In a sense, the whole city worships Aphrodite on the half-shell. Here Aphrodite is a mulata, extolled in every song, and appearing in person, in the tiniest of bikinis, on many a float, and revelling with many a tamborinist in groups of two men and one woman, known as *passistas*. The archetypal mulata was an eighteenth-century "lady," Chica da Silva, who became a provincial governor's mistress and dominated men by her lambent, even heroic sexual prowess. Many movies and TV series have been made about her. Blacks and mulattos form the very core of Carnaval, since they provide the central organization of every samba school, while white celebrities clamor to be allowed into its *desfile*, or pageant, as the total procession of *sambistas* and *sambeiros* is called. The anthropologist Roberto Da Matta calls this kind of organization "a comet-like structure." The permanent, relatively solid "head" is the Palacio do Samba, the large building in a mainly black *favela* or slum, where the organizing committee of the samba school has its offices, a bureaucratic structure matching in complexity those of government and business. It is also the site of intense rehearsals which begin almost as soon as the previous Carnaval is over. The floating "tail" of the comet consists of the "one-day trippers" who wish to form part of the parade on the great night and participate in its glory, and also, the upper-class Brazilian *brancos* (whites) and the foreign notables. This type of grouping, which cuts across class and ethnic divisions, Da Matta regards as typical of Brazilian social organization. The famous football (soccer) clubs are similarly organized.[19] It is encouraged, Da Matta argues, by the military oligarchy ruling this hierarchical system, where, nevertheless, uncontrollable industrial growth exerts a mounting pressure in the direction of liberalization, for aggressive, capitalistic business is hostile to red tape and rigid bureaucratic controls.

It is clear that such comet-like structures retard the emergence of explicitly political groups with a single class basis, that is, political parties, contending with the establishment for real power and influence. On the other hand, one might regard the samba school, with its multitudinous organizational problems and decisions being made daily, as a school in governance and administration wherein countless poor blacks learn the skills of politics at the grass-roots level. And since a great samba school like Mangueira or Portela represents a sizable constituency in itself, it can be expected to be wooed by local, even national politicians and administrators. There is also an intimate, secret connection between the leadership of Rio samba schools and the operators of the illegal kind of lottery, known as *jogo do bicho*, a numbers game involving animal symbols (*bicho* = "any animal, excepting fowl and fish"). At one Carnaval, that of Niteroi across the bay from Rio, Edie and I found ourselves with Da Matta's help in the mayor's box or cabin, along with the novelist Jorge Amado, who wrote *Doña Flor and her Two Husbands* and *Tent of Miracles*.[20] We discovered that a samba school had taken for its plot (*enredo*) the entire body of Amado's work based on life in the state of Bahia, which always has a romantic glow and patina for Brazilians, and dedicated its samba to him. The group in the box pointed out to me a number of "mobsters" who were deep in the numbers game and who had contributed munificently to the expenses of the occasion and to particular samba schools. One of these took as its plot or theme "The Wheel of Fortune," and each of its segments and floats and its samba libretto proclaimed the praises of Brazilian games of chance, cards, roulette wheels, *jogo de bicho*, betting at the races, and so on. One mobster, a huge man with a pendulous belly, was on the best of terms not only with dignitaries of the local government but also with officials and leading role-players of the samba schools as they passed the booths where their performances were given marks according to traditional criteria. Here there is a clear association between competition and chance, *agôn* and *alea*, in the parlance of Roger Caillois! As a matter of fact, Caillois himself remarked half approvingly that "in Brazil gambling is king. It is the land of speculation and chance."[21]

If one could say that "antistructure" was merely vertigo and mimicry one could agree with Professor Maria Goldwasser of the University of Rio de Janeiro when she describes the basic idea which explained for her the functioning of the samba school known as Mangueira studied by her in detail for a full year as "the crystallization of antistructure." Naturally I was delighted to find that she had used my book *The Ritual Process*[22] before it came out in Portuguese as an aid in analyzing the social aspects of the Escola de Samba Estação Primeira de Mangueira in her book *O Palacio do Samba*. Here is what she says about the "crystallization" process:

> Antistructure is represented here by Carnaval, and is defined as a transitional phase in which differences of (pre-Carnaval) status are annulled, with the aim of creating among the participants a relationship of *communitas*. Communitas is the domain of equality, where all are placed without distinction on an identical level of social evaluation, but the equivalence which is established among them has a ritual character. In communitas we find an inversion of the structured situations of everyday reality marked by routinization and the conferment of structural status. The status system and communitas—or structure and antistructure (which

also possesses its own systematic character)—confront one another as two homologous series in opposition.

The carioca Carnaval is the exemplary representation of antistructure. "To make a Carnaval" is equivalent "to making a chaos," where everything is confused and no one knows where anything is. In Carnaval, men can dress as women, adults as babies, the poor as princes and, even more, "what means what" becomes an open possibility by a magical inversion of real statuses and a cancellation or readjustment of the barriers between the social classes and categories.[23]

Yet Maria Goldwasser found that Mangueira, or "Old Manga," the name by which the school is everywhere known, is complicatedly organized and structured. She presents a chart of the organization which resembles that of a major firm or government department. I won't burden you with details but there is a major division into two directorates, the Directory of the School, whose function is mainly administrative, and the Carnaval Commission, which operates in the Esfera Artistica, the artistic realm. The first is subdivided into three parts: (1) the Wing (ala) of the Composers (of the year's main samba and other musical items, which deals with the technical supplies and emoluments of the composers themselves; (2) the Wing of the Battery, divided again between artistic and administrative spheres—the bateria is the awe-inspiring, compact mass of drummers and other percussion instrumentalists who bring up the rear of a samba school. By law only percussion instruments may be used in a school's desfile, its grand parade down the Avenida Getulio Vargas or the Praca Onze on the Segunda do Entrudo, the second day of Carnaval on the Sunday before Ash Wednesday. Some schools, notably O Imperio de Serrano, are known for their great "batteries," which earn them high marks from the judges. Then there is (3) the Committee of the Combined Wings, whose job is to integrate the numerous components of the school's parade. Under the battery officials are the ritmistas, the drummers themselves, who are also partly organized by the composers' officials. The puxadores and "crooners" also come under the Wing of the Composers. I won't go on, except to mention that in addition to this pattern of technical control, there is a parallel hierarchy in the artistic sphere which attends to such matters as overall design, the plot or libretto, and its apportionment among the various components of the desfile, the synchronization of dance, song, music, and miming, the tastefulness of the whole presentation, the designing and decoration of floats, costuming and coiffeuring, and the rest. It takes an awful lot of order to produce "a sweet disorder," a great deal of structuring to create a sacred play space and time for antistructure. If "flowing"—and communitas is "shared flow"—denotes "the holistic sensation when we act with total involvement," when action and awareness are one, and one ceases to flow if one becomes aware that one is doing it, then, just as a river needs a bed and banks to flow, so do people need framing and structuring rules to do their kind of flowing. But here the rules crystallize out of the flow rather than being imposed on it from without. William Blake said a similar thing using the metaphor of heat: "Fire finds its own form." This is not dead structure, but living form; Isadora Duncan, not classical ballet. The structure described by Goldwasser is akin to the rules of sport, belonging to the domain of ludus and not to the politico-economic order.

The competition among samba schools, indeed their very existence in their present form, is a fairly recent Carnaval phenomenon. The first escola de samba was named Deixa Falar ("Let 'em talk") and was formally constituted on August 12, 1928, in Estacio, a city ward which then was—and still is—a traditional stronghold of carnival. Until about 1952, according to authors Eneida de Moraes,[24] Wilson Louzada,[25] and Olavo Bilac,[26] Carnaval was a rather brutal revel, the heir of the Portuguese *entrudo* (Shrovetide), chiefly consisting of a vulgar battle where pails of water were thrown about indiscriminately at people in the streets and plazas. Such customs die hard, for I saw fraternity brethren on Saturday, April 19, doing exactly the same thing on University Avenue SE, at the University of Minnesota, during the University Carnival! My wife saw Cambridge University students doing this in the 1930s on Shrove Tuesday. The wide diffusion of similar carnival customs is perhaps due first to the spread of the Roman Empire which introduced such antistructural rites as Saturnalia and Lupercalia to its distant provinces, and second to that of the Catholic church which took with it around the world not only a common liturgy and liturgical year, but also a host of popular feasts and customs representing in some cases "baptized" circum-Mediterranean pre-Christian rituals.

Entrudo drenching was banned by an edict of 1853, and there succeeded a number of new forms of merrymaking. The popular inventiveness of Carnaval is limitless; there is a constant mutation in the type and scope of the revels. There is no time to even mention most of them. But one should mention the *rancho* of the early 1900s, a group of masqueraders which included a band and a chorus, specializing in the so-called *marchas-rancho*, which have a markedly slow cadence, in *choros*, a sentimental musical form, and later in sambas. The *ranchos* opened up the carnival to young women. Their costumes became richer and more luxurious, with a profusion of silks, velvets, spangles, plumes, and sequins. Usually the *ranchos'* names were rather flowery: "Flower of the Avocado," "Solace of the Flowers," "Pleasurable Mignonette" (Ameno Reseda). But in the twenties and thirties the tempo of life changed and the young rejected the sugariness of the rancho style, desiring a lighter and different flow of rhythm and short and less elaborate lyrics. The samba came into its own, and the units that played it were, first, the *blocos*, and soon after, the samba schools. *Bloco* is a genus, applying originally to any informal group of carnivalesques, usually from the lower and humbler social strata. In the film, *Doña Flor and Her Two Husbands*, the carnivalesque first husband has his fatal heart attack while dancing in a *bloco*. A species of this genus is the *bloco de sujos* (bloc of dirty ones), designating either a loosely organized band of ragamuffins, or a group of revelers that paint their faces with charcoal and rouge and dress in loud colors in artless fashion. These groups have a chaotic, disarrayed appearance, and seem to portray best the "vertigo" component of carnival play. Another species is called *bloco de arrastão* (bloc of the fishing net), for, as the group moves along, the seduction of its rhythmic chanting and the dancing of its members prove irresistible to spectators, who totally unable to resist, are "pulled in" (*puxados*), "netted," to sing and dance with the *bloco*, "dirties" or otherwise.

Hundreds of *blocos* still exist in Rio, and one of our four Carnaval nights, the first, was devoted to watching their parade in 1979. They rejoice in such names as Vem Amor (Do Come, Love), Vai Quem Quer (Come Who Will), Bafo da Onça (Jaguar's Breath), Namorar Eu Sei (In Loving, I Know), Suspiro da Cobra (Sigh of a Snake),

Canarios das Laranjeiras (Canaries from Laranjeiras, a ward of Rio), and Bloco do Gelo (Ice Block).

What usually happens is that a large and well-organized *bloco* eventually becomes an *escola de samba*. Like the *escolas*, large *blocos* have detailed regulations and by-laws, are governed by a board of directors democratically elected by all the members at a general assembly, have adopted heraldic colors of their own, and members appear at carnival time wearing uniform costumes which have been especially made for the occasion. Lastly, some of the better-off *blocos*—like the major samba schools—are the proprietors of the club house where they have their headquarters and of the place where they hold their rehearsals.

The samba schools are organized into three leagues with demotion of the last two schools in the first and second leagues and promotion of two schools from the second and third to replace them. To judge them there is an awards committee. Although their numbers fluctuate, my best information suggests that there are now nine jurors. The first evaluates the guild's flag since each "school" is officially a guild (*gremio*) and the line of its officials known as the *comissão de frente*, usually fifteen, who march at the head of the parade, often in frock coats and top hats. The second juror evaluates the performance of the flag bearer, the *porta-bandeira*, and the major-domo, or *mestre-sala*; usually the *porta-bandeira* is the most beautiful woman of the *escola* and the best dancer—always she appears in the dress of an eighteenth-century lady. At every carnival the *escola* presents a different, beautifully embroidered flag, showing on one side the emblem of the guild and on the other some design allusive of the plot which is presented in that particular pageant. Until 1967 the flag itself was awarded points, but not subsequently. The major-domo is also called *baliza*, literally a signpost or a landmark. This is apt for he is really the pivot round which the choreography revolves. He is usually tall and slim, agile and graceful. He appears either in seventeenth-century attire, with short cape and plumed hat, like one of Dumas's musketeers, or in the silk and satin knee-length coat of the eighteenth century, with powdered wig in the style of Louis XV. He carries a small fan in his left hand, or a lace handkerchief, and with his right he holds his partner's hand or her waist, as the dance may require. They dance together and then separate. She then gyrates swiftly, the silk of the flag sighs as it cuts the air, while he dances round her, inventing complicated steps, kneeling, bowing as gracefully and delicately, as if he were in Versailles in the days of Louis-le-Bienaimé. While these blacks from poor *favelas* display the elegance of a vanished feudalism in their liminality, the white "beautiful people" in the restricted entry indoor Carnaval of the Clubs revert to the almost naked barbarism of the night revels of *La Dolce Vita*.

Back to the judges! The third evaluates the *escola*'s current plot (*enredo*) and the lyrics of the samba, which always refers to the plot and indeed creates its emotional tone. The fourth evaluates the appearance of the *escola* as a whole and the choreography of the ensemble: the main components are the *alas* (wings), consisting of about ten to thirty persons, often of the same sex, who are organized around a subplot, which must conform to the school's main plot. In addition to the *alas*, there are the *destaques*, or *figuras de destaque* (the stand-outs or individual items), persons wearing sumptuous and magnificent costumes and plumes, who strut down the avenue in solitary, solar, lunar, or rainbow splendor. Quite often, these are transvestites, some with silicon implants to almost caricature femininity, and not rarely they are well-known Rio socialites. Floats are also a carnival component, limited by regulation to four per school, including the float which spearheads the pageant—known as the *Abre-alas* (literally "Wings opener or usher"). Its purpose is to proclaim the name of the Escola and the title of its plot for the year. An *Abre-alas* may represent an open book, a large portal, or a baroque cartouche (like those which appear in old maps and charts— "heere be mermaids, theer be gryphons," and so on). By tradition, the text is as follows: "G.R.E.S. [an acronym for Grêmio Recreativo Escola de Samba Mangueira— or Portela, Mocidade Independente, Beija Flor, Império Serrano, Academicos de Salgueiro, or whatever] pays its compliments to the People of Rio, presents [here follows the plot's title], and requests permission to pass through." Some of the floats are unbelievable. It is recorded that the Portela, in 1965, exhibited a float which was an exact replica of the library of Princess Isabel, in which she signed the Act of Abolition of Slavery! Another example of black Brazilian elegance. Some floats are in rank bad taste, however, and some schools have substituted for them painted panels and screens and a series of gonfalons (standards with two or three streamers) and oriflammes (red silk banners split at one end) carried by members of the *escola*— much more dramatic, I think!

The fifth judge evaluates the tunefulness and musical texture of the samba and the performance of the *bateria* (percussion battery). An *escola* without a *bateria* would be unthinkable. The number of bandsmen—or *ritmistas*—may vary greatly. A small *bateria* may make great music. Last year in Rio, Edie and I vividly recall the exact moment when the Academicos de Cubango entered the main downtown Avenue of Niteroi. It was well after dawn on Shrove Tuesday. The huge crowd around us had been there since before nightfall on Monday. We had seen school after school go by, including the one whose plot was based on the novels of Jorge Amado, a glittering world of samba, imagination, and luxury. What could top it? Would the last pageant fall with a thud? Then we heard the magnificent contralto of a *puxadora*, the first female we had heard in this role, a renowned television singer, doing something completely magical with the theme song of the samba—*Afoxé*, which, among other things, means a cult group of the Candomblé Afro-Brazilian religion strongly rooted in Bahia. The school itself in its *alas* and *destaques* portrayed this religion, the gods and their altars, the devotees. The technical term for portraying a plot is *defender o enredo*, "defending" the plot, that is, convincing everyone, judges and public, that the plot is authentic and its Carnaval expression beautiful and powerful. This the Academicos had done by the time their incomparable *bateria* arrived and literally took the Avenida by storm. We were all swept away on the great tide of the samba played on drums by hundreds of *ritmistas*—as I have mentioned, only percussion instruments are permitted, but they include not only large and small drums such as *cotixa*, the military drum, and many others, but also friction drums (*cuicas*) which can make several sounds at once in syncopation, *agogos* derived from African hunting bells, tambourines, *pandeiros* or timbrels, polished saucepans, and many more. The smaller instruments are played by *passistas*, dextrous leapers and contortionists, who often cavort, two men to one girl, in the sexiest of postures. At Niteroi we all fell in behind the *ritmistas* and *passistas* in a Dionysiac abandonment I have never experienced before or since. What is it like to be a *sambista* or *sambeiro*? One journalist, Sergio Bitencourt, writing in the *Correio da Manha*, claims that the Carnaval for him or her is "a mission, a mandate, a supreme moment of deliverance and self-sufficiency." He adds: "The drops of perspiration which cover the face of the sambista have the savor of drops of blood." Here we have what Huizinga calls "the deep earnestness in play," even a hint of the Via Dolorosa, the Way of the Cross. Festival at times is not too far from its ritual origins, and can give its participants something not too far from a religious experience. Remember Ash Wednesday is not too far behind Mardi Gras, and Death is implicitly present—the movie *Black Orpheus* stressed his presence in his guise of *Exu* of the cemeteries, the chaos deity of the Umbanda religion *Exu sem Luz*.

The sixth juror evaluates the masquerades and the individual floats. I cannot here describe the universe of mimicry these terms point toward. No one, to my knowledge, in anthropology at any rate, has done an adequate study, either aesthetic or semiotic, of the costumes, masks, disguises, ritual nakedness, color symbolism, and the structural oppositions and mediations among all these, that can be found in any Rio Carnaval—a veritable surplus of signifiers. To round off my tally of the jurors, three are appointed to be placed at different locations on the parade route, to assign negative votes as penalties for any delays caused by wilful negligence. There is further anthropological material in the politicking that goes on around the Awards Committee, and the hostility, often leading to violence, even homicide and suicide, which greets their final assessment of the various schools' performances. The jurors are drawn from the ranks of professional artists or art critics, dress designers, newspaper persons or television professionals, professional ballet dancers and choreographers, professional musicians and composers. But umpires and referees are seldom popular in any of the fields of play we have been talking about! When play makes serious statements about the human condition, people take its outcomes seriously.

I also have no time to discuss the elaborate nightlong balls in the city's clubs, beginning on Tuesday and lasting to Ash Wednesday's hungover dawn, hosted by the wealthy and the organizations to which they belong, or by renowned soccer clubs, such as Flamengo and Fluminense, or by yacht clubs. Nor can I home in on the improvised street carnivals that mushroom in every neighborhood. Just one word. It is a Brazilian point of honor that if one is going to wear a costume, or *fantasia*, it must communicate one's most private or intimate fantasy in the most artistic way possible. Repression must be lifted. One might even talk about the aestheticization of the repressed, making the very private very public in the mode of beauty. The secret of Brazilian culture perhaps lies in this, that it has created a "palace of Carnaval," a palace of samba, out of fantasies suppressed through the rest of the year by immersion in industrial labor, by submission to an autocratic regime, by tenacious vestiges of feudal attitudes in the relations between men and women, young and old. Even more, it has raised a traditional ritual of reversal to the scale of a great industrial nation, in every way equivalent, in its subjunctive mood and at the unconscious and preconscious levels, to the complex modern industrial system that is Brazil's indicative mood and conscious reality. In so doing, it serves as a kind of paradigm, or model, for the whole modern and postmodern world. It is no Aldous Huxleyan "orgy porgy" as in *Brave New World*—its ironical, whimsical, urbane, and genial touch dispels such a thought. Rather it is the creative antistructure of mechanized modernity. Carnaval is the reverse of fiction or fake: it demands validity of feeling, sad or glad. It is mostly glad, and there is no mistaking the authenticity of radiant joy that pours out of faces and songs, and makes the samba live up to one of its names, *arrasta-pé*, netter or snarer of feet. No one can feel embarrassed in the many-dimensioned world of carnival. "Shame is absent from Carnaval," the saying goes. It is a world oblivious of original sin, as its own lyrics dare to say in a Christian country . . . *Aquele mundo encantado*, that enchanted world. The Golden Age really does return. Naturally, there are many Brazilians who are skeptical, regarding Carnaval as "opium for the people" (though "speed" would be perhaps a better metaphor). Again, the roads at Carnaval time leading from Rio are choked with the cars of the new middle class, fleeing the revelries of the carnavalesque reversal of their hard-won bourgeois values.

What has Caillois and his theories of play to do with all this? Only that Carnaval engulfs all his categories in a dynamic many-leveled, liminal domain of multiframed antistructures and spontaneous communitas. *Paidia, ludus, agôn, alea, mimicry,* and *ilinx* are spun together indistinguishably in the spangled tapestry of the nocturnal *desfile* of the Carioca samba schools.[27] As the poet Cassiano Ricardo put it: "A bit of Brazil in the hearts of angry men—Wouldn't it be a solution?"[28]

Notes

[1]. For Saturnalia, see Ambrosius Aurelius Theodosius Macrobius, *The Saturnalia,* trans. and ed. Percival Vaughan Davis (New York: Columbia University Press, 1969). On Lupercalia, A. W. J. Holleman, *Pope Gelasius I and the Lupercalia* (Amsterdam: Hakkert, 1974).

[2]. For Independence Day, see Henry James, *The Social Significance of Our Institution: An Oration Delivered by Request of the Citizens at Newport, Rhode Island, July 4th 1861* (Boston: Ticknor and Fields, 1861). For Cinco de Mayo, see Jane M. Hatch, *The American Book of Days* (New York: Wilson, 1978), pp. 420–21.

3. Jean-Richard Bloch, *Carnaval est mort: Premiers essais pour mieux comprendre mon temps,* 4th ed. (Paris: Editions de la Nouvelle Revue Française, 1920); (1910–14) articles reprinted from *L'Effort Libre.*

4. Julio Caro Baroja, *El Carnaval, analisis historico-cultural* (Madrid: Taurus, 1965).

[5]. Victor Turner and Edith Turner, *Image and Pilgrimage in Christian Culture: Anthropological Perspectives* (New York: Columbia University Press, 1978); Victor Turner, *Process, Performance and Pilgrimage: A Study in Comparative Symbology* (New Delhi: Concept, 1979).

6. On the Trinidad Carnival, see Erroll Hill, *The Trinidad Carnival* (Austin: University of Texas Press, 1972). On New Orleans,

see Munro Edmondson: "New Orleans Carnival," *Caribbean Quarterly* [Trinidad Carnival issue] 4 (1956): 233–45. On *Fastnacht,* see Ursula Hagen, ed., *Masken und Narren: Traditionen der Fastnacht* (Cologne: Kölnisches Stadtmuseum, 1972).

[7]. For the Tokyo Festival, see Meirô Koma, *Kyôto no Matsuri* (Festivals of Kyoto) (Kyoto: Tankosha, 1973). For the Holi, see K. Gnanambal, *Festivals of India* (Calcutta: Government of India [Anthropological Survey of India], 1967), pp. 20–22; and McKim Marriott, "The Feast of Love," in Milton Singer, ed., *Krishna: Myths, Rites, and Attitudes* (Honolulu: East-West Center Press, 1966), pp. 200–212.

8. Johann Huizinga, *Homo Ludens: A Study of the Play-Element in Culture* (New York: Roy Publishers, 1950), p. 13.

9. Roger Caillois, *Man, Play, and Games,* trans. Meyer Barash (New York: Schocken Books, 1979), p. 13.

10. Ibid., p. 13.

11. Ibid., p. 23.

12. Ibid., p. 14.

13. Ibid., p. 17.

14. Ibid., p. 19.

15. Ibid., p. 22.

16. Ibid., p. 25.

17. Ibid., p. 87.

[18]. Antonin Artaud, *The Theater and Its Double,* trans. M. C. Richards (New York: Grove Press, 1958).

[19]. Roberto da Matta et al., *Universo do futebol: esporte e societate brasileira* (Rio de Janeiro: Edicoes Pinakoteke, 1982).

20. Jorge Amado, *Doña Flor and Her Two Husbands* (New York: Knopf, 1969) and *Tent of Miracles* (New York: Knopf, 1971).

21. Caillois, p. 159.

[22]. Victor Turner, *The Ritual Process: Structure and Anti-Structure* (Chicago: Aldine, 1969).

23. Maria Goldwasser, *O Palacio do Samba: estudo antropológico da Escola de Samba Estaçao Primeira da Mangueira* (Rio de Janeiro: Zahar Editores, 1975), p. 82.

24. Eneida de Moraes, *Historia do Carnaval Carioca* (Rio de Janeiro: Civilizaçao Brasileira, 1958).

25. Wilson Louzada, ed., *Antologia de Carnaval* (Rio de Janeiro: O Cruzeiro, 1945).

26. Olavo Bilac, *Carnavalescos Poesias*, 18th ed. (Rio de Janeiro: F. Alves, 1940).

[27]. On the Rio de Janeiro Carnival, see also Roberto da Matta, *Ritual, Frames and Reflexions* (Philadelphia: ISHI Press, in press). Also see his "Carnival in Multiple Planes," in John J. MacAloon, ed., *Rite, Drama, Festival, Spectacle* (Philadelphia: ISHI Press, 1984), pp. 202–24 and his "O Carnaval como un rito de Passagem," in his *Ensaios de Antropologia Estrutural* (Petrópolis: Vozes, 1973), pp. 121–68; *Carnavais, malandros e heroís* (Rio de Janeiro: Zahar, 1979), pp. 1–138; Sergio Calzal, *As Escolas de Samba* (Rio de Janeiro: Fontana, 1974); José Sario Leopoldi, *Escola de Samba: Ritual e Sociadade* (Petró-

polis: Vozes, 1978); Francisco Guimarães, *Na roda do Samba*, 2d ed. (Rio de Janeiro: FUNARTE, 1978); Edigar de Alecar, *O Carnaval carioca através da música*, 3d ed. (Rio de Janeiro: Livraria Francisco Alvas Editora, 1979); Luís Delgado Gardel, *Escolas da samba: An Affectionate Descriptive Account of the Carnival Guilds of Rio de Janeiro* (Rio de Janeiro: Livraria Kosmos Editora, 1967); Ari Araujo and Erika Franziska Herd, *Espressões da Cultura Popular: As Escolas de Samba do Rio de Janeiro e o Amigo da Madrugada* (Rio de Janeiro: Editora Vozes/Secretaria Estadual de Educação e Cultura, 1978); Melo Morais Filho, "O Carnaval (Rio de Janeiro)," in *Festas e Tradiçoes Populares do Brasil* (Rio de Janeiro: Briguiet, 1946), pp. 27–45; Alison Raphael, "Samba and Social Control: Popular Culture and Racial Democracy in Rio de Janeiro" (Ph.D. dissertation) (New York: Columbia University, 1981); João Ferreira Gomes, *Ameno Resedá, o rancho que foi escola; documentario do carnaval carioca* (Rio de Janeiro: Editòra Letras e Artes, 1965); Olga R. de Moraes von Simon, "Family and Carnival in Brazil during the Nineteenth Century," *Society and Leisure* 1 (1978) no. 2: 325–52.

[28]. Julie Taylor, "The Politics of Aesthetic Debate: The Case of Brazilian Carnival," *Ethnology* 21 (1982): 301–11; Umberto Eco, Vjaceslav V. Ivanov, and Monica Rector, *Carnival!* (Berlin–New York–Amsterdam: Mouton, 1984); Cassiano Ricardo, *Poesias Completas* (Rio de Janeiro: Livraria José Olympia, 1957).

PART II

Continuity and Change:
The Emergence of New Festivals

8 / The Place of Festival in the Worldview of the Seventeenth-Century Quakers

Richard Bauman

Festivals have always been the object of considerable religious controversy, as they are related to worldview, beliefs, and symbols. The Catholic church, from its beginnings, has thundered against "pagan" spectacles, celebrations, masks, and carnivals. In the Middle Ages, Pope Gelasius I (405–96) wrote a famous letter against the survivals of the Roman Lupercalia; in the Renaissance the Council of Trent (1545–63) condemned festivals, bullfights, and rites of reversal such as the boy bishop celebration, or the "carmina turpia atque luxuriosa" (vile and lusty songs) which ritually profaned churches and sacred places in medieval carnivals. In the baroque period, treaties "contra mascaras" (against masks) abounded, and Jesuit writers contributed sharp, learned condemnations of festivals such as the famous 1609 Tratado contra los juegos publicos *by Father Juan de Mariana (1536–1624). The Catholic polemic against festival, however, was essentially a matter of form, mostly aimed at modifying and substituting symbols, supernatural beings, and actors, replacing the profane with the sacred, the literal with the metaphoric, the old gods with the new saints. Catholics dedicated May festivities to the Virgin Mary, who replaced both Flora, the goddess of flowers, and Maia, the goddess who had been the month's namegiver. The various subterranean black earth-*

93

mother goddesses became black Madonnas; twin Brazilian gods became saints Cosmas and Damian. In seventeenth-century Rome, in the middle of celebrations, the many masks of Carnival were forbidden for one day dedicated to the worship of the Veronica, allegedly the one and only "vera icon," the true mask of Christ.

In contrast, the Protestant polemic against festival was not a formal but a substantive one. It was aimed at drastically simplifying festivities or, in radical versions like the Quakers', at eliminating them altogether in favor of an all-serious life without festivals. For Quakers, as Bauman points out, God was not placed in a distant Paradise. He was actually present and speaking within each believer. Such belief had as a logical consequence the disregard or elimination of all intermediary personae and rituals in the relationship with God. Festival and festival behavior were intrinsically incompatible with the Quakers' Protestant beliefs.

Fertility rituals of harvest festivals, with their overt sexual symbolism, were the opposite of the "silence of the flesh" praised by the Quakers. The glorious beauty of the queens of May (forerunners of contemporary beauty queens) and the triumphant strength and prowess of the winners of athletic competitions were the marks of worldly pride and vainglory. The same held for maypoles, immoderate eating, and drinking—in brief, for all festive behavior. Furthermore, Bauman shows, drawing on the classic works of Max Weber, that incompatibility between festival and the Quakers' Protestant ethic came also from economic conflict. The Quakers' economic credo praised rationalization of labor and saw progressive accumulation of wealth as a sign of God's blessing. Nothing was more foreign to this attitude than festive gambling or conspicuous consumption— irrational, capricious, and destructive wastes of individual and collective wealth.

The Place of Festival in the Worldview of the Seventeenth-Century Quakers*

Richard Bauman

The religious Society of Friends, or Quakers, as they are more commonly known, originated as a radical Puritan movement in the early 1650s, a time of great religious ferment in England. In doctrine and practice, the Quakers approached the extreme of the Protestant tendency toward stripping away all intermediary symbols, rituals, and functionaries that stood between the individual and the experience of God. For the Quakers, the spirit of God was located *within* the soul of every person, most commonly identified as the Inward Light or "the small, still voice" of God, speaking within. The core experience of Quakerism was a communion with this indwelling spirit of God, which could only be achieved in a "silence" of the flesh.[1]

As one might expect, the early Quakers shared the well-known Puritan antipathy toward festivity, so consistent with the Protestant ethic illuminated by Max Weber[2] and those who have built upon his work. While Quaker views of festival illuminate the emergence of modern anti-festival ideology, the early Quaker position also suggests the need to qualify certain aspects of current theory concerning festival as a symbolic form.

*Written originally for this volume. Previously published in *Western Folklore* 43 (1984), no. 2: 133–38.

A reasonably comprehensive and representative picture of the seventeenth-century Quakers' view of festival and their moral objections to it is contained in an early tract by Stephen Crisp, an influential early minister, entitled "A Word in Due Season: or Some Harvest Meditations."[3] Morally distressed by the disorderly and licentious harvest celebrations he witnessed in June 1666, Crisp was moved to issue a warning against them. One portion of his argument is directed at economic concerns, consistent with Christopher Hill's suggestion that the extensive festival calendar of traditional, agrarian Europe was ill-suited to the need of the emergent capitalist economic system for regular, disciplined labor and the rational accumulation of capital.[4] (The seventeenth-century Quakers figure prominently in Weber's exploration of the Protestant ethic and the spirit of capitalism.) Crisp focuses his economic argument on the "inordinate feasting" and drinking that so frequently characterize festival. "The reward of the glutton shall be poverty," he declares, exhorting his readers to Christian moderation, a quality notably foreign to the spirit of excess that is part of the essence of festival.[5]

William Penn, the great Quaker founder of Pennsylvania, underscores the economic ethos implicit in the condemnation of festivals as wasteful. "It helps persons of mean substance to improve their small stocks," Penn writes, "that they may not expend their dear earning and hard-gotten wages upon . . . May-games . . . and the like folly and intemperance."[6] Where the goal is the rational *accumulation* of wealth, such indulgences as feasts, festivals, and holidays "which end, vanish, or perish with the using" have no worth.[7] Moreover, excess in eating and drinking are injurious to the health, spiritually as well as physically harmful because man is God's creature, and thus to bring injury on oneself by intemperance is to sin against God.[8]

The Quakers' principles against festival were not, of course, framed exclusively in economic terms. They were, after all, preeminently a religious movement, with a God-given prophetic mission to turn people to the Inward Light of Christ by which they might find salvation. The major obstacle to the advancement of their effort, they felt, was the hegemony of the "world's religions," bogged down with the accumulated weight of their vain, corrupt, and man-made forms, and degenerated from the pure integrity and power of the primitive church of Christ and the saints. Thus, the customs and traditions that the Quakers perceived to be rooted in the "fasts, feasts and holy-days" of Roman Catholicism or in the "heathenish" practices assimilated by the Catholic church were anathema to them.[9]

Crisp, for example, exhorts his readers to abandon "the abominable [harvest] custom of shouting in the fields . . . which is derived from generation to generation from the heathen, and from the papists."[10] He refers here to the custom widespread in Britain of exultantly announcing the completion of the harvest and sometimes the revels to follow.[11] The Quakers were especially affronted by the popular custom of erecting maypoles and the festivities associated with them, which they saw as idolatrous displays, and by "savage" morris-dancing, yet another custom rooted in heathen practice.[12]

The Protestant asceticism of the Quaker faith also led them to an especially strong condemnation of all manifestations of fleshly pride, which, in turn, drew Friends to attack certain other festival customs that they saw as means of glorifying the earthly self. Crisp singles out, for instance, "that wicked and abominable custom of making lords and ladies amongst you in the harvest fields," which would extend as well to

similar forms of symbolic status elevation, such as lords and ladies of the May celebrations.[13] Such practices are to be abandoned, he insists, as "tending to nothing
but to exalt the pride of men's heart."[14] Similarly, the athletic contests, such as
wrestling, that were a prominent feature of harvest and other festivities, had the ill-
effect of leading men to "boast and glory in [their] strength over him that is weaker,"
forgetting that all of their ability is given by God, "and so to be used in his fear,
without vain-glory."[15] Here we see reflected the fundamental Puritan religious principle
that men's actions while on earth, however mundane, are all to be done for the greater
glory of God, and not for the serving of human will, pride, or fleshly indulgence.
Rooted also in Quaker asceticism was the vehement condemnation of singing "corrupt
and vain harvest-songs," which are "filthy and abominable" and tend to "the subverting
and removing of modesty and chastity from the face of the earth."[16] From bawdy songs
to sexual license, it was feared, was but a small step.

Thus far, I have summarized the early Quakers' attitudes toward festival in terms
of their condemnation of some of its common elements, the components or means out
of which festivals are constructed. Building on this foundation, we may now examine
the problem in broader perspective: how did the Quakers conceive of the nature of
festivity in general within the larger scope of human existence? Here I believe that
the Quakers' understanding of the place of festivals in the lives of those who celebrate
them is especially instructive, for it sheds light, by opposition, upon their conception
of their own proper, godly life.

According to certain contemporary theories, the essence of festival depends upon
what Harvey Cox calls *juxtaposition,* by which he means that "festivity must display
contrast. It must be noticeably different from 'everyday life.'" "The reality of festivity,"
he continues, "depends upon an alternation with the everyday schedule of work,
convention, and moderation."[17] Edmund Leach echoes Cox's point in structuralist
terms in his influential essay, "Time and False Noses." "Each festival," Leach suggests,
"represents . . . a temporary shift from the Normal-Profane order of existence into
the Abnormal-Sacred order and back again."[18] By means of this alternation and contrast
between orders of existence, periodicity is established in the social life of traditional
societies, and thus, social time is created. These complementary perspectives, then,
ground the essence of festival in a fundamental contrast between normal, everyday,
mundane existence, and festival, which is special and stands in symbolic opposition
to it. Orders of time and existence, in this view, are *discontinuous, uneven, irregular.*

Such conceptions of the unevenness of time, as Keith Thomas points out, are
the natural product of agrarian societies, in which the flow of life and work is subject
to the vagaries of the weather and the seasons.[19] A rationally organized industrial
economy, such as was emerging in seventeenth-century England, required a more
regular, continuous, constant system of reckoning time, made possible by the intellectual efforts of Newton and the invention (in 1657) of the pendulum clock.[20] This
emergent sense of the uniform flow of time was sustained by the powerful Puritan
impulse toward plainness and uniformity of life in general, identified by Weber as a
major underpinning of the capitalist interest in the standardization of production.[21]
Of special interest in all of this for our purposes is the way in which this radical shift
in worldview was expressed in Quaker views of festival and its place in the lives of
non-Quakers.

The Quakers, we must remember, saw the festival means we have identified—

immoderate feasting, excessive drinking, singing, music, dance, sexual license, may-poles, athletic contests, and so on—as carnal indulgences, idle, wasteful, sinful pleasures of the flesh. It is noteworthy, then, that in the eyes of the Quakers, those who took part in festivals were in fact engaged in such sinful practices *all the time*. This view is summed up in Thomas Taylor's description of the "eating, and drinking, and sporting, and playing" characteristic of festival as "vain customs that the evil world loves and *lives in*" (emphasis added), "the miserable and woeful condition of the *most* part of people, that in these days bear the name of Christians."[22] Thus, for Quakers, scheduled festivals were not in contrast to the everyday lives of these people, but rather an additional excuse for indulging in the sinful practices that characterized their lives at all times. There is no alternation in this view between a workaday world and a festival world, only a constant world of festive indulgence.

Furthermore, the Quakers held that while festivity was sinful at any time, it was especially so when done on so-called holydays, in the name of religion. In excoriating "the world's vain fashions and customs, in their feastings, and revelings and ban-quetings, and wakes, and other vain feastings," George Fox, generally considered as the chief founder of Quakerism, emphasizes that those who indulge in such carnal activities "dishonor the Lord God more those times and days, which they call holy days, and feast days, than any other times and days."[23] In his attack on Christmas festivities, Taylor makes the same point:

> those that make most provision for the flesh, to satisfy it in the lusts
> thereof, let the time be what it may, are the greatest enemies to Christ,
> and their own souls; so let things be well weighed and considered, and it
> will appear to the open eye, that God is not more dishonored many twelve
> days of the year, than in these that people pretend most to honor him.[24]

That is, the sinful people of the world, "the most part of people," dishonor God at all times by the fleshly, festive indulgence they "love and live in," but they dishonor him all the more when they pretend to honor him by their festive behavior.

Having established this image of the sinful people "that live in their pleasures and lusts of the world,"[25] the Quakers then used it as a basis to define themselves, their own moral way of life, by opposition. Casting themselves in the image of the prophets and the apostles, the early Quakers made frequent use of the biblical topos of the world turned upside down, comparing themselves to Paul and Silas at Thes-salonica (Acts 17.6), who were perceived as agents of such overturning. Specifically, the established world that the Quakers aimed to overturn was conceived of as a world dominated by festivity, "where there is nothing to be seen but lightness and vanity, wantonness and obscenity, contrived to draw men from fear or being serious, and therefore no doubt calculated for the service of the devil."[26] By inversion, then, the Quakers were "the serious people,"[27] who lived their lives in the constant "fear of the Lord, to stand in awe before him, to walk as in his presence."[28]

Thus, for the Quakers, like those in traditional agrarian society, festival estab-lished existential contrasts. In their worldview, however, the contrast was not mani-fested in *alternations* between the conditions of everyday existence and the spirit of festival, but in a contrast between the *consistent* exemplars of two uniform but opposed ways of life: the carnal, profane life of festivity and the serious, sacred life of Friends.

In contemporary societies that are the cultural—if not fully the spiritual—heirs to the Puritan ethos out of which Quakerism emerged, "serious" is still a symbolic classifier of persons and actions—and religious behavior[29]—retaining a strong positive connotation. In such societies, because of this Puritan legacy and the concomitant rational economic ideology that dominates modern life, it still remains difficult to reconcile participation in festival with being a "serious" person. Traditional preindustrial people, of course, understand otherwise.

Notes

1. Richard Bauman, *Let Your Words be Few: Symbolism of Speaking and Silence among Seventeenth-Century Quakers* (New York: Cambridge University Press, 1983).

2. Max Weber, *The Protestant Ethic and the Spirit of Capitalism* (New York: Scribners, 1958).

3. Stephen Crisp, *The Christian Experience, Gospel Labours and Writings of . . . Stephen Crisp* (Philadelphia, 1822; orig. publ. 1666), pp. 118–122.

4. Christopher Hill, *Society and Puritanism in Pre-Revolutionary England* (London: Secker and Working, 1964), pp. 146–59, 183–94, 209.

5. Crisp, p. 119.

6. William Penn, *No Cross, No Crown* (Philadelphia, 1865; orig. publ. 1682), p. 246.

7. William Shewen, *The True Christian's Faith and Experience* (London, 1830; orig. publ. 1684–85), p. 127.

8. Crisp, p. 119; George Fox, "Epistle 302," in *The Works of George Fox*, vol. 8 (Philadelphia, 1831; written 1673), pp. 52–54.

9. Francis Howgill, "Concerning Fasts, Feasts, and Holy-days," in *The Dawnings of the Gospel Day* (London, 1676; orig. publ. 1662), pp. 428–30.

10. Crisp, p. 120.

11. Cf. William Henderson, *Notes on the Folk-Lore of the Northern Counties of England and the Borders*, Publications of the Folk-Lore Society no. 2 (London, 1879), pp. 87 and 89; A. R. Wright and T. E. Lones, *British Calendar Customs: England*, vol. I, Publications of the Folk-Lore Society no. 97 (London, 1936), pp. 188–90.

12. Thomas Taylor, "Against May-poles," in *Truth's Innocency and Simplicity* (London,

1679; orig. publ. 1660), p. 116; Penn, p. 246.

13. Crisp, p. 121.

14. Ibid.

15. Ibid.

16. Ibid., p. 120.

17. Harvey Cox, *The Feast of Fools* (Cambridge, Mass.: Harvard University Press, 1969), p. 23.

18. Edmund Leach, "Time and False Noses," in *Rethinking Anthropology* (New York: Humanities Press, 1966), p. 134.

19. Keith Thomas, *Religion and the Decline of Magic* (New York: Scribner's, 1971), p. 622.

20. Ibid., p. 623.

21. Weber, p. 169.

22. Thomas Taylor, "A Testimony Against Sporting and Playing," in *Truth's Innocency and Simplicity* (London, 1679; orig. publ. 1666), pp. 160–61.

23. Fox, p. 52.

24. Taylor, "A Testimony Against Sporting and Playing," p. 161.

25. George Fox, "The Serious People's Reasoning and Speech, with the World's Teachers and Professors," in *The Works of George Fox*, vol. 4 (Philadelphia, 1831; orig. publ. 1659), p. 199.

26. Robert Barclay, *Apology for the True Christian Divinity*, in *Truth Triumphant*, vol. 2 (Philadelphia, 1831; orig. publ. 1676), p. 538.

27. Fox, "The Serious People's Reasoning and Speech," p. 199.

28. Barclay, p. 538.

29. Emile Durkheim, *The Elementary Forms of the Religious Life* (New York: Free Press, 1965; orig. publ. 1915), p. 427.

9 / Three Fêtes of the French Revolution (1793–1796)

Adolphe Thiers

Festivals often commemorate the mythological or legendary origin of a culture, but they may also be given to celebrate the historical origins of a political regime. Newly established regimes which long for legitimacy, continuity, and popular support almost invariably introduce new festivals. The French revolutionary fêtes were explicitly created to replace the festivities of the freshly overthrown "enemies of the people," the Catholic church and the monarchy. But as Nietzche ironically remarked, it is not enough to give a festival, there ought to be people participating in it. To be sure of a large popular participation, and to elaborate new and spectacular choreography, the Parisian Revolutionary Directory enlisted the services of artist Jean-Louis David, the forty-year-old celebrated leader of the Parisian school. David had already painted such famous pictures as Joseph Bara, the portrait of a drummer boy shot by the royalists; The Oath of the Tennis Court of 1793, picturing the beginning of the French Revolution; and The Dead Marat called Pietà of the Revolution for its pathos and Jacobin inspiration. David was also a political figure. A member of the Convention Nationale and the Comité de Salut Publique, friend of Robespierre, he had voted for the execution of Louis XVI. In August 1793, Robespierre had orchestrated, under David's direction, the first new revolutionary festival, the Fête of Reunion, aimed at introducing the new religion of the Supreme Being. In opposition, Hébert, Chaumette, and their group of popular avant-garde organized the Fête of Reason (the first one described here) to further their campaign of de-Christianization, against the Catholic attempts at a counterrevolution in the Vandée region. In Notre Dame, refurbished after eliminating any sign of Catholic religion, the Fête of Reason reached its peak: a beautiful woman acclaimed as the Goddess Reason sat triumphantly clad in the colors of the new flag, as the congregation sang to her: "You, Holy Liberty, come live in this temple, be the Goddess of the French People." This festivity inspired violent anticlericalism. All over Paris the sansculottes broke into churches, pillaged and burned sacred images and objects, used sacred garments to improvise blasphemous masquerades and skits, and paraded in the streets dragging skeletons stolen from burial places. Church archives were burned; priests and high prelates abjured Catholic religion. In the Church of St. Sulpice, on November 30, the official speaker solemnly dared God to prove His existence by striking him by lightning and annihilating him on the spot. After a few minutes, since nothing happened, he solemnly deduced that God was an invention of the priests. The works of the convention were interrupted continuously by masquerades of people wearing clerical garments who wanted to show their allegiance to the Republic. Trees of Freedom, mock processions, allegorical floats, dances in churches, young women dressed as Goddess Reason, comic shows improvised in the tradition of the Feasts of Fools, burning of confessionals occurred all over France. Such disorderly celebrations became a way to live the holidays, to restate a political and revolutionary creed. The Fêtes of Reason somehow proposed a familiar model of enactment and collective representations, which exalted a collective truth. Tradition became political strength and, furthermore, revolutionary consciousness. But Robespierre whose Fête had been a label for power looking for consensus, understood the explosive, destabilizing potential of these festivities for the public order. Chaumette and Hébert were obliged to recognize his Religion of the Supreme Being. Then they were executed.

On May 7, 1794, Robespierre gave his famous speech on the religion of the Supreme Being and read to the convention the list of the official fêtes to be observed. On June 8 the Fête of the Supreme Being (the second described below) was celebrated. With the help of David, Robespierre embarked on a formidable attempt at constituting the liturgy of a new religion. The Fête wanted to obtain from the whole city of Paris, in the name of the whole people of France, a plebiscitary acceptance of the existence of the Supreme Being and of the immortality of the soul. The vital revolutionary crowd had to become a passive orderly mass of subjects, everyone in his own place, serious and dignified. Rousseau was often quoted to give sanction to public virtue and religion. The main symbol was now Wisdom, the principle of orderly reason, the logic that respects laws and honors God. Robespierre acted out his role by affecting cheerfulness, giving speeches and setting fire to statues of the old idols. All age groups, jobs, and professions paraded in this deliberate show of the new revolutionary society. Robespierre and the deputies appeared wearing official garments that characterized them: new uniforms introduced to convey uniformity. The departments of France did not parade as they had before to show the national and political basis of power: the new establishment wanted to claim instead an abstract metaphysical sanction. The people which had collectively enacted the chaotic and indecent representations of its enemies, the clergy and aristocracy, was to become the orderly, passive, and deferential crowd contemplating new idols. To replace living goddesses, David produced national monuments which Hitler would later praise.

Festivals often use the device of symbolic reversal to turn everyday life upside down. It is interesting to note that in some cases, as in the third fête described here, this operation is explicitly applied to former celebrations. While festivals normally celebrate kings' birthdays, in 1796 French revolutionaries introduced instead the anniversary celebration of the king's death. And instead of the customary oath of allegiance, ceremonies were centered on a ritual oath of hatred of monarchy. The creative, utopian potential of the first chaotic festivals was substantially reduced to follow prerevolutionary routines. A skeptical Thiers submits that nothing changed; one belief was simply substituted for another. In more modern terms, the issue is as Barthes and others posed it for the revolutionary languages of the 1960s: is it possible to further—or even to imagine—a revolutionary process while using the symbolic language of the system overthrown? Is the adoption of former symbolic structures an implicitly reactionary statement of continuity, soon bound to nullify any substitution of contents?

Revolutionary fêtes fell, along with the regime, to Napoleon and then restoration, and paradoxically David, the genial choreographer of Robespierre's fêtes, became the Emperor's official painter.

Three Fêtes of the French Revolution (1793–1796)*

Adolphe Thiers

1. The Worship of Reason Substituted for Christianity (1793)

The sections soon met, and came one after another to declare that they renounced the errors of superstition, and that they acknowledged no other worship than that of reason. The section of L'Homme-Armé declared that it acknowledged no other worship than that of truth and reason, no other fanaticism than that of liberty and equality, no other doctrine than that of fraternity and the republican laws decreed since the 31st of May, 1793. The section of La Réunion intimated that it would make a bonfire of all the confessionals, and of all the books used by the catholics, and that it would cause the church of Saint Méry to be closed. The section of William Tell renounced for ever what it termed the worship of error and imposture. The section of Mucius Scaevola abjured Catholicism, and declared that on the next decadi it would celebrate at the high altar of Saint Sulpice the inauguration of the busts of Marat, Lepelletier, and Mucius Scaevola. The section of Les Piques that it would adore no other god than the god of liberty and equality. The section of the Arsenal also abjured the Catholic religion.

Thus the sections, taking the initiative, abjured Catholicism as the established religion, and took possession of its edifices and its treasures, as it would of buildings and treasures appurtenant to the communal demesnes. The deputies on mission in the departments had already incited a great number of communes to seize the moveable property of the churches, which they said was not necessary for religion, and which, besides, like all public property, belonged to the state, and might therefore be ap-

*Reprinted from Adolphe Thiers, *The History of the French Revolution. Translated from the last Paris edition, with notes* (London and Edinburgh: P. Nimmo, 1877), pp. 373–74, 446–47, 614. Originally published as *Histoire de la Revolution Française* (Paris: Furne et Cie, 1850).

propriated for its purposes. Fouché had sent several chests of plate from the department of L'Allier. A great quantity had arrived from the other departments. This example, followed in Paris and the environs, soon brought piles of wealth to the bar of the convention. All the churches were stripped, and the communes sent deputations with the gold and silver accumulated in the shrines of saints, or in places consecrated by antique devotion. They went in procession to the convention, and the rabble indulging their taste for the burlesque, caricatured in the most ludicrous manner the ceremonies of religion, and took as much delight in profaning as they had formerly done in celebrating them. Men wearing surplices, chasubles, and copes, came singing *Alleluia*, and dancing the *carmagnole* at the bar of the convention; there they deposited the ostensories and the boxes in which the host was kept, and the images of gold and silver; they delivered themselves of satirical speeches, and sometimes addressed the most singular harangues to the saints themselves. "O ye," exclaimed a deputation from Saint Denis, "O ye instruments of fanaticism! blessed saints of every degree, be at last patriots, rise *en masse*, serve the country by going to be melted for money, and give us in this world that felicity which you desired to obtain for us in the other!" These scenes of merriment were followed all at once by scenes of reverence and devotion. The same persons who trampled underfoot the saints of Christianity bore a canopy; the curtains were thrown back, and pointing to the busts of Marat and Lepelletier, "These," said they, "are not gods made by men, but the images of worthy citizens assassinated by the slaves of kings." They then filed off before the convention, again singing *alleluia* and dancing the *carmagnole*; they then carried the rich spoils of the altars to the mint, and placed the revered busts of Marat and Lepelletier in the churches, now become the temples of a new worship.

At the requisition of Chaumette, it was resolved that the metropolitan church of Notre Dame should be converted into a republican edifice, called the *Temple of Reason*. A fête was appointed for the days of the decades, which fête was to supersede the catholic ceremonies of Sunday. The mayor, the municipal officers, and the public functionaries, repaired to the temple of reason, where they read the declaration of the rights of man, as also the constitutional act, discussed the news from the armies, and related the brilliant actions which had been performed during the decade. A letter-box of truth (*une bouche de vérité*), resembling the letter-boxes of denunciation which formerly existed at Venice, was placed in the temple of reason, to receive opinions, censures, or advice, likely to prove of utility to the public. These letters were examined and read upon every decade, an orator then delivered a moral sermon, after which pieces of music were performed, and the performance concluded by singing republican hymns. There were in the temple two tribunes, one for aged men, the other for pregnant women, with these inscriptions: *Reverence for old age—Respect and attention to pregnant women*.

The first festival of reason was held with pomp on the 20th of Brumaire (the 10th of November.) All the sections, together with the constituted authorities, repaired thither; a young woman representing the Goddess of Reason. She was the wife of Momoro, the printer, one of the friends of Vincent, Ronsin, Chaumette, Hébert, and the like. She was dressed in a white drapery; a mantle of azure blue hung from her shoulders; her flowing hair was covered with the cap of liberty. She was seated upon an antique seat, entwined with ivy, and borne by four citizens. Young girls dressed in white, and crowned with roses, preceded and followed the goddess. Then came the busts of Lepelletier and Marat, musicians, troops, and all the armed sections. Speeches were delivered, and hymns sung in the temple of reason; they then proceeded to the convention; Chaumette spoke in these terms:—

"Legislators! fanaticism has given way to reason. Her bleared eyes could not endure the brilliancy of the light. This day an immense concourse has assembled beneath these fretted vaults, which for the first time have echoed to the voice of truth. There it is that the French have celebrated the only true worship, that of liberty, that of reason. There it is that we have formed wishes for the prosperity of the arms of the republic. There it is that we have abandoned inanimate idols, for reason, for that animated image, the masterpiece of nature." As he uttered these words, Chaumette pointed to the living goddess of reason. The young and beautiful woman descended from her seat, and went up to the president, who gave her the fraternal embrace, amidst universal bravos, and shouts of *The republic for ever! Reason for ever! Down with fanaticism!* The convention, who had not yet taken any part in these representations, was hurried away, and obliged to follow the procession, which returned to the temple of reason, and there sang a patriotic hymn. An important piece of intelligence, that of the re-taking of Noirmourtiers from Charette, augmented the general joy, and furnished a more substantial cause for this rejoicing, than the mere abolition of fanaticism.

It is impossible to view with any other feeling than that of disgust these scenes, possessing neither reflection or sincerity, exhibited by a nation that had changed its worship, without comprehending either the previous, or the present, form of adoration.

When is the multitude sincere? When is it capable of comprehending the doctrines that are submitted to its belief? What does it generally want? Great meetings, which pander to its desire of being assembled, symbolic spectacles, which incessantly remind it of a power superior to its own; lastly, festivals, in which homage is paid to those who have made the nearest approach to what is good, noble, or great; in short, temples, ceremonies, and saints. There were now temples to Reason, Marat, and Lepelletier. The people were assembled, they adored a mysterious power, they celebrated those two men. All their desires were satisfied, and they gave themselves up to their passion on this occasion, in no other manner than as they always have done.

The procession at length reached the Champ de Mars. There, instead of the former altar of the country, was to be observed a lofty mountain. At the top of this mountain was a tree, beneath the boughs of which the convention seated itself. On each side of the mountain were placed different groups of boys, old men, and women. A symphony commenced; the groups then chanted a *chorus*, alternately responsive to each other. At length, on a given signal, the youths drew their swords, and swore between the hands* of the old men to defend the country; the matrons lifted their infants in their arms; all present raised their hands towards heaven, and the oath to conquer was mingled with the homage paid to the Supreme Being. They then returned to the garden of the Tuileries, and the *fête* concluded with public diversions.

Such was the famous *fête* celebrated in honour of the Supreme Being. Robespierre had on that day attained the summit of honours, but he had only gained this pinnacle to be hurled from it. Everybody had been wounded by his pride. The sarcasms had

---

*The ancient form of making a solemn declaration or oath before another.

reached his ear, and he had observed in some of his colleagues a boldness that was unusual in them. Next day he went to the committee of public welfare, and expressed his indignation against the deputies who had insulted him on the preceding day. He complained of those friends of Danton's, those impure relics of the *indulgent corruptionist* party, and demanded the sacrifice of them. Billaud-Varennes and Collot d'Herbois, who were not less wounded than their colleagues at the part which Robespierre had performed the day before, appeared extremely cold, and by no means over-anxious to avenge him. They did not indeed justify the deputies of whom Robespierre complained, but, recurring to the *fête* itself, they expressed apprehensions concerning its effects. It had, they said, alienated many minds. Besides, those ideas of the Supreme Being, of the immortality of the soul, those pompous ceremonies, looked like a return to the superstitions of old, and were likely to impart a retrograde impulse to the revolution. Robespierre was irritated by these remarks. He maintained that it never was his intent that the revolution should retrograde; that, on the contrary, he had done every thing to accelerate its course.

II. *Fête to the Supreme Being (1794)*

The 20th Prairial (June 8) was at hand; this was the day appointed for the *fête* in honour of the Supreme Being. On the 16th [Prairial] they were to name a president; the convention unanimously appointed Robespierre to take the presidency. This was conferring on him the principal part on the 20th. His colleagues, we see, still strove to flatter and to soothe him by dint of honours. Preparations had been made on a very large scale, according to the plan conceived by David. The *fête* was expected to be magnificent. On the morning of the 20th the sun shone forth in all its brightness. The multitude, ever ready to attend the sights afforded them by public authority, had collected. Robespierre kept them waiting a considerable time. At length he appeared amidst the convention. He was dressed with extraordinary care. His head was covered with feathers, and in his hand he held, as did every one of the representatives, a bunch of flowers, fruit, and ears of corn. On his countenance, usually so gloomy, was manifested a cheerfulness that was very uncommon with him. An amphitheatre was erected in the centre of the garden of the Tuileries. This was occupied by the convention; and on the right and left were several groups of boys, men, aged persons, and females. The boys wore wreaths of violets, the youths wreaths of myrtle, the men wreaths of oak, and the aged people wreaths of ivy and olive. The women held their daughters by the hand, and carried baskets of flowers. On the other side of the amphitheatre were figures representing Atheism, Discord, and Egotism. These were to be burned. As soon as the convention had taken its place, the ceremony commenced with music. The president then delivered an introductory discourse upon the object of the festival. "Republican Frenchmen!" said he, "At length has arrived that ever-to-be-remembered day of happiness which the French people consecrate to the Supreme Being. Never did the world, which he created, exhibit a spectacle so worthy of his attention. He has beholden tyranny, crime, and imposture reigning upon earth. He beholds at this moment an individual nation at war with all the oppressors of mankind, suspending the course of its heroic labours, to lift its thoughts and its prayers towards the Supreme Being, who gave it the mission to undertake and the courage to execute them."

After having spoken for a few minutes, the president descended from the amphitheatre, and, seizing a torch, set fire to the figures of Atheism, Discord, and Egotism. From amidst the ashes arose the statue of Wisdom; but it was remarked that it was smoked by the flames from whence it had to make its appearance. Robespierre returned to his place, and delivered a second speech upon the extirpation of the vices leagued against the republic. After this ceremony, the assembly set out in procession for the Champ de Mars. The self-sufficiency of Robespierre seemed extraordinarily increased, and he affected to walk considerably in advance of his colleagues. But some of them, feeling indignant, kept up with him, and lavished on him the keenest sarcasms. Some laughed at the new pontiff, and said, in allusion to the smoky statue of Wisdom, that his wisdom was obscured. Others uttered the word "tyrant," and exclaimed that there were *still some Brutuses left*. Bourdon (of the Oise) addressed to him these prophetic words: *"The Tarpeian rock is hard by the capitol."*

III. *An Anniversary Fête Instituted in Memory of the Death of Louis XVI (1796)*

The conventionalists seized the opportunity with which the anniversary of the 21st of January was about to afford them, to subject their colleagues suspected of royalism to a disagreeable test. They proposed a *fête* to celebrate, every 21st of January, the death of the late king; and they caused it to be settled that on this day every member of the two councils and of the directory should take an oath of hatred to royalty. This formality of an oath, so frequently employed by the parties, never could be considered as a guarantee; it has never been any thing else than an unjust infliction of the conquering party, who have wanted to force the conquered to a perjury. The proposal was adopted by the two councils. The conventionalists awaited with impatience the sitting of the 1st Pluviôse, year IV. (January 21st), to see their colleagues of the new third one by one appear before the tribune. Each council sat that day in solemn state. A *fête* was prepared in Paris, and the directory and all the authorities were to attend it. When the oath had to be taken, some of the newly-elected appeared embarrassed. The ex-constituent Dupont, of Nemours, who was a member of the ancients, and retained to an advanced age a great liveliness of temper, and showed the boldest opposition to the existing government,—Dupont, of Nemours, showed some spiteful feeling, and after pronouncing the words, *I swear hatred to royalty*, added, *and to every kind of tyranny*. This was one way of revenging himself, and of swearing hatred to the directory under evasive words. Great disapprobation was manifested, and Dupont was compelled to adhere to the official form. In the five hundred, one André would have had recourse to the same expression as Dupont, but he was in like manner obliged to confine himself to the formula. The president of the directory delivered an energetic speech, and the whole government thus made the most revolutionary confession of faith.

Editor's Note

Adolphe Thiers (1797–1877) was a prominent statesman, historian, journalist, essayist, and a master of parliamentary eloquence matched by few statesmen in Europe. He was prime minister in 1871, when he negotiated peace and crushed the revolutionary commune that had taken over Paris. He sided with the Orleans against the Bourbons. Chateaubriand classified him as the head of the "fatalist school," which saw the Terror as a necessary evil. His fluid prose aimed at "being simply true, being what things themselves are, being nothing more, being only through them, like them, as long as them." Thiers had no real interest in history of ideas, or social history, as these "journalistic" pages show.

On Thiers, see Rene Albrecht-Carrié, *Adolphe Thiers, or, The Triumph of the Bourgeoisie* (Boston: Twayne, 1977), and John M. S. Allison, *Monsieur Thiers* (New York: Norton, 1932).

On the French Revolution, see Georges Lefebvre, *The French Revolution*, 2 vols., trans. Elizabeth Moss Evanson (London: Routledge & Kegan Paul; New York: Columbia University Press, 1962–64). On the period of the fêtes described by Thiers, see also Albert Soboul, *The French Revolution, 1787–1799, from the Storming of the Bastille to Napoleon*, trans. Allan Forest and Colin Jones (New York: Vintage Books, 1974).

The fêtes of the French Revolution were anticipated by some observations by J. J. Rousseau. See Jean-Jacques Rousseau, *Oeuvres complètes*, 13 vols. (Paris: Hachette, 1907), 1: 187–88; 230; 269; 5: 245–46. Their choreography was influenced by the artist David. See David L. Dowd, *Pageant-Master of the Republic, Jacques-Louis David and the French Revolution* (Lincoln: University of Nebraska Press, 1948).

On the relationship between the revolutionary governments, church, and religion, see, for instance, Pierre de la Gorge, *Histoire Religieuse de la Revolution Française*, 4 vols. (Paris: Plon, 1909–21); François Victor Alphonse Aulard, *Christianity and the French Revolution*, trans. Lady Frazer (London: Bell, 1927); John McManners, *The French Revolution and the Church* (London: S.P.C.K. for the Church Historical Society, 1969); D. Charlton, *Secular Religions in France* (Oxford: Oxford University Press, 1963).

On the French fêtes of the revolution, see François Victor Alphonse Aulard, *Le culte de la raison et le culte de l'être supreme (1793–1794). Essai historique* (Paris: Alcan, 1892); Julien Tiersot, *Les fêtes et les chants de la révolution française* (Paris: Hachette, 1908); Mona Ozouf, "Le cortège et la ville. Les itinéraires parisiens des fêtes révolutionnaires," *Annales Economies Sociétés Civilizations* 26 (1971) no. 5: 889–916; Albert Mathiez, *Les Origines des cultes révolutionnaires, 1789–1792* (Paris: Bellais, 1904); C. Bessonnet-Favre, *Les Fêtes Républicaines depuis 1789 jusqu' à nos jours, d'après des documents authentiques* (Paris, 1909); Claude Fortuné Ruggieri, *Précis Historique sur les Fêtes, les Spectacles et les réjouissances publiques* (Paris, 1830); Gaston Bonet-Maury, *De la Signification morale et réligieuse des fêtes publiques dans les Républiques modernes* (Dole: Bernin, 1896). See especially Mona Ozouf, *La fête révolutionnaire 1789–1799* (Paris: Gallimard, 1976), pp. 125–48; she includes consistent references to the pamphlets and official literature of the time. For an overview of public celebrations from the French Revolution to Nazi Germany, see George L. Mosse, *Masses and Man: Nationalist and Fascist Perceptions of Reality* (New York: Howard Fertig, 1980), pp. 104–18. For a general discussion, see Yves-Marie Bercé, *Fête et Révolte* (Paris: Hachette, 1976).

For the latest manifestations of revolutionary festivities in France, see Sherry Turkle, "Symbol and Festival in the French Student Uprising (May–June 1968)" in Sally Moore and Barbara Myerhoff, eds., *Symbols and Politics in Communal Ideology: Cases and Questions* (Ithaca and London: Cornell University Press, 1975), pp. 68–103.

10 / Nazi Festival: The 1936 Berlin Olympics

Moyra Byrne

In spite of their ecumenical philosophy, modern Olympics have always been used by the organizing countries as a unique occasion to showcase their historical past and their present achievements. But on no occasion was this effort greater than for the German Olympics of 1936. Adolf Hitler had seized power in 1933, had achieved the nationalization of the masses, and was beginning their mobilization. His formidable team of propaganda experts, headed by Josef Goebbels, seized the opportunity of staging the Olympics, an established festival carrying international prestige, and turning the games into the cultural debut of Nazi Germany before the world.

As Byrne's essay points out, the German games had to be first of all the utopian Olympic festival of brotherly friendship and chivalrous competition envisioned by Baron Pierre de Coubertin. In the second place, they had to make a worldwide official statement of the organizational capabilities and cultural achievements of the new Germany. At the internal policy level, the Olympics were an occasion to foster the national pride of the German masses in the new Reich state and in its alter ego, the Nazi Party. The Games were also an occasion to test on the athletic fields the fitness and superiority of the Aryan race, in view of other upcoming tests in the battlefields. As the essay shows, the organizers, with the full backing of the Nazi state and its propaganda machine, set out to fulfill these tasks, and, in spite of their contradictory essence, fulfilled them brilliantly. In effect they fashioned two festivals in one: the orthodox Olympic festival for the international community of participants and spectators, and a nationalistic German festival, a self-enactment of Nazi Germany. Modern Olympics derive an aura of prestige from a postulated link with ancient Olympics and classical humanism. German organizers tried to present the image of a peaceful Germany, loving classical antiquity and rediscovering and spreading the message of Olympia to the new world through its historians, archaeologists, and scholars. Implied was the statement that Germany was to the new world what Greece had been to the old. In the opening speech of the games, the president of the Olympic Committee referred to the Olympic fire as creating a bond between Germany and "the sacred places of Greece founded nearly 4,000 years ago by Nordic immigrants"; Dr. Diem, the chief of the organizing committee, had the brilliant idea of introducing the new Olympic ritual of the torch run, a spectacular perambulatory fire festival. The fire was lit at Olympia by a lens designed by Zeiss, and was carried by safety torches, manufactured by Krupp, through seven countries and some 3,000 kilometers all the way to Berlin. German organizers indeed went out of their way to impress visitors and the world at large. The rate of exchange was kept artificially low, food and lodging were inexpensive, crime was virtually eliminated in Berlin—then the fourth largest city in the world—which was inundated by flags and festive decorations. A "week of mirth and happiness" was declared. Some 100,000 doves and pigeons flew as a sign of festive goodwill. The most powerful, moving German music was performed at the Olympic ceremonies, including Handel's Hallelujah Chorus and the choral movement of Beethoven's Ninth Symphony; Richard Strauss directed his new Olympic hymn. A dazzling dimension of spectacle was applied to the whole production in such a way that the participants and international public were thrust into the role of spectators at the celebration of Nazi Germany's greatness. In 1935–36 an Olympic exhibition toured the major German cities to illustrate the origins and development of modern Olympics. As for the provinces and rural areas of Germany, there was the Olympia-Zug. This Olympic caravan transported a traveling exhibit by means of four huge Mercedes diesel trucks, each hauling two trailers. The caravan formed a large pavilion and exhibition hall. The show presented and praised New Germany as the organizer of the Olympics and as the cultural vanguard of the twentieth century.

Hitler's public image was unusually restrained; his public appearances were short and measured, and his speeches reduced to a few moving words. He appeared moved and benevolent even if in private he complained that everything had been built too small, and entertained the idea of making a pharaonic Berlin the permanent site of postwar Olympics.

Racism was tuned down to the point of appearing to many a superseded policy. The all-Aryan crowds cheered the feats of Jesse Owens and the other black athletes, even if the media insisted on calling them "Negro auxiliaries," and Hitler hurriedly left the tribune of honor so as not to acknowledge Owens's four gold medals.

Byrne's essay refers to current theoretical work on festival such as Stoeltje's structural-semiotic approach, MacAloon's performance-oriented typology and Turner's liminal/liminoid categories, to show the structural differences between the components of the two-festivals-in-one staged successfully by the Nazi organizers. Festival usually implies a discontinuous reality with periodical regeneration, argues the author, but the

Nazi festival was in fact promoting the idea of the permanence of the new Reich and was inserted into the continuous series of festivities supporting the Nazi regime from beginning to end. Festival usually constitutes a temporary utopia in which the everyday order of life is suspended or inverted, but the Nazi festival in fact offered an intensified representation of Nazi Germany: Nazi salutes, brown-shirted Hitler youth, and storm troopers were a visible part of the rituals. In Olympic advertisements, Hitler was portrayed next to the Walter E. Lemcke's bell, as if he also was summoning to Berlin the world's youth. All over the city, the flag with the swastika flew side by side with the flag with the Olympic rings. Elaborating on an ominous observation of Roger Caillois, made on the eve of World War II, the article finally discusses how the Berlin Games were in fact a metaphor for peace and for war.

Nazi Festival: The 1936 Berlin Olympics

Moyra Byrne

On August 1, 1936, in the huge newly built stadium of Berlin, Adolf Hitler officially opened the games celebrating the Eleventh Olympiad of the modern era. The official *Diplomatische Korrespondenz* addressed the occasion with Olympic aplomb: "Amidst the plaudits of the world, the Olympic flame will enter the arena of peaceful combat exactly on that day when 22 years ago the torch of war was destined to afflict the world for four years. The entire German people read in this coincidence a happy omen of goodwill and the readiness of the nations to dedicate all their forces and faculties to the pursuit of friendly combat for the benefit of mankind." And the *New York Times* added, "This is undoubtedly the way the great body of the German people feels about the games."[1]

The honor and job of hosting the 1936 Olympics had been awarded to Berlin by the International Olympic Committee (I.O.C.) shortly before the Los Angeles summer Olympics of 1932. This was a coup for the German Olympic Committee organizers, whose hopes and preparations for a 1916 Berlin Games had been dashed by the war, and for Germany, whose teams had only been readmitted to the Olympic community in 1928. Hitler and especially his minister for propaganda, Josef Goebbels, recognized the extraordinary instrument that the Berlin Olympic Games could become for the new regime, and soon put all the power of the state behind an effort to make this the biggest and most splendid festival in history. They keenly saw the need to pave the way for Hitler's expansionist ambitions with a propaganda effort which would create the image of a "new" Germany. This new image should redeem both the image of a defeated nation, and that of a dangerously warlike people; it should command respect, even intimidate, yet blunt suspicions of aggressive aims.[2] The hosting of the Olympic Games would be an otherwise unimaginable opportunity to associate Nazi Germany with the sacred ideals of modern Olympism while placing it at the center of the world's attention.

At the same time, on the national front, the Berlin Olympics could fulfill a special role in the system of festivities which were already proving so effective in galvanizing and coordinating the Germans under Nazi leadership; participation and success in the festival endeavor would give them the strength of a new self-confidence in relation to the world.

This became the first Olympics since the beginning of the modern Olympic era in 1896 to be organized by state authorities. With state resources and facilities at their disposal, the Nazi organizers went to work on three planes of operation. Their first task was to organize and stage the international event. At the same time, they set to work to make this a festival of great national significance, a self-enactment and celebration of Nazi Germany. On a third plane the event was to be an artfully conceived, grandiose spectacle of Nazi Germany for as wide a world audience as possible. The intent of the spectacle was also for these three planes to appear a logical whole, and this demanded inspired and meticulous attention to the congruences and divergences in means and in aims among the three planes. The international event and Olympic ideals occupied the matrix plane; sufficient congruence between this and the other planes could disguise or even legitimize purposeful or inevitable divergences.

Modern Olympism and the New German Image:
Congruence and Divergence

The German organizers fell heir to a young but by then vigorous festival tradition. The modern Olympic Games cycle had been founded by the French baron Pierre de Coubertin (1863–1937), and inaugurated at the Athens Games of 1896. Baruch Hazan points out that "it is often overlooked that the origin of the modern Olympic games was political at heart. . . . Pierre de Coubertin was convinced that the lack of physical education in French schools had been the fundamental cause of France's defeat against Germany in 1870, and international sport competitions were to help set this right."[3] Nevertheless, by the time Coubertin's tenacity had seen the modern Olympic Games through the uncertainties of their first recurrences and beyond the First World War, his thought had matured into a genuine altruistic internationalism and pacifism, and he had rallied many sincere followers. The believers in the new "Olympism" saw the "peaceful combat" of the modern Olympic Games, with its carefully nurtured and controlled frame of ritual and festivity, as metaphoric behavior which could influence the behavior of mankind in everyday reality and lead to a peaceful coexistence based on mutual respect among individuals and nations. The idea of a lasting peace for which the Olympic Games could provide the model and the basis is of course a radical transformation of the principle of the armistice which in ancient Greece was enforced for the period of the Games.

To preserve the integrity of his festival Coubertin was particularly adamant about two basic tenets. The first is the recurrence of the Games at—and only at—four-year intervals which take their reference directly from the four-year Olympiads sanctified by Greek antiquity. The other rule of supreme importance is that the host city and country change each time, so that no nation can lay its national claim on the Olympics: the idea is that each site symbolically and temporarily becomes the international festive space of the "New Olympia." This is a reversal of the ancient tradition, which summoned its participants to Olympia from as far as the Greek colonies in Spain, North Africa, and the Black Sea, thus confirming Olympic Greece as the focus of the civilized world.

The propaganda task of the Nazi organizers of the Berlin Olympics was to fashion according to appropriate congruences with official Olympic ideals both a new self-image for the Germans under Nazi leadership, and the image which Germany could most usefully present to the world. The identification of modern Olympism with the glory of ancient Greek civilization was particularly apt. Germany had a rich intellectual heritage of enthusiasm for classical Greece as exemplified by the great eighteenth-century humanist scholar Johann Joachim Winckelmann, or the nineteenth-century archaeologist Ernst Curtius, who had directed excavations at Olympia itself. Much publicity was given to Germany's cultural heritage. Nazi Germany was to see herself and be seen as the apotheosis of her glorious cultural past fused with her vigorous present. One of the many instruments of this propaganda was the "Deutschland" Olympia exhibition which opened in Berlin on July 18, 1936, in time for the early influx of Olympia visitors. At the opening ceremony Dr. Goebbels defined the exhibit as not only an opportunity for Germans to learn about their own country, but as also the carrying out of an imperative national obligation to let foreign visitors observe for themselves the admirable facts of the new Reich.[4] Addressing an exhibition which ranged from Goethe's carriage (gaily driven across Germany to Berlin) to depictions of the most modern German technology and production, Goebbels said, "May the rhythm of a reawakened, reborn nation, pulsating with the desire to create, fill the whole exhibition. . . . This exhibition must not only be a testimony to the new Germany, to her ambitions and achievements, it must also be a statement of the great Germany of the past—in short, of the 'Eternal Germany.'"[5] Aided by the mediating identification of Berlin with "Olympia," Nazi propaganda implicitly constructed an equation between the focal position of Olympic Greece in the ancient world, and that of Nazi Germany in the modern world: the "Aryan" Germans under National Socialism were the new Greeks, and their culture the new Humanism.[6]

The cult of amateur athletics was the other identifying characteristic of Olympism which the Nazi planners had to tend. If the Berlin Olympic festival was to be a full success in terms both of the national celebration of a unified German will and self-confidence, and in terms of a spectacle of Germany's eminence in the world, German athletes must show high achievement in the competitions.

The nationalistic interpretation of the outcome of Olympic competition goes directly against the precepts of orthodox modern Olympism according to Coubertin's mature philosophy; the I.O.C., in fact, officially refuses to recognize any national scores and rankings. But the concept of the nationalistic utility of sports was a nineteenth-century ideological heritage very much present in the real-life context of the modern Olympics. Germany in particular enjoyed a conveniently home-grown version deriving from the doctrine of Friedrich Ludwig "Vater" Jahn (1778–1852), founder of the influential massed gymnastics movement. Three of the fundamental themes of Nazi culture—racial superiority, the health of the *Volk*, and military education—were already present in Jahn.[7]

Since excellence in sport, according to Nazi theory, was to be interpreted as evidence of racial superiority, the plane of the festival which was designed to be an intensified representation of the new Germany, by and for her people, called for strict adherence to Nazi anti-Semitic principles. However, anti-Semitism, which was fast taking on hideous forms and proportions, proved to be an aspect of Nazi doctrine that could in no way be expressed within the model of Olympism which the Nazi propagandists were obliged to follow for this occasion. As the Nazis began implementing a series of measures that would make it impossible for German Jews to compete in the Olympics, and when they even removed the internationally esteemed long-time president of the German Olympic Committee, Dr. Theodore Lewald, from his post because it was revealed that he was part Jewish, and, also, as much wider-ranging measures against German Jews became known, the international outcry was such that Germany came close to losing its festival. The actual compromises to which the Germans agreed in order to avoid this were temporary, limited, and definitely ambiguous. Nevertheless, when the crisis was past, Nazi leaders had sacrificed the completeness of the festival as a nationalistic expression in favor of its international value.

Fashioning the Festival

As a Nazi festival grafted onto the international event, the Berlin Olympic festival was a new event and presumably a one-time affair. The International Olympic Games, whose host in 1936 was to be Berlin, were a recent but established tradition with a strong principle of quadrennial recurrence. However, the modern Olympics are themselves different from a traditional festival which is celebrated by a homogeneous, self-evident community and whose rituals and distinguishing symbols grow out of the implicit ideology of that community. Coubertin's festival, inaugurated only forty years earlier, addressed the abstract community of humankind and had to gain and maintain its actual diffuse participants by winning them over to at least some part of the explicit philosophy of the new Olympism. This was necessarily an ongoing effort. The type of activity required for promoting Olympism and staging the Olympic festival opened up two realms admirably suited to the Nazi propaganda effort. The first of these realms of activity is in the space and freedom in this young, artificial tradition for the proliferation and creative manipulation of symbols and rituals. The other is the one in which the message of the festival is disseminated as widely as possible, enlarging and redefining its base of participation. Olympism's preference for non-Christian symbols also suited Nazi purposes well.

Festival Modes of Communication and Festival Temporal Dimensions.[8]   It is certain that the careful and lavish organization of this festival exploited a wide repertoire of intense artistic communication, from the colors of veritable walls of flags and banners (the white Olympic standard with the five colored rings, and the red Nazi one with the black swastika), to special exhibits, to elaborate pageantry and parties. On the evening of the opening day a spectacular "Pageant of Youth" in five acts, involving 10,000 participants engaged in gymnastic displays, dramatic dance, music and choral song, was presented in the Olympic stadium. But all Berlin was set up as a festive stage, from the daily fanfare wake-up by military bands parading through the streets, to the extreme hospitality the Berliners were exhorted to show their guests, the flowers they had been instructed to put on their balconies and in their window boxes, the uncustomary elegance with which the women were urged to dress, or the excitement and efficiency of the speeded-up subway trains. Music was a favorite form of festive communication. A particularly intriguing instance of its careful use to translate and underscore festival experience was only appreciated by the radio audience: a special piece of music was composed to bridge the intervals between the commentaries by the sportscasters reporting the more-than-two-hour marathon race. The Olympia World Station's report recounts that "this succeeded astonishingly well. The listener listened at [sic] the Marathon in its greatness and unendingness, in its battle and its decision, as at one great uninterrupted dramatic happening. It was certainly a chance happening that the collapse of the former Marathon victor Zabala found exciting and even terrible expression in the music immediately after."[9]

Two main principles underlie the temporal dimension of festival: the principle of periodicity and recurrence, which may have either a cosmic or a historical association; and the dialectical process of tradition and change whereby festival action, adapted to the present, interacts with festival's emphasis on the past, thus fostering social change. The role of the temporal feature in the contrived festival of the modern Olympics, and the Berlin Olympics in particular, is revealing.

Coubertin was very aware of the function of periodicity and recurrence, and therefore insisted on the four-year rule at all costs. He declared this to be a *revival* of the ancient Olympiad, thus borrowing an aura of pagan sacrality as well as appropriating the modern intellectual sacredness of the ideals of humanism. At first it was only his personal force, and that of his hardworking fellow Olympic officials, that saw the principle through. But as the recurrences accumulated, the four-year recurrence did begin to take on the sense of a cosmic ordering of time and the function of an impersonal stimulus toward the next Olympic festival. As for the play between past and present reality, Olympic philosophy and Olympic symbols and rituals explicitly proclaimed the difference between the internationalistic festival and its classical antecedent and also proclaimed the *aim* to effect social change. At the same time, spontaneous changes, reflecting and effecting social changes, were taking place in the festival, in particular its development into spectacle which will be discussed ahead.

These temporal features of the modern Olympics were rich resources for the Nazi organizers as they traced over them with the new self-celebratory and propagandistic Nazi festival. But there was one obvious difference in the temporal reality of the Nazi plane of the festival. The Nazi festival was not itself grounded in the principle of periodicity and recurrence. This is related to another basic difference which I will discuss in the investigation of "symbolic action." At this point it is enough to say that the Nazi Olympics of 1936 were part of an ongoing, more than periodic, reality of mass pageantry and festivity. Richard Mandell believes that "Hitler's success as a whole is inconceivable without the application of the contrived festivity that enveloped Nazism from beginning to end."[10]

The Festival Structures: Dominance through Congruence. Bound as modern Olympism is to an explicit idea, and given Coubertin's belief in the importance of ceremony and ritual in consecrating that idea, his Olympic festival's structures are made very visible. At the same time, much is volatile in this festival and open to creative planning, which is what the Nazis turned to fullest advantage in Germanizing it.

Underpinning the Nazis' propaganda windfall was of course the modern Olympic tradition of designating a different place, a different host city, for each occurrence of the festival. Berlin was designated, and by metonymy and by the state appropriation of the festival organization, Nazi Germany became the host of the Eleventh Olympiad. The very fact of the importance of ceremonies to the modern Olympics seemed to authorize the Nazi hosts to express them in as magnificent a manner as possible— outdoing even the Americans at Los Angeles, and implicitly and explicitly reaping the prestige for Nazi Germany (despite Olympic philosophy). The Berlin "Olympia" was given the form of an extraordinary sports complex spread over 356 acres on the western edge of the city. Its monumental heart was the huge stadium seating 110,000 and built for permanence. Then, inspired by the "Olympic Village" housing provided for the athletes by the Californians in 1932, the Germans created their own version. In contrast to the urban expression of the great sports complex, the Berlin Olympic Village was set in idyllic isolation on specially landscaped grounds among birch trees and small lakes ten miles from the sports complex. The buildings, comprised of meeting halls, an Olympic post office, shops and services, and 160 small houses (all also built to last, since they were to serve afterward for a military academy) were planned to house some 3,000 male athletes and their assistants.

The opening ceremony on August 1 and also the closing ceremony on August 16 were superbly planned and as gorgeous as could be imagined. Ritual was emphasized inside the stadium and in other settings. Contest, another common structural element of festival, is of course the heart of the Olympic Games festival. The "Pageant of Youth" exemplified festival use of drama while it put on exhibit disciplined German youth and professional dancers and musicians. Music's role was pervasive. At the crowning of the winners after each event, the national anthem of each winner was played; the crowning of German athletes took longer, because Nazi Germany had two anthems, "Deutschland Uber Alles" and the "Horst Wessellied," and both pieces had to be played. Somehow, too, the Germans succeeded in having their new Olympic hymn, the music to which was commissioned to the most famous living German composer, Richard Strauss, declared the permanent official Olympic hymn in place of the Bradley-Keeler hymn presented at the Los Angeles Games and at first declared the permanent Olympic hymn by the I.O.C.

The Nazi hosts also had a great deal of influence on the structure of *participation*. The most pervasive influence was Hitler's role in the festival. On the plane of the nationalistic performance the Fuehrer was unequivocally the mighty patron of it all, spiritually present in every successful aspect. On the international plane Hitler's image and behavior had to be carefully managed so that they did not too blatantly contradict the respectable illusion of Olympic internationalism, since this could seriously damage the propaganda value of the event. Even so, his fairly faithful presence at the games, his official drives across Berlin standing upright in the open car, and the public adulation of the crowds all put his stamp on the structure of participation on the international plane as well.

Symbolic Action: Dominance Through Divergence. The Nazi organizers' attention to the structures of the festival was designed to culminate in Nazi domination of the festival's *symbolic action* and, further, to direct its effect onto outside reality. The Nazis devised festival structures apparently appropriate to the Olympic spirit but which allowed them to superimpose the symbolic action of the Nazi festival model on that of the Olympic model. The startling difference between these two festival planes was that the reality of the orthodox Olympic festival, with its principles of periodicity and change of locality, suspended and even inverted many norms of everyday reality (even though the philosophers of Olympism envisioned an eventual transference of the festival norm of peaceful competition to behavior beyond the festival), while Nazi festival reality was intended as an intensification, not a suspension nor inversion, of normal Nazi reality (the very state of festive intensity was to carry over into daily life).

The Nazis' strategy of superimposing their festival plane on that of the Olympic festival is fascinating with regard to the strong element of religious pilgrimage in the Olympic festival. With the dramatic exception of the Olympic torch relay, little emphasis was given to the voyage aspect of such a pilgrimage festival, but, rather, to the kind of centripetal force that was to concentrate people (or attention) on the festival place. Special consideration was also given to that place, the Berlin Olympia, as a sort of pilgrimage shrine where visitors and Berliners were to gather in a state of sacred "communitas"—an intense type of experience in which the usual hierarchical order of society and the usual barriers between individuals temporarily give way to a spontaneous sense of communion among equals.[11]

A celebrated symbol of the centripetal force drawing the world into Berlin was a massive bell, which itself made a ceremonial journey from the foundry in the Rhineland to Berlin and to its place at the top of the 249-foot Fuehrer tower on the sports complex. On the bell were various further symbols of Olympia, Berlin, and Germany, and the inscription *"Ich rufe die Jugend der Welt"* ("I summon the youth of the world"). The summons to Berlin was not limited to the young athletes and the spectators to the Games. Nazi organizers saw to it that many others—especially Germans—gathered in various configurations to share this period of communitas. There was, for instance, an International Sporting Press Congress. And an international congress on physical education which lasted a month, together with a great gathering of the "Strength Through Joy" movement, brought in tens of thousands of young people—very few of whom had any chance of being spectators at the Games.

The communitas atmosphere was fostered by all kinds of planning. The severe restrictions that had been put on Berlin's nightlife were removed for this period. Sausages were to be sold for a set price, not by quality but by weight only; other prices for food, lodging, and goods in Berlin were frozen or reduced, and the measures strictly enforced. Lodging was organized for visitors in many thousands of private homes. Berliners were instructed to be extraordinarily hospitable and helpful to visitors, especially foreign ones, and many accepted the assignment with genuine enthusiasm. The most complete equipment for sacred communitas was that of the Olympic Village. Its remote location and idyllic character magically evoked the site of a pagan shrine. It was a "womanless republic"—no woman could even set foot in the compound: the precedent for this departure from normal social structure had been set by the Los Angeles Olympic Village, but at Berlin it was a rather accurate intensification of Nazi social theory.[12] Each of the small houses of the Village was named for a different town in Germany, and decorated with views of that town: Olympia became a concentrated image of Germany.

One brilliantly conceived and executed ritual did indeed dramatize the idea of sacred journey. This was the torch relay from the site of ancient Olympia in Greece to the "New Olympia" Berlin. Four years earlier the Los Angelenos had invented the symbol of an "Olympic flame" which burned in a big brazier for the duration of the Games. For the Berlin Olympics the idea was born of lighting an Olympic flame by the rays of the sun at the ancient stadium in Olympia and bringing the "sacred fire" to the stadium in Berlin. Some 3,000 runners passed the flame from torch to silvery torch (specially designed to meet all the difficult conditions of the race) over some 3,000 kilometers and seven countries day and night from July 22 to August 1. At important cities along the route the sacred flame rested at special altars while elaborate ceremonies were performed. A book about the torch relay printed in Berlin in four languages describes the scene as the runners reached "the mountainous villages of Arcadia": "The inhabitants shout: Hurrah for Germany! With raised arms they call out: Hail Hitler!"[13]

This extraordinary ritual—so extraordinary that it was not expected to be repeated for later Olympics—was in effect a two-way pilgrimage: first to the sacred past at Olympia in Greece, and then to the modern Olympia (the latter voyage symbolically both a link and a transformative move between the past and the present). As the runners of the different countries took part in the relay, and as men, women, and children from all levels of society, in the towns and in the countryside, turned out to see it, the relay did seem to represent their initiation to the great festival of world communitas about to take place in Berlin. At the same time, the destination of the sacred flame was very much Berlin, the capital of Adolf Hitler's German Reich.[14] The link thus symbolically enacted was that between Nazi Germany and its supreme claim to the humanist heritage. This was underscored, for instance, by Hitler's announcement at the opening ceremony of the Games that Nazi Germany would resume and bring to completion the archaeological excavations begun by Germans at Olympia from 1875 to 1881—a proposal which the *Berliner Morgenpost* titled "Adolf Hitler's Gift to the World."[15] By its authorship, reception along the way, destination, and symbology the relay expressed German hegemony at almost every step. It was one more element in the planned centripetal force which established the 1936 Olympic festival site at Berlin as a spiritual center for the civilized world while postulating this centrality as *German* and *permanent*.

Since the Nazi celebration of the 1936 Olympics was designed for the most part as an intensified representation of Nazi reality, actual or projected into the near future, the social order it displayed, such as Hitler's deity-like position in the festival, tended to be the normal order. Even hierarchy established in the competitions could be expected to carry over into nonfestival reality. In fact, Olympic winners who were employed in the army, in Hitler's special units, or in governmental agencies all received promotions. Furthermore, of course, the victory of Germany's athletic team in the Games was to stand for Nazi military, political, and economic superiority—actual or potential. The whole success in hosting the Games was to be seen as a corroboration of Germany's astonishing recovery and shining future thanks to Nazi leadership.

The tenet of Aryan racial supremacy was the one important theme that could not be given full symbolic expression in the Nazi Olympic festival. Besides the pre-game concessions that were made (such as the reinstatement of the partly Jewish German Olympic Committee president Dr. Lewald, the admission of one Jewish and one half-Jewish athlete to the German team, and the temporary removal of road signs with vicious anti-Jewish slogans), the playing out of the games dealt an apparently hard blow to the theory of Aryan supremacy. The American team swept the most prestigious section of the games, the track and field events, mainly through the prowess of its black athletes. Jesse Owens was the biggest winner. The German public was as enthralled as everyone else by him, and everyone was also entranced to observe the friendship that blossomed between Owens and the perfectly Aryan Lutz Long, his only serious rival in the broad-jump event. However, to a great extent, this undoing of Nazi theory and order could be perceived as a temporary phenomenon of communitas and thus be, as it were, absorbed by the Olympic festival plane of reality.

The Making of a Nazi Spectacle

The Nazi organizers were determined to make the 1936 Olympics a splendid spectacle. The spectacle dimension of the festival answered both to Hitler's passion for grandeur and monumentality, and to the aim of projecting the Nazi image as far and as seductively as possible. Spectacle had been part of the Olympic Games from the start, but at first not in such a way as directly or significantly to affect people's perception of the real purpose and function of that festival. John J. MacAloon analyzes the Games' "shift into spectacle," which was already in evidence by the late 1920s and early 1930s, in tandem with "the penetration of the stuff of ordinary life into the public liminality of the Games."[16]

MacAloon rightly defines the modern Olympics as a "ramified performance type" which comprises *spectacle, festival, ritual,* and *game*—each discrete but tightly interrelated genres of performance. This order reflects an inward progression from spectacle as "the most diffuse and ideologically centrifugal" genre to game as "the most concentrated and ideologically centripetal."[17] He goes on to show that with the emergence of the spectacle frame the identity and functions of the other three genres, and the Olympic ideal on which they were based, came into question; the connotation of intellectual and moral ambiguity adhering to spectacle in modern times, the sense that the images which spectacles communicate are "impressive and alluring but should be viewed with suspicion," made the meaning of the whole performance doubtful or ambiguous. In the light of MacAloon's hypothesis one can deduce that the Berlin Games took place at a stage in this process when the old model held well enough so that doubt was not conspicuous, and ambiguity was a fact which the Nazis could turn to their advantage.

The Projection of the Spectacle.   The organizers of the 1936 Nazi spectacle were concerned with fashioning a persuasive image of Nazi Germany and projecting it as much as possible in concurrence with the internationally sanctioned image of the Olympic festival. This projection can be seen as an outward movement and a counterpart to the effort to draw people and action *into* Berlin. Together they worked to make Berlin and Germany a symbolic center of the world. On the one hand the visitors, who were drawn into that center to be intimate spectators at the festival and to view the new Germany for themselves, were expected to go back out into the world as ambassadors of Nazi German "truth." The national commission for foreign tourist travel issued the statement that "foreign tourist travel is an important instrument in winning back Germany's respect and influence in the world"; it was every citizen's responsibility toward the National Socialist State to show extraordinary hospitality and bring no disgrace to the fatherland.[18]

Modern mass media was the other important outward-moving force in the hands of the Olympic festival organizers. The many foreign reporters were pampered with prime seating and an abundance of technical facilities. Putting to use also the most advanced technology, the German national radio set up an "Olympia World Station," and for the first time the Olympic Games were broadcast all over the world. "We could thus in imagination expand the vast space of the arena . . . into a gigantic forum in which all the peoples of the earth were participants and listeners at the Olympic Games," exulted the *Olympia Weltsender*.[19]

MacAloon points out that "spectacles institutionalize the bicameral roles of actors and audience, performance and spectators,"[20] and that this differs from festival's less clear distinction between actors and spectators and is in sharp contrast with ritual's principle of active participation. He also notes that spectacle emphasizes the visual. A brave attempt was made at television broadcasting (local) of the Games, but the medium was too young and the technical results proved very disappointing. However, one tremendous visual spectacle-making project that was successfully undertaken is Leni Riefenstahl's filming of the festival starting from the torch relay. The Nazi Party commissioned the work and provided almost unlimited funds. Riefenstahl and her crew, the only ones allowed to film at the Games, were everywhere—themselves part of the festival and spectacle scene. The resulting film, *Olympia,* in two parts, "Festival of the Nations" and "Festival of Beauty," and five hours long in all, was an artistic creation of great emotional and symbolic power. Most significantly, the film *Olympia* provided a special way to extend the 1936 Olympic festival beyond the festival time as well as space. Riefenstahl's film beautifully captured the effect of the powerful searchlights ringing the stadium that shot their beams into the night sky and then tipped them inward until they met and created a vast temple vault over the closing ceremony on August 16. Soon after the searchlights—and the Olympic flame—were turned off, the artificial reality of the XIth Olympiad dissolved. But the "Olympia" film could regenerate the spectacle at will for many other audiences. In Germany, at least, it was made to serve well in this way (despite the film's loving attention to Jesse Owens!).[21]

The Manipulation of Ambiguity. Ambiguity was created and also masked by the Nazi promotion of the 1936 Olympics as spectacle. The obvious dimension of spectacle in the ritual of the torch relay, for instance, was greatly responsible for its becoming as much a Germanized rite as a rite of active international participation. Moreover, the importance placed on the 1936 Olympic event as both a self-celebratory Nazi German festival and as a propagandistic Nazi spectacle for the world meant that the German people were repeatedly exhorted to the adequate performance of the festival as a "duty" and "obligation" to the National Socialist State and its leader. Thus in some ways festival making was more akin to performance of *ritual.* Festive codes could be ambiguous. For instance, Berliners were directed to put their town in festive costume in ways that would please and impress the foreign visitors. The streets were to be kept clean, the balconies bedecked with flowers, and merchants were to greatly increase their lighting since it had been calculated that "for Berlin to compete with other great cities of the world" its illumination needed to be about five times as strong as it was (the price of electric current for commercial uses would be lowered for the period of the Games)[22]—all as if this were not really festival costume, but the everyday true face of the new Germany.

Game, already paradoxical by nature, was the most explicitly affected Olympic performance genre. On the one hand the words of Reichssportfuehrer (director of all German athletics) Captain von Tschammer und Osten to a gathering of the German Olympic Committee and Olympic athletes left no doubt about the serious spectacle venture that the contests were to be: "Public opinion in the world and in every single country values only absolute achievement in the Olympic Games. The one who wins is the joyfully acclaimed darling of the masses, while the one whose strength or luck was not sufficient is left in the shadows. And what is true for individuals goes for nations as well."[23] This statement also touches on the reason for the popularity of athletic contest for demonstrating relative prestige: the objective measurability of the results. Von Tschammer und Osten went on in his speech to oppose to this mentality of the crass spectator masses the "clear-sightedness of responsible German sportsmen who can judge true achievement quite apart from the winning of gold medals." The Reichssportfuehrer then turned his audience's attention to the great accomplishments of the whole production of the Olympic festival, including the unparalleled structures of the sports complex: in this way he made an appeal for the self-celebratory festival effort (perhaps partly in case the scores in the contest should be disappointing), and also set up a certain legitimizing congruence with the "Olympic Idea" according to which, as Coubertin's recorded voice declared over the loudspeakers at the opening ceremony, "at the Olympic Games it is not important to win, but to take part, just as in life it is more important to play our part bravely than to conquer."

Olympic Games: Metaphor for Peace or for War

There were winners and, in varying relation to them, losers, plainly revealed by the national scores at the end of the Games. Since these scores had to be unofficial, the Germans and the Americans (the two most interested score-keepers) had different scoring systems, but the general results were the same. Germany, which had not shone at previous Olympics, amazingly had both the greatest number of gold medals and the highest overall score. The United States was a not-very-close second on both scores, but could argue that she was the winner in the field events, by far the most prestigious part of the program, while Germany had only been supreme in some of the so-called lesser sports.[24]

All other nations lagged far behind the first two, but conclusions were drawn from the relative strength and prestige of the "lesser" nations as displayed on the rest of the scorecard—conclusions which were clearly applied beyond the special reality of the Games. In the words of Richard Mandell:

> A lesson drawn from the results of the 1936 Olympics was that the totalitarian politics could indeed produce wonders in fields of endeavor that were traditionally believed to be out of bounds for political ideologues. Inspired fascists could defeat decadent democrats in areas where the liberals and democrats had traditionally been supreme. . . . In the light of their performances in the 1936 Olympics the British who were the inventors of both modern sport and of the ideas of justice and democracy were far inferior to the Italians, Hungarians, and Japanese.[25]

There was no question but that this Olympic game "play" was serious, in that there was a readiness on everybody's part to see the hierarchy established by the Games as carrying over into the reality of international politics. The question remains whether the games' oxymoronic "peaceful combat" was at least a metaphor for peaceful rivalry in the world, or not.

Pious words of peace pervaded the 1936 Olympic festival. Everything was heralded as a symbol or an omen for lasting peace. But metaphors and symbols have a notorious potential for multiple meanings which can also point simultaneously in different directions. Competitive games themselves of course have a basic structural similarity to war. It is on that very basis that this metaphor functions—although its active transference to everyday reality goes beyond metaphor. And everyday reality was emitting constant signals of militarism and war. Nations in that reality were very much defined by their armies and, in other words, by their ability to make war—although the tenuous theory was paraded that armies were for protecting the peace. As newspapers of the time reported, all the larger nations were intent on building up their armed forces and their weapons systems. Even Germany's rearmament was no secret, and earlier that year Hitler had daringly moved his troops into the demilitarized zone of the Rhineland. Meanwhile, actual war had burst into Europe in July in the form of a civil war in Spain. The newspapers were full of its extremely bloody events and also of the clear indications of military intervention from other nations.

Within the symbolic sphere of the Olympic festival the idea of war was always ready to be triggered. The very mention of peace implied war. War was represented in artistic form in one section of the "Pageant of Youth," a sword dance in which both dancers died in rhythmic agony: this was supposed to convey the moral that modern war destroys both the victor and the vanquished. The Nazi propagandists had set themselves the tricky double objective of keeping the nations at bay who might too early try to thwart Hitler's plans by intimidating them with indications of Germany's military strength, and also by reassuring them that Germany was not an aggressive nation. Declarations of peace and peacefulness were made repeatedly. At the same time, military and other uniforms were on festive display everywhere. One instance of militaristic display inserted into the festival frame is interesting for having misfired because it was perceived as a clear breach of frame. The French correspondent for the Paris *Figaro* reported the reaction to the inclusion, in one evening's program of film at the Olympic Village, of a film on German youth which ended with views of the German army and parades of weaponry: "unanimous protests showed the Germans that it would be more elegant not to push it," and the film was not given a second showing.[26]

At the opening ceremony in the stadium 20,000 (or by some counts 30,000) white doves, or homing pigeons, were released "like a cloud of peace over the peaceful contests" that were about to begin.[27] This spectacular gesture was a direct answer to the 3,000 doves which had flown up over the stadium at Los Angeles, which in turn was an inflated revival of the flight of some 300 doves at the first Games in Athens in 1896. These 20,000 homing pigeons and some 100,000 more had arrived in Berlin by train in shipment after shipment "from every country in which the homing pigeon sport exists." The other 100,000 were released earlier on the same day from the military playing field in the Spandau district of Berlin. Most of the participants at the stadium knew nothing of this greater flight of doves from unequivocally German territory, but it can serve to remind us that the Olympic athletic complex itself was built by army engineers on land that belonged to the army. The newly built Olympic Village was also army property and had been handed over by the army to the Olympic Committee, for the temporary reign of "Olympia," in a ceremony on July 1.

The Nazi organizers of the 1936 Olympics apparently succeeded in their aim to make of the event a vehicle for the image of a powerful but peace-loving Germany. But this image was a mask with limited utility; the ways in which it diverged from reality soon became irrelevant to the Nazi program. On the other hand, the Olympic festival enactment of Nazi German vigor, joy, competence, unity, progress, cultural grandeur, and physical superiority was designed to be extended into everyday reality and projected into the future in a never-before-attained intensity of politically coordinated socialization, productive activity, and joy fed on a steady diet of Nazi festivity. The Germanizing of the 1936 Olympics was also not necessarily a one-shot affair; Hitler had dreams of giving that transformation monumental permanence too.[28]

With the outcome of the Second World War the dream of a permanently Nazi German Olympic Games went under along with every other aspiration of the Nazi regime. Roger Caillois, writing not long after the Second World War, identified war, "the paroxysm of modern society," as the only phenomenon of our time that offers an analogue to "true, primitive" festival. Their similarity is in "their absolute grandeur, their function in the life of the collectivity, the image which they impress into the soul of the individual."[29] It was surely true, as the *New York Times* correspondent wrote, that the great body of the German people participated in the Olympic Games festival with hope in their hearts for a future of peace. Many of them, especially, who had suffered the horrors of the first war fervently hoped never to see war again. But the ever more intensely coordinated, militarized, and nationalistically exhilarated tenor of Hitler's Germany merged almost naturally into the paroxysm of war.

NOTES

1. Quoted in the *New York Times*, August 1, 1936.

2. This kind of propaganda effort is clearly an example of what Baruch Hazan terms *impregnational propaganda*, as opposed to *operational propaganda*. See Baruch Hazan, *Olympic Sports and Propaganda Games: Moscow 1980* (New Brunswick and London: Transaction Books, 1982), p. 15.

3. Ibid., p. 1.

4. Dr. Josef Goebbels, quoted in the *Berliner Morgenpost*, July 19, 1936.

5. Ibid.

6. It is ironic that this model of Nazi Germany does correspond remarkably to the position of Sparta which made possible the era of Olympia's greatest glory. This powerful militaristic city-state imposed its political protection on the Olympic Games and used them to further its dominance over the variously allied and warring states of the Peloponnesus.

7. See John Hoberman, *Sport and Political Ideology* (Austin, Texas: University of Texas Press, 1984), p. 163.

8. See Beverly J. Stoeltje, "Festival in America," in Richard M. Dorson, ed., *Handbook of American Folklore* (Bloomington: Indiana University Press, 1983), pp. 239–44.

9. *Olympia Weltsender* (Olympia World Station) (Berlin: Reichs-Rundfunk-Gesellschaft m.b.H., 1936), p. 90.

10. Richard D. Mandell, *The Nazi Olympics* (New York: MacMillan, 1971), p. x.

11. See Victor Turner, "Liminal to Liminoid, in Play, Flow and Ritual," *Rice University Studies* 60 (1974): 53–92.

12. The much smaller number of women athletes were housed in drabber fashion elsewhere, including a women's dormitory under the supervision of the Baroness von Wangenheim, near the sports complex. Interestingly, there was also one man in charge there.

13. Victor Kuron, *The Messengers of Peace from Olympia to Berlin* (Berlin: R. Hobbing, 1936), p. 12.

14. The *Berliner Morgenpost* of August 1, 1936, p. 1, heralded the minutely timed arrival of the flame in Berlin saying, "When at 12:50 the Olympic fire reaches the old museum, then the great bridge between the holy city-states of classical Hellenism and the cap-

ital of Adolf Hitler's German Reich will have been consummated."

15. *Berliner Morgenpost*, Aug. 2, 1936.

16. John J. MacAloon, "Olympic Games and the Theory of Spectacle in Modern Societies," in J. J. MacAloon, ed., *Rite, Drama, Festival, Spectacle* (Philadelphia: ISHI Press, 1984), pp. 262–63.

17. Ibid., p. 242.

18. *Berliner Morgenpost*, July 5, 1936.

19. *Olympia Weltsender*, p. 6.

20. MacAloon, p. 243.

21. See Mandell, pp. 270–71 for notes on this, and also on the film's unfortunate fate outside of Germany.

22. *Berliner Morgenpost*, July 11.

23. Quoted in the *Berliner Morgenpost*, July 16, 1936.

24. The tally of German and American medals in Berlin was:

	GOLD	SILVER	BRONZE
Germany	33	26	30
U.S.A.	24	20	12

in Los Angeles, 1932:

Germany	3	13	4
U.S.A.	40	30	28

25. Mandell, p. 205.

26. *Le Figaro*, Aug. 10, 1936.

27. *Berliner Morgenpost*, July 31, 1936.

28. According to Hitler's architect Albert Speer, Hitler dreamed of holding the Olympic Games in the "stadium of the four-hundred-thousand" in Nueremberg "for all time to come." See Mandell, pp. 292–93.

29. Roger Caillois, "War and the Sacred," Appendix III to *Man and the Sacred*, trans. Meyer Barash (Glencoe, Illinois: Free Press, 1959), pp. 168–80. On German festivals of the years preceding the Nazi era, see George Mosse, *The Nationalization of the Masses* (New York: Fertig, 1975), ch. 4 and 5, pp. 73–126. On Nazi propaganda see, for instance, Derrick Sington and Arthur Weidenfeld, *The Goebbels Experiment: A Study of the Nazi Propaganda Machine* (New Haven: Yale University Press, 1943).

11 / Rules of Misrule: Notes on the Doo Dah Parade in Pasadena

Denise L. Lawrence

In spite of their aiming to be valid and representative for all members of their community of reference, festivals sometimes do not succeed in gaining universal consensus. Alternative festivals may then be organized by groups who refuse to identify with the dominant celebration and the values that underlie it. This phenomenon has been observed in American culture since the time of black slaves' festivals. But since the 1960s it has gained nationwide dimension and attention. Segments of urban communities have originated intentional alternatives to the richer, better known, and more glamorous official festivals. Famous examples among many are Santa Barbara's Summer Solstice Parade, New York City's Greenwich Village Halloween, and the Calithumpian Parade in Eastport, Maine. But the most striking of such events is Pasadena's Doo Dah Parade. Initiated in 1978 as an improvised spoof to replace the postponed official Rose Parade, it has rapidly grown into a festive event in its own right.

The detailed description provided here shows first the relationship between the two events: the Rose Parade utilizes a corporate model of organization and is staged with commercially sponsored floral floats dedicated to uncontroversial themes, parading polished, innocuous images of beauty and happiness, and an abundance of smiling beauty queens. The Doo Dah Parade uses instead, as rituals of rebellion typically do, costume, play, and drama for parody and irony, protest and satire, jest and license. Its first target is the Rose Parade, whose formal and symbolic features are systematically reversed, parodied, and amusingly manipulated. In addition, the Doo Dah Parade addresses an autonomous and active message to the Pasadena community: the themes of a number of parading groups deal with crucial political issues such as urban planning and redevelopment, resource management, and the political and economic control of the city by the local elites. Furthermore, a third kind of skit staged by parading groups has as its theme American society, its political figures and key issues, and its way of life at large. Both parades, the author infers, reflect the normative, socioeconomic, and ideological basis of their support groups.

The article then discusses the evolution of the Doo Dah Parade, showing how changes in organization and content result from bureaucratic, economic, ideological, and political factors. The dialectic relationship between civic administration and the parade is largely mediated and interpreted by the lone organizer of the parade, the self-appointed "czar" left in the shadow by the article. As the need arises, this "deus ex machina" develops rules and guidelines to meet bureaucratic requirements without betraying the original character of the event.

As the article's conclusions show, drawing on theoretical statements by Max Weber and Victor Turner, the Doo Dah Parade is a case in point for some fundamental issues in the study of festival: with its explicit programmatic chart of "no rules, no theme, no contest, no prizes, no parade order," the event is now almost ten years old. Is repeated spontaneity going to generate its own rules, or fall within pre-set ones? How long is the demiurgic presence of the czar going to guarantee the parade's free-flowing style? And finally, is such a volatile structure going to survive him? In any case, the Doo Dah Parade has successfully met for a decade a self-imposed challenge: creating rules only to maintain its liberating rule-lessness.

Rules of Misrule:
Notes on the Doo Dah Parade in Pasadena[1]

Denise L. Lawrence

On the first of January 1978, several thousand people who had waited patiently on Pasadena's Colorado Boulevard for the city's annual Rose Parade were greeted instead by the First Occasional Doo Dah Parade. According to custom, the Rose Parade is always postponed one day when the New Year begins on Sunday. Thus, 1978's first Sunday created the ritual void that encouraged a community of artists and counter-culture misfits, led by their "czar," to cavort in the streets. Originally conceived as the "loyal opposition" to the Rose Parade, the Doo Dah intentionally inverted a number of key features of the dominant event. Where the Rose Parade featured innocuous floral beauty and emphasized competition and regulation, the Doo Dah Parade was associated with the expression of outlandish and unconventional behavior and had no rules and no prizes. Although begun in perpetual rebellion, with repetition the Doo Dah has begun to change. This discussion will explore the manner in which the Doo Dah Parade has become an established fact of Pasadena's ceremonial life, and the processes of rule-making which continue to affect its character.

Doo Dah: An American Parade

Pasadena's Doo Dah Parade has many features of a typical American parade. It is a collective linear performance, a procession, by participants for an audience. Participants engage in "special" behavior characterized by costume, mask, dance, marching, music, carrying signs and props, and other dramatic devices. Entries take the form of bands, drill teams, dancers, costumed performers and impersonators, floats, roller skaters, cyclists, and an assortment of animals including dogs, horses, and an occasional elephant. The Doo Dah Parade is a leisure time event; it is held between noon and 2:00 P.M. on the Sunday following Thanksgiving, approximately one month before the Rose Parade. The parade also recaptures the original site of the Rose Parade by proceeding down the streets of Pasadena's historic Old Town. Temporally and spatially the Doo Dah is organized into three parts: a formation area in which participants gather roughly two hours before the parade begins; the actual two-hour procession which weaves its way along the parade route; and a point of dispersal located in a public park where the parade ends.

The Doo Dah Parade has always been a more or less organized event, although its formal structure is a bit unusual. Organizational responsibility rests in the hands of a man who calls himself "czar"—a youngish, occasionally employed public relations professional who emerged as the self-appointed leader from an initial group of Old Town enthusiasts. The czar assumes overall responsibility for coordinating entrants and volunteers, collecting fees, negotiating with the city for the parade permit, and working with various local officials on parade logistics. Ironically, the title *czar* implies an absolute authority which he does not have. While the czar may make decisions about the planning and execution of the parade, he must also submit to city authorities and is concerned about public attendance and approval, especially from the Old Town community, of which the parade is still very much a part.

As a result of the Doo Dah's growing popularity, the numbers of audience members, participants, and volunteers have increased. From 1978 to 1984 the audience grew from several thousand to an estimated 60,000.[2] To accommodate the larger audience, the parade route expanded from its original .4 mile to the current 1.25 miles. The new one weaves back and forth through the streets of the Old Town in order to retain its original sentimental focus. The number of parade participants has also continued to increase; only about 250 individuals appeared in the first years but by 1984 there were roughly 2,500 performers.

Origins

The origins of the Doo Dah Parade are symbolically expressed in a number of rules which constitute a kind of charter for the event. Organizers consciously began in the shadow of the Rose Parade, intentionally inverting the dominant festival's overly rigid organization and innocuous character.[3] The thirteen-hundred-member Tournament of Roses Association consists of a volunteer bureaucracy, while the Doo Dah's minimal organization was vested in the sole authority of the czar. The Rose Parade required competition to gain entry into the parade; the Doo Dah permitted anyone. The Rose Parade had developed an elaborate code of rules and standards for setting parade themes, building the massive floral floats, and awarding prizes;[4] in contrast, the Doo Dah promoted its special lack of censorship and restrictions.

A second series of anti–Rose Parade rules was generated in the early days; these focused primarily on parody, drawing directly on positive aspects of Pasadena's Old Town as a symbolic protest against issues that concerned community members at the time. In Doo Dah's early days, the Old Town was a charming but impoverished and declining section of the city inhabited by members of the counterculture, artists, and the disenfranchised. It had become the object of an urban redevelopment plan which has since transformed the character of the community. The Doo Dah Parade originated as a community protest by focusing on the symbol of the economic and political forces behind the redevelopment scheme: the Rose Parade.[5]

Doo Dah rules that parody the Rose Parade and positively draw on the sense of community are those specifying a Queen (and/or King), a Grand Marshal (or two), and a coronation. Selection of the Queen is based on the czar's decision, after he has consulted with members of the community. Unlike the Rose Queen, the Doo Dah Queen is not chosen according to typical American beauty pageant criteria. A sixty-year-old former Old Town bar and hotel owner, who had created a family atmosphere for her transient and indigent male boarders but lost her operation to urban redevelopment, was honored one year. Once a middle-aged housewife who had never been a "queen" but always wanted to be one volunteered and was accepted for the job. Grand Marshals, selected by similar criteria, have tended to include Old Town bar owners and managers who support the Doo Dah Parade.

There is a tendency for official personages and occasions to lend official order to a parade, a risk the Doo Dah takes. Each year a celebration for the parade is held in an Old Town bar on the occasion of the coronation of the Queen. Typically, a local rock band such as Snotty Scotty and the Hankies plays. None of the local rock bands, however, has been appointed as the official band of the Doo Dah Parade; this honor is reserved for the Loch Ness Monster Pub Pipe Band. The pipe band became "official" one night in the Old Town's Loch Ness Monster Pub when its manager won a bet with the slightly inebriated czar—or so the legend goes. In spite of Doo Dah's rule-less rule specifying no parade order, the pipe band has been the first to lead the parade since it became the official band. Nevertheless, it is the only entry to have a regular place in the parade; the Queen and Grand Marshal must find their own places in line like everyone else. Even the czar and volunteers drift anonymously and unrecognized through the parade as it is performed.

Influences of Civic Government

A parade or festival where crowds assemble in public requires a permit in Pasadena as in most American cities. The permit represents a contract between the parade organizer and the local government for payment of city services in connection with the parade. The city of Pasadena charges the Doo Dah Parade an administrative fee and requires payment for services such as security, public works set-up of barricades and cleaning up afterward, and rental of portable toilets. The permit for the parade also requires the organizer to secure general liability insurance. While the insurance fees are set and paid in advance of the parade, the charges for city services vary each year and are billed to the czar after the event. These city requirements mean that money must be generated for the continuation of the event. If the bills are not paid, a permit request the following year will surely be denied.

The city also has the option of fixing the time and place as a condition for issuing the permit. All city parades, including the Rose Parade, are limited to two hours' duration; normally no other restrictions are placed on the date and location unless there is an obvious logistical conflict. In the case of the Doo Dah Parade, however, the city became involved as a mediator between the parade and community members who opposed the spoof of their "sacred" Rose Parade. In 1979 a local resident wrote to the editor of the city's newspaper:

> The Doo-Dah (it rhymes with "blah") Parade is not only a blatant
> slap in the face to our magnificent Rose Parade, but it is a cheap, tawdry,
> tasteless community affront.
> The Rose Parade represents the epitome of artistic endeavor. It is a
> grand display of community creativity and affords the nation a yearly
> glimpse of the real Pasadena.
> The Doo-Dah Disaster is a pathetically unimaginative hodge-podge of
> thrift-shop assemblages providing a background, and excuse, for a
> mawkish exhibition of public cavorting by welfare beneficiaries who
> should be seeking employment.[6]

Similar sentiments were voiced in a conflict brought by local businessmen to the city to arbitrate. The Doo Dah Parade was always held on the Sunday between Christmas and New Year's Day to sharpen its contrast with the Rose Parade. As the Doo Dah Parade's popularity grew, so did the crowds. By the fifth year local businessmen were complaining that the parade crowds were interfering with after-Christmas sales. The city directors were ostensibly neutral, but some were known to harbor hostile feelings toward the Doo Dah Parade. The manipulation of the date and place of the parade could dilute its effect while officially resolving the conflict. One director, for example, argued for changing the date to the middle of summer, or the site to a remote park in Pasadena, since the Christmas season was already filled with major events in Pasadena. Through the czar's perseverance and the cooperation of a handful of sympathetic city officials, the date was finally set for the fourth Sunday of November, where it now stands. This decision occurred not without renewed opposition from local businessmen, who now argued that the parade would conflict with before-Christmas sales. The continuing protests were ultimately ignored, and the route was changed slightly to avoid interfering with the customers of one very vocal shop owner.

Organizer Rules: Pragmatics

As organizer of the parade, the "czar" is solely responsible for dealing with the parade's logistical problems. He must formulate all the official rules and guidelines and must translate the city's requirements into a workable plan. Similarly, he maintains and articulates the Doo Dah's essential character, its rule-lessness. That some rules are necessary for pragmatic purposes has long been recognized by the Doo Dah community, but these rules are treated either as an unavoidable but necessary evil to be minimally articulated, or as candidates for transformation into spoofs themselves. The czar's general approach to parade organization has been a kind of laissez-faire; if there is a problem, fix it, but otherwise leave well enough alone. In formulating rules and guidelines he takes an experimental attitude, fiddling with the organization to see what works. Finally, the czar maintains one personal rule about rule making: "Never make a rule you can't enforce."

The czar has formulated what he calls "official rules" and a number of guidelines or "rules of thumb" that he and his volunteer helpers use. The official rules, the only ones formally recognized by parade participants and audience members, pertain only to the content of parade performance. One rule requires all animal entries to have a "pooper-scooper" to pick up animal droppings on the parade route. This rule was created the first year of the parade at the suggestion of a city official who was concerned with helping the czar keep clean-up costs at a minimum.

Most other parade rules and guidelines have been created with a more serious intent, usually following a negative experience with the parade. The czar isolates roughly two "crisis" years when he felt it imperative to instigate major organizational changes. The first of these occurred in 1979, the third year of the parade. The biggest problem had been getting the parade to finish within the two-hour limit set by the city. The czar attributed his problem to too many people, to "crashers" who entered the parade without registering, and to too much "dawdling" along the parade route. According to the czar, the parade's growth required him to impose an organizational rule limiting the number of entries to 125. He avoided formulating any rules for the selection of entries, but advertised to participants: "First come, first served." The same year the czar began to ride his bicycle in the parade to supervise the participants and keep the parade flowing. In spite of these minor changes, the parade was, by his own admission, a "mess," and the czar set about to make more drastic changes the following year. Because of the noise, pollution, and audience complaints about the lack of imagination in the automobile entries, a second "official" rule banned all motor vehicles except motorized wheelchairs. Additionally, the czar decided to change the way in which volunteer helpers were recruited. Up to this time he had informally invited a number of his friends to help out, but some of them disappeared during the parade or otherwise failed to assist with important tasks. The czar began to select people on whom he could depend—people he recognized as responsible or experienced in managing parade performers. These volunteer helpers later helped to recruit and train others, which is the system that continues to the present.

By the fifth year, 1981, the czar had initiated additional changes in parade organization. Until this time he had charged participant fees according to the size or type of group: $15 for individuals and groups up to six individuals; $20 for larger groups; and $29.95 for businesses. Some participants felt that the fees were unfair to individuals in small groups who had to shoulder a greater proportion of the costs than individuals in larger groups. Also, because parade costs were increasing, the czar needed to generate more revenues. In 1981 an individual entry fee was established, and by 1984 it cost an adult $4 and a child $2 to participate in the Doo Dah Parade. Still, a major and lingering problem continued to plague the czar: keeping the parade moving. One strategy the czar adopted was to have each entry meet with a parade volunteer before the event to review the logistics and emphasize the importance of finishing the parade on time. By 1984 a new laconic rule was issued: "Keep Moving!" This rule is one the czar realizes he will have trouble enforcing.

Organizing the Organization

Applying for city permits, arranging insurance, paying bills, promoting the event, and coordinating entrants has always involved a certain amount of paperwork and time. With the growth of the parade, the czar has become slightly more sophisticated in its management and coordination. Until 1981 the czar responded personally to telephone and mail requests for application forms. Although he still handles all the paperwork himself, the czar has invested in an answering machine. By 1983 he was renting an official Doo Dah Parade office rather than conducting all business from his home, and around the same time he began investigating the possibilities of establishing a nonprofit corporation to run the parade. When he discovered the problems of leadership among his hand-picked board of directors, he quickly withdrew the proposal. Today the czar runs the event as a "sole proprietor doing business as the Doo Dah Parade," ostensibly a money-making venture. Although the czar has yet to realize any tangible profits from the venture, it has brought him some prestige in the local community. In 1985 he was named to the city's Centennial Celebration Committee.

The Moral Order of the Parade

In spite of the creation of a number of rules and guidelines in recent years, the Doo Dah Parade's original emphasis on rule-lessness has remained relatively intact. There is still no theme, no contests or prizes, and no formal parade order. There is still a strong aversion to censorship, control, or even the subtle direction of entrants' choices of expression and performance. Most of the rules have been adopted to ensure the parade's continuation. The essence of the Doo Dah continues to be found in the participants' collective spontaneous performances. While some types of entries make single appearances, others become regular features. Some of these have evolved over the years, and some types of entries characteristic of the early Doo Dah days have altogether disappeared. These are the ones which made overt and direct satirical references to the Rose Parade or local Pasadena politics.

During the early years, when the Doo Dah Parade still represented a conscious protest against Pasadena's established order, a number of unique but obvious parodies of the Rose Parade appeared regularly. In 1979 an entry entitled the Torment of Roses, featuring a scruffy male impersonator of a Rose Queen, verbally parodied the Rose Parade's sponsoring organization, the Tournament of Roses. The same year, the Sweepstakes Trophie and the Grand Dog Award ridiculed the Tournament's practice of awarding prizes to Rose Parade entries. From time to time "floral floats" have appeared in the Doo Dah Parade; usually these have been "performed" by participants with their heads or torsos decorated in paper flowers. A number of entries have also explicitly satirized Pasadena's political scene. Since roughly 1981, however, there have been almost no entries making symbolic reference to the Rose Parade or local city issues.

The reasons for the gradual change away from symbolic protests against Pasadena's established order are several. During the early years as many as three-quarters of the participants and audience were Pasadena residents, while in more recent years, as the popularity of the parade has grown, non-Pasadenans have dominated. In addition, the Doo Dah Parade itself has finally become accepted by Pasadena officials and by many conservative community members who once opposed it.[7] Without intense opposition by the local elite, the need to parody the established order has largely disappeared.

The moral order of actual Doo Dah Parade performances consists of several tacit rules of participation which have gradually evolved in the absence of any official direction; they have emerged from the continued collective participation of parade performers. Perhaps the most important of these is that all entries have a message. This rule was made very clear by one participant who, after reflecting on the entry of which she was a part, made the point, "Well, everyone here is making a statement, and we thought we wouldn't." Messages may be serious or frivolous, but they must be conveyed with humor and wit. Satire and parody are the vehicles for many clever entries. The judgment of successful, witty entries is diffuse, although at least one audience group consistently attends the parade to flash numbered cards signaling the degree of their approval to parade performers. Another rule is that entries should be of the type that one would not see in the Rose Parade. The Doo Dah's emphasis has been on re-creating the home-town parade without professional performers or organizers.[8] Since "anyone" can legitimately appear in the Doo Dah Parade, entries tend intentionally to lack polish and focus on home-made props, costumes, and performance. Participants often use music supplied by a radio, tape recorder, or nearby band; they may sing or chant; they may dance, march, or perform in other dramatic ways. In fact, most Doo Dah entries include typical parade behavior executed in outrageous, incongruous, or inverted styles. These include costumed marching drill teams; queens, kings, or otherwise distinguished individuals self-appointed or impersonated by entrants; equestrian or other animal entries (dogs and horses are most popular, but elephants, mules, and armadillos have also made appearances); and bands. In addition to the bands, parade entries can be roughly classified into three thematic types: performers who exploit current events; those who elaborate on general social issues; and entries in which participants exaggerate themselves or "clown."

Bands are an essential element of any parade. Doo Dah bands, however, are a little different from those seen in most American parades. Frequent musical participants include the Great American Yankee (GAY) Band, and UCLA and USC Alumni Marching Bands, the Hyperion Outfall Serenaders (the "official band of Manhattan Beach," named after a local sewage treatment plant), and the Humboldt State Marching Band complete with "Kiss Our Axe" firmly imprinted on the seats of their shorts. Kazoo bands are also popular, such as the Marching Leech Kazoo Band whose members dress as giant bloodsuckers. Although kazoo bands do not make a significant musical impact because they lack volume, other bands help provide spacing in parade order. Since there is no deliberate attempt to bring order to participants, entrants simply gather in the formation area before the parade according to their order of arrival. As they rehearse before the parade, bands tend to space themselves so that the volume of music from one group does not compete with another. As groups of participants assemble, they may locate themselves near particular bands in order to use a musical background for their parade performance.

Entries with messages that capitalize on current events usually appear in only one Doo Dah Parade, although the individual performers or the group may reappear in new forms in other years. Almost all the current news entries focus on political issues. Impersonation of key figures and biting satire are the key devices employed.

In 1981, for example, a Nancy Reagan impersonator inspired the entry entitled Let Them Eat Ketchup. Nancy was seated on a throne-like chair before a large banquet table set on a platform that was pulled down the parade route by a motley assortment of raggedly dressed "slaves." She threw what appeared to be table scraps to the poor slaves and audience. The reference was to the Reagan government's attempt that year to have ketchup classified as a vegetable in school lunch programs. On another level, however, this parody referred to Marie Antoinette's infamous remark on the eve of the French Revolution: "They have no bread; let them eat cake."

Such humor is typical of the parade in general. In 1979 a Richard Nixon impersonator appeared carrying a sign claiming "I'm No Crook!" Two years later a protest against the California Peripheral Water Canal state ballot measure appeared in the parade. Featured were a group of tuxedoed "fat-cat" politicians in collusion with an impersonator of Jerry Brown, then governor of California, and Central Valley agribusinessmen. The performers carried signs and attacked observers with water-filled squirt guns. In 1982 a Ronald Reagan impersonator led a group of blind men who walked with canes down the parade route, chanting in unison "Trickle-Down, Trickle Down" in direct reference to Reagan's theories of income redistribution.

More recently a number of entries have appeared carrying MX Missiles or signs announcing "Get the US Out of El Segundo" (a local southern California harbor, the site of multinational oil refineries, whose name sounds like a Latin American country). In 1983 one entry capitalized on the recent U.S. invasion of the Caribbean island of Grenada by carrying signs asking "Which way to Grenada Club Med?" and featuring a Ronald Reagan impersonator dressed as a caveman toting a sign declaring "2 Wrongs Make It Right." In 1982 a group had sought to ridicule then–Secretary of the Interior James Watt by carrying a sign listing the members of the "James Watt Committee: A Woman, A Black, Two Jews, and A Cripple." Other members of this entry carried signs calling for the "nuking" of whales. In Doo Dah Parades preceding and following the 1984 Summer Olympic Games, held in the Los Angeles area that includes Pasadena, a few spoofs appeared. Before the event, some participants carried signs advertising counterfeit tickets and gas masks to help visitors cope with the smog. After the event one entry with over 100 participants reviewed memorable moments of the Games including the opening ceremonies, with performers playing toy pianos hanging from their necks, and several sports competitions, including water polo and synchronized swimming.

Closely related to these politically oriented "single-issue" satires are entries that parody general social issues. These groups also feature impersonation of important individuals and can incorporate specific issues each year to vary their performances. Generally, however, such entries appear in roughly the same garb every year and become well known among parade enthusiasts. In the early years of the parade, the "Immoral Minority" made several appearances. Symbolically inverting the Moral Majority movement visually as well as verbally, members of this entry marched in mock drills and flagged "left wings," fringed affairs attached to their left arms. In 1981 the Ladies Against Women made the first of a continuing series of appearances. The Ladies, members of a local university's women's center, appeared as impersonators known as Phyllis Shifty (Schlafly) and Virginia Cholesterol, who were accompanied by "real men": The Reverend Gerry Fallgood (Fallwell) and Generalissimo Alexander Hog (Haig). The Ladies carried signs announcing "Make Virginity a Requirement for

High School Graduation" and "Ladies—Rock the Cradle, Not The Boat!" In 1984 one member of this entry exploited a current news item by carrying a sign that referred to one of the year's presidential campaign issues, saying, "Reagan Is Not Senile. He Can Recall Everything, Including Missiles."

The Cancerettes have also made repeated appearances with an entry of less political interest but an equally biting social commentary. Organized by a group of ex- and current smokers who work for the American Cancer Society, the entry was conceived as a means to both protest against and educate the public about the falsely glamorous image of smoking promoted by commercial advertising. In an intentional spoof of 1950s television ads featuring dancing girls dressed in cigarette package costumes, the participants wear similar costumes, each clearly labeled with a cigarette brand name: "Old Mold" (Old Gold), "Bad Air" (Bel Air), "Yukky Strike" (Lucky Strike), "Fool" (Kool), and "Chest-a-Fire" (Chesterfield). Not to be outdone by the Cancerettes are the Mutant Queens who have also been appearing in the parade since 1981. The Queens began by wearing 1950s chiffon cocktail dresses, sporting black lips and nails, with rhinestone tiaras gracing their "cone heads." Their message is that if our society's fascination with nuclear power continues, future standards of feminine aesthetics may of necessity change to include some rather bizarre mutant forms. In more recent years the Mutant Queens have continued with their head gear and makeup but have changed their dresses to other flamboyant attire such as striped, plaid, and flower-printed shorts, shirts, and dresses.

A number of groups who make repeat performances, some of which have become Doo Dah "classics," appear as exaggerations of themselves, or at least exaggerate one of their many roles. Sometimes no exaggeration is necessary because simply appearing as oneself within the context of the parade is funny; for example, the elderly residents of a local convalescent hospital paraded in their wheelchairs one year. Many entries, however, appear in drill-team performances dramatizing some exaggerated aspect of their everyday life by marching, chanting, and employing other dramatic actions. Perhaps the most famous of all Doo Dah performers is the Synchronized Briefcase Drill Team. The drill team members are male and female bank loan officers who wear gray flannel suits and execute precision drill performances with their briefcases. The original intent of this group was to have a good time by making fun of themselves, and to try to improve the stodgy public image of bankers. So successful is this group that they have appeared on television and, recently, in a rock video; in 1984 each member reportedly earned $6,000 for public performances.

The drill team format has been so appealing that a number of other entries have employed this device. The bankers' closest competition appeared in 1982 as the Dull Men of Newport Beach. Also dressed in dark business suits, they carried portable leaf blowers with strings of ivy permanently attached. The second year their drill team carried large screw-shaped "drill bits" as props. Since 1980 the Stewardesses, dressed in regulation airline uniforms, have toted suitcases and asked the audience if they want "Coffee, tea, or milk?" They have recently expanded their performance to include a demonstration of the use of airplane oxygen masks which supposedly fall from the ceiling when cabin pressure drops. Also popular is Toro, Toro, Toro which performs its drills with gas-powered lawn mowers; the Keep It Clean entry which features bathers, each "wearing" a portable shower and scrubbing one another with long-armed brushes; and the Unknown Shoppers who, with paper bags over their heads, push shopping carts.

Finally, several entries use extensive props to convey an exaggerated image of themselves. Dr. Jim the Dentist has added new props almost every year since he first appeared in 1980. In addition to the oversized tube of toothpaste and brush, the tooth villain Mr. Decay dressed in black, Dental Flossie, and the Tooth Fairy, Dr. Jim has recently added a "mouth" consisting of a hinged teeth-and-gums affair with a wiggly pink tongue inside. The "mouth" opens and shuts as the prop is pushed down the parade route while Dr. Jim demonstrates proper teeth-cleaning techniques. Dr. Jim's goal, besides having a good time with his office staff who volunteer to perform, is to improve dental awareness among the public. A similar type of entry which uses extensive props is The Press. Since 1983 this group has made regular appearances with cameras flashing, tape recorders running, and pencil and paper in hand, by rushing into the audience on one side of the parade route, then the other, in order to "get their story."

A number of individuals who come as themselves, or as exaggerated aspects of themselves, and appear as clowns are also to be found in the Doo Dah Parade. Three in particular have been popular performers. In 1983 Lynn Klein, a Jewish American Princess (JAP), flew in from Miami Beach to make an appearance in the Doo Dah Parade. She wore a Bloomingdale's University sweatshirt and calmly filed her nails as she walked down the parade route. A buxom older lady wearing a T-shirt reading "Skateboarding Grandma" has made a number of regular appearances on her skateboard. Weaving her way back and forth between both sides of the street, she usually cycles through each parade at least twice. Finally, there is Zeke the Sheik who talks in rhyme, dresses in a white sheet, and drags along with him his "pet" reinforcing bar on wheels. It is impossible to have a "normal" conversation with Zeke, even outside the context of the parade, and yet his nonsensical wit seems to capture the very essence of the Doo Dah Parade. Says he,

> I am
> Zeke the Sheik with the sleek physique from Battle Creek,
> The man with the plan in the caftan,
> With Levar the rebar from Corona Del Mar,
> The brightest, most bizarre
> Popular
> Star
> By far
> And, "Baby, you can drive my car."[9]

Conclusion

Although unique in character, the Doo Dah Parade is not an isolated phenomenon in contemporary American culture. It belongs, as do a number of similar events, to a class of festivals that have appeared since 1975, which I have termed "alternative parades."[10] In Santa Barbara, California, the Summer Solstice Parade provides a noncommercial, nonalcoholic, community arts festival that directly contrasts with the city's historical, elite-sponsored Fiesta Days celebration. Residents of New York City's

Greenwich Village created a Halloween Parade which spoofs the city's better-known Macy's Thanksgiving Day Parade by having the audience move along a route dotted with mini-theatrical performances before they join the milling crowds of costumed ghosts and ghoulies. Each parade consciously borrows critical formal features from the major event (procession, props, costumes, drama) and ritually reverses their expression in order to symbolize an alternate set of community values.

While the creators of Santa Barbara's and New York City's festivals consciously provide their events with a specific alternative theme and organizing structure, Doo Dah was created with an aversion to and explicit avoidance of rules. As a doubly rebellious creation, the Doo Dah sought to protest against the overly rigid Rose Parade by perpetually undoing it. As the Doo Dah Parade approaches nearly a decade of annual performances, however, repetition has given way to regularity, apparent in the increasing number and formality of its rules and guidelines. Many of the rules have emerged as a result of the parade's growing popularity and increasing size in the context of a bureaucratized urban environment. On the other hand, the parade's ideological emphasis and the founders' intentions are carefully preserved by its charter and spontaneously expressed within the protected arena of parade performance. The moral order of the Doo Dah Parade, established in rule-lessness, has taken on its own "traditional" character, reveling in parody and satirical dissent.

Institutionalizing inherently unstable sociocultural forms, such as ritual disorder and spontaneity, is theoretically as well as pragmatically problematic.[11] Conceptually, and at a gross structural level, the states of order and disorder contradict and oppose one another. In preliterate societies symbolic and ritual inversions take on specific recognizable forms.[12] Ritual disorder is often safely contained within the liminal phase, where it acts to encourage members of small-scale homogeneous communities to achieve communitas, the elevated sense of collective belonging.[13] In these societies rules can be ritually broken in order to heighten social awareness of values and norms. Because these rebellious aspects of ritual are embedded within a larger ritual context, they are sacred; and because they are played out in a holistic cultural setting where norms are largely unquestioned, they act to reinforce the social order.

Ritual disorder in modern society is problematic because, although ritual processes are similar, the forms they take in complex societies are not easily identified. Some argue that tribal rites of rebellion cannot be maintained in complex and highly fragmented modern societies because they are too threatening to the social order and those in power.[14] When aspects of ritual and symbolic disorder are institutionalized, however, they represent a process of transition from collective spontaneity to social structure. Turner exemplifies one approach in his definition of *normative communitas:* "the attempt to capture and preserve spontaneous communitas in a system of ethical precepts and legal rules."[15] Turner emphasizes that organization may be directed at protecting ideological features that permit liminality and communitas to continue for a particular community after repetition and regularization of social relations have occurred.[16] In the case of the Doo Dah Parade, rules have been consciously created to protect and maintain the rapidly growing event in the face of potential bureaucratic encroachments. It is clear, however, that a single integrated community, engaging in spontaneous and existential communitas, did not create the Doo Dah Parade. Rather, Doo Dah grew from an already fragmented societal structure and, as its appeal has grown and spread, the community of supporters has become even more heterogeneous.

Doo Dah is what Turner calls a liminoid experience; liminal-like but clearly belonging to the partial realm of play and leisure-time pursuits of modern society rather than to the realm of sacred ritual.[17]

Weber also treats the topic of regularizing spontaneous phenomena by the routinization of charismatic authority.[18] He argues that the economic survival of a group of followers and the need for smooth succession of leadership are paramount in changing an organization from otherworldly to routine.[19] By focusing on the considerations of internal organization, Weber finds the ultimate structural expression of routinization in traditional or legal-rational bureaucratic forms, or a combination of both. Although the Doo Dah might be said to be routinizing along traditional and legal-rational, as well as inverted legal-rational, lines, this regularization is not the result of the needs of followers. The Doo Dah does not constitute a charismatic movement; rather, routinization seems to be related to the necessities of surviving in an already overbureaucratized environment.

Doo Dah does have, however, a kind of charismatic leader in the czar, from whom the parade derives much of its organization and impetus for a continued existence. As Weber points out, the succession of a leader is paramount to the maintenance of any movement, although it may be yet too early to know about succession for Doo Dah Parade leadership. While a decade seems like a long time to maintain an American ritual of rebellion, the event has not yet extended beyond the lifetime (or midlife crisis) of one man. Perhaps the real verdict on the regularization and maintenance of the Doo Dah Parade cannot be delivered for several more decades.

Notes

1. Continuing field research on the Doo Dah Parade, Pasadena, California, began in 1980. In addition to participant observation and intensive interviewing of volunteers, community members, and performers, research methods include the continued use of videotape recordings and photographic documentation of the parade. A preliminary version of this paper was presented at the International Congress of Americanists meetings, October 1982, Manchester, England.

2. *Los Angeles Times*, November 26, 1984. Because the first Doo Dah Parade was held on January 1, 1978, to an audience mistakenly awaiting the Rose Parade, the audience was unusually large. The second Doo Dah Parade, held in December of the same year, attracted far fewer observers but did so on its own merit.

3. Denise Lawrence, "Parades, Politics, and Competing Urban Images: Doo Dah and Roses," *Urban Anthropology* 11 (1982): 155–76.

4. Arnold Rubin, "The Pasadena Tournament of Roses," in *The Visual Arts: Plastic and Graphics*, ed. Justine Cordwell (The Hague: Mouton, 1979), pp. 669–716.

5. Lawrence, "Parades, Politics."

6. *Pasadena Star News*, February 14, 1979.

7. See the interview with the czar on the front page of the local paper, *Pasadena Star News*, November 23, 1984.

8. In recent years many local Southern Californian municipalities have been able to hire professional parade organizers and performers to put on their so-called "community" parades. This mode has been overwhelmingly rejected by Doo Dah supporters and sympathizers.

9. Zeke the Sheik, quoted in *A Pictorial History of the Pasadena Doo Dah Parade*, ed. Peter Apanel (Pasadena: Pasadena Doo Dah Parade, 1982), p. 12.

10. It is obvious that the creation of new parades is a continuous historical process; however, the several parades noted here, and

others which capitalize on already established events also begun since 1975, share certain features in common. For example, each of the parades was initiated by young (age 25–35-year-old) artists and have attracted the attention of community residents of generally the same age group. Also, the fact that these parades are focused on particular communities, rather than national movements, seems to reflect the interests of post–Viet Nam young people.

11. Sally Falk Moore and Barbara G. Myerhoff, "Introduction to Part One" in *Symbol and Politics in Communal Ideology: Cases and Questions* (Ithaca: Cornell University Press, 1975), pp. 27–32.

12. Arnold van Gennep, *The Rites of Passage*, trans. Monika B. Vizedom and Gabrielle L. Caffee (Chicago: University of Chicago Press, 1960); Max Gluckman, *Custom and Conflict in Africa* (New York: Barnes and Noble, 1956); Victor Turner, *The Ritual Process* (Chicago: Aldine, 1969).

13. Turner, *The Ritual Process*, p. 96.

14. Gluckman, *Custom and Conflict*, p. 134.

15. Victor Turner, "Variations on a Theme of Liminality," in *Secular Ritual*, ed. Sally Falk Moore and Barbara G. Myerhoff (Assen, The Netherlands: Van Gorcum, 1977), p. 46.

16. Victor Turner, *Dramas, Fields and Metaphors* (Ithaca: Cornell University Press, 1974), p. 269.

17. Idem, "Liminal to Liminoid, in Play, Flow, and Ritual: An Essay in Comparative Symbology" in *From Ritual to Theater* (New York: Performing Arts Journal Publications, 1982), pp. 20–60.

18. Max Weber, *The Theory of Social and Economic Organization* (New York: Free Press, 1947), pp. 363–86.

19. Ibid.

12 / Riding, Roping, and Reunion: Cowboy Festival

Beverly J. Stoeltje

On occasion, new festivals become established in a cultural setting to celebrate not an ethnic or religious group, a ruling class or a monarch, but instead an occupational group. One of the most famous and widespread of these in the United States is the festival of cattle-raising people which features rodeo as its biggest attraction. The rodeo, surrounded by music, dancing, feasting, and ritual, for many Americans still represents the true spirit of the West and the frontier heritage, and has captured the imagination of people all over the world as the most eloquent embodiment of the Spirit of America. This event was elaborated into a meaningful festivity using the idiom offered by the cowboys' life-style and cattlemen's culture.

This study concentrates on one traditional, regional, noncommercial festival, known as cowboy reunion, held annually for four days in West Texas. Organizers, audience, and participants are mostly residents of the region and active bearers of traditional cattle culture. With friends and visitors, they participate in feasts, dance, and rodeo.

While a particular festival is described and discussed here, the analysis bears on the theory and interpretation of rodeo as a genre, and of festival at large. Using methodology based on the classic works of Kenneth Burke and Victor Turner, the dis-

cussion analyzes rodeo as a symbolic enactment of cowboy culture, organized according to the principles of ritual drama. And since the social interaction and dynamics of this microcosm, argues the author, include conflict as well as harmony, the rodeo orchestrates events of two different kinds: contexts symbolizing work relationships and clown acts symbolizing play forms into a ritual drama. Occupational skills and worldview are represented, displayed, and dramatized in each segment of the rodeo. In the analysis, a set of implicit associations of images and ideas are developed into an explicit series of opposing terms arranged into a "dramatic alignment" between the opening and closing terms. A dialectical movement oscillating between the opposing principles structures the system, and the rodeo performance progresses through this alternation, which allows for the maturation of a "happy route" to the end, in spite of the expression of conflict resulting in competition, victory, and victimization.

Turning to social context, Stoeltje shows how cowboy culture rests upon an economic enterprise in which animals are central. Therefore it is not surprising that in rodeo animals are designated as the symbolic vehicles for the enactment of social meanings, specifically the attitude toward nature and wilderness, the relationships between the cowboy employee and the cattleman employer, and between female and male. Furthermore, the analysis shows that rodeo events express an American ideological conflict which opposes play forms to work forms and, through the changing relationship between human and animal realms, alternates the dominance of work and the dominance of play. Far from being resolved, the dialectics between the wild and the tame continue in this All-American show, featuring the challenge of the wild and the cowboy's determination to win and tame it.

Riding, Roping, and Reunion: Cowboy Festival

Beverly J. Stoeltje

John Adams wrote in 1776 that independence would be celebrated as the great anniversary festival of the United States. He believed the festival should include acts of devotion to God and "pomp and parade, with shows, games and sports, guns, bells, bonfires and illuminations, from one end of this continent to the other from time forward, forevermore."[1]

Since their beginning these festivals have reflected the interests of local populations. In the American West the national holiday has been wedded to the cowboy rodeo in many communities. The four-day Texas Cowboy Reunion, since 1930 one of these traditional July 4th rodeo celebrations, is held in Stamford, Texas.

The old-time cowboy occupies a position of honor at the Reunion, for the event was initially conceived as a reunion for the older cowboys who had been the first to work on the large ranches of the area. The occasion has evolved to mean reunion for all those who feel that they belong to this tradition or have ties to the region.

As in festivals everywhere, many activities attract the attention of the participants, including a memorial service for deceased cowboys, fiddle contests, a horse show, and private parties at homes and campsites. However, the central and largest event is the rodeo itself, held once each day of the celebration in the arena built for the performance. Here the significant features of life in cattle culture are enacted in contest form. Because this rodeo-reunion is embedded in the tradition of a cattle-ranching region, it is appropriate to interpret rodeo in a social context, and, therefore, possible to comprehend it as a symbolic performance.

While humans and animals are clearly in competition with each other when a cowboy attempts to ride a bucking horse or a bull or to rope a calf, staying on the animal's back or catching the calf seem like small matters to those who have witnessed the life-or-death contest of a bullfight, or even the intensity of a horse race. Yet the cowboy rodeo communicates its message through action and words as do other cultural performances, using the animals as symbolic resources to say more than might appear at first glance. In addition to the textual relationship between human and animal, rodeo expresses contextual tensions inherent in the social life of cattle people, and, on a more abstract level an ambivalence basic to American culture.

While the people of America are so diverse that it is impossible to generalize about all groups, certain themes have long been a preoccupation with a majority of the people. Preeminent among these has been work, a subject of concern to philosophers and politicians as well as economists, educators, and the working class.[2] Yet a concern with work must inevitably lead to a confrontation with play. Many voices in the United States were engaged in a dialogue on the relationship between work and play in the second half of the nineteenth century, while cowboys and cattle people were settling the West and establishing a society based on cattle raising. On the ranges of the West, however, in contrast to the factories of the East, the boundaries between work and play were malleable. Although the cowboy was a wage earner who worked for a cattleman who was striving to make a profit, the nature of the work itself was determined by the seasons and the animals, not by a clock or factory. Cattle raising then by its very nature incorporates elements of nature and elements of the capitalist economy, and the cowboy role integrates both the demands of the economy and those of nature, defining him as a worker in economic terms but a player in terms of the free choice and license granted him periodically by the natural cycle of his work. It is no coincidence then that the cowboy serves as a vehicle for the enactment of this conflict in ideology over work/play.

At the sociological level, cattle raising attracted large investors and monopolists as well as cowboys and small ranchers. Social conditions on the cattle frontier did not provide institutional means for mediating the conflicts of interest which so frequently arose between the two types. But the factors which set the corporate ranch and the individual cowboy in opposition were incorporated into the social structure of cattle-raising society. Thus, as open conflict was reduced on the range and permanent settlements were established, two separate social groups became apparent: the cattleman (a business man) and the cowboy (a wage earner or small family rancher).

Rodeo developed as a public event simultaneously with the settlement of the West, and incorporated these social tensions from within cattle-raising society as well as the tensions of the larger American culture between work and play. Consequently, both social and ideological concerns permeate rodeo. The two levels of meaning are expressed in rodeo through the actions of humans and animals. As animals are the substance of everyday life, it is not surprising that they serve as the means for enactment, the symbolic vehicles.

The event, rodeo, however, sets up a series of actions that place man and animal in competition. The question then arises as to the meaning of animals if rodeo is about social relations and ideology. From the point of view of symbolism, one may question why the contests between man and animal do not drastically alter the state of the animal or the cowboy. That is, neither animal nor man is subdued, killed, or consumed by the other as in many ritual events of other cultures that involve animals.

Answers to these questions are embedded in the very nature of cattle culture. Involvement with animals defines the lives of cattle-raising people regardless of the degree of modernization utilized in the process. Therefore, the structure of this occupationally based social group is very strongly influenced by the processes of nature—rain and drought, fertility, birth, and death, disease and health. Yet the motivation for this full time occupation with animals and nature is to sell cattle for a profit in a sophisticated economic system.[3] Cattle then integrate primary natural processes with an economic system. Such a wide range of features results in a complex social order that defines meaning at a point where human, animal, and economics intersect. The motive of this occupationally based culture being the production of cattle for profit, relationships between human and animals and humans and humans reflect roles in the production of cattle. As the social order is built upon the system of animal production, social meaning then is bound up in relationships that involve animals. More concretely, cowboys are defined as those who handle cattle, and cattlemen are those who own cattle. Cowboys earn a monthly or daily wage, and cattlemen collect profits from the sale of cattle. Cowboys or cowhands manage cattle, primarily by means of riding a horse trained as a cow horse, and cattlemen manage money. Cattle signify money, their value being determined by the current price per pound they command on the market.

The cowboy is defined occupationally by his special skills. He must be able to tame unbroken horses (broncos), rope cattle, and, as is often said, "to know" cattle—how they move around, how to manage them, herd them, doctor them, sort them out, castrate them, and care for them so that they will thrive and grow. As he does not often work directly under the eye of his boss, he must be trustworthy as well. As a cowboy does not always own his own horse, he must ride one that belongs to his boss, so the cattleman values the cowboy's skills as a horseman. The cowboy values a boss who respects these skills and demonstrates respect for the cowboy's work. Thus the relationship between cowboy and cowman, and that between cowboy and animals, give *cowboy* specific meanings beyond that of labor. As these relationships involve skills with animals and certain shared values, the actions of rodeo represent these social and cultural meanings through the relationships presented. Thus what cattle people do in relation to animals reflects information about *social order,* and consequently animals serve as symbolic vehicles, as through them the available resources—human, animal, economic—are arranged into meaningful units of action.

In rodeo, the major public performance of cattle people, the performance action is derived from actions recognizable to cattle people as basic to raising cattle which thus carry certain meanings. However, by framing, sequencing, and defining these actions as competition with rules and judges, the rodeo transforms familiar actions into ritual, drama, and sport.

During the past hundred years rodeo has developed a standardized form and sequence of actions with rules governing the contest events. Although variations may occur certain events and rules have become standard procedure for traditional and professional rodeo. The sequence of events occasionally varies also, but a certain pattern is always evident. Professional rodeos are required to hold the basic events so that cowboys can compete in rodeo all over the nation and total up points from each one, but local nonprofessional rodeos generally follow similar patterns.

The usual sequence of events in rodeo looks like this:

> Grand Entry
> Introductions
> Bareback Bronc Riding
> Cowgirl Barrel Race
> Special Act
> Saddle Bronc Riding
> Calf Roping
> Wild Mare Race
> Double Mugging
> Special Act
> Bull Riding

A formal rodeo always opens with a *Grand Entry*, during which the arena fills with horses and riders moving in a serpentine pattern, crisscrossing the space and exiting through the same gate that serves as the entrance. Riders carrying the national and state flags enter the arena first and stand at the entrance while the riders pass by single file but grouped into categories of cowgirl sponsors, riding groups, judges, and individual contestants. When the arena has emptied, rodeo officials and prominent individuals are introduced in the arena, and the national anthem is played.

Rodeo contests actually begin with the *Bareback Bronc Riding*. In this event a cowboy attempts to ride a bucking horse (bronc) without a saddle for eight seconds. A "pick-up man," a man on a horse, lifts the cowboy off the horse if he is not bucked off. Points are awarded by judges for a successful ride based on the style of the cowboy's ride and the wildness of the horse. Here, as in the other riding events, the cowboy with the highest score is the winner.

In the *Cowgirl Barrel Race*, a cowgirl races her horse around three barrels set in the arena, forming a cloverleaf pattern. The cowgirl who makes the run in the fastest time wins.

Saddle Bronc Riding, similar to Bareback Bronc Riding, requires a cowboy to ride a saddle bucking horse (bronc) for eight seconds. Here too a "pick-up man" removes the cowboy from the horse after the ride, and a judge scores the ride on the basis of style if the cowboy rode for eight seconds.

A *Special Act* brings a clown into the arena to perform a rehearsed act with a trained animal. Alternatively, the act may consist of one or two trick riders performing a variety of difficult tricks on their trained horses.

A cowboy contestant in the *Calf-Roping* event rides a horse trained for rodeo roping and chases a small calf, ropes it, gets off the horse, and throws the calf to the ground and ties three legs together. The tie must hold for six seconds, timed by a mounted judge in the arena. The cowboy who completes the action fastest wins.

Three untamed horses without saddles and with a rope around the neck are released into the arena for the *Wild Mare Race*. Three teams of three cowboys each attempt simultaneously to catch the horses and saddle them, and one cowboy from the team then rides the saddled horse the length of the arena and back to the starting point. The team to complete this set of actions first wins the contest.

Another roping event, *Double Mugging*, allows two cowboys to rope together as a team. A very large yearling calf is the animal to be roped, and either of the cowboys can rope the calf, while both men together throw the calf and tie its legs together. Only one contestant or team appears in the arena at a time. When each cowboy or set of cowboys has attempted to rope the calf, the times are compared, and the fastest time wins.

In the *Special Act*, the audience is again entertained by a clown performance or trick riding or trick roping. These performers are under contract for their performance, and there is no contest involved. Because they are rehearsed dramatic presentations and are not competitive they are labeled *acts* in contrast to the contest *events*.

Although the final event, *Bull Riding*, is a bucking event, it is significantly different from the three earlier events of this type. The animal that the cowboy attempts to ride in this event is a large bucking bull, and the cowboy must stay on for the minimum eight seconds. In place of the pick-up man on a horse who rescues the bronc riders, in this event a clown performs antics in close proximity to the bull in order both to stimulate his bucking and to distract him from the cowboy when he is bucked off, whether it is before or after the eight-second buzzer has sounded. (The clown is not on a horse and has no protection.) For this event the clown is known as a bullfighter but is dressed as a clown. The cowboy who stays on the bull for eight seconds and receives the most points from a judge for his style wins the contest. When the last bull ride is completed, the rodeo performance is over.

Addressing attention to the setting of the ritual drama, the Texas Cowboy Reunion (and many other important rodeos as well as the original of the related form, the Wild West Show), occurs on the holiday of national independence, July 4. This blending of the cowboy ritual drama with Independence Day constitutes "a matching of the important with the important,"[4] each feature contributing something of its significance to the other and thereby ritualizing the actions, for art converts "truth" into a symbolic process by excluding the irrelevancies and providing form.

The rodeo begins with a ceremony, the *Grand Entry*, ritualizing the cowboy act of riding by matching riders and horses with the national holiday, the flags, and the national anthem. Further, this ceremony "opens" the work, presenting the statement of the situation from which it arose, demonstrating the social order of cattle culture in the procession of riders moving through the arena.

Following this statement, the rodeo then begins the dialectical movement, playing out the competitive collaboration of opposing principles through variations on riding until the cowboy achieves a transformation and enacts a counterstatement in the bull riding with the aid of the clown.

The "emic" classification of rodeo performance distinguishes the opening ceremony, the Grand Entry, from the action which follows, separated into contest events and special acts (the clown and trick rider performances). Contest events are of two kinds: riding or bucking, and roping. This distinction is based upon the relationship between human and animal as it is acted out in the event: the rodeo animal may represent (a) an untamed creature, (b) an animal trained for working cattle, or (c) an animal trained to perform as if it had human abilities. We can distinguish between action that represents the *work* of the cowboy—the contest events (a, b)—and action that represents *play* and is performed for entertainment only—the special acts (c). In the sequence of the rodeo, the latter separates the bucking events from the tamed horse events. As Figure 1 shows, the sequence of action alternates between the two kinds of contest events.

These two categories of contest events represent two opposing principles. The category on the right side presents the cowboy in a competition with a wild (bucking) animal. The animal dominates here, as the question is whether or not the cowboy will be able to ride the horse. The category on the left side (roping and barrel racing events) presents a team made up of tamed horse and rider. Thus this category is human dominated. Animal Dominance and Human Dominance constitute the opposing principles. As the rodeo progresses, each subsequent event borrows features from the opposing principle to increase the complexity and move the dialectic. To move from one of the opposing principles to the other, the Special Acts serve as contrastive action, mediating the dialectic as it progresses. Collaboration occurs here also, as the opposing principles eventually borrow from the mediator as well. The specific features of each act and event demonstrate this movement.

Human Dominance Events

These events are preceded by the Grand Entry, the uncontested statement of the social order, a procession of the population all riding tamed horses in a pattern through the arena. The contest events in this category include, in order, Cowgirl Barrel Racing, Calf Roping, Double Mugging (or another variation of roping). All of these events present a rider on a tamed horse, trained for the purpose of barrel racing or roping. Time takes on primary importance as a part of each of the contests: the question is which horse-and-rider team can accomplish the action in the fastest time. Not only then does the human dominate the animal, but the race against time functions as definitive, integrating a feature from the modern world of technology into the contest between man and animal.

When the female riders race through the arena, creating a cloverleaf pattern in the first contest of the Human Dominance principle, several features emerge for consideration, central to all of them being the significance of the female rider, the cowgirl.

Like the roping event to follow, the barrel race pairs horse and rider as a team, and together they engage in a race against the clock. There is no competition between human and animal, only that between the horse/rider team and the clock. Each cowgirl and her horse make their run individually in the arena; when the final contestant has exited from the arena and her time is announced (in seconds), the times are compared and the first, second, and third place winners can be determined on the basis of the fastest times.

Barrel racing is unique among the rodeo events in that it features females. Moreover, the female barrel race is the only contest event that follows a pattern, and does not set human and animal in competition at all. In place of the animal as opposition (the bucking events), or the animal as obstacle (the roping events), barrels are placed in the oval arena like the three points of a triangle, providing the reference points for the pattern to be created by horse and rider. Unlike the animate horses and cattle that are placed in opposition to cowboys, the inanimate barrels do not challenge the

Figure 1. Dialectical Movement of Opposing Principles in Rodeo

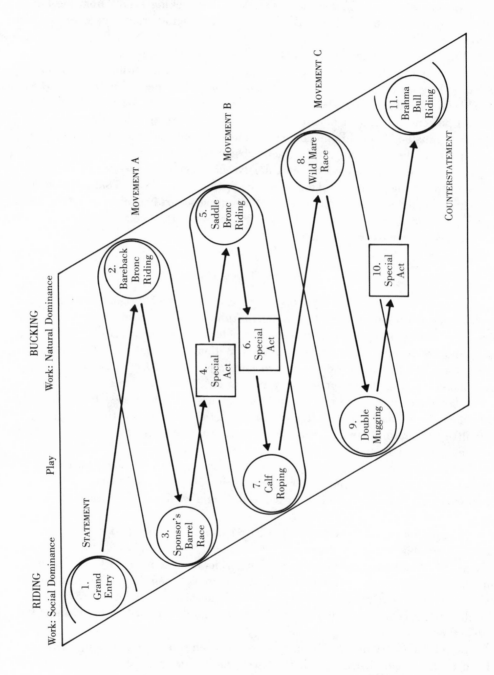

barrel racer but serve as markers to guide her in the creation of the cloverleaf pattern. Like other aesthetic acts, however, barrel racing demands that some skill be displayed, beyond the act of riding itself, the definitive act from which all rodeo action begins. Although each run happens so rapidly that it may appear easy to accomplish (approximately twenty seconds), the barrel race demands control and coordination from both horse and rider, for the goal is to create the pattern in minimum time; yet horse and rider must exercise control over speed. If not, the horse will make an unnecessarily wide circle around the barrel, adding seconds to the total time or, alternatively, with more speed than control, the horse and rider may hit the barrel, knocking it over and automatically adding five seconds to the contestant's time. The "art" of barrel racing then derives from the delicate balance between speed and control defined as circling the barrels as fast as possible.

Aesthetic appeal in the barrel race derives not only from this balance of qualities, but from the display of coordination between horse and cowgirl. A successful team moves together, the rider leaning with horse on a turn, communicating direction and speed with the knees, and leaning forward for the exit, the long straight run covering the length of the arena. Further, the Texas Cowboy Reunion insists that barrel racers wear "colorful Western attire" when competing in the arena. This final feature, color, combined with the display of speed, skill, and graceful movement of cowgirl and horse together in the creation of a pattern that exists only in its moment of creation, vanishing as the team disappears through the exit, defines this event as one of pure aesthetics.

The question remains as to the female significance of the contest. The above discussion strongly suggests that formal aesthetics in cattle culture are associated with the female, the cowgirl, who, like the male rides a horse, but for the purpose of creating pattern and beauty, not for establishing dominance over animals. The cloverleaf pattern itself (the local term) suggests a model for male/female relations if the barrels and the cloverleaf can be understood as symbols for male and female respectively. The male barrels remain immobile and permanently in place throughout the event while the female, on the horse, creates circles and pattern around the male in a few fleeting seconds and then fades from the public view. The origins of the term *cloverleaf pattern* are not known, except that this pattern as well as barrel racing itself originated at the Stamford, Texas Cowboy Reunion, and the pattern was first known as the Stamford pattern in contrast with others which are seldom ever used today.[5] For an unknown reason, however, this pattern has been unconsciously selected over the past fifty years by barrel racers everywhere and is now equated with the barrel race itself. Given that there is no cowgirl exegesis for the cloverleaf pattern, we may focus on its positional meaning as a symbol, its position in the enactment itself.[6] Clover has been associated with luck and abundance in the popular mind for centuries. If we equate the cloverleaf pattern with the female who runs it and interpret the standing barrel as a male symbol, the female then represents luck, abundance, beauty, control, and order, a patterned order that creates a design around the permanent and stable male symbol. The female then competes only with Time, a socially defined opposition, and in a cooperative relationship with animal (the horse), in an effort to create beauty, order, and abundance, determined in skeletal form by the male symbol.

A contest event that defines the female role in society, emphasizing order, seems logically placed as the first in the sequence of events representing Human Dominance. If the Grand Entry displays the whole social order as the opening statement of rodeo, it is not surprising that the first contest should elaborate on that order, identifying the female role in it.

Teamed with a tamed horse, riding in a saddle, representing control and aesthetics, the cowgirl contest situates the female in cattle culture, identifying her with the social order and questioning only her degree of competence by imposing speed as a measure.

Calf Roping, the second event in the Human Dominance principle, demonstrates in its differences from barrel racing the process of competitive collaboration. However, as in barrel racing, the animal and human relationship defines this as an event of human dominance from the beginning. The roper and his horse, saddled and specially trained for rodeo roping, work as a team toward the goal of catching and tying a calf. As in barrel racing also, time is the major opposition, for the roper who succeeds in achieving the goal in the fastest time wins first prize. Additionally, the roping event introduces a new skill of human dominance, the ability to catch a calf with a humanly produced tool, the rope. Thus, the features of human dominance have increased. Carried over from barrel racing are the trained horse and saddle and time as a competitive factor, but the rope and the skilled action of roping are added human features. But the event borrows significantly from the animal-dominated principle: the cowboy replaces the cowgirl in the team of horse and rider, and an untamed but small animal functions as the obstacle or the goal. The small calf belongs to the species, cattle, and it does not become domesticated on the range or in the rodeo, but remains in the category of undomesticated. These animals are the very ones a cowboy must be able to handle on the range, and one means of handling them is roping, another kind of cowboy work. The contest achieves considerable complexity by introducing the calf and the rope, yet human dominance is maintained as there is no doubt that the calf can be roped.

Whether or not it will be roped depends on the competence of the cowboy, and also as in the barrel race, the winner is determined by the roper who catches and ties his calf in the fastest time. However, in this case a judge sits on a horse in the arena and drops a red flag when the calf is tied, signaling to a man holding a stop watch. The judge then observes the calf to determine that it has been properly and securely tied. These judges, like the bronc riding judges, are experienced and respected men, representing a cowboy with seniority and authority.

Double Mugging (or other variations of roping) occupies the third slot in the Human Dominance events, and it increases the basic elements in size and number. The single roper becomes two in this event, and the calf grows to almost adult size. Thus both the human and animal principles have been strengthened, and there is much less certainty that the calf will be roped, even with two ropers, and even less certainty that the two will be able to throw and tie the larger animal. Time still functions as the major opposition since the winner is determined by the fastest roping time. As in the previous roping event, judges on horseback time and assess the quality of the tie.

This last event of the Human Dominance principle has more evenly balanced the contest through collaboration, just as the Wild Mare Race did in the opposing principle. While this event does not introduce chaos, it does intensify the difficulties of displaying the skill of roping and complicate the action with the second cowboy.

Animal Dominance Events

In each event of this category the animal to be ridden has not been tamed. The first event, the bareback bronc riding, presents the principle of animal dominance in its purest form—only a cowboy rider and the horse in a competition—representing the cowboy of the ranch through one of his work actions: breaking broncs (untamed horses). The element of *time* functions here to limit the bronc's opportunity to "buck off" the cowboy and to provide a fair measure for comparing the individual contestants. The presence of the pick-up man and the judge is significant. With them the social order comes into the arena. The pick-up man rides a horse, but unlike the cowboy, has the title of *man;* he supervises the action by efficiently removing the cowboy from the bronc and directing the riderless horse out of the arena. In this role he represents the cattleman just as a manager or foreman of a ranch represents the ranch owner by supervising the cowboys. The judge, who stands on the ground marking a score sheet, gives each cowboy points for his competence and style, taking into consideration the difficulty the horse posed to the cowboy. In this role he represents the older, experienced cowboy who exercised an informal authority on the ranch, teaching and evaluating the young cowboys, but maintaining good relations with the cattlemen. The structure of the event arranges the cowboy in opposition to the wild horse, representing the most uncomplicated of the contests.

The second contest event, saddle bronc riding, changes the action only slightly but introduces a major symbol. It involves riding a bronc that is saddled before the cowboy climbs on its back in the chute and enters the arena. The saddle increases the danger of bronc riding because the cowboy can become entangled in some part of the saddle, and get caught in the flying hooves of the horse or dragged around the arena by the horse with his head on the ground and feet in the air. At the level of meaning, the saddle is the equipment most essential to his occupation, the means by which the cowboy dominates the horse so that he can handle cattle. More than simply an instrumental means, however, the saddle is an aesthetic object, utilized and evaluated on the basis of both functional and aesthetic criteria. Its significance rests in its definition as an instrument of Human Dominance. The Animal Dominance principle has then borrowed an essential feature from the opposing principle. No other changes are effected, however, for the judges and pick-up men repeat their roles in this event, emphasizing the presence of the social order in the arena.

When the Wild Mare Race bursts into the arena, it considerably alters the Animal Dominance principle. The event arranges the action more like that of organized sport than of cowboy work, presenting teams of cowboys and a simultaneous contest rather than individuals as in the previous events. Moreover, the arena functions much like a playing field for it is marked off with white lines at either end which must be crossed by the rider once the horse is saddled and he has maintained his seat in it. Yet the untamed animal multiplies its effects in this event by its numbers—three wild horses in the arena at once, and further because the cowboys must catch, saddle, and seat themselves on the horse as part of the contest, the untamed horse has an advantage over the cowboy. It is so great, in fact, that some teams never succeed in even saddling the horse, much less crossing the finish line, defining this event firmly as one of Animal Dominance. There are no pick-up men, and the judges only stand near the white lines to determine that they are crossed and who crossed them first, functioning much like referees. The Wild Mare Race creates chaos in the arena and an intensity of crowd response unmatched by other events. For the duration of the race, brief though it is, the crowd screams in anticipation of and in response to every unpredictable action. One horse may simply lie down on the ground in protest, refusing to compete at all while on another team a cowboy wraps his arms around the horse's neck and bites her ear, an act designed to compel her to stand still while being saddled. One racing horse and rider may collide with another in their wild run while another cowboy might be driven away in an ambulance, having been kicked in the head.

Such planned chaos, incorporating and intensifying features of both opposing principles, foreshadows the transformation to come in the final event of the rodeo which is also the last of the Animal Dominance events.

Special Acts

Interspersed between the contest events are rehearsed, comical clown acts, highly trained trick riders, or other performances derived from the circus.[7] These acts involve animals and humans in relationships and actions which are clearly the reverse of the cowboy contests. Never any hint of the wild animal appears, but in its place a monkey, horse, or dog acts out the illusion that it has human capacities for thought and action and exercises what appears to be self-directed and controlled behavior. Not only does such action contrast with the wild bucking bronc or even the trained cowhorse, but the clown acts often reverse the human/animal relationship so that the animal appears superior to the bumbling fool, the clown. Human actors and animals are usually dressed in wild color combinations or glitter, sequins and feathers, emphasizing with the act of dress-up their performance role, contrasting with the cowboy who appears in work clothes and exhibits working skills. When we consider the importance of sequence once again, and note that these acts occur between those of the opposing principles, they may be seen to operate as the mediators, "through which the cooperation of the competing principles can take place."[8] These special acts then aid the contest events in their collaboration by introducing a radically changed scene, breaking up the set of features established in the previous contest events and opening the way for the transmission of features from one principle to the other.

Such contrasts as the Special Acts present serve also to sharpen the perceptions of humans and animals. When a horse behaves like an automobile, or miniature bulldogs appear with horns, pretending to be bulls, humor results from the mixing of categories as well as the accompanying sharpened awareness of the relations between animals and humans in the classification system.[9] Further, as Lévi-Strauss has pointed out, miniaturization, exaggeration, and other forms of alterations utilized in art allow for the comprehension of the subject as a whole.[10]

More specifically, however, the Special Acts provide entertainment, rehearsed miniature dramas enacted for their own sake which often incorporate jokes and tricks. More than just circus acts, clowns and performers illustrate humor and play so characteristic of the cowboy, but not so familiar perhaps as the work of the heroic cowboy. Seen as acts of play in which categories can be rearranged and taboo subjects publicly aired and treated as comic (sex, bodily functions, social relations), the Special Acts stand in sharp contrast to the contest events.[11] Whereas these latter represent the competition between cowboy and animal and therefore the *work* of the cowboy, undertaken for the production of cattle and the perpetuation of the social order, jokes and tricks represent the *play* of the cowboy engaged in for its own sake and often in opposition to the social order. Consequently, the mediating performers introduce the role of play into rodeo, in opposition to work, and remind us of the ambivalence, sometimes hostility, with which play was regarded by the social order of the range and of the larger American culture of the late nineteenth century.

Bull Riding

In the final event of the rodeo and the counterstatement of the Grand Entry, although the cowboy once again rides, in this contest he rides a bull, and, of great importance, his protector is a clown.

Riding bulls does not constitute cowboy work, and, in fact, rodeo programs often state that this contest is engaged in for "pure fun." Further, clowns in costume did not inhabit the range. Although this event involves a cowboy in the act of riding an animal, the relationships have been altered to the extent that a transformation has been brought about through the collaboration of the two opposing principles and the mediation of the special acts. That is, the bull, an untamed animal, clearly dominates in the contest with the cowboy for there is no question of his ever being tamed. Yet the character of the bull represents more than the wild, untamed animal. This animal represents male potency, the paternity of many young calves that will be produced on the range and sold on the market for a profit. Therefore, this creature brings not only great danger into the arena due to his strength and his horns, but the symbolic power of potency and economic gain. Profits from this potency will, of course, be garnered by his owner, the cattleman. When the cowboy attempts to ride this two-ton beast, he has thus placed himself in competition with the cattleman through his symbolic vehicle. No protection or assistance is offered from the pick-up men, representatives of the cattleman in the arena for this contest. (The explanation offered for this claims that the bulls would attack the horses.) However, the agent of reversal, the clown, brings his combined skills as fool and hero into the contest event to excite the bull and protect the cowboy when the bull bucks him off. True to the dual character of the clown,[12] this bullfighter entertains the crowds with scatological jokes between bull rides and often antagonizes the bull into chasing him around the arena, providing the crowd with additional thrills, and protecting the cowboy.

Moreover, the cowbell wrapped around the bull's belly signals a transition as it clangs wildly with every move of the bull, accompanied by the cacophonous noises from the band. Lévi-Strauss explains that noise occurs when a syntagmatic sequence has been broken and when a foreign element intrudes into this sequence, appropriating one term of the sequence and bringing about a distortion. Discussing the noise of charivari he states:

> It signified the breaking of a chain, the emergence of a social
> discontinuity, which could not be really corrected by the compensatory
> continuity of noise . . . but which it indicates objectively and which it
> seems to be able, metaphorically to counterbalance.[13]

And Needham's comments on percussion and transition also suggest a transformation when he observes that there is a conjunction of two fundamental features: "1) the affective impact of percussion, 2) the logical structure of category-change."[14]

With this final event the syntagmatic sequence of collaboration between animal and human opposing principles has been broken. These were based on the work of the cowboy, always combining cowboy and horse, and representing the social order. As the collaboration progressed, the competition between human and animal, the symbolic vehicles, intensified, and the special acts contrasted play with the contest events of work, inverting the norms of the social order.

In this final event the bull replaces the horse as the animal for riding, and thus redefines the cowboy as a player instead of worker; the pick-up men have been replaced by the foreign element, the clown, thus removing all final evidence of the social order and declaring that Play is in command. Through the rearrangement of man and animal, achieved gradually by the dialectical movement and mediated acts in the rodeo, the social order of the Grand Entry, representing work on the range, has been inverted. The counterstatement introduces the symbol of potency and appropriates the symbol of reversal, establishing deep play as the reigning category.[15] In this conjunction and inversion, the bullrider has taken on a new identity, that of symbolic cowboy, replacing the working cowboy, the bull has become a contest animal as well as the potent member of an edible species, and the clown reveals himself as a courageous hero as well as an unsocialized fool. Thus, the opening statement of the rodeo has been countered in an act of metaphor featuring a bull, cowboy, and clown.

When the last bull ride is completed, the rodeo performance is over, and the crowds quickly empty the stands. Most participants and spectators flow to the dance halls where dancing is well under way, while others load up their horses and "haul" down the road as far as a hundred miles away to their homes.

The melodies of the bands playing traditional country music in one dance hall and progressive country rock in another, the gravitation of hundreds of cowboys and cowgirls in varying states of sobriety to the dances, and the sounds of moving vehicles and horses fill the hot dusty summer night with a mixture of release from the performance tension and anticipation of the night ahead. While some casually set about locating their crowd and a dancing partner, others relive the day's best times and scores, adjusting to their disappointment or building hope that they will maintain their position in the next day's performance. As the fireworks shoot overhead, we are once again reminded that this festival of the West occurs on Independence Day.

NOTES

1. Quoted in William H. Cohn, "A National Celebration: The Fourth of July in American History," *Cultures* 3 (1976) no. 1: 112–89.

2. See James Gilbert, *Work Without Salvation* (Baltimore: Johns Hopkins University Press, 1977); Daniel T. Rodgers, *The Work Ethic in Industrial America, 1850–1920* (Chicago: University of Chicago Press, 1974); Irwin Yellowitz, *The Position of the Worker in American Society, 1865–96* (Englewood Cliffs: Prentice-Hall, 1969).

3. See Arnold Strickon, "The Euro-American Ranching Complex," in *Man, Culture and Animals*, ed. Anthony Leeds and A. Vayda, Publication 78 of the American Association for the Advancement of Science (Washington, D.C., 1965), pp. 229–58.

4. Kenneth Burke, *Lexicon-Rhetoricae in Counter Statement*, 2d ed. (Berkeley and Los

Angeles: University of California Press, 1968), p. 213.

5. Cleo Tom Terry and Osie Wilson, *The Rawhide Tree: The Story of Florence Reynolds in Rodeo* (Texas: Clarendon Press, 1957).

6. Victor Turner, *The Forest of Symbols: Aspects of Ndembu Ritual* (Ithaca: Cornell University Press, 1967), pp. 50–51.

7. See Beverly J. Stoeltje, "Cowboys and Clowns: Rodeo Specialists and the Ideology of Work and Play," in *And Other Neighborly Names: Social Process and Cultural Image in Texas Folklore,* ed. Richard Bauman and Roger D. Abrahams (Austin: University of Texas Press, 1981), pp. 123–51.

8. Kenneth Burke, *The Philosophy of Literary Form: Studies in Symbolic Action* (New York: Vintage Books, 1957), p. 64.

9. Victor Turner, "Betwixt and Between: The Liminal Period in Rites de Passage," in *Reader in Comparative Religion: An Anthropological Approach,* ed. William A. Lessa and Evon Z. Vogt, 3d ed. (New York: Harper and Row, 1972), p. 345.

10. Claude Lévi-Strauss, "The Science of the Concrete," in *The Savage Mind* (Chicago: University of Chicago Press, 1966).

11. See Paul Bouissac, *Circus and Culture: A Semiotic Approach* (Bloomington: Indiana University Press, 1976).

12. See John Towsen, *Clowns* (New York: Hawthorn Books, 1976), p. 134.

13. Claude Lévi-Strauss, *The Raw and the Cooked: Introduction to a Science of Mythology* (New York: Harper and Row, 1969), 1: 338.

14. Rodney Needham, "Percussion and Transition," in Lessa and Vogt, op. cit., p. 396.

15. See Clifford Geertz, "Deep Play," in *The Interpretation of Cultures* (New York: Basic Books, 1973).

Editor's Note

For more on rodeo, see for general background Joe B. Frantz and Julian Choate, *The American Cowboy: The Myth and the Reality* (Norman: University of Oklahoma Press, 1955) and Douglas Kent Hall, *Rodeo* (New York: Ballantine Books, 1976). Also valuable is Elizabeth Atwood Lawrence, *Rodeo: An Anthropologist Looks at the Wild and the Tame* (Knoxville: University of Tennessee Press, 1982).

13 / Folk Festival and Festival Folk in Twentieth-Century America

Angus K. Gillespie

In the study of the still-fluid phenomenon of folk festivals in the United States, little attention is usually given to audience composition, behavior, and typology. Here, however, Angus Gillespie chooses to focus on the problem of identifying and classifying the festival goers, their mannerisms, motivation, and esprit de corps. He starts with a number of preliminary questions: Who comes to a folk festival? What do they customarily do? What do they want? Why do they keep coming? Is the audience looking for the things the director wants them to find? And, finally, are festivals worth the effort? What do they really accomplish? To answer these questions, the author decided to set aside his own folk festival management experience and to attend a number of U.S. festivals in the early 1980s strictly as an observer. His essay is based mostly on direct observation, and suggests that there are three audience "archetypes" in attendance at a folk festival: the family, the folknik, and the outlaw. The family is looking for wholesome outdoor recreation and entertainment on a consumer basis. The folknik is a counterculture snob who sees himself as an arbiter of taste. To him, the festival is an opportunity to act out his life-style and values and a social occasion to be seen in the right place at the right time, and by the right people. The outlaw is readily recognizable by his attire, which closely resembles that of the motorcycle gang member. He comes to the festival not to listen but to make himself heard. Actual violence is rare, but he is noisy and disruptive. Each type of festival goer, argues the author, is in some fundamental way inattentive: the family is interested in buying things; the folknik wants to make music himself; the outlaw wants to be noticed. The author's profiles of the three types of audiences are deliberately comic. This approach stirred up considerable controversy and criticism when the author anticipated this article in a paper delivered at Washington, D.C. in 1980. Although most people in the audience were visibly amused by the presentation, remembers the author, several folklorists were offended by his portrayal of the folk festival audience and more by his suggestion that the audiences were fundamentally inattentive; some festival organizers, "funding agencies types," and prominent people in the field were overtly hostile after the talk. Obviously, if his view was correct, "then folk festivals were simply not achieving the public educational goals which festival administrators were claiming," commented Gillespie. Lost in the heat of the moment was the article's fundamental point, which is a serious one in spite of the breezy presentation. The inattention of the audience, argues the author, is understandable and comes mainly from the fact that at a U.S. folk festival it is not unusual to have a solid line-up of musical and other performances from twelve noon until ten at night several days in a row. But audience attention is not a relevant index for the festival's success, value, and justification. This point has been made before, notably by Paul C. Tate in the 1965 Newport Folk Festival program book. There he stressed that the festival had played an important role in the preservation of Cajun music. Here Gillespie reiterates the argument. For a folk festival to be a success, argues the author, it is not necessary for the crowd to be consistently attentive to all of the formal proceedings. In 1980, fifteen years after Tate's original observation, Gillespie interviewed Louisiana tradition bearers, musicians and craftsmen, about the relationship between the folk festival and their art. Both musicians and craftsmen confirmed that their festival experience had given them renewed confidence, enthusiasm, and pride.

Although it is disappointing to festival managers to see widespread audience inattention, concludes the author, it should be remembered that the most important effect of the festival, and the justification for the trouble and expense producing it, lies not in audience education, but in perpetuation of tradition, and in the stamp of approval which it gives to the folk artists themselves. They gain something even more important than money: a sense of pride and a validation of their art and their culture.

Folk Festival and Festival Folk in Twentieth-Century America

Angus K. Gillespie

Since annually there are more than 3,000 festivals held in the United States, the student of festivals is confronted with a bewildering variety of events.[1] Joe Wilson and Lee Udall have made a commendable effort to classify the existing festivals into five categories. (1) *Indigenous Festivals:* "These celebrations grow from particular cultures and are a part of them. Control is by individuals from a culture and the event is directed toward the culture at large." (2) *Evolving Indigenous Festivals:* "These events are similar to indigenous festivals in that they grow from the culture depicted, are monocultural, are directed and controlled by persons from within the culture. They differ in that they include conscious attempts to adapt cultural material to persons who are not of the group." (3) *Commercialized Indigenous Festivals:* "As Chambers of Commerce, tourist organizations and some private promoters have discovered that folk celebrations can attract broad audiences, they have moved to promote festivals to attract more consumers. This had the effect of moving the event partially into popular culture even while it retains support from folk culture." (4) *Non-Community Mono-cultural Festivals:* "Some monocultural festivals are organized by persons from outside the culture presented, have no base of support from the cultural group depicted, and make no attempt to involve persons of the culture as members of the audience. At the same time, the organizers may hold to a highly 'authentic' format in performer selection and presentation. The classifying factor is that the organizers are not of the culture presented and prepare the presentation for others not of the culture." (5) *Multi-Cultural Folk Arts Festivals:* "These festivals, a relatively new phenomenon, present the cultural materials of many cultures. Their audiences, with few exceptions, tend to be people who are not of the cultures presented. The organizers of such festivals tend to be eclectic fans of the folk arts or academics and control of the event is likely to be in the hands of an institution, usually a non-profit institution. Such festivals vary to a considerable extent in their adherence to the cultures they present. Some feature persons reared in the cultures presented; others present only persons who learned to perform materials drawn from cultures which are not their own. Still others present both. Most of these festivals are primarily presentations of folk music, crafts, or hobby crafts, but a few present other genres of folklore."[2]

Our focus in this essay is on the last category, the Multi-Cultural Folk Arts Festival. This category includes most of the biggest and best known festivals, including the Philadelphia Folk Festival, the Mariposa Folk Festival (Canada), the San Diego Folk Festival, the Smithsonian Festival of American Folklife, and the National Folk Festival. These festivals are of particular interest to folklorists because they often involve professional folklorists as managers and staff members and because they are widely perceived as models by smaller regional and local festivals.

To speak of the customs of folk festivals requires a certain leap of the imagination. To be sure folk festivals do involve learned behavior, being repeated in the same, or similar, context over a period of time. One problem is that the context is contrived; that is, it is planned, managed, and manipulated by directors in a conscious and deliberate manner. Another problem is that the customs of folk festival audiences have evolved over a relatively brief period of time, over the last fifty years, from about 1930 to the present. Thus the customs of folk festival audiences are twentieth-century customs of mass entertainment and are perhaps best thought of as popular customs rather than folk customs. With these limitations in mind, it is possible to observe repeated patterns of behavior—customs—at twentieth-century Multi-Cultural Folk Arts Festivals.

The scholarly literature on folk festivals is surprisingly sparse. What little study has been done tends to be by folklorists who themselves have had some festival management experience. Understandably these studies have been addressed to other folklorists who share concerns about such issues as authenticity and the politics of culture. The primary concern of the professional folklorist has been to find and to showcase authentically traditional participants.[3] Some festivals have evolved from the presentation of hobby crafters and revival performers to featuring pure traditional folk artists. The Blue Ridge Festival in Virginia and the Western Regional Festival in California are two among the many that have followed this evolutionary pattern under the guidance of professional folklorists.[4] There is also a strong concern with developing innovative and appropriate performance contexts. Folk festival directors strive to suit the presentation to the performer as well as to the art.[5]

In their concern with authenticity and context, festival directors and folklorists largely ignore the customs of their audiences. They are also interested in having an orderly and manageable crowd. And, in a general way, directors are interested in having a satisfied audience. If the audience gets its money's worth, perhaps the people will tell their friends and neighbors about the festival.

But there was more than a little truth when Joe Wilson, director of the National Folk Festival, said jokingly at the staff meeting on the eve of the 1980 Festival: "We all know that the real reason we put on the festival is so that the staff and the performers can have a good time." There really is not much they can do about the members of the audience other than hope that they keep coming and buying tickets.

Yet, if we are really to understand the customs of the folk festival, we must look at the composition and motivation of the audience. Without audiences, there would be no folk festivals. The questions are, Who comes to a folk festival? What do they customarily do? What do they want? Why do they keep coming? Is the audience looking for the things the director wants them to find? And, finally, are festivals worth the effort? What do they really accomplish?

At first the task of describing folk festival customs seems daunting and overwhelming. Even the smallest folk festival attracts dozens of tradition bearers and hundreds of visitors. To describe, classify, and catalogue the thousands of diverse interactions taking place at such a complex event is a real challenge. Yet, for all this complexity, patterns do emerge.

For the festival director, the festival is a statement of taste, a managerial challenge. For the staff, a festival represents hard work, a chance to meet old friends, and an opportunity to have intimate backstage access to the performers. At its best, the festival is to tradition bearers, both musicians and craftspeople, a validation and affirmation of their art and of their culture. It is somewhat harder to say just what the festival means to its audience. Festival organizers seldom make inquiry about their audiences, beyond making a count. Some festival directors have tried various strategies to identify and attract a given audience. For example, Charles Camp wanted a local audience for the most recent Maryland regional folklife festival. He did not want the "urban culture consumer." Therefore he did not send out press releases, did not list the festival in the NCTA calendar, and did not advertise the festival outside of a three-county area. Within the three-county area, he advertised heavily, as well as relying on word of mouth. Camp feels that through this strategy he did attract a local audience.[6] At the National Folk Festival, Joe Wilson wanted to attract audiences of people from whom the tradition carriers were drawn. He also advertised heavily in ways appropriate for each group. Although he feels that he has been successful in attracting white mountaineers to the National Folk Festival, he has not been able to draw the black community.[7]

Festivals that charge admission know the size of their audience with precision, but free festivals typically rely on police estimates, which are unreliable and usually inflated.

Who comes to a folk festival? I would suggest that there are three audience archetypes: (1) the family, (2) the folknik, and (3) the outlaw. Not all festival goers will match one of these three patterns, but most will bear marked resemblance to one of them. In relating the "language" of folk music to the larger social structure of the festival audience, we assume that folk music can only be fully understood in terms of the criteria of the groups that appreciate the music. This assumption, of course, contrasts with that of some established musicologists who use an "objectively" conceived aesthetic.[8] With this in mind, let us examine these three models.

1. The Family. Typically the term *folk festival* is coded to mean wholesome outdoor recreation suitable for the whole family. This is a message conveyed in press releases, posters, and public service announcements for radio and television. As Peter Hartman of the Blue Ridge Folklife Festival said, "I would bring my grandparents to a folk festival. I wouldn't bring them to a rock concert."[9]

Thus the folk festival is a family-oriented activity scheduled for the weekend. The targeted family will probably be white, suburban, and middle-class with an automobile for easy access to a park-like setting on the edge of a large city. The idea that a folk festival must be in a rural setting is rather firmly entrenched. For example, Charles Seeman, director of the Western Regional Folk Festival, held in rural Marin County, wanted to move the festival into the city of San Francisco to attract a larger, more heterogeneous audience. However, the Park Service, which sponsors the festival, conforms to the conventional bias toward a pastoral festival setting and wants to keep it in the country.[10]

The folk festival will be chosen as a special alternative entertainment for a given weekend. Since it is usually an annual event, occurring more or less at the same time every year, many families will watch for it year after year. Indeed such repeat visitors are the bread-and-butter for any festival. Thus the folk festival is like a state fair, or a concert, or a circus. One must plan on going. In this respect it is unlike a visit to a museum, or a zoo, or a theme park, which will be open for a long season, if not year-round.

The family-oriented image of the festival is well deserved. Typically there is something to appeal to every member of the family at a different level. For parents the music may constitute an alternative entertainment to the usual mainstream commercial offerings. For children, the park-like environment may in itself be attractive. Perhaps the setting, like Wolf Trap Farm Park, will offer a stream to play in and hills to roll down. For grandparents, the crafts exhibits may offer a tangible link with the past.

An inescapable fact about our hypothetical folk-festival-going family is that they come for recreation and entertainment. Like other American recreational activities, folk festival attendance can be seen as a consumer activity. Our family may be arriving by car, paying for parking, and for admission, then buying a program with the activities of the day and background information. Festival sponsors also offer a number of souvenirs—typically T-shirts and posters. Laden with these treasures, our family begins to survey the festival grounds, where they are urged to purchase an LP album right away because, "it's available here but not readily available in a regular record shop." Moving on to the crafts area, our family may encounter furniture makers with chairs for sale, or a duck decoy carver with ornamental birds for sale. Farther down the line, it may be hard to resist the jar of honey offered by the beekeeper or the miniature horseshoe (with your child's name custom-embossed on the spot) offered by the blacksmith.

Tired out by their long stroll in the hot sun, burdened by souvenirs, our family may decide on a visit to the food concession stand for lunch. After lunch our family may return briefly to their car to store their souvenirs in the trunk. They may resume strolling the festival grounds and decide to watch the local historical pageant at 2:00 P.M. on the main stage, for which there is an extra admission fee.

By midafternoon Dad will probably want a few beers from the beer truck and Mom may have gone back to the chairmaker, checkbook in hand, to negotiate seriously about a hand-made rocker. The children, by now having developed a serious interest in folk music, may want to buy a limberjack, or a set of spoons, or a harmonica. By now it is time for dinner so that family may stay and buy tickets for the special country supper prepared by the ladies' auxiliary of the local volunteer fire company. Sometimes these dinners feature local dishes with a particular regional identity, but most often the food is simply inexpensive mainstream American cookout fare—perhaps barbecued chicken and potato salad washed down with large quantities of beer. After a satisfying dinner under the green-and-white striped tent, our family gravitates toward the impromptu jam session over in the parking lot while waiting for the evening concert. After the concert, the family buys some gas and heads home.

2. The Folknik. Now let us examine the second archetype—the folknik. A couple is likely to arrive in a battered Volkswagen bus rather than in a Buick station wagon. They take care to park down the highway in order to avoid the parking fee. He is dressed in Levis or cut-offs and is likely to sport a cowboy hat or leather vest or both. He has been described as "the cosmic cowboy."[11] She may wear a granny dress with a calico print, sporting a wide-brimmed hat, going barefoot, and carrying a guitar case. There is really no need for them to buy a program since they already know everybody. There is no need for him to buy a folk festival T-shirt, since he is already wearing a faded one from an out-of-state festival held five years ago. The older and more faraway T-shirts are highly prized as status symbols.

Around the festival grounds, they are in their element, warmly embracing old friends who also travel the folk festival circuit. If it is early in the season, they may not have seen each other for nearly a year, and there is a lot of catching up to do. In cruising the festival grounds, he may pass by the chairmaker or the blacksmith, but he naturally gravitates to the instrument maker, with whom he chats knowledgeably. Generally avoiding the fire department hamburgers and the rescue squad hot dogs, she returns to the van for a granola meal around noon. Indeed the van may become the site for an impromptu jam session.

The entire day has the character of a family reunion, of a gathering of the clan. It is an extended family devoted to folk music as a social symbol of a particular life-style. Members of the family generally agree on a wide range of social and political issues. They all agree on a certain musical aesthetic, but their shared assumptions go much further: mainstream American culture is plastic and artificial. Popular music in general reflects this culture. Folk music, on the other hand, connotes a vague commitment to left-wing politics, peace, truth, and beauty. Thus the seasoned folknik may have an antiwar background and may have been involved in forms of social protest ranging from grape boycotts to nuclear plant sit-ins. Taken collectively, the bumper stickers in the parking lot express an entire political philosophy: "Save the Whales," "Split Wood Not Atoms," and even an occasional faded "McGovern for President." The music at the evening concert is expected to carry, articulate, and express this entire life-style.

But oddly enough, the folkniks may not really pay much attention to the music itself at the concert. They already know the music. They have significant collections of records and tapes at home. The evening concert, like the rest of the day, is another opportunity to be seen in the right place by the right people. It is a stage for the folkniks to act out their life-style and their values. Rural is better than urban. Natural is better than artificial. Acoustic is better than amplified. *A cappella* is better than accompanied. Old is better than new. The folknik feels like an arbiter of taste.

The main reason the folkniks do not pay close attention to the evening concert is that to them it is fundamentally unimportant. The main event of the day is the informal musical jam held late at night. These customary events have the appearance of spontaneity, but are actually highly structured. Participation in these events is the folkniks' ultimate badge of acceptance to the in-group. Here at last is an opportunity for the folknik, or deeply committed fan, to play with the on-stage performers. The rules for participation are never made explicit, but they still are very much present. It is best to bring along a six-pack of imported Canadian beer, either Molson's or Labatt's. This is an outward and visible sign of good taste. It is not necessary to bring along whiskey, but the preferred brand is Jack Daniels, for two reasons. First, the advertising photographs for Jack Daniels have established it as rural, down-home, and authentic. Secondly, the label on the bottle has an old-timey appearance, much admired by folkniks. Bringing along a generous supply of an acceptable beverage is certainly a good entree into a small group. The newcomer must not be too eager to join in but must hang back until an appropriate moment, often cued by a nod from someone already playing. Even then, the newcomer must not play too loud or too long, or the group may just walk away.

As the night slips away, songs are exchanged, the beer is consumed, and marijuana is smoked. The later one stays up, the better. It is not unusual to see musicians straggling back to their tents and sleeping bags with the first light of dawn. Indeed the most prestige accrues to those who do not go to bed at all. Predictably, the folknik is exhausted by the end of a three-day festival. Before he leaves the grounds on Sunday, he picks up a few T-shirts. By now they are being sold at half price. She also remembers to pick up a discarded program to tuck into her guitar case to save as a souvenir.[12]

3. The Outlaw. The third archetype is the outlaw. Like the folknik, he tends to hang out in a large group with his peers. Unlike the folknik, he arrives without an instrument. The outlaw behaves as if he were at a rock concert.[13] He appears in large numbers at bluegrass festivals; in smaller numbers at folk festivals. But folk festival directors who feature bluegrass may find him in their midst. He arrives about noon on a Harley-Davidson motorcycle, or in a Chevy pickup with a shotgun rack above the rear window, or a Dodge van heavily laden with cases of beer, bearing bumper stickers like "Bluegrass: Love That Shit-Kickin' Music," or "If You See This Van Rockin', Don't Come Knockin'."

The outlaw is discouraged by most folk festival promoters, but actually courted by some bluegrass promoters anxious for his business. The key lies in the advertising. If the promoter wants to maximize the gate, regardless of the conduct of his audience, he may advertise using appropriate code words: "A Weekend of Peace, Blues, and Bluegrass. Come out to the Farm for a Foot-Stomping Good Time." This will bring the outlaws. If the promoter is really concerned about the crowd's deportment, he will use a different set of code words. For example, in the summer of 1980, the Berkshire Mountain Blue Grass Festival advertised: "No Drugs—No Alcohol in Performance Area—No Open Fires—No Private Sound Systems—All Pets Must Be Leashed—Motorcycles Must Be Left at Main Gate—A 100% Family Show." The recital of "No's" is enough to discourage most outlaws. A simple statement like "No Alcoholic Beverages" alone is not enough. The statement must be very emphatic if it is really to be believed.

The outlaw is readily recognizable by his costume, which closely resembles that of the motorcycle gang, rather than that of the cosmic cowboy. He may be a construction worker in his daily life. He arrives at the festival in a sleeveless faded denim shirt so as to reveal his bronzed biceps. Headwear is revealing and important, but varied rather than standardized. Favorites include the Greek fisherman's cap, a red bandana, or an olive-drab Army fatigue cap. The outlaw congregates with his friends to one side of the mainstream audience—perhaps under a large shade tree—where he spreads out his blankets and places his beer coolers.

Basically the outlaw comes to the festival not to listen, but to make himself heard. Actual violence is rare, but he is noisy and disruptive. If alcoholic beverages are permitted, he may make a spectacular show of breaking empty beer bottles to dramatize his bad behavior. If alcoholic beverages are not permitted, he probably won't break bottles, but he will drink openly from the bottle rather than discretely from paper cups like the mainstreamers. Some festival promoters actually sell beer themselves directly from vending trucks, a move which sanctions drunkenness and disorder. If drinkers are forced to bring in their own supply in coolers, this limits what they can consume. But if a beer truck is right there, the only limit is what one wants to spend. Though the drinking and shouting become more brazen and open by midafternoon, few security guards want to tangle with the outlaw. The guards usually just look the other way and avoid that part of the field.

The outlaw draws attention to himself by noisy verbal outbursts. He claps if the music is loud or fast. If it isn't, he roars for "Rocky Top" or "Orange Blossom Special" or "Panama Red." The emcee who interrupts the fast flow of music is hooted off the stage. The solo female vocalist is greeted by cries of "Take it off!" When not drawing attention to himself by shouting or drinking, the outlaw may turn to dancing. For partners, he favors young women in cut-offs and halter tops. The best place to dance is right in front of the main stage, so that the audience will see him rather than the musicians. However, his female companion can easily steal the show from him at this point if she takes off some of her clothes. As the day wears on, and the alcohol starts to take effect, his behavior becomes more and more clownish and outrageous. He may circulate among the family groups, shaking hands and introducing himself. He may parade about with an American flag in one hand and a window-washing bottle in the other, playfully squirting everyone in his path. Underneath the play, of course, is a provocation.

For the outlaw the festival is a stage for his own performance—loud, obnoxious, rude, and inconsiderate. Still, his behavior is so stylized and customary that it cannot really be called outrageous or unexpected. He assumes the pose of rebel without a cause, of bad boy. If he attends enough festivals, he gets very good at it.

Like his mainstream counterpart the outlaw takes his dinner at the concession stand. A period of relative quiet may come immediately following dinner. The food has a mellowing effect. Rarely does the outlaw drink himself into insensibility. As the evening sun goes down and the temperature starts to drop, the drinking resumes and with it the hollering. As it gets later and later, mainstream families begin to drift away, leaving the festival to the folkniks and the outlaws. At the end of the concert the outlaw makes his noisy departure—leaving the festival to the folkniks for jamming. As the last motorcycle roars off into the distance, music is still being played here and there in small circles. For today, the outlaw has left.[14]

Up to this point we have sketched three archetypal festival goers, and we have argued that each is in some fundamental way inattentive. The family is interested in buying things. The folknik wants to make music himself. The outlaw wants to be noticed. No one seems to be paying attention. One problem is that the festival is a long event. It is not unusual to have a solid line-up of music from twelve noon until ten at night. This may go on for two or three days or even longer. No one can possibly pay close attention to the music for such a long stretch of time, so people wander around and do other things, as we have described. The format, usually long hours in an open field, invites such wandering. A festival is not quite a concert, and so a different set of customs has evolved.

If the festival goer is not really attentive or critical of what he is seeing and hearing, then perhaps festival directors could schedule anything and get a positive response. Indeed Charles Camp has argued that a tourist audience can be counted on to respond positively to *any* exhibit or performance, including a "dead monkey."

If the festival audience will be entertained by anything, what do festivals accomplish that is different from other entertainment? The staff has a good time. If they are revival musicians or craftspeople themselves, they may learn more about their art from the folk performers. Some establish relationships which develop into friendships either with each other or with the folk performers. Staff and performers enjoy the backstage partying and good times that accompany most festivals.

What does a festival do for the folk artists? Charles Camp feels that a folk festival is "an instrument for the distribution of public funds to traditional artists and secondarily an event to educate and motivate a local audience to understand the artists in their midst." For this reason 80 percent of his festival budget was spent on artists' fees. Camp is the extreme, however, since many folk festivals pay little more than a symbolic fee which may not even cover artists' expenses.

What else then do the folk artists derive from festival participation? Something much more important than money—a sense of pride and a validation of their art and their culture.

We have seen that the folk festival audience is made up of three archetypes. The family is interested in entertainment and purchases. The folknik is interested in finding an environment that reflects his taste and life-style. The outlaw wishes to draw attention to himself. In general, the audience's attention to folk artists is limited and their interest is superficial. Nonetheless, they do show enough interest that the performers are rewarded emotionally and artistically through their participation in a folk festival.

NOTES

1. A complete list of folk festivals is available from the National Council for the Traditional Arts, 1346 Connecticut Avenue N.W., Washington, D.C. 20036. American Indian Festivals, not treated in this essay, are listed on the American Indian Calendar, available from the Bureau of Indian Affairs, Information Office, 1951 Constitution Avenue N.W., Washington, D.C. 20540. A selective list of major folk festivals is given in Larry Sandberg and Dick Weissman, *The Folk Music Sourcebook* (New York: Alfred A. Knopf, 1976), p. 232. Current information on folk festivals can be found in magazines such as *Bluegrass Unlimited*, *Muleskinner News*, *Pickin'*, and *Sing Out!*

2. Lee Udall and Joe Wilson, *Presenting Folk Culture: A Handbook on Folk Festival Organization and Management* (Washington, D.C.: National Council for the Traditional Arts, 1978), pp. A2–A5.

3. For a theoretical overview see Robert J. Smith, "Festivals and Celebrations," in Richard M. Dorson, ed., *Folklore and Folklife: An Introduction* (Chicago: University of Chicago Press, 1972); Roger D. Abrahams, *Rituals in Culture*, Folklore Preprints Series, vol. 5, no. 1 (Bloomington, Indiana: Folklore Publications Group, 1977); Robert J. Smith, *The Art of the Festival*, University of Kansas Publications in Anthropology, 6 (Lawrence: University of Kansas, 1975); A. W. Saddler, *The Form and Meaning of the Festival*, Asian Folklore Studies 28 (1969); and David Whisnant, ed., *Folk Festival Issues* (Los Angeles: John Edwards Memorial Foundation).

4. Information on the Blue Ridge Folklife Festival from AG interview with Peter Hartman, July 11, 1980, Vienna, Virginia; information on the Western Regional Festival from AG interview with Charles Seeman, July 12, 1980, Vienna, Virginia.

5. AG interview with Joe Wilson, July 18, 1980, Piscataway, New Jersey.

6. AG interview with Charles Camp, July 10, 1980, Baltimore, Maryland.

7. AG interview with Joe Wilson.

8. Cf. John Shepherd, Phil Virden, Graham Vulliamy, and Trevor Wishart, *Whose Music? A Sociology of Musical Languages* (New Brunswick: Transaction Books, 1979), p. 1.

9. AG interview with Peter Hartman.

10. AG interview with Charles Seeman.

11. For a discussion of the "Cosmic Cowboy," see Bill C. Malone, *Southern Music: American Music* (Lexington: University Press of Kentucky, 1979), p. 136. For more on cowboy costume generally, see Sandra Kauffman, *The Cowboy Catalog* (New York: Crown Publishers, 1980).

12. Description of the folknik was written after a helpful discussion with Tom Ayres, July 24, 1980, Malden, Massachusetts. For more on the relationship between folk music and political activism, see Jerome L. Rodnitzky, *Minstrels of the Dawn: The Folk Protest Singer As a Cultural Hero* (Chicago: Nelson-Hall, 1976). The late-night postfestival jam session may be seen as small-group festive gathering (SGFG). See Linda T. Humphrey, "Small Group Festive Gatherings," *Journal of the Folklore Institute* 16 (1979) no. 3: 190–201.

13. Though the outlaw behaves badly, the problems of the rock concert are much more severe. See, for example, the three-part series "Rock Concerts: How Safe Are They?" in *The New York Times*, "Ghost of Cincinnati Rock Tragedy Still Haunting Festival Promoters," August 13, 1980, p. A-1; "Despite Tragedy, Rock Promoters Back 'Festival Seating' Policy," August 14, 1980, p. C-19; and "Lawmakers Seek Guidelines to Insure Safety at Rock Concerts," August 15, 1980, p. C-22.

14. Description of the outlaw was written after a helpful discussion with Joe Wilson, July 18, 1980, Piscataway, New Jersey.

14 / Pacific Festivals and Ethnic Identity

Adrienne L. Kaeppler

Festivals are an important communicative vehicle to build, reinforce, or affirm ethnic identity. Emerging nations may stage them for this purpose, sometimes choosing to join forces to increase the importance of the event and reach a wider public. Such was the case for the South Pacific Festival of Arts, introduced in 1972 and held every four years at a different location in the South Pacific. Its third edition, discussed here, was held in 1980 in New Guinea, with the title "Celebrating Pacific Awareness." It was intended to emphasize cultural diversities and similarities; to teach younger generations about their own ethnic roots and those of their neighbors; and finally to educate outsiders, including Western academics, to the true South Pacific cultural ways.

But festival is a multifaceted communicative event, and as the author shows in the discussion of this case, the message intended by the organizers, the one conveyed by the performers, and the one received by the audiences may differ substantially. In fact, when the event took place, interaction with Westerners was negligible, since they were really not encouraged to attend. Performed out of context and in local languages, drama, music, and dance were not clearly understood, nor was it clear to audiences which reaction was appropriate, or which part of the performance was traditional and which had been choreographed according to the expressive languages of the Western world.

In spite of these external and internal communication problems, in spite of drastically different and separate ethnic identities that surfaced, the festival accomplished the establishment of personal friendships and the preservation as well as the updating of folklore: island brotherhood and fellowship were celebrated after all.

A drastically different situation is presented by the second festival discussed, the July Tiurai held annually in Tahiti since the last century. Here the festival appears to be the playground of dialectics between two conflicting projects. The French establishment introduced the festival in all Polynesia to celebrate overseas the mainland's national festivities, whether those of Bastille Day on July 14, or those formerly given for the emperor's birthday. The Polynesians instead seem to consider the festival as a July celebration continuing the tradition of the ancient indigenous harvest festivals. The French establishment still sponsors the festival to celebrate common identity, unity, consensus, and pacification for all people belonging to greater overseas France, and to reinforce ties with the distant mainland. The Tahitians see it, on the contrary, as an occasion to reaffirm their ethnic identity and diversity, helped in this by the presence and solidarity of the "cousins" of neighboring islands who come not only to participate and perform in the highly competitive "spectacles folkloriques" but also to further their common Polynesian ethnic identity and separate heritage, and more or less explicitly use the festival to reiterate their claim to political independence.

The third South Pacific case discussed is the Merrie Monarch Festival, introduced in Hawaii in 1964, which seems to present a markedly divisive character. The competitions between performers show apparent similarities to the other South Pacific events analyzed before, but, unlike the others, here the importance is placed on winning, not on participating, and competition is very hard, recalling the tribal wars of old. This, claims the author, may be due to a number of factors: the lack of overall unity of the groups, the absence of traditional leadership formerly entrusted to chiefs, the reduction of ethnic identity to the 'ohana (the extended bilateral kin group), and the massive presence of American society and its non-Hawaiian values.

Nevertheless, the Merrie Monarch Festival sets apart the identity of the Hawaiian ethnic groups from the larger communities of reference, the Aloha State, American society, and Western culture in general.

The discussion of these prominent South Pacific celebrations gives a wide variety of references for the understanding of new festivals and their principal goals, namely communicating ethnic identity through the staging of events in a multicultural social setting; preserving ethnic identity while updating folklore to meet the challenge of Western culture and postindustrial economics; and furthering political unitary action from a common situation of ambivalence toward the ex-colonizers. These issues are especially relevant if the Pacific is destined to become in the near future the most important meeting place of disparate cultures, and possibly the birthplace of new ones.

Pacific Festivals and Ethnic Identity

Adrienne L. Kaeppler[1]

The influence of outsiders on Pacific Island societies has been uneven, ranging from some areas of New Guinea where the only direct contact has been with patrol officers and possibly anthropologists, to important overseas possessions of major outside powers such as the Society Islands and France, Irian Jaya (West New Guinea) and Indonesia, or Hawai'i, now the fiftieth of the United States. Between these extremes are Tonga, an independent kingdom (which, although extensively influenced by England was never completely a colony but only a Protected State), a number of newly independent states such as the Solomon Islands, Fiji, Kiribati (formerly the Gilbert Islands), and those still attached to a larger political power such as the Cook Islands and New Zealand, or Guam and the United States.

The varied cultures of the Pacific Island societies are usually divided into three major groupings—Polynesia, Micronesia, and Melanesia, including New Guinea. The cultures in these areas have certain core characteristics in common, but some societies do not easily fit into one of the major groups. New Caledonia, for example, has many elements in common with other Melanesian societies but has chiefs (which is more characteristic of Polynesia); Fiji is in many ways a transitional area between Melanesia and Polynesia. Many of the cultures of the Pacific are as different from each other as they are from any other culture in the world. For example, Melanesians may share physical characteristics (they are classified as Oceanic Negroids) with societies of Africa, but Polynesians (who do not share these physical characteristics) have more in common with some African social structures.

In recent years the peoples of the Pacific Islands have come to feel that they have more in common with each other than with outsiders and periodically come together to celebrate their brotherhood in the South Pacific Festival of Arts. These feelings of brotherhood are not trivial or manufactured for the occasion, however, but constitute real concerns as these societies face their separate futures. What these societies do have in common is the colonial experience and the love/hate relationship that has emerged with the colonizing power in the wake of efforts toward independence. An important element in independence is the interaction with other world societies in the international arena, such as at meetings of the United Nations and UNESCO, and the maintenance of embassies and other consul activities in foreign metropolitan areas. At the same time, the Pacific Islanders maintain their ethnic identity. Although politicians are usually not the same people who, for example, dance, they do legislate cultural policy—and it appears that throughout the Pacific ethnic identity is considered to be politically as well as socially valuable.

The third South Pacific Festival of Arts, held in Papua New Guinea (a political, not cultural, division of Melanesia)[2] in July 1980, had as its theme the "Celebration of Pacific Awareness." The Honorable Stephen Ogaji Tago, M.P., Minister for Culture, Science, and Tourism, noted that the festival would "once again emphasize our cultural diversities and similarities. Our young generation must be both directed and allowed the opportunity to know their roots and practice their traditional culture. They should also learn to appreciate their neighbours' cultural practices as well as their own. . . . Too many academics today claim to know much about our cultures, yet do not even try to scrape the surface of our knowledge and the wisdom of our way of life. It is now our responsibility to educate the outsider and show him our true cultural ways. The South Pacific Festival of Arts is one way of doing this."[3]

In spite of this laudable aim, few outsiders (i.e., non–Pacific Islanders) were there, and they were really not encouraged to come. The Pacific Islanders, however, were outsiders themselves. The performances could be understood as performance, but, for several reasons, they could not be understood as "true cultural ways." Many of the performances were, and still are, tied to language. Almost all were performed in local languages and therefore could not be understood by outsiders. Pacific Islanders communicate across cultural boundaries usually in English or Melanesian pidgin, but here there was usually no attempt to introduce or explain the performance. The audience did not understand if the performances were old or new, what part they played in the traditional culture, or how the audience was supposed to react.

For example, the Kamula tribe of the New Guinea Highlands performed an old, traditional dance. The Kamula have had little interaction beyond their own tribe and know little about the traditions of the outside world. Their dance, aesthetically appropriate in Kamula terms, is calculated to make the audience cry. The audience did not cry, found it incomprehensible and rather dull, and after a few minutes dispersed. In more sophisticated groups sometimes a buffoon was added to a traditional performance—he would communicate with the audience in a nontraditional way in order to hold their attention. The two groups that received the most acclaim from the large local New Guinea audiences were the dance troupes from Tahiti and Hawai'i. The meaning and function of their dances were not communicated, but the use of the hips and legs in ways unheard of and even taboo for New Guinea performers was a source of unending fascination. Groups more used to performing for audiences could alter their performances on the spot in order to capitalize on audience reaction.

In short, understanding each other's cultures through their arts was not accomplished in the abstract, but getting to know each other on a personal basis was accomplished. It was hoped that the South Pacific Festival of Arts would be instrumental in preserving old traditions as well as fostering new productions based on these old traditions but appropriate in the modern world. Another aim was intercultural understanding and lasting friendships between individuals who inhabit different cultural worlds. All of these elements are features of the Festival. Old dances which exist essentially in the minds of old dance leaders surface. New theatrical groups such as the Raun Raun Theatre condense universal problems into a form that can touch anyone, but filtered through the New Guinea experience. Outside observers have questioned the wisdom of using the arts to foster political aims, but Pacific Islanders have found that these are noncontroversial activities making it possible to meet on neutral ground and form friendships that might be useful elsewhere. It is a place where cultural diversities and similarities are explored on a grass-roots level; the festival is a celebration of island brotherhood but separate ethnic identity carried out in an atmosphere of sharing.

This low-key cooperative festival must be contrasted with the high-spirited competitive atmosphere of the Bastille Day Fête in French Polynesia known locally as "Tiurai" (or the July celebrations). Unlike the South Pacific Festival of Arts, which has no indigenous or historical counterpart and has been held only three times so far (Suva, Fiji, in 1972; Rotorua, New Zealand, in 1976, and Papua New Guinea, in 1980),[4] the Tiurai has been held annually since 1881. Although its distant roots may be in Polynesian harvest festivals, its more recent predecessor was the birthday celebrations of the French Emperor Napoléon III on August 15, celebrated annually until 1870.[5] Whereas in France the fête is celebrated primarily on July 14, in Tahiti and the rest of French Polynesia it is celebrated for much of the month of July.

Competition has become the key factor for the festival participants, while merry-making liberally laced with food and drink is most important for the general populace. Rather than the high-minded ideals of the South Pacific Festival, Tiurai is celebration *par excellence*. Beginning with the more European accoutrements, including a parade, visits to the Governor's residence, horse races, and a grand ball, the fête moves on to more Polynesian activities including outrigger canoe races and the reenactment of the enthronement of a Tahitian high chief in an outdoor temple complex. The days follow with competitions of javelin throwing, plaiting of mats, copra preparation, and races of fruit carriers, but the most important part of the Tiurai begins each evening at 9:00 P.M.—the *spectacle folklorique*. This competition of music and dance draws performing groups from throughout French Polynesia—Tahiti and the other Society Islands, the Austral Islands, Marquesas Islands, Tuamotu Islands, and Mangareva— as well as from the Cook Islands and occasionally Easter Island. As they are at the South Pacific Festival, the performances are in the local vernacular, but these languages (and cultures) are closely related and the intent of the performance is immediately understood. Indeed, widespread cultural borrowing of myths and legends as well as dance movements is a feature of this *spectacle folklorique*. And a spectacle it is.

Although the dance troupes may perform together throughout the year, they begin to put together their new repertoire for the Tiurai some months before July under the direction of a choreographer who may also be the group leader. The choreographer, working alone or with others of the troupe, often takes as a starting point a myth, legend, or historical event and forms his outline around it. The performances have a standardized form and include one or more of each major Tahitian dance genre— *'ōte'a, 'aparima, hivinau,* and *pā'ō'ā,* and, if there is an appropriate singing group associated with the dance troupe, *'utē* are also included. The choreographer must fit all these genres into an integrated performance based on his theme, choreograph each section, and teach the performers, who must practice until they have a flawless production. Meanwhile costumes are chosen which may help to illustrate the theme but must also have certain specified characteristics based on "tradition" and have different forms for the two most important genres *'ōte'a* and *'aparima*. Time to change costumes must be built into the choreography—usually while the singing group is performing. If the troupe includes an individual entering the solo dance competition, costumes are changed during his or her dance (*'ori Tahiti*). The theme, choreography, and costumes must all be kept secret from other performing groups, and secluded areas or buildings are found for practice. Even troupes from non–Society Island areas try to fit their performances into this format, although this is not actually necessary.

Each evening during the *spectacle folklorique* about six groups perform, each for about one half-hour and each attempting to outdo all the others with spectacular costumes, based often on modern versions of pre-European chiefs' costumes. This immediate visual impact is the first of a number of surprises calculated to display the creativity of the choreographer and the excellence of the performers. But recognizing that all groups are not equal, the entrants compete within a specified class—the most important division separating professional from nonprofessional groups. The professional groups put on the most creative spectacles while the nonprofessional groups, such as village or youth groups, put forth a maximum of exuberance even if timing, staging, and precision are less than perfect. Within the professional domain, although the highest prize goes to a performance with traditional antecedents, there may also be a special prize for creativity. In 1979 this latter prize was taken by "Tamaeva" under the direction of Coco. During that year Coco's group had worked on the Hollywood film *Hurricane*, set in Samoa. The choreographer for the film, who used many non-Polynesian movements, had at least a temporary influence on Coco, who choreographed his 1979 performance with nontraditional postures in which the body was bent foward and the dancers' fingers were widely spread to emphasize long false fingernails. During another sequence the men walked on six-foot-high stilts in an elaborated version of a Marquesan tradition. The 1979 winning professional group, "Fetia," did a relatively straightforward professional performance which, in the words of the judges, was distinguished by the unity of its theme and the quality of execution. But the crowd pleaser was the performance from the small island of Taha'a, which danced many sequences on movable trestles, reviving a tradition of the 1930s.

Tiurai is a typical Polynesian mixture which institutionalizes the love/hate relationship between the colony and the colonizer. Ostensibly celebrating the storming of the Bastille and the revolution that made France what it is today, the Tahitians have their own revolutionary reasons for wishing to be free from France as it is today.[6] Yet many of their attitudes and tastes are French. The Tahitians feel they must at all costs maintain their ethnic identity in spite of being considered simply an overseas part of greater France. Because of French opposition to the continued use of the Tahitian language in the schools, French has become the official language. The Tiurai celebrations, on the other hand, provide a forum for Polynesianness. Although the music and dance has changed during the 200 years since first European contact, it has evolved in Polynesian ways. The rhythmic and movement elements of the performances are difficult, and Europeans are not good at doing them. It is something that is their own and offers creative possibilities for indigenous people. The Tuamotu, Marquesan, Austral, Cook Island, and Easter Island participants are warmly welcomed. These closely related Polynesian cultures all perform with the same competitive spirit, but underlying it is support for their Tahitian cousins. The Society Islanders have consistently been the leaders in dealing with outside political powers, but they speak for all the central Polynesian groups. Separate identity is important among the islanders, but more important is Polynesian identity as a way to separate themselves as a group from outsiders. In contrast to the fictional brotherhood espoused by the South Pacific Festival of Arts, Tiurai is a boundary marker for prehistoric relationships of real cousinhood.

In Hawai'i, in recent years festivals have tended to take on a divisive rather than supportive aspect. Although the Aloha Week festival, during which a Hawaiian king, queen, and royal court are elected, has been around for some time, modern competitive festivals are relatively new. Competitive festivals do, however, have roots in Hawaiian culture. The *makahiki* festival was traditionally a three-month harvest and tax-collecting festival, during which competitive games and sports were played under the watchful eye of Lono, god of peace and agriculture. With the overthrow of the state gods in 1819, however, such festivals were attenuated and eventually disappeared. A modern descendant of this festival began in Hilo, Hawai'i, in 1964. Known as the Merrie Monarch Festival, after King Kalākaua (1836–91), who brought back traditional hula to the public domain in 1883, this annual festival is an integral part of the twentieth-century hula renaissance. In format the Merrie Monarch Festival is much like a shortened version of the Bastille Day Fête in Tahiti, including a royal parade, canoe parade, exhibitions of Hawaiian arts, crafts, and dance, and sometimes a symposium, such as the one in 1979 on "Future Direction of the Hula." The most important part of the festival is the hula competition, which is held on three consecutive evenings.

The first evening is the "Miss Aloha Hula" competition, in which solo dancers perform a traditional and a more recent hula and the awards are given that night. The next two evenings, from 6:00 P.M. until about midnight, dance groups from all the inhabited Hawaiian islands come to exhibit their dances in a charged competitive atmosphere that often ends in broken friendships and disappointment. Each group performs twice—the first evening in the "traditional" manner and the second evening in a "modern" style. What characterizes the traditional form is that the dances accompany a chant and traditional musical instruments—a sharkskin-covered drum, a gourd "drum," and rattles—and the costumes are (modern) versions of pre-European styles.[7] The performance in modern style is an accompaniment to melodic songs and modern musical instruments—'ukulele, Hawaiian guitar, slack key guitar, double bass, and sometimes other European instruments—and the costumes are based on late nineteenth-century dress made of ti leaves or long, fitted holoku made of velvet, satin, or other elegant materials. In 1981 there were twenty-two such groups, and each performed about fifteen minutes on each of the two evenings.

There is a similarity here between the Tahitian Tiurai competition and the Merrie Monarch competition. Each group has about the same length of time overall; each performs in both old and more recent styles accompanying both chant and song as well as traditional and modern musical instruments. Each group has a chance to demonstrate both learned and new choreography. In the Merrie Monarch the dance leader chooses an old dance (presumably performed as learned from the teacher's teacher based on a traditional chant) and all are given a contest song which each group leader must choreograph based on traditional forms.[8] The dance leader also choreographs the modern selection as well as the danced entrances and exits for both evenings. In Hawai'i, however, there is usually not an attempt to relate the whole performance to an overall theme based on myth, legend, or historical event. Instead, a group of unrelated dances are performed as showpieces without context. Occasionally a dance leader will relate his dances to a theme. For example, in 1981 the Johnny Lum Ho group related both his male and female groups to a story about Kamapua'a, the pig god. But although this group won second place that year, it was not because of this relationship.

Unlike Tahiti, the Merrie Monarch competitions are separated by sex and style. There are three awards for male groups and three awards for female groups in each of the traditional and modern categories as well as three awards for male groups and female groups in an overall category. The disappointment rate is high and often bitter. After the festival there is often a feeling of wasted time, energy, and money. The judges are often blamed for favoring their students or relatives. There is little feeling among the losers that simply having taken part in the festival is an important end in itself or that even if other groups win each group has supported the importance of the renaissance of traditional dance and its place in the life of modern Hawai'i. The important element here is not the celebration of dance and festival for its own sake, but winning. This rather non-Polynesian attitude can be related to both the non-Polynesian worldview that is accelerating in Hawai'i and to the fragmentation of Hawaiian groups in the absence of respected Hawaiian leadership based on chiefliness.

Although there is certainly a persistence of Hawaiian values in everyday life among Hawaiians, there is also the ambivalence of living in a modern American society. Being part of a dance group that performs for such important Hawaiian occasions as Merrie Monarch is a way to emphasize one's Hawaiian ethnic identity. Although most Hawaiians are also part something else—European, Chinese, Japanese, Korean, Filipino, or Portuguese—quite often their primary identification is with their Hawaiian ancestors. Of course, some dancers are not Hawaiian at all, but they seem somehow to attach themselves to others who are Hawaiian if they become full-fledged members of these groups. Hawaiians today, however, really do not have any overall unity. Now lacking traditional chiefs, who in former times organized confrontation and competition, most Hawaiian sentiment and mutual support is based on relationship within the *'ohana,* an extended bilateral kin group. Competition between unrelated kin groups, like the wars of old, is harsh and bitter. Not winning, in the Hawaiian worldview, means you have lost—and is, like losing a battle, degrading. Unfortunately, this has caused some excellent dance groups to drop out of the Merrie Monarch competition. This has led to the rise of other hula competitions where the stakes are not so high and tradition more important.

Most popular of these festivals is the hula competition held in conjunction with the annual King Kamehameha celebration. The emphasis here is on traditional forms— no *ti* leaf skirts or *holoku,* no ukelele or guitar, and little emphasis on showmanship that detracts from the basic performance. Groups interested in showmanship save their creative exuberance for Kanikapila, an annual performance at the University of Hawai'i amphitheater, where the link with tradition is tenuous indeed.

Unlike Tiurai, which celebrates cousinhood and mutual support among central Polynesian groups, Hawaiian festivals seem to celebrate the traditional ambivalence between unrelated Hawaiian groups—a modern emergence of the traditional jealousies among chiefs of warring lines. But this, too, is a form of ethnic identity—an identity that separates Hawaiians (and would-be Hawaiians) from the larger society whose values are primarily Western, and an identity which can be said to continue the values of respect and support for one's own in-group at the expense of other such groups, even if they, too, are Hawaiian.

NOTES

1. Fieldwork on which this paper is based includes attendance and study at the South Pacific Festival of Arts in Port Moresby in 1980, the Bastille Day fêtes in Papeete, Tahiti, in 1976 and 1979, and the Merrie Monarch festivals in Hilo, Hawai'i, in 1979 and 1981. For further reading, see Alfred Gell, *Metamorphoses of the Cassowaries: Umeda Society, Language and Ritual* (London: Athlone Press, 1975); Adrienne L. Kaeppler, "Structured Movement Systems in Tonga," in *Society and the Dance: The Social Anthropology of Process and Performance,* ed. Paul Spencer

(Cambridge: Cambridge University Press, in press); Ann Salmond, *Hui: A Study of Maori Ceremonial Gatherings* (Wellington: A. H. and A. W. Reed, 1975); and Andrew and Marilyn Strathern, *Self-Decoration in Mt. Hagen* (London: Duckworth, 1971).

2. Papua New Guinea includes the eastern half of the island of New Guinea, the culturally different areas of New Britain, New Ireland, Manus (formerly the Admiralty Islands), and part of the Solomon Islands, but does not include the closely related cultures of Irian Jaya (the western half of the island of New Guinea).

3. In the *Souvenir Programme*, 1980, pp. 4–5.

4. The fourth festival was scheduled for New Caledonia in 1984.

5. Bengt Danielsson, pers. comm. April 8, 1982.

6. One of the primary reasons is the nuclear testing by France in nearby Mururoa.

7. These costumes are never quite successful because in pre-Christian times women went topless, and this is not permitted in the festival.

8. This is not the place to discuss whether the results are "traditional" either for the contest song or the chosen song, but at least that is the intent.

PART III

Signs and Symbols of the Festival

15 / An American Vocabulary of Celebrations

Roger D. Abrahams

In confronting festive events, one preliminary theoretical concern of scholars should be nomenclature. In this article, Roger Abrahams outlines the semantics of the festive vocabulary for American English and the fields of meaning for several key terms.

The premises of Abrahams's discussion may be found in the works of John Dewey and the behaviorists which give a preliminary definition of social behavior. Individual experiences of special intensity and significance form an event. If the event takes place on a special occasion, it receives a further "charge" of semantic meaning. And if there is a preagreement as to how people might act and feel in common, the event constitutes a celebration which can be either festive or ceremonial. At this point the argument draws on a classic concept, Emile Durkheim's pair of opposites sacred *and* profane. *The statement has been updated by Victor Turner's parallel distinction between* liminal *(obligatory, highly formalized) and* liminoid *(optional, free-flowing) social events and behavior. In discussing religion and society, Robert Bellah pointed out the present progressive secularization of postindustrial Western culture. In many traditional cultures, elaborates the author, high fun and seriousness are strictly united in the "work of the gods." In postindustrial cultures, the new meaning of festival must be investigated after acknowledging the separation of holy work and revelry.*

Given the general background of these premises, Abrahams's argument remains based on the opposition between ritual (sacred) and festival (secular) in contemporary America. Both occur at highly charged times in community life, but their social function and consequences, their distinctive features and symbolic meaning are in opposition. Ritual arises out of shared apprehensions in the face of individual and social changes; devised in order to cope with them, it gives names and definite borders to transitions and transformations. Festival, in contrast, goes against customary confirmation and pacification, with subversive disorder and dramatic juxtaposition. Ritual underscores continuity and confirmation. It reinforces the harmony of society and intensifies authority. Festival questions authority and challenges social harmony. Ritual is "for real"— a serious occasion whose transformations and consequences carry into everyday life; festival is "for fun"—not to be taken seriously: its consequences should only affect the make-believe world. Ritual reenacts to some extent the way the natural and social world are put together; festival takes its meaning precisely from opposition to the everyday and the workaday, which it represents with symbolic inversion and the topsy-turvy in a game of distorting mirrors. Ritual takes energy already accrued in the social fabric and reinforces it regularly. Festival provides its own explosive energy and tears it to pieces periodically. Indeed, firecrackers and fireworks, suggests the author, are the most striking signs of festivals since they command attention and spectacularly consume themselves in a brief moment.

Besides presenting in his discussion a strong case for Durkheim's semantic pair of opposites sacred/profane and its classificatory importance for contemporary American celebrations, Abrahams's contribution is also important because it sketches the diachronic evolution of the meaning of his terms, the introduction of new ones, and the rising importance of others in America's festive vocabulary. The discussion then shows the rising importance of the fair, display of products of a rural year cycle celebrating the economy and glorifying the quality, merit, and usefulness of daily objects and produce.

Fair now tends to become synonymous with festival, especially in urban environments, says the author, and its stress on usefulness and production is replacing the festival's ancient, carnivalesque indulgence in conspicuous waste and destruction. To fair is now attached a connotation of nostalgia for an American Arcadia, a way of life with economy and technology simple enough to allow individuals to do everything by themselves.

The importance of festival in America is decreasing, states the author, and the variety and fragmentation of social life have introduced new "play events" into the festive vocabulary, with ceremonies intensified at the individual and familiar dimension. Holidays from quasi-religious occasions tend to become family-oriented functions; the party is more and more important for a society praising spontaneity, sincerity, "sharing," and egalitarianism in public occasions. And finally there is the weekend, the last novelty of postindustrial society. Successor to the day of the Lord devoted to rest, to restore energy and contemplate His works, the weekend is a longer time in today's miniaturized calendar which alternates work and holiday. It is devoted to play, fun, and festive activities on a private, individual basis in which Americans can also replay their imagined past of warriors, pilgrims, farmers, hunters, or gatherers.

On the whole, Abrahams's contemporary vocabulary of festive events reflects the

*postindustrial freeing-up of time and energies and their investment into different, frag-
mented social events and individualistic celebrations. The future of festival, it seems,
has already started.*

An American Vocabulary of Celebrations

Roger D. Abrahams

Let me begin with a self-evident observation: the study of any culture is affected by
the basic terms around which the description and analysis revolve, and where these
terms are also key ones in the language and culture of the observer, the description
itself will constantly be open to ethnocentric influence. Perhaps in humanistic and
anthropological studies there ought to be no necessity to state something so obvious.
Yet the degree of sensitivity in matters of this sort has been little greater than in any
other writings about other cultures. To be sure, many ethnographic reports today
attempt to couch their descriptions of key scenes or events of the culture under
observation with reference to the native terms for the event, its constituent parts, and
the shared feelings that emerge, ideally, as part of the experience. Yet we still employ
a great many of our own resonant terms without having analyzed their fields of meaning.
We cannot, therefore, make explicit where our patterns of practice and our approved
sentiments differ from those of the culture under analysis, and thus we do not regularly
check ourselves to see how our own way of thinking and organizing will affect the
ways in which we cast the practices of others.

The central terms of a discipline are especially subject to such semantic pressures:
not only do *tradition, civilization, community, society,* even *culture* itself have different
meanings in different languages, but the relationship between these terms is constantly
under negotiation in American English, both as they are used in everyday speech and
as terms of art in folklore and anthropology. This is equally true of the terms employed
in describing ceremonial acts and events: *ritual, festival, festivity, pageant, party,
game, get-together,* and *ceremony* itself. *Ceremony* and *ritual,* moreover, often refer
to the formalized and formulaic dimension of everyday activities in certain vernacular
uses, and thus may carry with them the feeling that such nonspontaneous activities
are examples of how empty and inauthentic formal social acts may become.[1]

It therefore seems useful to explore the range of meanings of some of these key
terms in American English as they are drawn on in the vernacular for two compelling
reasons: to bring any semantic "pull" to the surface, so that we can protect ourselves
from imposing our own meaning for the term on cognate phenomena found in other
cultures; and, conversely, to see if, by such reflexive examination, we can discover
ways to study ceremonial activities cross-culturally in a more responsible manner.
The exploration is especially appropriate in the vocabulary for celebrations in public
(that is, out of the home), inasmuch as American English commonly opposes *ritual*
and *festival* somewhat in contrast to the way in which the terms have been used in
previous ethnographic descriptions. For a number of reasons, most of them having to
do with the growing secularization of American life, we have assigned the names *ritual*
and *rite* primarily to activities taking place in sacralized spaces, and *festival, festivity,*
and related terms to our playful and profane domain.

This change in our discourse on public congregating has come about as a by-product of the proliferation of events celebrating our "secular religion," as Robert Bellah has called this complex of developments. But we can also cite the growing alienation from any kind of public formality in speech and carriage arising from the long-standing American tendency to distrust those ceremonial behaviors in which status or rank differences are dramatized. We reserve for such institutions as the church, the courts, and some other governmental activities the right to act formally and to maintain a discourse system by which the priests and judges may continue to act authoritatively. These are the only ones who have maintained the power of "performatives" in our system of speech acts, i.e., words which do what they say they are doing ("I find you guilty . . ."; "I now pronounce you man and wife . . ."), and even those performatives we don't trust or believe fully, as our divorce rate shows. On the other hand, talk in more casual situations has been shorn of the overtly formal. American speakers regard such talk as unfriendly and empty, even to the point of questioning the greeting system beginning "How are you?" if the speaker doesn't really care. Reflecting both this move toward sincerity and an egalitarian attitude toward talk, the American system of interaction seems to value exchanges that are freely and spontaneously carried out, in which the willingness simply to enter into a sharing of energies and information is the primary reason for conversing.

We now seem more concerned with the smaller meanings-in-common that go into personal encounters arising within self-constituted groups as they occur in our daily encounters. What are the assumptions, the "givens" that members of a group carry into life that assent to and maintain group membership? we seem to be asking. And can there be any doubt that it is precisely this concern that has brought about a change in the way the anthropological disciplines have redirected the use of the very term *culture*, shifting its center of gravity from institutional systems to the agreed-upon regular practices of a group.

This is not to argue that we have totally undercut the value of the activities by which institutions and ideals are made explicit—that is, in rituals, festivals, ceremonies, and other kinds of public events. But the change of emphasis has opened up a new set of questions, ones that ask for connections between everyday activities and "the rite side of life."

Here we take our cues from the ways in which the norms and practices of the everyday are intensified and social roles, statuses, memberships are thereby confirmed; but we also are highly tuned to the use of such norms as a point of departure in developing alternative worlds. These framed and prepared-for activities borrow from the everyday but are transformed by stylization and sometimes by the spirit of license which encourages the inversion of everyday values and practices, even to the point of acts of transgression. We will proceed in this analysis of activities from the term that lies at the center of the American discourse on culture: *experience*.

From such a perspective, recurrent patterns of experience provide the basis for the study of behavioral traditions. Here we are concerned with the distinction made in our vernacular between *experience*, or the flow of happenings as lived by individuals, and *an* experience, the recognition that this flow has somehow carried more pressure and volume, and has become more significant. These experiences steal up on us, enliven us as they produce fear and/or thrill. They produce the events that become our stories insofar as they are interesting, typical, and retellable. When the intensity and significance are shared by a number of people, an *event* is upon us. When these events are experiences for which people prepare and anticipate in common how they will act and feel, they are usually *celebrations*—either festive in intent or principally focused on ceremony. In either case, they are the most focused of all cultural encounters. But whether the event is anticipated or not, we can say that the more eventful the experience, the more focused the encounter will be. More simply stated, both the excitement of the acts and the meaning of the activity are available to shared meanings and feelings. Finally, the more tied the event to an *occasion*, the more ceremonial or festive it becomes.

Most important, perhaps all cultures build anticipation into life by having such celebratory events incorporated into the yearly calendar of community life. When these occasions re-enact, in some part, the way in which the social or natural world is put together, we interpret them as rites. These tend to be traditional—that is, memorable, learnable, repeatable, susceptible to accumulating important meanings and sentiments. The meanings, indeed, are often translated into *messages*, value-laden *lessons* explicitly spelled out. In the case of rituals and ceremonies attached to institutions such as church or school, they arise out of shared apprehensions in the face of the inexorability of somatic or social change.

There are other named and recurrent happenings, however, that have become detached from confirmation or transformation. Though they may also mark off important times in the flow of group life, they are often practiced "for the fun of it." Anthropological study has shown that in many societies, especially the noncosmopolitan ones, "the work of the gods" conjoins fun and seriousness, juxtaposing them as one means of attaining community. But as societies become tied to the marketplace as well as the temple and other holy places, the two tend to become disassociated. "High" seriousness becomes the special responsibility of the priest. "Low" play and the carnivalesque spirit is put in the hands of the strange ones, the free spirits, or those commonly excluded from the center of ceremonial life. In such a society, play is carried out in defiance as well as for renewal. This is the condition from which our contemporary sense of festival tends to emerge.

Yet festivals and rites still seem part of the same human impulse to intensify time and space within the community and to reveal mysteries while being engaged in revels. Cultural objects and actions become the foci of community actions carried out in common, when the deepest values of the group are simultaneously revealed and made mysterious. But in our secularized world there *is* a felt need to distinguish between holy work and revelry. While rites in contemporary culture are still often accompanied by festivities, and a festival often has a designating rite at its core, surely we have progressively associated rituals with being "for real" and festivals with "fun." While rituals alone are involved with developing our individual sense of the authoritative, both rituals and festivals enter into the process of self-authentication. The distinction is far from trivial, for it speaks about our most important states of being. Moreover, the primary vocabulary of ritual underscores such motives as continuity and confirmation; the transformations put into practice are responsible for maintaining the flow of life. Festivals, on the other hand, commonly operate in a manner that confronts and compounds cultural norms, and therefore operates for the moment in a way antagonistic to customary ritual confirmation.[2]

Rituals in such a discourse system are shared reactions to those disturbances arising as the result of a constant flow of changes. Rituals give names to these changes and draw on the group's shared anxieties in the face of the transitions and transformations. They provide focus, then, for undistributed energies, energies which arise naturally as a group confronts the changes in social state and marks them in marriages, funerals, or migrations.

Festivals, on the other hand, operate during those very times when the life of the group seems most stable, in the "flat" times of the year; festivals manufacture their own energies by upsetting things, creating a disturbance "for the fun of it." While ritual underscores the harmonies and continuities in the expressive resources of a culture, emphasizing the wholeness of the world's fabric, festivals work (at least at their inception) by apparently tearing the fabric to pieces, by displaying it upside-down, inside-out, wearing it as motley rags and tatters.

Festival—like other terms for complex traditional events, it takes a major semantic dimension from the ways it contrasts with the everyday, especially the workaday world, and the ways it differs from other such intense and planned-for cultural activities. It is through such dramatic contrasts that festivals achieve meaning within the idea of *tradition*. By this we mean that the festival has an existence apart from the specific participants as it is "put on" for any given occasion.

In addition to festivals, there are other events included in the domain of festive occasions. Especially important here are the less public occasions for "a good time," events like parties and other kinds of social gatherings, most of them occurring in enclosed places, ones not open to public scrutiny. There are also conventions, inaugurations, and other events connected with our civic lives which combine public and private activities. Such *festivities* often accompany focal ceremonial confirmations. *Festival* itself conjures up notions of openness, either through the opening of the doors of the community (and other such readjustments of the boundaries of private or family space), or through a taking to the streets. Festivities, in general, mean the evocation of the spirit of fun, of play and games. Festivals draw on the languages and techniques of play to intensify them.

Festivals seize on open spots and playfully enclose them. Spaces are found and are invested with the meaning of the moment and the power of the occasion. This is, of course, what happens on the streets during parades; spaces become transformed and activated, a place for diversity to be displayed within certain rules and between the boundaries made for the occasion. Festivals thus draw their own boundaries for the occasion and redraw the boundaries of the host community, ironically establishing themselves in areas that, in the everyday world, have their own boundaries.

In this place those who choose to play come together and play roles which, given the everyday ways of labeling, are usually marginal. Thus, the opening up is social as well as spatial and temporal. In this way, festivals embellish the edges and margins of the community under the closely monitored conduct of play; for in play of any sort, the codes of behavior, as well as the roles, role relationships, motives, and moves are severely restricted. Play events appear to be liberating only in contrast to selected features of the everyday world, inasmuch as they playfully depart from some of the most restrained features of social interaction. But it is enough to note that play is being carried on in festivals, involving a motive and a way of operating that are certainly encountered on many other occasions in our lives. Indeed, encounters in our everyday lives are often open to some kind of playfulness, even when serious discussions are carried out.

Openness, central to our experience of festival, is temporal as well as spatial. Festivals are complex, calendared events. Many of them come from the older agricultural year, and take place when nothing central to the cycle of production is occurring. In a sense, an open spot in the calendar is found, enclosed, and valorized. Ritual and festival both mark points of life transition in intensive and stylized traditional ways. But in ritual, the work of the gods is truly being carried out, inasmuch as personal and social transformations are made possible by being re-enacted according to the gods' examples. Transformations occurring within the spatial-temporal frame carry authority out of that frame, into the "real world." Rituals rely on the powers of the gods as served by ritual officers to bring the viability of these potential transformations to our notice. While play often occurs in a ritual—as when a minister uses a joke within a sermon—clearly it is not central to the proceedings. We certainly identify the ritual process with motives of serious purpose, and the process itself with the highly sequenced, the formal, and the ceremonial. Indeed, *ritual, ceremony,* and *serious occasion* have become virtually synonymous in our lexicon of acts and events. The invocation of the spirit of play occurs merely as one device among many to call attention to the significance of an event, to intensify it through employing all the stylized effects the community has available. And perhaps most important, rituals emerge at points of transition, even in the face of crisis. Unlike festivals arising in "open" areas of life, then, rituals emerge in impacted zones.

Both rite and festivity involve stylized, imitative, repeatable acts, carried out in highly charged times and places. Both invoke learned and rehearsed speaking and acting "routines," and gather their power to focus attention on the contrast between ordinary times and the extraordinary occasion. Both tend to transform the world and the individuals within it. But with festivals, the transformations are for fun, to be maintained only within the special world. With rituals, transformations, if they occur, are carried into the everyday. Thus the power of the transforming performer is quite different in the two, for in ritual the role tends to be an intensification (or perhaps a reauthorization) of an everyday role, while in festival, the transforming figures tend to be clowns or magicians, performers not to be taken seriously.

Perhaps the difference can be more keenly felt in the ways repetition is carried out in the two "worlds." In the ritual world, repetition is commonly carried out to intensify. Things done in unison convey the message that community exists and communion is possible. In festival, repetition is as central to the proceedings as it is in ritual, but with a different anticipation and result. Here, having fun is the key to the occasion, and having fun often means making fun, imitating for comic purposes.

What occurs at the point that imitation becomes mimicry? Is this not the point of dramatic transformation, whereby the real becomes, simultaneously, the real and the unreal? This leads to a dramatic juxtaposition of polar opposites so immediately contradictory that we can only respond by laughing: a paradox that we must experience every time we engage in fun-making. Under the *nul* conditions of festival, all social life becomes available for this inversive display in which everything is done with mirrors. But such imitation almost always results in distortion, a misshapenness which in "real life" would be regarded as grotesque. Indeed, the mirrors held up to society in festive times often resemble those one finds in the funhouse, the type that misshapes, miniaturizes, makes into a balloon.

Transformations brought about within the festive world are precisely the sort that cannot be carried into the world beyond festivities; to allow them here would be to open ourselves to charges of craziness.

The different worlds are also contrasted by the sources of their energies and how these energies are deployed. While rituals seize the accrued energies attendant on the common perception of transition (whether in crisis or not), festivals must provide their own energy source. The festival does this in the following ways: through enforced confrontation; by role play involving dressing up or dressing in rags; by making a lot of unusual noise and large-scale movement, including singing and dancing; by engineering arguments and developing heightened contests and notions of chance taking; and by invoking the spirit of nonsense and the topsy-turvy. The essence of the festival world is articulated by the temporary and fragmentary objects associated with this kind of celebration. Here I refer to festive employment of exploding devices, pieced-together costumes made in high-contrast and high-intensity colors, and to the temporary character of the inventions, like the decorations on animals, carts, floats, and people.

While festivals in the past provided a summary statement of community (and every community had its own festival), festivities of the present have become various and fragmentary.[3] Public open places are now used for other kinds of inversive behavior such as parades, protests, and other kinds of linear public displays. Surely it is significant that during festivals the major symbolic movement was "making the rounds," whether that meant mummery, caroling, or simply making a procession. Now, the one-way parade that goes only through the town or city center has become the most important statement of ensemble activity within the community.

In the form of *processions*, parade-like activities in the agricultural festival complex are the occasions on which the most powerful object of the community is brought forth and carried around to enliven it, perhaps even bring it back to life. But parades also have an ancestry of military muster, militia in uniform, practicing to go off to war, or re-enacting past bellicosities. Today the parade is a congeries of festival shapes, colors, and actions derived from the diverse displays, put in a line, "paraded by" a review stand, and judged by criteria of display, not power and awe. The gigantic and distended object, in the past associated with the major crop or with fertility in general, has literally ballooned; now it is transmuted through pageantry into any comic figure who can be represented in blown-up or stuffed form. The hock cart, developed into the pageant *triumph* now becomes the *float*, mysteriously propelled from within. And through it all, the special festive noisemakers intrude: the rattles, whistles, and firecrackers.

Perhaps the firecracker carries the message of festival most fully as a noisemaker that demands attention as it consumes itself. And, in the fireworks show, it becomes the most dramatic and temporary of all of the festival arts, made for the moment of display only, destined to self-destruct, come apart, and disappear. Like the firecracker, festivals "go off"; they are exciting and exist only for the seized moment.

Just as ceremony offers a useful contrast to festival on one side, the fair exists on the other, as a related cultural event which inhabits and valorizes the same kind of open spaces. Emerging again out of the agricultural calendar, and occurring in the inactivity between seasons, fairs are intended to display products of the growing season.

Though one encounters most of the same attractive devices and even the same range of play forms as in the festival, in fairs these features are found on the peripheries. Indeed, from the structural point of view, fairs and festivals seem like mirror images. For what is central to the festival is on the peripheries of the fair, and vice versa. Many of the same foods, drinks, and ways of decoration and display are found at both events. But at fairs, people come to discuss and judge the ways things of merit and usefulness are made, while the destruction of such items is central to the festival. The fair features private and homey things cleaned up for public viewing. But the objects remain things of the home, utilitarian objects and confections, and animals that are judged in terms of their breeding, feed, and care. Fair performances tend to be tied to occupations, such as stylizations of the old methods of working on the farm, the ranch, the lumber camp, and the mining camp. As the old ways fade, the fair becomes less oriented to the utilitarian and leans toward the languages and devices of display. Thus, in the urban environment especially, the *fair* and the *festival* merge to become almost synonymous.

Both fair and festival operate in the zone of nostalgia, as reminders of life in a simpler economy and technology, when individuals "could do for themselves." Now mainly consigned to weekends and rigidly calendared in to give us long weekends every quarter year, our major festivals ask us to remember and reminisce. Ironically, the communitarian message of agricultural festivals has been transmuted into the family morale, "the family" now meaning little more than whatever remains of the nuclear unit. Here the festive moment becomes more directed toward parties.

Festivals are ultimately community affairs. Indeed, they provide *the* occasion whereby a community may call attention to itself and, perhaps more important in our time, its willingness to display itself openly. It is the ultimate public activity, given its need for preparation and coordination of effort, and its topsy-turvyness, in which many of the basic notions of community are put to test. Inasmuch as communities no longer have such an important place in our symbolic lives, the place of festival in our system of celebrating has been largely taken over by family occasions focused on smaller groups and the individual's place within them.

We witness the direction of change in the history of the term *holiday*. For what was once a quasi-religious time of celebration becomes, rather, an occasion for a *family function*, a *get-together*, a *do*. Moreover, the word *season*, with its origin in agricultural festivals, is now associated with family occasions. "Christmas Season" and "Easter Season" have become events for getting together with "those we hold most dear." These seasons each call for a new costume or wardrobe, thus tying patterns of clothing to those of feasting. Once they were occasions of displaying production through conspicuous consumption, but now only the latter is evidenced. Holiday feasts now are "given" for the children and the old ones, the people least involved in producing anything. On most holidays, we try to stuff ourselves—especially the children—with food and gifts, almost as if they are an energy resource for the future.

The other successor to festivals as play events is, of course, the *party*. The party is grouped in our native category system with holiday dinners as *get-togethers*, or *functions*, and include such diverse types as *dinner parties*, *receptions*, and *cocktail parties*, among others.

Parties have become the most significant kind of planned-for event in American culture and elsewhere in the West. A great many of the occasions are calendared, but usually in reference to an individual or family activity. Parties are talked about and judged according to the degree they allow us to "be ourselves." Such discussions may contrast "good parties" with how we "have to act" on the other kinds of familiar big events, when either we have to dress up and be on our best behavior or we put on costumes to get away from our usual roles. "Being ourselves" seems to mean obeying the rules of casual conversation, "having a good talk" if you will, meeting new people and making new friends—friendship being defined in terms of the relationships that can develop out of discussing one's personal experiences and the meanings derived from them.

The importance of such occasions intended to encourage a certain kind of spontaneous behavior underscores the fact that the same values tend to be brought to the fore in everyday interactions and these more special times. A dialogue is established between the expressive resources of everyday interactions and those which commonly enliven these specially set-aside and planned-for events.

We carry on this dialogue within ourselves between the everyday workaday worlds and the "big" times, when we relax and have fun. Our latest calendrical invention, the *weekend*, is contrasted by us with the *week*, and our new "high holidays" are the long weekends fixed on the calendar. The contrasts are endowed with enormous meaning, for the week is when we work, when we do "what we have to do," and the weekend is when we devote our energies (at least ideally) to what we want to do.

To be sure, this contrast arose out of the old holidays that responded to the agricultural work year. Now however, relieved of the anxiety of food gathering, one of our luxuries is to replay our imagined past; we become weekend warriors, summer emigrants and pilgrims, farmers or hunter-gatherers. Thus we regularize our procedures for "getting away from it all," and connect our runaway acts with a structure of sentiments in which high entertainment value is placed on past practices, especially the "fun" ways of celebrating. Our repertoire of observance includes more festivities than ceremonies or other ritual devices, but the ceremonies of confirmation and commemoration of individual and familiar identity have been intensified. Not only have we preserved Thanksgiving, Christmas, and other such family occasions, but we have elaborated birthdays, anniversaries, reunions, and other such calendared occasions. To be sure, many of these planned-for events are "excuses" for having fun; they unite the generations in a spirit of license and permit them to depart from the strictures of family life. But at the center of such occasions is some kind of ceremonial dressing-up, using our best dishes and silverware compounded by attempts to be on our best behavior.

Our American vocabulary of celebrations reflects, then, the effects of a post-industrial liberation of our time and energy and their reallocation into a diversification of our display events.

NOTES

1. Any writing on the language of festivals today is indebted—directly or indirectly—to the work of Arnold van Gennep, especially *The Rites of Passage*, and the development of his ideas by Victor W. Turner in a series of works commencing with *The Ritual Process*. I am more directly in Turner's debt as I worked with him in a number of capacities, most

recently in an exhibition at the Renwick Gallery of the Smithsonian Institution entitled *Celebrations*, 1982–83. He edited a book that accompanies the exhibition, *Celebrations: Studies in Festivities and Ritual* (Washington: Smithsonian Institution Press, 1982), which includes my piece "The Language of Festivals" (pp. 161–77). A related essay examining the field of meaning of the term *experience*, especially in contrast to *event*, "Ordinary and Extraordinary Experience," is found in an anthology which Turner edited with Edward Bruner, *The Anthropology of Experience* (Champaign: University of Illinois Press, 1985).

2. Here this essay draws on the work of Mikhail Bakhtin, *Rabelais and His World* (Cambridge, Mass.: MIT Press, 1965) and Clifford Geertz's discussion of the Balinese cockfight in his *Interpretation of Culture* (New York: Basic Books, 1973), pp. 412–53. The notions of inversion explored by the contributors to *The Reversible World*, ed. Barbara A. Babcock (Ithaca and London: Cornell University Press, 1978), were very important in launching my thinking on the subject. And the work of Beverly Stoeltje on a West Texas rodeo (see her "Riding, Roping, and Reunion: Cowboy Festival" in the present volume) has provided a useful ongoing discussion of the subject.

3. This section on *experience* and *event* arises from my reading in the American pragmatists, especially William James (see esp. *The Writings of William James: A Comprehensive Edition*, ed. John McDermott [New York: Random House, 1967]), and John Dewey (see esp. his *Experience, Nature and Freedom*, ed. Richard J. Bernstein [New York: Liberal Arts Press, 1960]). Here I want to thank my colleague Ralph Ross, one of the editors of the Dewey papers, for leading me through the arguments of his mentors. Some of my previous articles in the area of festival and play include "Ranges of Festival Behavior" (with Richard Bauman), in *The Reversible World*, ed. Babcock, pp. 193–208, "Play," in *Proceedings of the Centennial of the Folklore Society*, ed. Venetia Newall (London: The Folklore Society, 1981), pp. 119–21, "Shouting Match at the Border: The Folklore of Display Events," in *And Other Neighborly Names*, ed. Richard Bauman and Roger D. Abrahams (Austin: University of Texas Press, 1981), pp. 308–21, "In and Out of Performances," in "Folklore and Oral Communication" in *Narodna Umjetnost* (Belgrade, Yugoslavia, 1981), pp. 69–78, "Play and Games," *Motif* 2 (June 1982), no. 1: 5–7. A number of the articles dealing with West Indian festive behaviors are reprinted in my *The Man-of-Words in the West Indies* (Baltimore: Johns Hopkins University Press, 1983).

16 / Place and Time in the Carnivalesque Festival

Marianne Mesnil

Folklorists and anthropologists have been increasingly aware of the importance of context in the events that they investigate, both the immediate performative context, and the abstract context of the worldview, with its set of norms and values that ultimately affect all social phenomena in a culture. In this essay, context is discussed as the primary basis for the definition of carnival, and for the classification of its different types. Furthermore, a series of fundamental issues is addressed. Is carnival sacred, or profane? Is it relevant to place it in the classic Carnival-Lent cycle proposed by van Gennep? How does historical change affect its meaning? Does carnival oppose or support the establishment and its value system? Does a counterculture tend to produce carnivalesque manifestations? And conversely, can a contemporary new festival produce an ephemeral community? To discuss such an extended range of issues, the author draws on important contributions by prominent scholars in different fields: social and cultural history, comparative religion, and semiotics. By context, Mesnil means the social and historical reality in which carnival participates, namely, the dimensions of place and time, with their respective social characters. Three models of context that define corresponding models of carnival are proposed: (a) the medieval and renaissance city; (b) the rural-agrarian society; (c) the modern industrial city.

184

   The medieval and renaissance city-state (in the classic humanistic model outlined by historian Michel Freitag) was an "autocephalous" system; it had its own economics, politics, ideology, identity, and legitimization. It constituted a fully integrated social system, that is, in the author's terminology, a community. *Festival time, in this social model, is drastically different from ordinary time: it is self-contained and has a universal and cosmic character. A desacralizing time of rupture, it returns cyclically, bringing back a festive explosion of opposition to the everyday rules: the liberating, revolutionary counterculture that Bakhtin analyzed in his famous essay on Rabelais and carnival.*

   The model of the peasant-village culture (presented in the essentially meta-historical formulation by Mircea Eliade) is also a community, an "autocephalous" world, a fully integrated system. It has its distinctive economic activity and political-institutional control based on the extended patriarchal family; its ideological and normative values are orally transmitted through folklore. The festive time of this traditional agrarian culture also breaks dramatically into the ordinary cyclical temporality. But unlike the other, it is sacred, as Eliade suggests, and brings about the return of the mythical "Great Time," when cosmos and order were created. This rebirth is represented in the festival, revitalizes the social order, and supports it.

   The model of the modern industrial city (the discussion returns to Freitag's models) presents instead a drastic structural difference. The city is no more a self-centered autonomous community; *it is a small part of a supra-urban system, the nation. Decisional centers for economics, politics, social values, and norms are distant; the city becomes the "means" for the integration of individuals in the larger society. Time in this model is generally informal and uniform. Festive time is not a time of rupture of any logically or symbolically relevant temporal dimension. It does not constitute a separate reality, apt to bring to life events of cosmic dimension. In this context, affirms the author, carnival proper cannot take place.*

   The discussion of these models allows the author to propose a definition of carnival as a festival that reaffirms the cohesion of an integrated social group by means of a time that brings about the group's revitalization by the representation of the cycle of birth-death-resurrection. Of course, depending on the context of the festival, such cohesion will be directed against official values (as in the case of the desacralizing medieval festival of Bakhtin), or in support of the existing cosmic and social order (as in Eliade's sacred festivities). What happens in the third model, the urbanized industrial society, is especially relevant also to its contemporary offspring, the present-day postindustrial city.

   The author suggests that since the third model lacks an integrated context, that is a structured, specific, and tangible present community of reference to support or to challenge, revitalization is no longer the function of its festive events. The birth-death-resurrection cycle, having lost its meaning, disappears, taking away the sacred character and the transcendent meaning of the festival. In this new context, carnival changes into something else, structurally different, termed a "folklorized festival." This new event keeps only some formal characters of former festivals, becoming a "show" with passive spectators, a "make-see" and no more a "make-do." The "semiotic indices" of this process of change in festive events are indicated from the work of leading semiotician Algirdas Greimas. In essence, a global mythical phenomenon dissolves, appearing in separate "idioms" such as poetry, music, dance. These lose their former sacred connotations and take new ludic or aesthetic functions. Performances use individual stylistics and do not produce collective meaning, but are aimed at individual consumption. To the crowds of postindustrial society, the new festival, this "complex semiotic object," seems to promise nothing but "fun, fun, fun."

Place and Time in the Carnivalesque Festival[1]

Marianne Mesnil*

Introduction

Among the fashionable topics that seem to rouse sudden and unexpected intellectual inquiry, "the festival" has now taken its place. It remains to be seen whether this phenomenon will suffer the fate of so many others; just as anthropologists discover their importance, the phenomena themselves have already begun to disappear.[2]

Folklore was "discovered" (in the etymological sense of the term) when the social categories underlying it were becoming marginal in relation to society as a whole. "Folk art" collections were created after the art had been perceived in terms of its "value." Similarly, only in recent decades have we observed the emergence of scientific interest in carnivalesque festivals and museum collections thematically oriented to the carnival or mask. These indications may perhaps be construed as signaling the decline of a fundamental expression of what is commonly referred to as "folk culture," as opposed to "literate" culture, or culture transmitted by written language.

In the following analysis, we shall attempt to define the phenomenon of the carnivalesque festival in relation to its "context," or the social reality in which it takes place.[3]

General Meaning of the "Carnivalesque Festival" and Its Folkloric Definition. The term "carnival" in the classic folkloric sense[4] represents those festivals that are primarily urban and take place in a seasonal cycle designated by van Gennep as the *cycle de carnaval-carême*, or a cycle of the Lenten carnival. It is in fact the precise meaning of the carnival, if one accepts the most probable etymology "carne levaris"[5] which refers to the ecclesiastical sanctions and interdictions associated with the Easter liturgical cycle. The historical development of Western society shows the particular vigor of this festival in the urban milieu. In Eastern European society, on the other hand, the festival has developed as a rural carnival. For both types of cultural phenomena, we would like to introduce a single integrative and descriptive quality.

In addition to these considerations, the general meaning of the carnivalesque festival will be retained as follows: a community expression suspending the rules of everyday life, with the mask providing material support.

From Eliade to Bakhtin Place and time, two criteria of the carnival's definition, must be examined if we are to approach our definition from the sociological perspective. The next two sections explore spatial and temporal factors involved in the carnivalesque festival.

---

*Translated with permission from *Trois Essais sur la Fête. Du Folklore à l'Ethno-* *Semiotique* (Brussels: Edition de l'Université, 1974), pp. 9–20. Translation by Fae Korsmo.

The Social Place of the Festival

Study of the carnivalesque festival reveals different types of social settings. To skirt the complexity of typologies, we shall refer to Freitag's two models of "urban" society,[6] noting that the distinction between them is fundamental to our analysis. The models are as follows:

(a) the urban community of the Middle Ages and the Renaissance; and

(b) industrial cities and urbanized society.

The Urban Community of the Middle Ages and the Renaissance   The first type of social setting has a dual nature. From Freitag's socioeconomic perspective, it is indeed "urban."[7] On the other hand, he posits that the societal character of the city exists to the extent that it corresponds to a "general system of institutional and cultural integration of society."[8]

Medieval society meets this requirement, developing as an autonomous unit in relation to the rural environs. The medieval city exhibits several levels of autonomy. First, at the levels of nonagricultural production, the trades organized themselves. Second, with regard to modes of exchange, the city became a marketplace subject to endogenous regulation.[9] Finally, autonomy is seen in the *sui generis* institutional and political structures acquired by the city. An autocephalous system is thus constructed on the ecological base of the city, consisting of the "collectivity of structural dimensions of the system of actions: economic activity, political control, and the ideological-cultural system of community identification and legitimization."[10]

To this system, furthermore, we can affix the label "official" or "serious" culture, the opposite of which Bakhtin saw as "folk culture." Bakhtin derived the term from the work of Rabelais who also provides a model of the festival.[11]

Describing the culture originating in the urban social milieu, Freitag speaks of a "classic humanist" culture which "expresses itself in perfect harmony with the ethico-political order insuring the community structure's legitimization and integration."[12] This culture is related to the *power* that it justifies in the same way as it participates in the process of institutionalizing urban society.[13] The "festive" concept shares the social framework described above: the urban, bourgeois, corporate community of the late Middle Ages and the Renaissance. However, the festival opposes the official value system whose role is one of legitimizing a new social order. The festival becomes external to social institutions; we shall investigate its quality of rebelliousness below.

For our present purposes, the most important feature of the festival in the late Middle Ages and the Renaissance is its embeddedness in the social framework of *community*; the "place" of the city represents more than a simple ecological structure separate from a societal presence. Freitag emphasizes its role as a "historical and social city structure . . . materialized within its ecological structure,"[14] or urban territory. This relationship constitutes a fundamental distinction between the first type of "urban" society and the second—industrialized cities and urbanized society.

Industrial Cities and Urbanized Society   Leaving aside the subcategories used by Freitag in describing historical processes of development, we see this major category as essential to the consideration of contemporary Western carnivalesque festivals, particularly the one in Binche (Belgium). As we shall discover, the setting can be either rural or urban, since we are dealing with a single system.[15]

The city in this category differs from the first type insofar as "the transformational principles of development and the systemic regulation of economic and social activities are no longer focused on the urban system as such, but directly on the *supra-urban* industrial system and the state system. . . ."[16] Therefore, the city does not appear as a social, autocephalous system, but as a "particular social framework in which the social function is situated above."[17] Unlike the traditional city, it is not directed inward toward integration or internal operations, but "must abandon its own capacity for self-government in exchange for the benefits of a larger system."[18]

As a result, established relations among the inhabitants also change. The case is no longer that of community members, because societal integration cannot exist at the level of the industrial city. According to Freitag, "inhabitants of the industrial city are thus more socially connected with the city. . . . Typically the city tends to function solely as the location of their participation in the *supra-urban* system of production."[19] The city-country dichotomy seen in the previous system of the Middle Ages and the Renaissance is superseded here by the emergence of *urbanized society*.

At the foundation of the evolutionary process, Freitag places the factor of *economic* transformation which, in its first stage, established the medieval mercantile town as the place where "the economists' abstract conjecture of the marketplace"[20] was made concrete. Subsequently, at the heart of advanced, industrial societies, there emerged a "natural and universal environment of social relations."[21] The city, then, lost its societal character and became "the place" and "the means" of participation in the system of *social integration*. In such a system, space external to the city would also be considered quasi-urban, or of an organized nature.

The urban-rural distinction no longer applies in this system; there is, rather, one urbanized environment, with its corresponding systems of economic and political organization that develops a new "type of cultural, consensual integration in direct opposition to the prevailing type of institutional integration characteristic of the nation-state."[22] Freitag barely touches on the latter thought, but it appears useful in expanding the typology of the festival when one wishes to account for the relevant social framework.

The two types of social settings we have discussed so far are "urban" according to Freitag's typology, but they should be distinguished from one another on the basis of their respective social mechanisms. To complete this explanation of the "social place" of the festival, we now turn to "rural traditional society," a context appropriate to festivals of Eastern Europe in particular, but equally relevant to the development of the European carnival in general.

Rural Traditional Society   Based on the preceding schema, we can say that the traditional village community, such as the medieval town, can be described in terms of its "societal" nature. Indeed, the autocephalous system in question presents different "structural dimensions of the action-based system," corresponding to the following three levels:

(1) the structure of economic activity, or means of production and exchange in a subsistence economy dominated by agriculture and pastoralism and functioning at the level of the family unit;

(2) the structure of politico-institutional control dominated by the unit of the family;

(3) the ideological-cultural system corresponding to "traditional peasant culture" (agro-pastoral), and characterized by the means of oral transmission.

This schema seems to be consistent with the social structure and cultural phenomena—especially those concerning religion—which were studied by Mircea Eliade.[23] Eliade refers to the village community as a global society, thereby placing the social unit outside a historical context with its potential for politico-institutional conflict. The community remains, then, in an equilibrium without tension, where the only reaffirmation of institutional power appears in the ideological-cultural system, a system analyzed by Eliade in terms of its religious aspect.

In comparing the two models described previously, we can establish the presence of an "oppositional culture" consistent with Bakhtin's analysis. The oppositional culture takes as its unit of reference society as a whole, or "official culture." In Eliade's analysis, however, the opposing forces do not constitute an organized social group in relation to the same unit of reference, and there is no "oppositional culture." We shall return to Bakhtin and Eliade and their analyses of the festival as the reaffirmation or verification of the social system.

The three models—urban communities of the Middle Ages and the Renaissance, industrial cities and urbanized society, and traditional rural society—will serve as backgrounds to the following analysis, in which we explore the "social" or "urbanized" nature of various festivals and their relationships to institutions.

Characteristics of "Carnival Time"

Whether the concept of "festival time" is placed in the first or second societal model, it implies the same event: a break with everyday life, a time that is qualitatively different and perceived as separate, a time permitting social actions that would be inconceivable outside the boundaries of festival (for example, inversion of rules and roles, the negation of certain values, etc.). Furthermore, it has a universal and cosmic aspect insofar as it allows a "revitalization" expressed through the "birth-death-resurrection" theme seen in the analyses by Bakhtin and Eliade. The concept represents the central theme of carnivalesque symbolism, having as its basis the cognizance of a cyclical time which is recurrent, capable of regeneration, and thus of reaffirming the existence of society. The reaffirmation can be of an oppositional nature (folk culture in the Middle Ages, for example) or it can reinforce the cohesion of the institutional system (as in the traditional rural community).

The same "world vision" of cyclical time lies at the foundation of Bakhtin's symbolic system in which grotesque imagery is revealed by the mask, an accessory *par excellence* of the festival that suspends the ordinary and everyday. Eliade describes this time as sacred, since it constitutes a "severance with the profane existence by a breakthrough of Great Time,"[24] which allows a reactualization of the Myth through the act of Rite. Bakhtin, on the other hand, places the medieval folk festival in a "desacralized time" because of the dichotomous relationship between folk culture and official culture.

With respect to the sacred-profane dualism, Greimas[25] observed "that which distinguishes the mythical from the aesthetic is the particular form of cultural connotation underlying either phenomenon."[26] He adds a comment by Y. Lotman regarding the typology of literary texts which "succeeds in demonstrating that the decisive factor determining whether a text is sacred, didactic, or literary is not necessarily within the text itself, but originates instead in the connotative attitudes of the reader, who is himself embedded in a particular cultural context."[27]

Extending this logic, we can interpret the "sacred" quality of the festival as nonintrinsic to the phenomenon itself, but rather as part of the social reference unit or the festival's role within the institutional system and the type of power relations entailed. In this sense, the Rabelaisian festival is desacralized only if its unit of reference is seen as global society, or the society that sustains the "classical humanist culture" mentioned by Freitag, and that "expresses itself in strict accordance with the ethico-political system assuring the legitimization and integration of the community structure."[28] In relation to this reference unit, the urban medieval carnival certainly appears to be an expression of an oppositional folk culture; further, we shall attempt to describe it as "desacralizing" in relation to literate culture and the institutional power against which folk culture arose.

This "desacralizing" culture, however, appears "sacred" as well, when one considers the cultural connotations and "world vision" belonging to the social group in question. It expresses, in this case and according to Bakhtin, resistance to the official medieval culture which, "through all its forms and images, through its system of abstract thought, attempted to inculcate the diametrically opposed belief in a static, unchanging world order and in the eternal static order of all existence."[29]

On the other hand, the traditional agricultural festival analyzed by Eliade exemplifies "traditional peasant culture" as the unit of reference corresponding to society as a whole. There is no oppositional culture in reference to a chosen referent, but a culture that places itself within society's institutional order. The potential for opposition is found outside the imagined order (for example, taking literate culture as the global society referent). The world vision underlying this type of festival is one of cosmic revitalization; it does not question the institutional order, but rather permits its reactualization and rebirth.

Definition of the "Carnivalesque Festival" Concept

In the preceding section, we explored the meaning of the two coordinates "place" and "time" in the context of the carnivalesque festival. We have seen that these concepts represent a "world vision" expressed at the festive-symbolic level (i.e., grotesque masks, death-resurrection scenarios, etc.).

Here, we offer a definition of the carnivalesque festival, in which the social framework is communitarian—or "societal," to use Freitag's terminology—and time is perceived as a rupture. This perception imbues time with qualities that allow for the *reaffirmation* of the group's social cohesion, a phenomenon that can occur only beyond the boundary of the ordinary. Time is thus dynamic, whether the group's values are those of the established order or the oppositional culture.

The dynamic nature of the carnivalesque festival is thus a function of the relation between the reference group and the global society in power. It will be "rebellious" (oppositional) in the first societal model (Bakhtin) and "institutional" in the second model (Eliade), depending on whether the festival's community support is leveled within the power structure or against it. Acceptance of this definition implies the insignificance of other classificatory criteria. For example, that a festival belongs to the "winter cycle" or to the "spring cycle" is important only in the historical sense (the festive calendar differs in Eastern and Western Europe). While the distinction between rural and urban festivals is significant in a communitarian society, it is no longer determinant in the "urbanized society."

From the "Carnivalesque" Festival to the "Folklorized" Festival

We must now return to the "urbanized society,"[30] and review the definition of its function. We conceptualized the carnivalesque phenomenon as a festival that reaffirms the cohesion of a social group to its communitarian structure through participation in a time of revitalization. Such revitalization is accomplished by the "birth-death-resurrection" cycle.

The "social place," as defined in the "urbanized society model" cannot, then, be described as communitarian (societal), since there is no "community" to speak of, and therefore no need to reaffirm a cohesion that never existed. The global society, functioning as a unit of reference, exists here at the supra-urban level, and the city consists of merely a "particular social frame"; in other words, the "frame" simply acquires an ecological delineation, while merging with the global society in all other respects. In such a context, festival "time" will also diverge from the two preceding models.

Time in the carnivalesque sense is a "rupture" in relation to sociocultural factors. If the social group whose values are projected into the festival ceases to constitute a "community," the ruptural connotations—which allow a revitalization expressed by birth-death-resurrection symbolism—must logically disappear from the festival; they have lost their correspondence to the world vision held by the societal group. It seems, then, that neither of the criteria used to define the carnivalesque festival are realized in the model of urbanized society; neither time nor place have an effect on "carnivalesque" features. In other words, "urbanized society" cannot experience a carnivalesque festival (at the level of theoretical models which can in reality interpenetrate).

The urbanized society can, however, experience a second type of festival, the "folklorized festival," which has retained the formal aspect of the carnival. Below, its characteristics are briefly reviewed.

The cultural characteristics of urbanized society serve to influence both coordinates of time and place in relation to the festival. Where time is concerned, the social group's informality and lack of cohesion at any level below that of society as a whole gives the festival a passive and "performance" dimension. In contrast, the dynamic "world vision" implies participation in the "Great Time." Material evidence of the performance aspect in the folklorized festival is often provided in the form of a "ramp" between actors and spectators.

From a semiotic perspective, Greimas describes the process leading to "folklorization" as a "passage from the ethnosemiotic to the sociosemiotic."[31] He lists the following indicators of this process:

(a) a dissolved global mythical phenomenon reappearing at the fringes of so-called "developed" societies as disconnected, autonomous discourse (poetry, music, dance);

(b) rather than sacred manifestations, the various autonomous languages of macrosocieties assume entertaining or aesthetic functions;

(c) as opposed to collective manifestations, expressions of poetry, music, or motion adopt individualistic styles for their production and utilization;

(d) contrary to collective productions of meaning, semiotic objects generated via languages become essentially objects for individual consumption.

Applying this general process of "folklorization" to the carnivalesque festival and the folklorized festival yields the following observations:

• the festival, as it corresponds to a "complex semiotic object," is "desemanti-cized" preserving only certain formal aspects of the original model; it conveys the symbolism of a world vision that has lost its relevance to any extant culture;

• the festival is desacralized, becoming a show or spectacle (the rupture acquires entertaining or aesthetic connotations);

• the festival becomes individualized, "consumed," and unreal (its support being an informal group rather than a community); it becomes a "make-see," not a "make-do."[32]

The two types of festival—carnivalesque and folklorized—resemble each other only in certain formal aspects. We can hypothesize an informal "community" created through participation in "carnivalesque" time and, inversely, "festival time," producing the "cohesion" of a momentary community that dissipates with the festival itself. Such a festival would have an oppositional relationship to the values held by the global society and could possibly be seen as a "valve" mechanism in that time is controlled by the festival. The other alternative would resemble a revolutionary process. By inverting the concepts of the hypothesis, one can observe the "festive" as well as "carnivalesque" connotations in demonstrations of protest like that of May 1968 and the hippie movement's search for a new way of life "outside the establishment."

We are now able to construct a relational diagram showing the different models and corresponding festivals. Figure 1 was obtained by using the Carnival of Binche and the Winter Carnival of the Balkan States as examples.[33] In this chart, the first column applies to "carnivalesque" festival, and the second corresponds to "folklorized" festivals. Additionally, it should be remembered that concrete examples of the festivals cannot be described by a single model; only the Rabelaisian festival excludes outside influences, since it constitutes a model in itself.

Figure 2 summarizes the types of power relationships that determine the dimensional aspects of the carnivalesque festival. The diagram also presents the world vision(s) expressed in the festival(s). (The singular applies to theoretical models, while the plural is used in the context of social reality and accounts for the inevitable interference produced by sociohistoric evolution.)

Returning to Figure 1, we see in the example of *Moldavie du Nord* two models. First, there is the expression of a "world vision" that reaffirms the values of the institutional system—namely, the patriarchical society—in a "sacred" time of rupture that allows "revitalization" (for example, the Myth of the Eternal Return and the Birth-Death-Resurrection scenario). Second, there is a world vision related to the supra-community level, or the "urbanized society" model, in which the festival becomes a "put-on performance."

The mutual interference between the two models stems from the dynamic tension between the different levels of the festival phenomenon. The two "world visions" are incompatible with the institutional system (or mechanisms of power), leading to the

Figure 1

	"Sacred"	"Performance"
Model I	Example of a peasant carnival: the cycle of 12 days in Moldavia (Rumania) —Binche in 1st aspect	*idem;* folklorized aspects example: Festival of the Masks "Les Kukeri de Pernik" in Bulgaria
Model II (medieval urban)	folk carnival (Rabelaisian festivals)	—
IIa (commercial town of the last century)	Binche—2nd aspect	*idem;* folklorized aspect
Model III	community of the moment (Binche in 4th aspect)	folklorized carnival (Binche in 3rd aspect)

Figure 2

Power Relationship in Social Place	Institutional	Oppositional
Model I	Cycle of 12 days (Central Europe—Balkans)	—
Model II	—	Rabelaisian festival
Model IIa	Binche—2nd aspect	—
Model III	Binche—3rd aspect	Binche—4th aspect

inevitable destruction of one of the festival types. At the time of this writing, the "rural community" system is being supplanted.

(1) The Rabelaisian Festival of the Middle Ages   As we have seen, the Rabelaisian festival represents a model of a festival expressing the "world vision" of a folk-urban class that makes up a "community." This community becomes immersed in a time of rupture—a time we can also call "sacred"—allowing for the reaffirmation of the community's own culture, as opposed to the culture in power (literate culture, the state, the church).

(2) The Binche Festival of Today   Finally, the case of Binche merits a more extensive treatment, since it offers an important example of interference between the models and the juxtaposition of two different festival types. Applying the above schema

to the Binche festival, the process appears to be one of "sedimentation," observed especially in the gestural and morphological symbolism of the festival's central character, the "Gille."[34] The action takes place as if each social model underlying the festival has fashioned its own symbols to bring forth its "world vision." The symbols then undergo successive transformations corresponding to the model itself and to the world vision.

This leads to a progressional pattern of "desemantization" and "resemantization" culminating in the carnival's transition to folklorization, or total desemantization in relation to the chosen societal unit of reference. We shall explore this process below through looking at several components of the Binche festival.

First, the origins and present use of the costume can be seen in light of Model I (the rural festival). The Binche festival has in fact retained a series of elements that cannot be explained unless they are placed within a semiotic system corresponding to a former culture. In this case, the use of the costume should be seen in the context of the culture in which the actual festival originated.

Second, with regard to Gille's appearance, the image we have of him is actually quite recent, dating back some 100 years. In fact, the Gille of the rural festival changed after 1850, precisely when the city of Binche began to experience economic prosperity and became an important center with a thriving middle class. Such prosperity caused the festival's "appropriation" by the dominant class, and a new "world vision" appeared; the "grotesque" faded with the emergence of prestige and luxury, the signs of which were donned by Gille. Gille's "metamorphosis" was not accidental. It was one aspect of the festival's fundamental transformation from one "world vision" to another and its appropriation by a social class desirous of proclaiming its existence and "power."

The incongruous features of Gille's character and his central role in the present-day carnival illustrate the third component of the Binche festival: the hidden festival core of the seemingly folklorized festival.

If we begin by considering the Carnival of Binche in relation to the global society of Model III (urbanized society), we can easily observe characteristics of "folklorization," in particular, the "putting on a show" aspect. The international reputation of the Binche festival is such that each year the crowds are as numerous as they are diverse.

If, however, we think of the "town" or the "Binche population" as the social reference unit, we return to a framework similar to that of Model II (urban and societal), keeping in mind, however, the necessary adjustment. Binche has its own historical and cultural characteristics; the festival is not an expression of "folk culture" values, but of those belonging to the prosperous commercial class. These exceptions aside, the fact remains that behind the vast "folklore" of the Carnival of Binche, in the inner city, there is a festival that is still authentically carnivalesque. It constitutes the reaffirmation of a "community" which brings to "carnival time" the expectation of yearly revitalization. This festival concerns only *les Binchois*, the people of Binche.

At the heart of the festival, a momentary and informal "community" recovers, through institutional methods, the conditions of the carnivalesque—a "communitarian" social place and a time of rupture experienced as "collective revitalization." The example of Binche serves to clarify the different aspects of the festival that we previously outlined through use of abstract models. As a whole, the Carnival of Binche represents the juxtaposition of two models: a carnivalesque festival and a folklorized festival, both intermingling in the more or less desemantized semiotic systems of which Gille is one of the foremost representations.

In conclusion, we have attempted to define the concept, "carnivalesque festival," as a return to complex reality, a direct reflection of society, and evidence of the society's value system. It is tempting to conclude that the festive-phenomenon approach leads one to the core of a sociological puzzle and thereby constitutes an advantageous mode of perception. The festival appears to be a crystallization of society's everyday reality.

NOTES

1. The examples are chosen in reference to the surveys conducted: Fieldwork on the Winter Masquerade in northern Moldavia, Rumania, 1969, 1970, 1971; on the carnival of the Center region (Binche and Leval-Trahegnies, Belgium); and to studies concerning the theme of the festival by Mircea Eliade (*The Myth of the Eternal Return* [New York: Pantheon, 1954]), and to the festivals described by Mikkaïl Bakhtin and Samuel Glotz (see below).

2. Mihai Pop. *Problèmes généraux de l'ethnologie européenne*, First International Congress of European Ethnology, Paris, August 24–28, 1971. Multigraph.

3. For the relationship between "text" and "context," refer to the controversy between Vladimir Propp and Claude Lévi-Strauss. See Claude Lévi-Strauss "L'analyse morphologique des contes russes," *International Journal of Slavic Linguistics and Poetics* 3 (1960): 122–49. Revised as "La structure et la forme. Réflexions sur un ouvrage de Vladimir Propp," *Cahiers de l'Institut de Science Économique Appliquée* 9 (1960): 3–36 and reprinted in Claude Lévi-Strauss, *Structural Anthropology*, vol. 2 (New York: Basic Books, 1976), pp. 115–45. See also Vladimir Propp, *Morphology of the Folktale* (Austin: University of Texas Press, 1966) and *Morphologie du conte*. *Les transformations des contes merveilleux*, with an introduction by Eleazar M. Meletinskij (Paris: Seuil, 1970), pp. 171–200. Refer also to Paul Bouissac's analyses of the circus, namely to his "Pour une analyse ethnologique des 'entrées de' clowns: construction de l'object et esquisse de la méthode," *Ethnologie*

Française (New Series) 1 (1971) no. 3–4: 7–17.

4. Arnold van Gennep, *Manuel de Folklore Contemporain*, vol. 1 (Paris: Picard, 1947).

5. Ibid., p. 876.

6. Michel Freitag, "De la ville-societé à la ville milieu," *Sociologie et société* (Les Presses de l'Université de Montreal) 3 (May 1971) no. 1: 25–57.

7. The notions of "urban" frame, of "urbanization," and of "urbanized society" are used here in the meaning that Freitag gives them. It would be useful, however, to revise these notions in accord with the contents that human geography can give them, and to distinguish not only the socio-economic dimension as the author does, but for instance the morphology of the social place, or also the type of "communication" within a social place.

8. Freitag, p. 26.

9. Ibid., p. 31.

10. Ibid., p. 31.

11. Mikkaïl Bakhtin, *L'oeuvre de François Rabelais et la culture populaire au Moyen Age et sous la Renaissance* (Paris: Gallimard, 1970).

12. Freitag, p. 37.

13. Ibid., p. 26.

14. Ibid., p. 36.

15. S. Glotz, *Le Carnaval de Binche* (Bruxelles: Editions du Folklore brabancon, 1948); "Le Carnaval de Binche et les Archives communales," in *Le carnaval traditionnel en Wallonie*, Catalog of the Exhibit Sept. 12–Oct. 21, 1962 (Mons: Fédération du Tourisme de la province du Hainaut, 1962); *L'Origine et l'évolution de quelques types carnavalesques de Wallonie (Belgique)* (Lisbon:

junta de investigaçoes do ultramar, 1965), Acts of the International Congress of Ethnography, 1963.

16. Freitag, p. 45.

17. Ibid., p. 46.

18. Ibid., p. 47.

19. Ibid., p. 48.

20. Ibid., p. 55.

21. Ibid., p. 56.

22. Ibid., p. 55.

23. Mircea Eliade, *The Sacred and the Profane: The Nature of Religion* (New York: Harper & Row, 1961); *Myth and Reality* (New York: Harper & Row, 1963).

24. Mircea Eliade, *Patterns in Comparative Religion* (London: Sheed and Ward, 1958), p. 396.

25. Algeirdas Greimas, "Reflexions sur les objects ethno-sémiotiques. Manifestations poétiques, musicales et gestuelles," paper delivered at First International Congress of European Ethnology, Paris, August 24–28, 1971.

26. Ibid., p. 3.

27. Ibid., p. 3.

28. Freitag, p. 37.

29. Bakhtin, p. 274.

30. Henri Lefebvre, *La vie quotidienne dans le monde moderne* (Paris: Gallimard, 1968).

31. Greimas, p. 4.

32. Ibid., p. 9.

33. These examples were selected with reference to fieldwork on the Winter Masquerade in North Moldavia, Rumania, 1969, 1970, and 1971; of the Carnival of the Center region (Binche and Leval-Trahegnies, Belgium); and to studies on festivals by Eliade (*The Myth of the Eternal Return*); Bakhtin (*L'oeuvre de Rabelais*); and Glotz (*Le Carnaval de Binche*).

34. For information on the Gille, see Dorothy Gladys Spicer, *Festivals of Western Europe* (New York: H. W. Wilson Co., 1958), pp. 6–7.

17 / Japanese Festivals: A Preliminary Semiotic Analysis

Maurice Coyaud

Since its appearance in 1928, Vladimir Propp's "Morphology of the Folktale" has had an enormous impact on folklorists, anthropologists, linguists, and literary critics. Propp described the structure and formal organization of narratives following the linear sequence of elements in the text. Such component parts were termed "functions," that is, acts performed by the story's personages and defined from the point of view of their significance for the course of the action. Propp individuated and organized thirty-one "functions" to form a morphology, that is, a description of the text according to its component parts and the relationship of these components to each other and to the whole.

After Propp, structuralism and more recently semiotics contributed further developments of the systematic approaches to cultural materials, often proposing to consider as "texts" such diverse corpuses as pictorial cycles, film genres, culinary systems, or circus acts.

In this article, Maurice Coyaud presents the results of his analysis of eighty-six festivals of contemporary Japan. The article indicates the main characters in the festival ceremonies: human, divine or demonic, or animal. Following is a list of eleven "func-

tions" at work in festivals of Japan: appeasing the souls of the dead; driving away evil spirits; building a sacred place; summoning the gods; exposing oneself to danger; installing a god in his proper location; procession; sharing of food; performing ritual plays; achieving welfare; and transferring life or living qualities to an object. Each "function" is explained and given a distinctive sign. The author then discusses the different combinations of these "functions" in the development of different festivals, and some of the main types that result from these linear patterns. Of course, not all "functions" appear to have the same importance in the progression of Japanese festivals, and the author focuses the discussion on festivals centered around the function "sharing" or "exorcism" or those without the latter, because the consistent absence of one function may also be a relevant indication for the analysis. He is also able to indicate, making a preliminary comparison between sequential developments of similar festivals, that for instance some festivals no longer have the religious function as a central theme, but have changed into "pure spectacle" in large towns, while similar festivals have maintained a religious character (and the religious function) in smaller towns. The author concludes his semiotic analysis by pointing out how Buddhism was intermingled with Japan's autochthonous religion, and how the resulting essential function of Japanese festivals is a prayer for security, health in this life and in the hereafter for people, and abundant rain and good rice harvests for the fields. As an appendix to the text, the author gives an index of the festivals with the time of the year and the place of occurrence. This semiotic approach is intended as preliminary, and the author does not hide the difficulties encountered in approaching such a large, non-Western symbolic system. Yet, even though the operation at first glance may seem to have produced only a dry list of exotic names, matched to commonsensical functions, it offers a viable and synthetic classification of the basic social purposes and symbolic meanings of calendrical customs, rites, and festivities in Japanese culture. It also shows the potential help of such a methodology for studies conducted in the more established approaches, be it the comparative study of festival, the study of the whole festive cycle, or the preliminary, complete contextual frame for the in-depth analysis of a single festival or festive thematic motif. It can also be a sound basis for a computerized classification and further analysis of folkloric materials based on folkloric theory. In more general terms, the article shows how the semiotic approach—the study of signs—once clarified and refined may offer useful insights into the meaning of distant cultural systems such as the "Empire of signs" of Japanese festivals.

Japanese Festivals: A Preliminary Semiotic Analysis*[1]

Maurice Coyaud

The encompassing term *semiotic analysis* includes both functional and structural approaches. Vladimir Propp's *Morphology of the Folktale* (University of Texas, Austin: 1968) is an example of a functional perspective in which tales are analyzed according to the functions of their *dramatis personae*; while the number of personages is shown to be quite large, the number of functions appears to be very small. Structuralism deals with the relationships, both linear and nonlinear, between such functions.

*From *L'Homme* 17 (1977) no. 4: 91–105.   Translation by Fae Korsmo.

Marianne Mesnil[2] is the first, to my knowledge, to have applied the methods of Lévi-Strauss and Greimas[3] to the analysis of folk festivals. Using as examples two festivals in Belgium (the Carnival of Binche and the "polecat hunt" in the Bastogne region), Mesnil offers a tentative definition of the festival as a structure of significant relations; for the "polecat hunt" in particular, she proposes four functions: displacement, acquisition, sharing, and consummation.

In a similar vein, the following analysis proposes 11 functions for more than 86 Japanese festivals. The functional patterns, or relationships between functions, will serve as a means to discover the principal goals of Japanese festivals.

The first section lists the actors, or festival participants, and is followed by definitions of the 11 types of functions. Section 3 provides examples of functional patterns, and the final section discusses religious aspects of three important festivals. An index of the festivals is appended, giving the names, dates, and locations for festivals numbered below (F1, F2, etc.).

I. Actors

Participants in Japanese festivals can be categorized as human, divine, or animal (though animals are often divine).

A. Human Actors

—children: F1, F2, F13 (festival of children aged 7, 5, and 3 years), etc.
—boys: F2 (*tango no sekku* "boys' festival"); adolescents and young men
—believers: F21 (*hi watari* "fire crossing")
—entire population: F24 (*neputa:* an ainu term of uncertain etymology; during this festival, the entire town dances)
—specialists
  • cart pullers: F4, F37, etc.
  • mimes: F4, F45 (*onden-asobi,* "games of the rice fields" and farm labor miming)
  • musicians: F3, F4, F37 (Gion), F47 (Chikuma)
  • dancers: F6 (the eight deer), etc.
—clergy (who may also be musicians or dancers)
  • *kannushi* (Shinto priest): F5, F6, F7, F13, and especially F45 and F47 (playing the *sho* or mouth organ)
  • *miko* (priestesses): F13, F37, etc.
  • *yamabushi* (mountain ascetics generally associated with the Buddhist Shingon sect): F21, F32, F20a (*yamabushi* shell players)

B. Divine or Demonic Actors

—a "good" god: F7
—sun and moon (played by children): F53
—*tengu* ("Sky Dog," a winged angel with phallic nose and red face; there are also *karasutengu* with beaks and green faces). During the *onden-asobi* or the

ta no asobi the *tengu* play the role of the agrarian god *Sarutahiko:* F22, F45, F66.

—*oni* demons
* *ushi oni* "cow demon": F5, F63
* *aka oni* or "red demon," and *ao oni,* "green demon": F20a, F60 (*setsubun, oni kenbai*)
* *namahage:* F71

C. Animal Actors

—*ushi* "cow": F22 (*ta-asobi*)

—*ushi oni* "cow demon": F5, F35, F63

—*shishi,* a mythical animal represented most often as a lion, but also as a tiger, a deer, or a wild boar, depending on the festival's location. F8, F51, F61

—*ryû,* a dragon: F9, F64 (Nagasaki *okunchi*)

—*karasu* and *usagi,* the crow-rabbit pair mimed by children in F57, or by *yamabushi* in F32

—*shika* or deer: F6, F63

II. Functions

Eleven principal functions can be derived. While this may seem to be too large a number, there are, I believe, more than eleven, due to the great diversity of the festivals. Furthermore, several of the eleven functions are quite abstract and encompass subfunctions. For example, sharing of food implies its consumption. Similarly, "welfare" (see H below) implies plentiful harvests as well as good health and security.

In another respect, the functions of certain episodes seem both obscure and marginal and have therefore been set aside for a more in-depth analysis. They are as follows:

—F71: *namahage,* "frightening the children." This can be considered a marginal function since it appears only in this festival;

—F66: *tengu o okoraseru, tengu warai,* "teasing the *tengu.*" The purpose of this festival is not clear;

—F30 and F34d: wooden dolls representing Dôsojin are thrown into the fire. It can be assumed that the Dôsojin dolls play the same role as the *hitogata,* effigies of oneself which are sent floating down a river, carrying with them all of one's ills, impurities, and diseases. What is not understood is the use of the name of the god Dôsojin to designate the dolls which are then burned.

The eleven functions we will consider are the following:

A: appeasing the souls of the dead (the *bon* [trays] festival) and especially those of suicides (F38)

B: building a sacred place (*temenos*)

C: convoking the gods and spirits, awakening the forces

D: driving away the souls of evil spirits, diseases, etc.

E: being preyed upon, exposing (or pretending to expose) oneself to danger

F: sharing and consuming food

H: health, welfare, and good harvests

I: installing a god in a location, be it inanimate (tree, temple, or *mikoshi,* or portable shrine that is bounced around during a boisterous festival) or animate (a child)

P: pursuit, procession

S: performance of a show, dance, mime, contest

T: transfer of one's life, one's name, one's diseases to an object

For each of these functions, examples and further explanation are given below.

1. *A:* In the festivals selected, appeasement is not frequently enacted, but it is nevertheless important for its primary role in Japan's most popular festival, the *bon,* or festival of the dead.

2. *B:* Construction of a sacred place, the *temenos,* for example, or a sacred vessel (F30). The *yamabushi* walk barefoot across live coals (F21); the *hoko* (halberd) floats of the Gion festival (F37) serve to attract the gods like lightning rods.

3. *C:* Convocation of the gods or benevolent spirits. Awakening of Hachiman (F65); making noise to rouse the spirits of dormant vegetation in wintertime (F34). There is slight interference between this function and function I.

4. *D:* Exorcism is practiced in a variety of ways. A few of these are listed here:

—hitting the ground with a bamboo stick (the role of the two *tengu* in F22)

—sweeping ashes on the observers (F44)

—shooting arrows toward the four directions—or six directions, counting the sky and the earth—(F21); shooting arrows at a target placed on the temple door (F22)

—brandishing an axe (the *yamabushi* in F21)

—burning (F21, F21a, F30 to F34d, F52, etc.)

—setting adrift an effigy of oneself which carries away the various ills threatening to harm the person; this is somewhat like using a "scapegoat" (F52, F50, F76)

—smearing oneself with soot (F40, F73) or mud (F74). A form of homeopathy? Soot and mud symbolize diseases and are easily washed away; "may the diseases leave us just as easily." However, there are those who also say, "We cover ourselves with soot to frighten away demons."

5. *E:* During their dangerous years, men risk death. The festival imitates such danger. In Nozawa (F30), men expose themselves to death by fire; similarly, the *yamabushi* expose their feet to hot coals (F21, F21a).

6. *F:* The sharing function is linked to function C, since the gods are often convoked for the sharing of a meal (F23).

7. *H:* Once the live coals have been crossed, the *yamabushi* are safe and sound (F21). In Nozawa, men in their dangerous years leap from a burning vessel onto the snow (F30).

8. *I:* Installation of the gods in their dwellings, using a tree or a child. In F57, a child fulfills the role of a god (*kami no yorishiro o yaku*).

9. *P:* The pursuit and/or procession function is linked to function D (the necessity of driving out impure spirits) and to function S.

10. *S:* Performance of sacred or non-sacred dances, mime (F45's simulation of coitus), miming the work of the rice fields (F22).

11. *T:* The transfer of one's life into another being (*mi-gawari*), generally a simplified effigy of oneself, so that the danger may harm only the substitute. Often, one's name is written on the object. Objects can be *hitogata* (F52); *kashima*, or straw dolls set afloat (F50); dolls on floating boats (*nagashi-bina*, F76); burnt wooden Dôsojin dolls (F30); burnt paper lanterns (F30); or burnt pieces of wood (F21). The destruction of these substitutes means that ills have been chased away and good health will follow. Note that T is linked to D and H.

Though it is easy to see that appeasement, function A, is linked to function D, I have singled it out because of its importance and specificity. The list of functions is neither perfect nor exhaustive, but may serve as a useful point of departure for the analysis of Japanese festivals.

III. Order of Functions in Japanese Festivals

Festivals involving a single function are rare; these are festivals in which the religious element is no longer present and which have been reduced to pure performance. (See, for example, function S in F25 and F26 and functions P and S in F28 and F29.)

The *tanabata* festival involves the convergence of two amorous stars—Vega the herdsman and Altair the weaver. The lovers meet every year on July 7. Originating in China and widespread in Korea, the *tanabata* has lost its religious function as it is celebrated in Sendai (F26), but in smaller towns like Matsumoto (F58), the religious function survives. In the Matsumoto *tanabata* festival, *kegare* (impurities) are placed on *hitogata* and set afloat.

1. Fire Festivals in Nozawa and Takao

To illustrate the various functions and their patterns, the scene of the fire festival in Nozawa can be reconstructed as follows (F30):

—*B:* A 15-meter tree is cut for the ship or vessel, and the vessel is built and heaped with cypress branches (*Cryptomeria japonica* or *sugi no ki*) and New Year's decorations (*shimenawa, kadomatsu*).

—*I:* Men at critical ages sit on the vessel; the aged ones come carrying Dôsojin dolls and *shotoro* lanterns, placing these items on the vessel; the torches are lit.

—*E:* The critical moment. The torches are thrown into the vessel, and the men on the vessel catch them in midair, risking their lives and singing.

—*H:* The vessel goes up in flames, and the men save themselves by leaping onto the snow, still singing. *Mochi* rice cakes are cooked on the coals; the Dôsojin and the *akurei* (evil spirits) return to the sky.

—*F:* The *mochi* are eaten.

The resulting sequence for F30 is B, I, E, H, F.

A similar pattern can be observed in the *hi watari* or "fire crossing" festival in Takao (F21): B, P, I, D, E, H.

—*B:* A large square is marked off with string, and the people then hang straw and pieces of paper on the string. At the center of the square is another square (10 m²) strewn with cypress branches. Pieces of wood bearing the names of believers are also tossed into the center square. This will become the pyre.

—*P:* Procession to the sound of seashells from the communal house.

—*I:* Installation of the actors in the sacred place, prayers at the door, and a procession around the square. The *yamabushi* then take their places according to rank.

—*D:* Prayers, singing, shooting of arrows to kill the demons; axes are brandished for the same purpose.

—*E:* Crossing live coals barefoot to dispel evils.

—*S:* Safety. Participants are assured immunity from disease, infernal fires, and earthly fires (which are frequent in Kantô during the dry season).

2. Examples of the Sharing Function in Festivals

—F38 (*kichigai matsuri*). By night—P, A, P: twelve men with torches flash through the town crying "Fire!" They then go to the lakeside grave of a female suicide, draw water, and sprinkle it over the grave, thus appeasing the suicide's soul. By day— P, F, P: the twelve men carry trays of nuts, *kaki,* and *mochi,* and run through the town streets. They arrive at the house of the *toya* (festival organizer). The twelve men throw the contents of the trays in the face of the *toya* who has come out to welcome them. This is a "violent" type of sharing, with the expected result of good harvests.

—F55 (*amazake butsu kake* or *bukkakke*): P, F. This festival offers yet another example of "violent" sharing. Participants throw sweet sake (*amazake butsukake matsuri*) in each others' faces.

—F20 (*setsubun*): D, P, F. In this case, the sharing consists of sowing dried peas, *mame-maki,* which have the power to chase away demons, by throwing them at the onlookers.

—F23 (*kangen sai*): P, F. The *mikoshi* shrine is carried out to sea; the *kannushi* offer food to the gods in a peaceful sharing.

—F47 (*nabe-kanmuri*): P, F. A *miko* (priestess), dressed in white, boils water in four large cauldrons; she cooks rice in the cauldrons, then offers it to the agricultural god Sarutahiko.

—F3 (*o-bon*): B, S, F, A, D. Construction of a stage for musicians; dance; sharing of food offered to the souls of the dead who have come to stay by their graves for three days. In this way, the *akurei* are driven away.

—F22 (Fujimori *ta-asobi*): D, S, F. The demons are chased away in two ways: two *tengu* hit the ground with large bamboo sticks; a *kannushi* fires arrows at a target hung from the *torii* (a portico, often painted red, an obligatory feature of all Shinto temples) at the entrance of the sacred place. Sixteen acts of mime and singing showing rice field work follow. Finally, a shared offering of sake and *ushi-no-shita* cakes (cows' tongues) to the god.

—F18 (*hadaka matsuri*): D, P, F, D. Purification by ice water; procession to the temple (actually by running); offering of *mochi,* tangerines, and fish to the god; small *mochi* and tangerines are thrown to the spectators who stand in a line.

—F19 (*bonten matsuri*): B, I, P, H, F. Construction of *bonten.* The *bonten* is a sacred object made from bamboo sticks in bundles (in Takao), separated (in Tokyo), or in the shape of sugar bread four or five meters long (Akita-shi, Yokote). The etymology of the term is uncertain, but it is known that the *bonten* are dwelling places of the gods or divine forces. After the *bonten* is made, there is a procession to the temple. Good health and safety are granted in return for prayers before the *bonten*. Food and sake are shared after the procession and the ritual combat between the *bonten*.

—F72 (*kamakura*): I, F. The *kamakura* are snow huts where children make an altar to Suijin, the god of water. Tangerines and *mochi* are offered to Suijin, and the children share their meal in the *kamakura*, eating the food offered to Suijin.

—F74 (*doronko matsuri*): D, P, F. Participants roll in the mud; the *mikoshi* is tossed into a muddy pit; there is a procession; the impurities, together with the mud, are washed away, and everyone eats heartily.

3. Festivals in Which the D Function Is Fundamental

In the preceding festivals, the D function was often present, but since these festivals were classified by the distinguishing function of "sharing," the D function was not emphasized. In the following festivals, the "sharing" function is not as obvious.

—F44 (*tenteko*): P, S, D, E, H. Procession to the temple, dancing around the *torii;* dispelling of demons; sweeping away ashes as protection from sickness and intellectual impotence; performance in the temple to dispel the dangers threatening 25-year-old men; good health will result for these men.

—F45 (*asuka onden-asobi*): D, S, E, T, H. A green *tengu* performs the ritual of *tsuyubarai* exorcism by hitting the ground. A first performance mimes work in the rice fields; a second simulates coitus. Fertilization symbolizes sowing (T: the fertility of the couple on stage is transferred to earth).

—F52 (*chi no wa kuguri*): T, D. Passage through a large ring of rice straw; infants and children must touch a paper figure for purification. The *hitogata* are either burned or set afloat, carrying with them all the ills which could have harmed the children.

—F50 (*kashima nagashi*): T, D. Dolls carrying potential ills are set adrift.

—F5 (*ushi oni*): P, D. The wooden cow knocks at the houses to drive away impurities, diseases, etc.

—F37 (Gion): B, D, P, S. Carts are built and decorated with *hoko* to expel the epidemic which struck Kyoto.

—F40 (*sumi-nuri*): D, P. Participants cover themselves with soot to rid themselves of sickness and demons.

—F51 (*ôtaue*): D. When the rice is transplanted, but before the work has begun, the demons (*akumabari*) are chased away.

—F61 (*shishi odori*): D, P, S. During a deer dance, the demons are driven away.

—F62 (*mushi-okuri*): D, P. In summer, a procession drives away the harmful insects and "accompanies" them (*okuri*) out of the village.

—F60 (*oni kenbai*): D, S. People in demon costumes dance and carry swords; the dance serves to drive out the demons.

—F24 (*neputa*): T, D, S. Originally, the various ills were transferred to enormous dolls, which even today are still sent out to sea (*akurei o nagasu*).

—F35 (*yamayaki*): A, D. The soul of the cow demon (*ushi oni*) is appeased, and annoying insects are chased away by "burning" the mountain.

—F34 (*sagichô*): B, C, D. Beds of coals are assembled with much noise to summon the spirits of vegetation which lie dormant under the earth; demons are driven away by the fire.

—F53 (Shiramatsu-*sai*): I, D, P, S. The god is installed in his abode (*kami no shuku*), demons are driven away, and there is a dancing processional with *sasara*, or multiple castanets.

4. Festivals Without Exorcism

The D function is extremely important and is present in the majority of festivals. According to my experience and available documentation, this function does not appear in the following festivals, though this may be due to insufficient documentation or observation.

—F82 (*goza kae*): B, I, S. Construction of new *tatami* to house the gods. Performance of dances: *sarugaku*, dance of the monkey; and *iwato-hiraki*, dance of the cave opening, a ritual related to the myth of the origins of Japan.[4]

—F2 (*tango-no sekku*): I, P. Installation of the god in the *mikoshi*. He is carried into the midst of general pandemonium.

—F4 and F14 (Kawagoe *matsuri*, Chichibu *yo matsuri*): P, S.

—F46 (Takaoka): I, P. The gods Ebisu, Sarutahiko, and Daikoku are placed in carts and carried about.

—F57 (*kodomo dengaku*): I, P, S. Placing the god in the body of a child.

—F41 (*baka-bayashi*): S, H. Mimes intended to attract the favor of Ubusuna, the goddess of childbirth.

—F65 (*yagorô-don*): C, P, S. Calling on the god Hachiman. Children are awakened in the middle of the night, and they in turn awaken the god.

IV. Shinto Religion in the Festivals

To conclude this rather brief study, I shall turn to the gods invoked during the festivals, and describe two festivals in which divine dwellings are constructed (F80 and F82) and one festival of meditation (F81: "fortifying the soul"). Finally, I will summarize the principal aims of Japanese festivals. A verification of the tentative semiotic analysis sketched above lies outside the scope of this article.

First, who are the gods? The Shinto festivals consist mainly of summoning the gods to request something of them. There are as many gods as there are creatures and objects. Every tree and every stone conceals a *kami* or spirit. Apparently these *kami* are no different from the higher god *kami* such as Amaterasu, the sun "who lights up the sky," Ama no uzume no mikoto, "an immodest maiden," or O kuni nushi no mikoto, "master of the country." For these major gods, the reader is referred to the *Kojiki*. The less personal gods are also those who are most frequently invoked: Yama no kami (god of the mountain), Ta no kami (god of the rice fields), Suijin (god of water), Saru ta hiko ("monkey rice field boy"), and Tengu ("Sky Dog").

The *kami* is the fundamental life force. Each being upon birth is endowed with a part of this force. It can be attacked and weakened by the *akuma* or *akurei* evil spirits. It is therefore necessary to reinforce or "fortify one's soul" (*tamashi zume*) through contact with the *kami*. These *kami* reside in specific locations (mountains, sky, trees, rocks, sea, earth), but also in certain privileged humans, including children (*chigo*, "kings of the festivals"), old men, and shamans (*noro* and *tsukasa* in Okinawa, *itako*,[5] the blind of Tohoku, and *miko* throughout Japan).

—F80 (*onabashira matsuri*). This festival takes place once every six years in Suwa, in the Nagano province; it is a festival of "posts" (*hashira*). Thirty fir trees, some as long as 30 meters, are cut down in the mountains and carried to the Suwa area. The work is done completely by hand, since any mechanical means would be considered profane. Strong, strapping fellows pull the trees down the mountains with ropes. According to Honda, the object of the festival is to place these tree trunks in each of the village's four temples, to "refresh" or revive the divinity. In reality, much of the true meaning of the festival has been lost and has been replaced by the sporting aspect of the event.[6]

Besides these fir tree pillars, the gods have other homes: *heisoku* (or *heigushi*), bundles of *gohei* (sticks decorated with cut-out paper charms, symbolizing the branch of the *sakaki*, a sacred tree); *bonten*, *hoko* swords, bows, arrows, and bundles of sticks (*shiba*); *kadomatsu*, pine trees placed at the door of one's house at New Year; *toshinawa*, ropes of rice straw, renewed each year and placed on the *torii* or under the door of the house. *Kadomatsu* and *toshinawa* are specific to Shogatsusama, the god of the New Year.

Each year the divine dwelling is renewed, providing the occasion for a festival:

—F82 (*goza kae matsuri*, festival for changing mats). This festival takes place on September 24, in Kashima, district of Yatsuka, in the Shimane province. As it is celebrated now, the ceremony is quite simplified. At one time, however, *igusa* reeds used for making *tatami* were cut from the sacred wet field (*shinden*). As they are destined in this case for the gods, they are named by the more solemn term, *goza*, rather than *tatami*. Once the new mats are ready, the *kannushi* of Izumo dance on them (*goza no mai*). The two main dances are the *sarugaku* or monkey dance (linked to Sarutahiko, the god of the rice fields) and the *iwato-hiraki* dance of the cave opening. The *kannushi* hold in their hands a twig of the sacred tree *sakaki* (*gohei*), a bow, arrows, or a sabre, depending on the dance.[7] This summary of the *goza kae* is based on Honda's description (1972).

An appropriate welcoming of the god of the New Year serves to "fortify the soul" (*tamashi zume*). A particular festival by this name takes place in the so-called Miyaza, in the Kansai.

—F81 (*tamashi zume*). This is a form of retreat, of meditation. First, one must empty oneself (*onore o muneshû suru*), leaving space for the new fortified soul. Then, by drinking the sacred sake (*omiki*), one allows the soul to be penetrated by the spirit of rice. Finally, one participates in the *kagura*, or sacred dance. The god of the parish (*ujigami*) then descends upon the house of the *toya*, and the villagers gather around the house and receive the blessings of the *tamashi zume*. Similarly, when one carries the *mikoshi* in procession, one is favored by a *tamishi zume*.

The aims of the festivals enumerated by Honda obviously confirm most of the functions identified here. According to Honda, the festivals serve seven purposes: (1) secure plentiful harvests; (2) ward off disease (and in particular the *ekirei*, "epidemic-carrying demons") as in the Gion festival in Kyoto; (3) chase away evil spirits (*akuma*, *akurei*); (4) avoid fires; (5) obtain rain (climbing mountains, imitating thunder with large drums, lighting fires, praying to Ryûjin the dragon god, the dance of thanksgiving once rain has fallen); (6) chase away insects (*mushiokuri*); and (7) have good fishing and safety at sea. Those festivals in which participants are nude are the agricultural festivals calling on the god (*kami-mukae*) to request plentiful harvests and good health.

Index of Festivals[8]

F30 (January 15) *hi matsuri* "fire festival," Nozawa, Nagano-ken[20]

F31 (July 14) *hi matsuri* "fire festival," Nachi, Wakayama-ken[21]

F32 (December 31) *shorei sai* (or *jorei sai*) "festival of the torches," Haguro-san, Yamagata-ken[22]

F33 (October 22) Kurama *hi matsuri* "Kurama fire festival," Kyoto[23]*

F34 (January 14) *sagichô, chiwara no tondo* "festival of the straw pyres" (*tondo* or *donto* according to region), Nara

F34a (August 16) *hi matsuri* "fire festival," Yoshida, Yamanashi-ken[24]

F34b (January 7) *oni yo no hi matsuri* "fire festival of the night demons," Shiroshima-cho, Fukuoko-ken[25]

F34c (March 14–15) *sagichô* "straw pyres," Ôe Hachiman-shi, Shiga-ken[26]

F34d (January) *sankurô yaki* "burning of the *sankurô*," Matsumoto, Nagano-ken[27]

F34e (August 26) *daichôchin* "great lanterns," Suwa-jinja, Hazu-gun, Aichi-ken[28]

F34f (August 15) *bon kuyô* "offering of the *bon*" or Shingen-tsuka *no hi ondori* "Shingen fire festival," Shinshiro-machi, Minami-shitaragun, Aichi-ken[29]

F35 (January 15) *yama yaki* "burnings of the mountain," Nara

F36 (May 15) *aoi matsuri* "mallow festival," Kyoto[30]

F37 (all of July) Gion *matsuri* "festival of the Gion district," Kyoto[31]

F38 (October 8) *kosai no kichigai matsuri* "festival of fools," Katada-ko, Shiga-ken[32]

F39 (October 1) *niyû no warai matsuri* "laughter festival," Kawabe-cho, Wakayama-ken[33]

F40 (January 15) *sumi-nuri matsuri* "festival where one covers oneself in soot," Matsu no yama onsen, Niigata-ken[34]

F41 (May 24) *baka-bayashi* "fools' music," Fukui-shi[35]

F42 (May) Atsuta *no hoho matsuri* "Atsuta humor festival," Mie-ken[36]

F43 (February 11) *ta-asobi* "rice field games," Itabashi, Tokyo[37]

F44 (January 3) *tenteko matsuri*, Nishi-o-shi, Fuku-chi-chô, Aichi-ken[38]

F45 (February 4) Asuka *no miya no onden-asobi* "Asuka temple rice field games," Asuka-mura[39]

F46 (May 1) Takaoka *matsuri* "Takaoka town festival," Toyama-ken*

F47 (May 3) *nabe kanmuri matsuri* "festival of the cooking pots," Chikuma, Maibara*

F48 (May 5) *bonden* or *bonten*, Sumida-ku, Tokyo[40]*

F49 (May 17) *sanja matsuri* "sanja festival," or festival of the three fishermen brothers, Asakusa, Tokyo[41]*

F50 (May 24) *kashima nagashi* "setting afloat of the *kashima*," Akita-ken[42]

F51 (July 12) *Ôtaue matsuri* "great transplanting festival," Fukushima-ken (S.)

F52 (June 30) *Chi no wa kuguri* "ring of straw," Hikawa-jinja, Ômiya, Saitama-ken (S.)

F53 (June 14) Shiramatsui-*sai* "festival of Shiramatsu," Chiba-ken (S.)

F54 (July 20) *sumomo matsuri* "plum festival," Tokyo (S.)

F55 (July 25) *amazake-butsu-kake* (or *bukkake*) "festival where people throw sweet sake on each other," Saitama-ken (S.)

F56 (July 27–28) *ki-bune matsuri* "festival of the yellow boats," Kanagawa-ken (S.)

F57 (August 1) *kodomo dengaku* "dance of the children," Fukushima-ken (S.)

F58 (July and August) *tanabata* and *bon*, Matsumoto, Nagano-ken (S.)

F59 (summer) *nenbutsu kenbai* "sabre dance for Buddha," Iwate-ken (S.)

F60 (summer) *oni kenbai* "ogres' sabre dance," Iwate-ken (S.)

F61 (summer) *shishi odori* "dance of the deer," Hanamaki, Iwate-ken (S.)

F62 (August 17) *mushi-okuri* "sending away of the bugs," Saitama-ken (S.)

F62a (July 10) *mushi-okuri*, Aichi-ken[43]

F62b (January 14) *tori-oi* "bird hunt," Nakano-jo, Gumma-ken[44]

F63 (November 3) *itsu shika to ushi oni* "the five deer and the cow demon," Ehime-ken (S.)

F64 (October 7) Nagasaki *okunchi* "offering to Nagasaki" (S.)[45]

F65 (November 3–5) *yagorô-don* "yagorô-don festival," Kagoshima-ken (S.)[46]

F66 (November 15) *tengô matsuri* "tengu festival," Saitama-ken (S.)

F67 (November 17–18) *Sanzorô matsuri* "sanzorô festival" (with the seven gods of happiness), Aichi-ken (S.)

F68 (December 7) *yama no kami matsuri* "festival of the mountain divinity," Mie-ken (S.)

F69 (January 15) *hotohoto*, Okayama-ken (S.)

F70 (January 7) *shichi fuku jin* "seven gods of happiness," Shirasawa, Fukushima-ken (S.)[47]

F71 (December 31) *namahage* "home visiting by the ogres," Oga-hanto, Akita-ken (S.)[48]

F72 (February 15) *kamakura* "snow huts," Yokote, Akita-ken (S.)

F73 (February 15) *sumi tsuke* "smearing oneself with soot," Gumma-ken (S.)

F74 (February 15) *doronko* "covering oneself with mud," Inba-hun, Chiba-ken (S.)

F75 (April 3) *doronko*, Noda, Chiba-ken (S.)

F76 (March 3) *nagashi-bina* "setting the dolls afloat," Tottori-ken (S.)

F77 (April 15) Nagahama *no kodomo kabuki* "kabuki of the children of Nagahama," Shiga-ken (S.)

F78 (June 5) *ja-maki* "festival of the snake," Nara-ken (S.)

F79 (June 11) *tako gassen* "contest of the flying deer," Shirane, Niigata-ken (S.)

F80 (April) *onbashira matsuri* "festival of the sacred pillar," Suwa, Nagano-ken[49]

F81 (New Year) *tamashi zume* "fortifying one's soul," Kansai[50]

F82 (September 24) *goza kae matsuri* "changing of the sacred mats," Shimane-ken[51]

F83 (June 20) Tsugaru *no itako bon* "the *bon* of the mediums of Tsugaru," Aomori-ken[52]

F84 (March 2) *mizu okuri* "sending away the water," Wakasa, Fukui-ken[53]

F85 (November 30) *kennô matsuri* "offerings," Sawara, Katori-jinja, Chiba-ken

F86 (April 30) *yamata no orochi* "expedition against the eight-forked serpent," Izumo, Shimane-ken

Each year, several books on Japanese festivals are published in Japanese. The bibliographical references we have cited are therefore incomplete (the list of functions, however, seems to be fundamentally complete).[54]

NOTES

1. A more comprehensive description of the contents of this article in Maurice Coyaud, *Fêtes au Japon* (Paris: P.A.F. [Pour l'Analyse du Folklore], 1978).

2. Marianne Mesnil, *Trois Essais sur le Fête* (Brussels: Editions de l'Université de Bruxelles, 1974).

3. Claude Lévi-Strauss, *Structural Anthropology*, 2 vols. (New York: Basic Books, 1963–76). Algirdas Greimas, *Sémantique Structurale* (Paris: Larousse, 1966).

4. Compare chapter 17 of the first book of the *Kojiki*, trans. Donald L. Philippi (Tokyo: University of Tokyo Press; Princeton: Princeton University Press, 1969), pp. 80 ff.

5. Compare the book by Sakurai Tokutarô, *Nihon no shamanizumu* (Tokyo: Yoshikawa-Kôbunkan, 1974), reviewed by M. Coyaud in *Études Mongoles* 8 (1977): 127–40.

6. I saw a very detailed report of this festival on Japanese television. The journalist concluded his commentary by saying: *"baka na matsuri"* (stupid festival!) adding however

"omoshirokatta" (it was fun!). The religious element is no longer perceived at all.

7. At Izumo, in 1975, I had the opportunity of seeing the Kannushi of *yamata no orochi*, on April 30, the Emperor's birthday. The kannushi playing the role of Susanoo carried the sacred signs *gohei* and *sakaki*. Cf. chapter 19 of book 1 of the *Kojiki*, or, for a popular but more recent version, see tale 180 of the anthology by Maurice Coyaud *Cent quatre-vingts contes populaires du Japon* (Paris: Maisonneuve et Larose, 1975), pp. 169–71.

8. Festivals involving a similar theme are grouped under the same number followed by a letter. The name of the festival is followed, in certain instances, by the name of the temple where it takes place, by the names of the village, borough, district, and finally province (-*ken*); it is followed only by the name of the town if the town is an important one. The festivals at which I was present are marked with an asterisk.

9. K. Nagata, *Matsuri* (Festivals) (Tokyo: Sogensha, 1957).

10. R. Koiké and Y. Kubo, *Tôkyô no matsuri* (Festivals of Tokyo) (Tôkyô: Kijisha, 1972), p. 12.

11. Seiichirô Asami, *Chichibu: matsuri to minkan shinkô* (Festival and folk customs in Chichibu) (Tokyo: Yugishoten, 1969).

12. Yasuji Honda, *Kyôdo no matsuri* (Festival of the soil) (Tokyo: le no hikari Kyôkai, 1972), pp. 84, 142.

13. Nagata, p. 156.

14. K. Yamada, *Yamato no matsuri* (Festivals of Yamato) (Tokyo: Asahishinbunsha, 1974), p. 132.

15. Tôkai Television Chain, ed., *Furusato no matsuri* (Country Festivals) (Tokyo: 1973), pp. 70–73 and multicopied document of the Oigawa city hall.

16. Hideji Hôjô, *Matsuri Kikô* (Itinerary of festivals) (Tokyo: Shôbunsha, 1972), pp. 159–70.

17. Shuzaburô Hagiwara, *Omatsuri junikagetsu no tabi* (Journeys for twelve months of festivals) (Tokyo, Deiskabaa Japan bukksu 12), 1973; Tokai Television Chain, op. cit.; Kenji Maeda, *Nihon no matsuri* (Festivals of Japan) (Tokyo: Zôkeisha, 1976).

18. Nagata, p. 202.

19. Yamakei (guidebook in color) *Nihon no matsuri* (Festivals of Japan) (Tokyo: Yama to Keikokusha), 1967, p. 31.

20. Tôkai Television Chain, op. cit., p. 44.

21. Hagiwara, p. 95; Hôjô, pp. 113–30.

22. Hagiwara, p. 192; T. Tachibana, *Omatsuri jikoku hyô* (Handbook and schedule of the festivals) (Osaka: Dokubai shinbunsha, 1973), p. 39.

23. Hagiwara, p. 135.

24. Honda, p. 137; Nagata, p. 248.

25. Honda, p. 139.

26. Ibid., p. 139.

27. Hideji Hôjô, *Kisai junrei* (Pilgrimage to strange festivals) (Kyoto: Tankosha, 1969), pp. 65–77.

28. Hôjô, *Matsuri Kikô*, pp. 83–90.

29. Ibid., pp. 145–56; Masayoshi Nishitsunoi, *Nenjû gyôji jiten* (Dictionary of the yearly festivals) (Tokyo: Tokyôdo, 1957), p. 402.

30. Yamakei, p. 71; Maeda, pp. 217–25; Nagata, p. 190.

31. Yutaka Kondô, *Gion matsuri* (The Gion festival) (Tokyo: Taiga shuppan, 1973).

32. Tôkai Television Chain, op. cit., pp. 182 ff.

33. Ibid., pp. 186 ff.

34. Honda, p. 137.

35. Tôkai Television Chain, op. cit., pp. 106 ff.

36. Hôjô, *Kisai junrei*, pp. 130–37.

37. Honda, p. 124; Nagata, p. 165.

38. Hôjô, *Kisai junrei*, pp. 23–24; Tachibana, p. 140.

39. Hôjô, *Kisai junrei*, pp. 95–106.

40. Koiké and Kubo, op. cit.

41. Maeda, pp. 147–56; Nagata, op. cit., p. 192.

42. M. Sugawara, *Matsuri to Kodomo* (Festivals and children), 4 vols. (Tokyo: Saera shobô, 1972). See also festival *infra* followed by (S.).

43. Hideo Haga, *Japanese Folk Festivals* (Tokyo: Mura, 1970), p. 9.

44. Hôjô, *Matsuri Kikô*, pp. 91–111.

45. Maeda, pp. 157–66.

46. Ibid., pp. 57–68.

47. Haga, p. 13.

48. Maeda, pp. 5–16.

49. Honda; Maeda, pp. 31–44; Nagata, p. 185.

50. Honda.

51. Ibid.

52. Hôjô, *Matsuri Kikô*, pp. 27–41.

53. Tachibana, p. 108.

54. See, for instance, Helen Bauer and Sherwin Carlquist, *Japanese Festivals* (New York: Doubleday, 1965); Laurence Berthier, *Les fêtes saisonnières au Japon* (Paris: P. O. F.), 1981; Yasuji Honda, *Nihon no matsuri to geinô* (Festivals and arts of Japan) (Tokyo: Kinsaisha, 1974); Meirô Koma, *Kyôto no Matsuri* (Festivals of Kyoto) (Kyoto: Tankôsha, 1973); Gerard Martzel, *La Fête d'Ôgi et le nô de Kurokawa* (Paris: Publications Orientalistes de France [Pof-Études], 1975); Narimitsu Matsudaira, *Les Fêtes saisonnières au Japon* (Paris: Maisonneuve et Larose, 1935), and *Le Rituel des prémices au Japon* (Paris: PUF [Bulletin de la Maison franco-japonaise], 1956); Iwao Oba, *Matsuri* (Festivals) (Tokyo: Gakuseisha, 1967); K. Shibasaki, *Shinshû no matsuri* (Festivals of the province of Shinshu) (Nagano: Shinjuro, 1972); K. Yamada, *Yamato no matsuri* (Festivals of Yamato) (Tokyo: Asahi shinbunsha, 1974).

18 / Festival Masks: A Typology

David Napier

Within the morphology of festival, certain signs hold a prominent place. Masks may be indicated as the most expressive sign of festival, since they have an especially complex and important symbolic value. In fact, they "mask," i.e., hide, the identity of the person wearing them; but at the same time they reveal another persona by bringing to the outside what in daily life is an invisible entity, a hidden double personality, or a secret dream. Furthermore, masks manifest artifice itself; they signal by their mere presence that a representation is being held, a symbolic message is being conveyed.

A festival mask, Napier states, may be understood as a vehicle through which a persona is manifested at a particular public event. Though such events occur almost universally, typically they also reaffirm categories of thought that are culture-specific. For Westerners, an ethnocentric bias interferes with the analysis of festival masks from other cultures: their legitimacy is undermined by the presupposition that the world is governed by a single omniscient deity. Since masks seem to represent the many faces of many gods, Westerners will necessarily develop a vocabulary for dealing with groups of masked personae that implies their superficiality. For monotheists, in other words, talking about masks in anything but a pejorative vocabulary is difficult indeed. In fact, for the

newly established Christianity, the infinite variety of masks was considered the mani-
festation of the devil's many faces. The only "legitimate mask" could be the Veronica,
literally the vera *icon, i.e., the true image, allegedly the mask of the passion of Christ,*
miraculously imprinted on the venerated linen kept by Saint Veronica and then entrusted
to the church.

Discussing the uncertain etymology of the term mask, *Napier reviews the meaning*
of masks in classical antiquity and in the "pagan" demonology and shows how the
drastic change from polytheism to monotheism affected mask iconography. The author
then discusses the usually overlooked physiology of masks. By covering the face or the
entire head of those who wear them, masks come into contact with major organs of
sensory perception. While the rituals performed by the masked individuals provoke
psychological states of alteration, masks themselves also induce states of altered phys-
iological perception. The author suggests that the significance of festival masks may
derive both from their ability to manipulate appearances in order to invoke transitions
that are culturally meaningful, and also from their ability to enhance certain altered
states of consciousness that affect social transitions.

In order to understand why festival masks are significant, it is essential to elaborate
a typology that individuates the basic kinds of masks. Traditional typologies have been
based on the sacred/profane character of the mask, or on the content of the entities
represented, or on the shape or size of the mask (masks that cover part of the face, all
the face, all the head, all the person). Here instead the author presents an essentially
"semiotic" typology, based on the communicative functions and symbolic meaning of
masks. He argues that beyond their apparently infinite variety, masks fall within a very
limited number of types. Placing them on a theoretical continuum, it is possible to
isolate two radically opposite kinds of masks that seem particularly appropriate to the
goals of festival activity and dramatic representation. These types present two antithetical
theses about the nature of change. The first focuses iconographically on evolutionary
transformations, as in the mask of Harlequin, the sign of mutability par excellence,
while the second has as its focus those changes that are sudden and cathartic, as in
the mask of Medusa, the permanent and petrified fixity.

Festival Masks: A Typology

David Napier

What Is a Festival Mask?

If we may define a festival as a public event at which an inclusive set of cultural
symbols is manifested,[1] a festival mask must be defined as an image that in some way
reflects certain elements of that set of symbols. In order, therefore, to understand what
may be the meaning of any festival mask, it is important to address the relationship
between the origins of the meaning of *mask* and the social role of the festival in general.

Considering the etymology of the word *mask*, it must be stressed that the origin
of the term is very unclear. The English *mask* has cognates in virtually every European
language; this fact assures the widespread use of a related concept but it also makes
understanding the evolution of the term a complex matter. Nonetheless, we can be
assured that from the Middle Ages onward the concept existed in a form compatible

with the common meaning of a covering which conceals the face. However, the Late Latin *masca* meant not only "mask," but also "daimon, spectre, or witch."[2] *Mask*, in other words, referred to a manifestation as well as to an object that covered the face. As for the etymology of *mascus, masca*, its origin may be either Arabic (*maskharah*) or Teutonic (*maskwo*)[3]—the former referring to virtually "anything ridiculous or mirthful"[4] and being the most commonly accepted origin of the word *mask*.

In either case, the foundation for the Western concept of mask—that is, a disguise that is usually deceitful—may be readily connected to specific medieval, and especially Patristic, concerns. It is clear, for example, from what we know of the use of terms such as *lamia*[5] that the daimons of Teutonic culture were very much the object of what Bernheimer has referred to as the "codification by the pseudoscience of demonology."[6] The Christian attempt to redefine non-Christian metaphysical terms was, naturally, most emphatically directed toward pagan daimons; it was also directed toward achieving a new thesis about appearances in general. With specific regard to masks, the most remarkable example of this redefining process was, as Marshall has pointed out,[7] the Church's alteration of the concept of *persona*—the word that, in antiquity, stood not only for the mask, but the entire manifested character.[8]

Why did the *persona* become concretized into the basis of our word *person?* Why did the Church Fathers, for example, study Boethius carefully while omitting his considerations about the meaning of *persona?* These are difficult questions; however, two points are particularly relevant to masks and to the further understanding of festival masks in particular. The first is the fact that the pre-Patristic—that is, the Roman, and before that the Greek—terms (*persona/prosopon*) were much more inclusive than the concealing visage which we call a mask. For the Greeks, as John Jones has pointed out,[9] the emphasis of the mask's meaning was on the visible manifestation of character; to ask who is behind the mask would be to undermine the masking convention. For Christians, conversely, a mutable visage made no sense in the presence of an omnipotent God; appearances were, thus, rigidly controlled and standardized, as icon painting in general, and Veronica's veil (the *vera icon*) in particular, attest.[10] The second point is that the theatrical events at which masks were worn in antiquity were originally seasonal—that is, they were restricted, as in the Dionysia, to religious holidays occurring at the festival time. Plays were part of a larger ritual context and priests of the cult stood in judgment of the performances. The masks were, in other words, festival masks in the fullest sense. This fact is borne out not only in ancient art and literature, but in the scholarly conviction, from Mannhardt to Dumézil,[11] that the Centaurs of Greek mythology have their counterpart in the *personae* that are impersonated in important European folk plays and festivals to the present day. That these *personae* were conflated with the "wild men" of Teutonic folklore, and thus, the object of the Christian codification of pagan spirits into a proper demonology, suggests that the original meaning of the festival mask rests not only in the cases of masking that have survived Patristic times but in the earliest known examples of festival masks within western civilization—that is, the refined prototypes of Classical and Preclassical Greece. From this point of view, we may suppose that the Preclassical Greek masks are part of an even more ancient—and, perhaps, in part an Indo-European—tradition: a tradition that may be traced from Greece to Rome; one whose original meaning is suggested in the difficulties posed by festival masks for a radical monotheism.

Masks and the Physiology of the Festival

Though it is clear that the iconography of the mask can tell us something particular about the meaning of the festival, does it also tell us something more specific about the act of wearing masks—about the physiology of masking? While we already have a great deal of evidence for the sensuous nature of masks and the social events at which they are worn (e.g., the "fleshy" etymology of the word *carnival* or the connection between the word *masque* and impudence),[12] we have never really addressed the question of whether any of the changes that are credited to masks relate in any way to the fact of covering the face or head. However, since sensual experience is so much a part of festivals, and the effect of the festival upon the senses so critical to our appreciation of the event, we must ask if there are any specific consequences of wearing a mask for the senses—especially because a mask covers all or part of the face, and often the entire head, and because it, therefore, comes into contact with our major organs of perception.

Of the senses that masks affect, certainly the most important is sight. It is quite obvious that the visual transformation of the face and the way this transformation appears to the viewer is the concern to which masks are primarily addressed. Masks are about appearance, and appearance is a visual phenomenon. However, there is also something to be said for the effects of masking on the other senses as well, and especially in the case where the design of the mask itself causes a direct change in the way the senses are stimulated. Here, no doubt, the most important relationship is that of the effects of the festival upon the sense of hearing. Thanks to Needham's exemplary analysis of the connection between the general phenomenon of percussion and states of transition,[13] we can see how percussive devices (such as the bells that are found throughout Europe in conjunction with festival masks) are the auditory correspondent to the festival mask's visual concerns. Huxley, moreover,[14] has pointed specifically to the relationship between trance states and the inner ear. In this instance, one can see how a helmet mask that covers the ears and head in general could affect the senses through both auditory and visual deprivation. That sensory deprivation is an integral part of transitory states is a fact that has been known for a long time, and one that is noted in the role of seclusion in almost every rite of passage. Through deprivation, no doubt, the senses are made ready for the transformation itself.

What kinds of sensory deprivation, then, can be specifically associated with mask wearing? In the first place, as we have seen, masks affect the sense of sight—not only from the fact that they usually inhibit our ability to see (perhaps making us more dependent on our sense of touch), but also by virtue of the powerful images they portray. Second, masks worn in dances would, by Huxley's reasoning, affect our sense of balance; they deny the wearer his ability to have a firm sense of place and may even induce vertigo. Third, in most cases masks at least partially cover the nose and mouth. Not only, therefore, may they inhibit our senses of smell and taste, but, more importantly, anyone who has worn a mask for more than a few minutes knows that there can be great discomfort in having to breathe through the small opening provided by most masks. With respect to transitory states, it is interesting to note that there is a well-known cure for hysterical hyperventilation which employs a very mask-like treatment. Here the dizziness caused by the loss of carbon dioxide is cured by partially covering the head. The result of this therapy is not unlike the placing of blinders on an excited horse, except that the physiology involved is quite different, since in the case of masks, the wearer reintroduces air that is richer in carbon dioxide.

Now just what a cure for hysteria has to do with festival masks and rites of revivification may not be immediately evident to us; but to the Greeks hysteria was thought to be directly connected to disorders of the uterus—to birth, and hence to trauma generally.[15] The transformation in emotional states through the medium of festival masks, thus, has a historical foundation both in the notion of hysteria and in the correspondence between human birth and the rebirth realized within the context of the festival. The connection between masks and reproductive imagery, therefore, is not only reflected in the common occurrence of lascivious behavior during festivals; it is associated specifically, and from the earliest times, both with sexuality and with the expression of arrest on the human face. We are not surprised, then, to find that masks again and again are especially meaningful in festivals of revivification—in cultural events in which something dies and is brought to life again.[16] Once this physiology of transformation is perceived—once, that is, the contrast between evolution and sudden change is described iconographically—a categorization of festival masks can be rendered in terms of a synthetic typology.

Types of Festival Masks

If a festival mask may be described as a mask that brings to life certain cultural *personae* at a particular time of year, what role do specific types of masks play in the festival? The answer to this question involves coming to terms not only with the staging of the masked event but with the structure and meaning of the festival as a whole. Thus, we know of a wide variety of festival masks based upon the nature of the specific festival in which they appear. There are funerary and death masks, the *imagines* of ancient Rome and the masks of All Souls—all of which are dedicated in some way to the dead. There are the masks that bring to life some semihuman animal or vegetable form (such as the "wild man" and *masque feuillu* of European folklore). There are the masks of carnival which run from the comic stock characters such as Harlequin and Pulcinella to the horrific satyr-like creatures who dance so frantically as to be the death of any poor human caught up in their frenzied celebration. And there are the masks of the truly animistic underworld cults whose celebrating may climax in the masked appearance of an ambivalent, horrific spirit, or a performance that is dedicated entirely to the staging of one incredible cathartic scene (such as the Rangda figures of the Balinese trance dance). There are masks—for example, those of the carnival or masked ball—that may be worn by anyone and that personify the free spirit of celebration, and masks that are so sacred that they can only be looked upon and worn after specific observances by the wearers and complex preparations by the community as a whole. (Again, the Balinese provide many cogent examples.) Then there are explicit inversion masks such as those employed in the Feast of Fools or the transsexual masks of certain fertility cults (such as the Yoruba Gelede masks). These are only some examples among which an infinite number of intermediary types and various combinations may occur.

Yet, it seems that an analytical synthesis is possible once we accept the fact that all masks address some sort of transformation—some shift between planes of existence. Even a mask that reproduces in the finest detail the face of the mask wearer is, by virtue of being placed over the face, a statement about the nature of change, since the mask covers the essential features by which we make empirical judgments about the status of others. To put on a mask is, therefore, to undermine our capacity to be assured that something has remained as it was. Once this fact is understood, the nature of our classification is greatly clarified. If all masks can be said to concern the phenomenon of transformation, then a proper classification of masks ought rightly to be made by reference to types of transformations, to the modes of change that determine the metaphysics of masking. Such a classification, moreover, is faithful to our definition of a festival, since, fundamentally, the festival is an event, a specific occurrence, a time of transformation. The connection of masks with festivals, in other words, is among the best indicators that not only the masks but the festivals themselves are concerned primarily with the phenomenon of transformation. It is important, therefore, to say something of the structure of festivals so far as they pertain to masks in order that we may more directly ascertain what types of festival masks may be viewed in some sense as archetypes of transformation.

Sir Edmund Leach, in his paper, "Time and False Noses,"[17] offers a framework for discussing the structuring of masked events within the context of a festival. Leach's interpretation is essentially Durkheimian; it juxtaposes the profane time of daily life with the sacred festival interval. In this respect his description resembles that of the *rites de passage* as characterized by Hubert and Mauss and van Gennep.[18] However, Leach also attempts to relate the problem of inversion by disguise to the apparent contradiction between the sacred and profane within the context of the festival itself— to answer the question of where, in a celebration of a religious nature, "the funny hats come in."[19] By Leach's account, festivals are sacred events that order time; festivals, therefore, typically involve role reversals that, through opposition, distinguish the sacred time of the festival from the profane period of daily life. This contradistinction accounts for why the forms of festival behavior are often so contradictory— why on the one hand, festivals can incorporate the highly solemn and rigidly formal and, on the other, that which is truly outrageous (what Eliade refers to as the reactualization of primordial chaos).[20] For Leach, both forms are necessary opposites in the structuring of the ritual, the sacred time of the festival itself: "A rite which starts with formality (e.g., a wedding) is likely to end in a masquerade; a rite which starts with a masquerade (e.g., New Year's Eve; Carnival) is likely to end in formality."[21] If Leach is right, it is easy to see how masks or "false noses" contribute to the realization of the extremes that must be illustrated in defining the scope of the sacred.

However, if we could define the exact scope of innovation made possible by the festival context, we would by definition undermine Leach's idea, since it is, in part, dependent upon a structure that can accommodate extremes—and not only those extremes that we now know, but ones that have yet to be invented (or, rather, ones that are continually reinvented).[22] It is because this sacred demand for extremism is precisely what is at issue that Leach's idea at once escapes verification yet seems inescapably true. And though we must therefore conclude that it is quite impossible ever to be capable of establishing the limits of the human imagination (because the limits themselves are continually transforming), we are assured in assuming that the mask types, and especially the mask types that are archetypal, can direct us toward answering this question—that the capacity of masks to elaborate ever new imaginative extremes is precisely what makes them an integral part of the festival. What mask types, then, form the core of the archetype of the festival mask? What types, that is, strike at the essence of what the festival seeks to bring to life? Here we must return to classical mythology and to the time at which ritual participation in the festival gave way to the theater, to the pleasure of observing and theorizing about the transforming event.

To my mind, there are two fundamental notions of transformation to which masks are especially applicable. The first is the protean capacity for mutability. This is the fine art of transformation and in science it is what is called evolution. While it may occur rather quickly—as with Kafka's Gregor—it may also take place over such a long period that the change escapes our capacity to perceive it until it has taken full effect. In either case, recognition of the change depends upon a recognition of related steps, of family resemblances. Formal variations of masking—such as masks that only cover part of the face, or the alteration of facial appearance through make-up—are visual steps along this path of mutability. The second is the cathartic: the capacity of the human mind to be arrested, to be petrified by a sudden and completely unprecedented change. These two modes, the evolutionary and the cathartic—the mutable and the transfixed, as it were—provide the parameters of transformation within the context of the festival. As masks, they show us, on the one hand, how change may manifest itself through a process, while, on the other, how it may be governed by saltation. In both cases we can at some point experience the phenomena of arrest and astonishment; but in the first it is the astonishment of recognizing that change is occurring in a gradual, even undetectable, way, while in the second it is the astonishment of sudden change itself. The first recalls the Satyr of classical antiquity (effective because he is so nearly human); the second the Gorgon (the petrifying force, the horrible apparition). Now how are these two sentiments manifested in masks, and what, specifically, do they have to do with the experiencing of the festival?

To answer these questions we must first realize that the astonishment of transformation can, especially in a festival rite, be the avenue for contacting something supernatural, for achieving, that is, some new or higher state of awareness. In other words, the festival provides the scheme through which astonishment may be experienced—what Huxley has called the context for the staging of the transformation scene.[23] For masks, this means that the festival must be so structured as to hand over the stage to the masked transformer at the appropriate point in the process. And here, suddenly, the meaning and function of the mask is given; for we realize that in making the transformation possible, the mask must incorporate the contradiction that is implicit in the transformation, whether it be evolutionary or cathartic, and that the iconography of the mask must try in some way to epitomize the precise nature of this change. Let us, then, return to the Satyr and Gorgon and see how, in the context of these two extremes, such change is accomplished.

What I have done in the past description is reduce the actual iconography of festival masks—the infinite number of facial types that the mask may assume—to two types of facial icons that between them encompass the extremes in modes of transformation. Thus, on the one hand, we have a face that is so subtle as often to defy our attempts to isolate peculiar iconographical features, while on the other hand we have a mask that expresses the extreme instance of emotional tension, of cathartic astonishment, of arrest. Of course there is an infinite number of mask types that may occupy the space between these two poles; but for the purpose of definition, these two types constitute the radical cases so far as the iconography of transformation is concerned. What we need now do is point out the common feature shared by these two radical opposites which enables them both to epitomize the point of transformation within the festival. Here I am speaking of the need for recognizing the importance of the expression of ambivalence on festival masks, the expression of a set of facial icons that informs us that some kind of change is underway. It is here that we begin to see the logic behind the role of masks in those seasonal festivals and rites of revivification that have always been among the most salient features of culture; for ambivalence not only enables us to understand how a single festival can incorporate such extremes of formality and informality through the masked *persona* or *personae* to which the festival gives life, it also tells us something about why the festival happens in the first place. The festival, that is, is a demonstration—a visible sign—that the forces of nature, the powers that can either kill or cure, are proceeding according to an ordered, but complex plan. It is, thus, the mask of ambivalence that best characterizes the structure of transformation; it is the face that designates the precise point of transformation, the contradiction that marks both the end and the beginning.

NOTES

1. For a working definition of *festival*, see editor's introduction to this volume. On masks, see—in addition to the general literature— I. Madé Bandem and Fredrik Eugene deBoer, Kaja and Kelod: *Balinese Dance in Transition* (Kuala Lumpur: Oxford University Press, 1981); Jane Belo, *Bali: Rangda and Barong*, Monographs of the American Ethnological Society, 16 (Seattle: University of Washington Press, 1949); Samuël Glotz, ed., *Le Masque dans la tradition Européenne* (Binche: Musée international du Carnaval et du Masque, 1975); M. H. Goonatilleka, *Masks and Mask Systems of Sri Lanka* (Colombo: Tamarind Books, 1978); Marcel Griaule, *Masques Dogon*, Travaux et mémoires de l'Institut d'Ethnologie, 33 (Paris: Institut d'Ethnologie, 1938); Simon Ottenberg, *Masked Rituals of Afikpo: The Context of an African Art*, Index of Art in the Pacific Northwest, No. 9 (Seattle: University of Washington Press for the Henry Art Gallery, 1925; rpt. Seattle: University of Washington Press, 1975).

2. See, among others, Oscar Bloch and Walther von Wartburg, *Dictionnaire étymologique de la langue française*, 2d ed. (Paris, 1950); André Chastel, "Les Temps moderne: masque, mascarade, mascaron," *Le Masque* (Paris: Musée Guimet, 1959), pp. 87–93; John William Cunliffe, "Italian Prototypes of the Masque and Dumb Show," *PMLA* 22 (1907): 140–56; Carlo Battisti and Giovanni Alessio, *Dizionario Etimologico Italiano* (Florence: Barbera, 1952) 3: 2381, entry *maschera;* Charles Du Cange, *Glossarium Mediae et Infimae Latinitatis* (Niort Favre, 1885) 5: 293, entries *"masca," "mascara," "mascarata," "mascarati";* James A. H. Murray, ed., *A New English Dictionary on Historical Principles* (Oxford: Clarendon Press, 1905); Charles Talbut Onions, *The Oxford Dictionary of English Etymology* (Oxford: Clarendon Press, 1966); Eric Partridge, *Origins: A Short Etymological Dictionary of Modern English* (London: Routledge & Kegan Paul, 1966); Julius Pokorny, *Indogermanisches etymologisches Wörterbuch* (Bern, 1959); Walter W. Skeat, *An Etymological Dictionary of the English Language* (Oxford: Clarendon Press, 1910).

3. The former origin is preferred, for example, by Partridge and Skeat and the latter by Murray.

4. Skeat, p. 364.

5. Richard Bernheimer, *Wild Men in the Middle Ages: A Study in Art, Sentiment, and Demonology* (Cambridge, Mass.: Harvard University Press, 1952); Chastel; Arthur Percival Rossiter, *English Drama from Early Times*

to the Elizabethans: Its Background, Origins, and Development* (London, 1950).

6. Bernheimer, p. 101.

7. Mary H. Marshall, "Boethius' Definition of *Persona* and Mediaeval Understanding of the Roman Theatre," *Speculum* 25 (1950): 471–82.

8. See A. David Napier, *Masks: Transformation and Paradox* (Berkeley and Los Angeles: University of California Press, 1986).

9. John Jones, *On Aristotle and Greek Tragedy* (London: Chatto & Windus, 1971), p. 45.

10. See Claude Gaignebet, "Veronique ou l'image vraie," *Anagrom* 7–8 (1976): 45–70. [I would like to thank Alessandro Falassi for calling my attention to this source.]

11. Wilhelm Mannhardt, *Antike Wald- und Feldkulte aus nord-europäischer Überlieferung* (Berlin, 1877); Georges Dumézil, *Le Problème des centaures: Étude de mythologie comparée indo-européene*, Annales du Musée Guimet, 41 (Paris: Musée Guimet, 1929).

12. For a discussion, see Chastel.

13. Rodney Needham, "Percussion and Transition," *Man*, N.S., 2 (1967): 606–14.

14. Francis Huxley, "The Ritual of Voodoo and the Symbolism of the Body," *Philosophical Transactions, The Royal Society of London*, Series B, 251 (1966): 423–27; Huxley, "Anthropology and ESP," *Science and ESP*, ed. John Raymond Smythies (London: Routledge & Kegan Paul, 1967). See also Alfred Gell, "The Gods at Play: Vertigo and Possession in Muria Religion," *Man* 15 (1980) no. 2: 219–48.

15. I am grateful to Francis Huxley for first calling my attention to the correspondence between birth trauma and apotopaic imagery.

16. See especially Mircea Eliade, *The Myth of the Eternal Return or, Cosmos and History*, trans. Willard R. Trask (Princeton: Princeton University Press, 1965).

17. Edmund R. Leach, *Rethinking Anthropology* (London: Athlone, 1961).

18. Henri Hubert and Marcel Mauss, "Étude sommaire de la représentation du temps dans la religion et la magie," *Mélanges d'histoire des religions* (Paris, 1909); Arnold van Gennep, *The Rites of Passage* (London, 1960).

19. Leach, p. 134; on inversion and the meaning of masks, see Claude Lévi-Strauss, *La Voie des masques*, 2 vols. (Geneva: Skira, 1975).

20. Eliade, pp. 62 ff.

21. Leach, p. 136.

22. This is basically the Aristotelian notion that "if new forms are produced only by isolating existing tendencies the end result would be a dead level of nonvarying, enclosed types" (Stephen R. L. Clark, *Aristotle's Man: Speculations upon Aristotelian Anthropology* [Oxford: Clarendon Press, 1975], p. 39; see also Napier, 1986).

23. Francis Huxley, *The Way of the Sacred* (New York: Dell, 1976), p. 284. See also Elizabeth Tonkin, "Masks and Powers," *Man*, N.S., 14 (1979) no. 2: 237–48.

19 / Notes on a Semiotic Approach to *Parade, Cortege,* and *Procession*

Louis Marin

Significant elements of festival are usually organized in patterns. Perhaps the most widespread among them is a perambulatory event which takes several different names— pageant, parade, procession, cortege, demonstration, and others. It may practically constitute an entire festivity all by itself, or it may be staged explicitly as one of the focal points of the festival.

    In this article Louis Marin discusses festive perambulatory events, indicating the main types and the semiotic and symbolic aspects of each. The argument is built starting from French materials, but its development and conclusions have also a general applicability. Marin reviews the meaning of key lexical terms and events, observing how they are related to domains crucial for any social system: cortege to political power, procession to religion, parade to war. These events are also performances, but the usual distinctions among actors, roles, and spectators are not rigid as in most performances; contact and distance between actors and audience alternate; the varied physical viewpoint of the spectators also has important implications for their reading of the message conveyed by the event.

    Corteges, parades, and processions produce time and space of a special symbolic quality. The duration of the event acquires its own artificial length, with parts and "movements" governed by an internal logic. Since the perambulatory event chooses a series of locations and a particular route touching them, it creates "spaces" and organizes them into "places."

Routes themselves are a significant element carrying symbolic meaning. Three major types of them are indicated: (a) the one-way route that signifies irreversibility and focuses on a cathartic final point; (b) the round trip that attaches special meaning to "pendular" reversibility and stresses the turning point, which is an end and a beginning at the same time; (c) the closed circuit, whose movement encloses and excludes, that tends to eliminate the special value of beginning and ending points. Routes can take on—and convey—the political connotations of the perambulation's events. Marin gives examples of left-wing, right-wing, and "erratic" routes in Paris, showing how names of places chosen for inclusion in the route recount their own different stories about political ideologies. Furthermore, gathering and dispersion points are especially important, being "liminal" areas where the passage into and from the special ritual dimension may take place in a disorderly manner and ignite unforeseen, potentially explosive behavior.

The order of parading individuals, groups, and symbols as well as their relative position is another important aspect of perambulatory events: there are key places and key rows, whose reciprocal position suggests social and ideological hierarchies.

Besides analyzing the component parts of the perambulatory events, the article also discusses the phenomenon as a whole. In parades and corteges, processions and demonstrations, states the author, solidarity and community, agonism and antagonism are at play, and in general what he terms the "great semantic apparatuses" of ritual production, which try, if not to resolve, at least to signify and moderate society's most crucial contradictions.

The article makes the point in one particular area of festival study, but the author indicates issues and problems open to further scholarship. The discussion uses a series of examples, each one of which is implicitly proposed for significant study: the Christian Via Crucis of Holy Friday; a 1794 parade celebrating the taking of Toulon, copied faithfully from the procession of Corpus Christi; the demonstration in Paris during May 1968; the parade in the revolutionary fêtes of Marat, designed to build his legend and to constitute an edifying "exemplum"; the royal entries into cities in the Middle Ages and the Renaissance, and their evolution from an egalitarian encounter into an act of submission to the sovereign. More abstract theoretical questions are raised by the author as he suggests explicitly what to do in order to broaden and further his discussion: furthering the schema "death and rebirth" proposed by E. Leach for all festive sequences; refining the semiotics of festive time and its different types; studying the parade as a case of the passage from metaphor to metonymy indicated by Mauss and Lévi-Strauss. Indeed, this is a series of themes showing the richness of festival scholarship.

Notes on a Semiotic Approach to Parade, Cortege, and Procession*

Louis Marin

This survey is less concerned with defining the "complex ethno-semiotic object"[1] of parade, cortege, or procession, than with exploring the various symbolic and semiotic aspects of each. Here, the complexity of forms and historical diversity of the object are not only assumed qualities but can also be taken as our point of departure. For

---

*Translation by Fae Korsmo.

example, how did our object of study acquire these names? Which derivations, evolutions, shifts, and transfers of meaning affected this group of lexical items? Which semantic fields are associated with it? What shared or unshared elements can a study reveal? What is the dictionary's response concerning such terms as *cortege, parade, procession, demonstration, march, funeral procession, military review*, etc., terms which we use intuitively in our everyday language. Just as intuitively, we see that the first four of the above-mentioned terms express different domains which we shall consider below.

According to Furetière, *cortege* is "the company kept by a Prince or an eminent person during a ceremony, including carriages, horses, or other items used to honor him." Littré takes up the same idea: "a retinue which accompanies another person to honor him during a ceremony," but he also records a secondary, more generalized meaning of the word: "a meeting of persons who walk with great pomp," and then adds, "any large retinue of people."

As for *procession*, Furetière notes the primary meaning as "the prayers uttered by followers of the clergy on a pilgrimage to a holy place, a church," and then gives the "proverbial" meaning of a "long retinue of people moving in a line, one after the other." Littré echoes the latter meaning in his second definition, "a solemn march of clergy and people which takes place inside or outside a church and during which hymns, psalms, or litanies are sung," a definition equally valid for pagan ceremonies analogous to Christian processions.

With regard to the term *parade*, Littré points out the military and warlike aspects in "the marching of a troop of soldiers in column formation, passing before a leader." Or, more precisely, "the movement which, after an inspection, consists of all departing troops marching past the officer who just reviewed them," and more generally, "this same movement performed by soldiers assembled in a group who must now file out one by one to begin their march and pass through narrow places."[2]

To the constellation of terms surrounding the three words, we must add *demonstration*, a movement of people assembled to express a political intention. A demonstration can take the form of either a parade or a cortege. We could also consider *march* and *review*, two terms that enter the military domain; *review* also overlaps with *parade* in that it consists of the inspection of troops arranged to file past spectators.

What then, are the social functions and roles implied by these terms? Using lexical definitions, we can isolate some essential traits. First, the "processional cortege" contains the indispensable aspect of collectivity. In other words, every assembly is not necessarily a cortege, parade, or procession, but there can be no "processional cortege" without an assembly. This grouping of people constitutes the birth, existence, and end of the processional cortege. To parade or to form a cortege or procession implies that the individuals constitute a totality and collectively "take shape," whatever the modalities of this coming together or the characteristics of the constituted product might be. This grouping also has a complex and diversified structure, simultaneously real and symbolic, axial and teleological.[3]

Second, because the notions of following or succeeding, marching or moving, and line or order recur constantly in the definitions, it seems that the lexical group is itself a type of body moving through a particular space with a certain orientation and in a certain order. All parades, processions, or corteges can thus be viewed as a group of proceedings which, while manipulating space, engender space specific to each one according to determined rules and norms. In turn, these norms and rules constrain the movements of the parade, procession, or cortege, while enhancing their value. The same can be said of time. A parade, procession, or cortege, arranged in chronological time, structures time according to its own particular temporality and through the structuring, produces a specific time period that both interrupts and establishes chronological time.[4]

Furthermore, *parade, procession,* and *cortege,* not to mention *march* and *review,* imply bipolar structures such as activity and passivity. These bipartite "roles" are assumed by actors and spectators and do not necessarily remain fixed throughout the duration of a parade, cortege, or procession. In sum, a general structure of theatricality appears to interrelate the participants.[5]

Finally, *cortege, parade, procession,* and more generally, the complex object whose profile we have attempted to outline, seem to emanate from the domain of rite or ritual ceremony, whether it be profane or religious, civil or military, festive, diversionary, or directly functional. *Cortege, parade,* and *procession* contain the repetitive structure characteristic of ritual systems, whether the system be syntagmatic or paradigmatic. In other words, the rite in question may correspond to calendar time, such as, for example, the Corpus Christi procession which takes place in the Catholic world on the Sunday following Trinity Sunday, at the end of May or in early June, the military parade on July 14 in France, or the Fourth of July celebration in the United States. In the second, paradigmatic situation, the rite corresponds to a series of occasional circumstances and is performed according to a determined paradigm. Examples of this type include processions in the fields to prevent drought and the ceremony of royal entry into a Western European city as practiced from the fourteenth to eighteenth centuries.[6]

The study of rite can be applied to *parade, cortege, procession,* and *demonstration,* since each constitutes a part of ritual in general, and an aspect of rite, in particular. In terms of the symbolic structure of rite, then, we shall examine the syntactic, semantic, and pragmatic elements of the ethno-semiotic object.

Questions concerning the syntax of a cortege are derived directly from its temporal and spatial characteristics. *Parade, cortege, procession,* and *demonstration* unfold as they move through a pre-existing space already articulated by certain named or marked places: streets, squares, intersections, bridges, buildings, monuments, districts, neighborhoods, and boundaries within the city; paths, roads, hamlets, farms, fields, fences, and woods in the country. In and from this space, a parade will extract its stage and decor. Because certain stretches of a route will be chosen in favor of others, some places will be kept on the program while others are discarded, some buildings or monuments will be visited while others are ignored. A parade thus manipulates space and the places that already exist. A parade gives space a meaningful structure, and the places chosen for its route articulate the "sentences" of a spatial discourse. On the other hand, those places bypassed or avoided by the parade deploy a counter-discourse of denial or repression. This counter-discourse helps to form the background of the first discourse, thereby giving it another dimension of meaning.

Use of existing space is necessarily accompanied by production of another, more specific space, space which is forbidden, off limits to normal circulation, divided, or whose permanent everyday decor is dissimulated or modified. In the process of spatialization, a parade creates a specific order of places which both determines the route and is implied by the route.

This process is apparent in the Stations of the Cross, a religious procession re-enacting the Passion of Jesus Christ. The route transforms the order of sanctuary places—the side aisles, the nave, the choir, etc.—into another specific area through the re-enactment of Christ's route. This example also shows that the starting and finishing points of *parade*, *cortege*, or *procession* are markedly distinct from those places connected together along the route, since they constitute the epiphanic place of the parade. Additionally, the finishing point is where a parade disappears as it reaches its "finality"; the group disappears once its performance has been accomplished, or even when the march has ended in failure.

Likewise, the start and finish can be "dangerous" places for the group(s) involved in a procession such as, for example, a political demonstration. At the beginning of a protest march, at either the gathering point or the march's immediate outset, police and the forces of order try to intercept those isolated individuals who are not yet participants in the parading mass. At the end of a march, at its point of dissolution, *provocateurs* join the mass, become uncontrollable elements, and instigate disorder. The assembly and dispersion points thus represent borders between the law of "normal" everyday spaces and places and the law of the parade and its route. They can also be thought of as passages from one law to another; they are themselves outside either law and are therefore dangerous.

The possibilities for such points or passages are in part dictated by the spaces produced. One-way parades, round-trip (one-way plus the return) parades, and closed-circuit or circular parades create very different spaces.

A one-way direction implies an irreversible movement whose temporality may be expressed by, for example, the schematic reproduction of a story or the story's scenario. For a walking collectivity, the end point of a one-way march represents a symbolic victory over those ideas or persons defied by the march.

A round trip emphasizes a reversible, bi-directional spatialization. In the coming and going, the turning point is heavily invested, since it is both the end and the origin of "retrogradation." This duality helps to free a round-trip parade from chronological forms of temporality and from the succession of events, allowing it to become a "presentation of places" through repetition. Similarly, the point of departure is locally identical to the arrival point, but is not identical spatially, or in terms of the space created by the route. By taking place after the departure, a march "legitimizes" the point by reaching it again at the end.[7]

In a closed-circuit or circular route, the movement encloses a space by creating a real or ideal limit and protects the enclosed space with a symbolically closed border. This type of route can also "lock up" the enemy, symbolically forbidding any escape. Such was the parade of the ancient Hebrews around the walls of Jericho. Their march can be understood as an effort to substitute for "real" walls a symbolic encirclement that became conquest and destruction. A closed-circuit route, therefore, turns the encircling action into a local order, transforming motion into respite by obliterating the specific values of the starting and end points.

The above considerations of the syntax of parades, corteges, marches, etc., open up the possibility of a typology in which time and space would be linked in diverse ways. Time can be unidirectional and linear, bidirectional and linear, cyclical and durative, punctual, static, inchoate, or terminal. These different temporal categories, in turn, are integrated with the various spatializing processes. For example, portions of unidirectional linear time may be present with closed-circuit routes, or the inverse. This relationship can be observed in carnival parades where farandoles, merry-go-rounds, or rounds danced on the city squares may be incorporated into the route at any point between start and finish.

Rather than examine a parade in terms of its places, spaces, and times, we can instead look at it in terms of its own internal syntax, isolating such factors as order, ranks of participants, and the composition of the totality. From the Panathenes or funeral marches of antiquity[8] to the demonstrations of the labor unions, political parties, and "groupuscles" of May 1968 in Paris, from the Corpus Christi procession of the High Renaissance to the Red Square parades during the anniversary celebration of the October Revolution, we can see that order is an essential means for getting across the "message," be that message religious, civic, political, philosophical, or social. Often the intended message becomes complex due to the participants' reciprocal relationships and relative positions within the parade.[9]

The composition of a cortege also signifies a message about the intended message. An incident stemming from the French Revolution is a noteworthy example. In 1794, an alpine village celebrated the taking of Toulon.[10] The parade consisted of the municipal authorities, followed by justices of the peace, working classes, eight chosen cantors, and all other cantors and citizens. The "Constitution, however, was carried on a stretcher under a red canopy by the four eldest."[11] Not only was the Constitution being solemnly celebrated as the firmest guarantor of unity among all groups (categorized by age, sex, profession, etc.) and governmental bodies (municipal, judiciary, etc.) forming the indivisible Nation, but this unity was seen as the sacred political body of France. This politico-religious quality was evident to the participants since the organization, instruments, and symbols of the celebration were the same as those used in the procession and display of the Holy Sacrament.

The composition of the cortege thus acts as a syntactical signifier, placing the Constitution in a "here and now" context. It also functions as a semantic signifier, using the metaphor of the Holy Sacrament to emphasize the sacred quality of national unity.

Turning to the semantic values of a parade, we note the importance of toponyms or place names. One illustration of the significance of place comes from contemporary Paris. In recent years, most political demonstrations by the Left, starting from the Place de la Nation and going to the Place de la République, used the streets of Faubourg St. Antoine and Boulevard Beaumarchais via the Place de la Bastille, whereas the few demonstrations of the Right took place between the Tuileries and the Place de l'Etoile using the Champs Elysées. Onto the order of places is superimposed an order of names, and the naming is rarely arbitrary. Sometimes the place transfers its history to the name as in, for example, the street of Faubourg St. Antoine whose name is semantically charged by the revolutionary and controversial activity that has taken place there since the sixteenth century. Sometimes the place is named for its history as in the case of the Place de la Bastille, where the prison fortress of the Bastille was built during the fourteenth century and was later burned by the Parisians on July 14, 1789. Still other places are semantically charged by their names, such as the Place de la Nation or Place de la République.

Consequently, we may say that a parade, by moving through these named places, re-enacts a myth, legend, or story by narrating what is already inscribed in the places, their order, and their names. The parade can also create a new political discourse in addition to providing historical narration. The May 1968 demonstrations in Paris, for instance, showed a certain novelty in the names of places where the demonstrators met and a degree of creativity in that the route seemed to be improvised section by section, thus proclaiming the political and ideological spontaneity of the groups involved.

More generally, *parade, cortege*, and *procession* create through their narrative aspect a system of values from which any parade, cortege, procession, or demonstration derives its legitimacy. The process of legitimization or actualization may, in turn, serve to formalize relationships between participants, such as the political relationship between a sovereign and a city.

Using a historical example of the cortege, we note that the entry of a King into one of his cities is both a means of maintaining the monarchical aura and of ritually opening a political and institutional dialogue between the sovereign and the city's inhabitants. While several traits of royal entries have disappeared or changed, visits by chiefs-of-state to cities of the countries they govern remain essentially similar. The royal entry is, "first of all, the encounter of two corteges, a royal and a civic, at the city gates. The ordering of persons and groups as well as the royal itinerary for inside the city are fixed by custom, and the decorations and theater of the street are always found at the same points."[12]

In certain situations during the fifteenth century, the King, surrounded by his own in addition to the city's cortege at the city gates, sometimes made an oath to the city. He swore to maintain the rights and liberties of the community, and the community responded with another oath swearing allegiance to the King. But more often, from the sixteenth century on, this mark of obedience and subjugation consisted of presenting the keys to the King "*in signum majoris obedientie et subjectionis.*"[13]

In other words, if the city's cortege meeting the King outside the city wall obtained from him a promise to respect the city's rights, the King submitted the city to himself by passing with his entourage through the door whose keys he had received. A pact was thus formed which later became a political contract, abetted by the encounter of the two corteges and their stops in significant places along the way. In terms of the spatialization process and the ordering of places, the royal entry affirms the existence of the space inside the route as part of the larger kingdom and at the same time as a unitary political entity with specific rights. The royal entry not only legitimizes a political relationship, but also seeks to signify and moderate political contradictions. We are reminded here of the semantic apparatuses and their symbolic productions that anthropologists have observed in ritual.[14]

Another semantic dimension of a parade is its repetition. A parade revives a story in a certain way, not so much telling it as reliving it. A parade organized to commemorate a historical hero, like the cortege described by M. Ozouf for the feast of Marat,[15] provides a valuable example for focusing on this semantic dimension. One of the organizers, who is also a theoretician of corteges, writes that he wanted "to present at different points along the route of the cortege, as if in a moving picture, all of the principal circumstances in the life of Marat, retracing it with characteristic titles and emblems in each successive, different grouping." Everything is done, it seems, so that the onlooker may tell himself the story of Marat's life as it progressively unfolds; the telling is made easier through titles that are displayed to sustain the narrative.

Ozouf writes, though, that "what the cortege distributes in space is not . . . the circumstances in Marat's life revealed in . . . order . . . but the separation of legendary characteristics." What pass before the spectators are not the episodes of Marat's life, but wagons carrying "his public virtues," "his private virtues," the "rewards," and finally the "examples." Furthermore, different ages are incorporated into the examples, so that "everyone can derive, from Marat's life, an example adapted to his own role and abilities." This grouping of different ages in human life with the examples of deeds helps to terminate the cortege with the practical injunction that to participate in the parade, if only by watching, is in a way to become Marat through one's own specific abilities and characteristics.

A commemorative parade not only revives but re-establishes, that is, gives legitimacy to a past by making it a basis and an origin. The performance aspect of a commemorative parade contributes to this construction, transforming the spectators and actors into a living monument to the past. A parade is thus an apparatus in the art of memory.[16]

The performance aspect of *parade, cortege,* and *procession* brings us to the pragmatic dimension. In fact, to the degree that a parade, be it a religious procession, a royal cortege, or a working class demonstration, is more or less a narrative scenario, a legible text, a visible spectacle, a ritual and a ceremony, the syntactic and semantic apparatuses discussed above are also pragmatic ones. The operation of a parade is more than a sequence of movements and gestures. As in all ritual, a parade is organized around significant nodal acts. Concerning the pragmatic dimension, our questions focus on the effectiveness of these acts.

It appears that the major effect of a parade results from the articulation of two domains—the spectators' and the actors'. Unlike theater, where actors perform a story in front of a passive audience, the parade implicates the "audience" of spectators as actors. In many political demonstrations as well as military parades and religious processions, the so-called cortege, while winding its way from marked place to marked place, is viewed at various key points by spectators installed on balconies or at windows, sometimes even on platforms constructed for this purpose.[17] Depending on the personalities involved, or the offices they hold, it can be just as important for the spectators to be seen by the "actors" or by other spectators as it is for the viewers to watch the parade.

It is nevertheless impossible to view a cortege in its entirety from one privileged point of view along the route. "The cortege is an art of time as well as space; it belies simultaneity. It obliges the spectator to choose an observation point and thus limit his vision."[18] Here is an argument implicating the spectator as actor in a parade. He cannot theoretically dominate time in its unfolding in space. It is in succession that he comes to know the episodes. That is why, in a political parade, spectators are often implored with gestures and shouts to descend into the streets and participate. Some can chant the slogan of the marching group, others can applaud. We can also observe that some parades continuously incorporate spectators into their march, spectators who pass gradually from immobile observation to joining in, and finally marching.

The role of spectators as actors is obvious in the royal entry. The symbolic effectiveness of this ceremony is in fact due to the dialogue between two performances, one given by the monarch to the city, and the other given by the city to its sovereign. In this exchange, a dual process of recognition takes place: recognition on the one hand of the might and glory of the monarch manifested by the glitter of his cortege, and, on the other, of the unity and harmony of the city, shown by the diversity of its group.[19]

In sum, we can use Turner's idea (1969) that ritual feast (in this case a parade or cortege) transforms one or more real and specific social relations into "communitas" both temporal and symbolic.[20] Extending this view, *parade, cortege,* and *procession* could evoke two larger types of communitas: one that symbolically enacts a real, internal antagonism in the society through amicable competition, and one that symbolically rehearses a confrontation with an enemy external to the group. For the first type, we could cite as examples the parade of soccer "fans" before the game and a procession of religious confraternities such as the one in Noto, Sicily, where, on Easter morning, two processions, one carrying a statue of Jesus Christ, the other carrying a statue of the Virgin Mary, race through the city and meet at the cathedral square. Examples of the second type of communitas include military parades on national feast days or the cavalcades that introduced tournaments of the Renaissance.[21] Either of these could provide interesting material for analysis.

NOTES

1. A. J. Greimas, *Sémiotique et sciences sociales* (Paris: Le Seuil, 1976).

2. Definitions taken from *Dictionnaire de Spiritualité ascetique et mystique* (Paris: Beauchesne, 1981) and *Dictionnaire d'Archéologie chretienne et de liturgie* (Paris: Le Touzey, 1948).

3. Victor Turner, *The Drums of Affliction* (New York: Oxford University Press, 1968).

4. Michel de Certeau, "La Cérémonie," *Traverses*, nos. 21–22 (Paris: Minuit); Louis Marin, *Utopiques, jeux d'espaces* (Paris: Minuit, 1973).

5. G. R. Kernodle, *From Art to Theater* (Chicago: University of Chicago Press, 1949).

6. J. Jacquot, "Joyeuse et triomphante entrée," in *Les Fêtes de la Renaissance* (Paris, 1956).

7. Louis Marin, *Le Portrait du Roi* (Paris: Minuit, 1981).

8. N. Loraux, *L'Invention d'Athenes* (The Hague: Mouton, 1981).

9. M. Vovelle, *Les Métamorphoses de la fête en Provence de 1750 à 1820* (Paris: Flammarion, 1976).

10. Toulon, the capital city of the Var, was delivered by the royalists to the British in 1793, but Dugommier, aided by Napoleon Bonaparte, regained it.

11. Vovelle.

12. Jacquot.

13. B. Guénée and F. Lahous, *Les Entrées royales françaises* (Paris: C.N.R.S., 1968).

14. Gregory Bateson, *Naven* (Stanford: Stanford University Press, 1958); Raymond Firth, *The Works of Gods in Tikopia* (London: Athlone, 1967); A. Gell, *Metamorphosis of the Cassovaries* (London: Athlone, 1975).

15. Jean-Paul Marat (1743–93) was a doctor and politician during the aftermath of the French Revolution. Editor of *L'Ami du Peuple*, he was one of the instigators of the September massacres. He was assassinated by Charlotte Corday. See M. Ozouf, *La Fête Révolutionnaire 1789–1799* (Paris: Gallimard, 1976).

16. F. A. Yates, *The Art of Memory* (London: Routledge and Kegan Paul, 1966).

17. S. Carandini Dell'Arco, *L'Effimero Barocco, Strutture della Festa Nella Roma del '600*, 2 vols. (Rome: Bulzoni, 1978).

18. Ozouf.

19. Jacquot; Kernodle.

20. Victor Turner, *The Ritual Process* (Chicago: Aldine, 1969).

21. André Chastel, "Le Lieu de la Fête," *Les Fêtes de la Renaissance* (Paris, 1956).

PART IV

Social Functions and Ritual Meanings of the Festival

20 / The Commemoration of the Dead

Vladimir Propp

As each individual festival is made of many component elements, one festive theme may be found in several festivities distributed along the year cycle of the same culture. In this little-known essay, Vladimir Propp, the celebrated author of the seminal Morphology of the Folktale, *provides a comprehensive discussion of the different ceremonies concerning the cult of the dead in agrarian prerevolutionary Russia. The topic is of primary importance, because the commemoration of the dead appears to be one constant element in Russian agrarian festivals, as Propp shows by reviewing the scholarship on the subject.*

The first part of the essay sketches the festive calendar in prerevolutionary Russia, showing how the reference points in the older division of time were the two solstices and the two equinoxes. In different epochs, all four of them had served to determine the beginning of the year. As religious, secular, and folk calendars later coexisted without coinciding, celebrations for the dead related to all three of them, and took place on many occasions, but always between Christmas and the Feast of Trinity.

Propp's discussion shows the importance of a preliminary reconstruction of the festive cycle for the study of festival. The calendrical context not only indicates the rationale of an apparently random repetition of rituals during the year cycle, but it also shows that for one part of the cycle such celebrations did not take place, and allows the author to discuss the reasons for this absence.

In the commemoration of the dead, ritual foods held a great importance. The kut'ja was a dish of millet and barley, also eaten at marriages, births, and baptisms. Being prepared with seeds that embody and multiply life, the author argues, this food symbolized the constant rebirth of life in spite of death. The bliny, possibly the most ancient way of cooking a dish made of flour, had the symbolic meaning of food that fed to satiety. Eggs, and dishes made with them, especially around Easter, conveyed a similar meaning. Having the quality of conserving, containing, and reproducing life, eggs were used as a sign of immortality. The article illustrates how ritual food was consumed on the different occasions: eaten at the family table, or during the picnics at the cemetery, placed or rolled over the tombstones, put on the window for the dead who had no descendants and were wandering around, or donated to the beggar fraternities. On all these occasions, it was believed that the deceased people of each family would actually be invisibly present and eat together with the living ones, as in the traditions of Rome or classical Greece.

Other practices commemorating the dead are discussed in the article, such as the visit to the tombstones to ask the dead for forgiveness, or the big bonfires to which the dead were called to warm themselves. The article also shows the progression of the cult of the dead during the year cycle: at Christmas the commemoration took place in the homes, at Carnival families went individually to the cemeteries, and finally at the feast of the radunica, *immediately after Easter, the commemoration involved the whole community, and became more and more solemn: functions were held in churches, and people who had not been properly buried received appropriate funerals. At the cemeteries, people prayed for the dead and lamented their loss, "fed the dead," and then feasted themselves. Sadness changed to merriment and sometimes revelry with song and dance, and even "indecent amusements," as older reports suggest. Propp indicates the pagan forerunners of the* radunica, *but refuses cultural or historical borrowings as an explanation. To him, the relevant point is that there is a constant tie between forms of work and forms of thought, and ritual practices express both of them.*

The cult of the dead, argues the author, was tied to the needs and interests of the peasants, and therefore took place in the period between the winter and spring solstices, when the ancestors could help to awaken the forces of nature necessary to agriculture. When these forces were in full bloom, propitiation was no longer necessary or useful, and ceremonies for the dead ceased until the next winter solstice. In passing, Propp also touches upon the problem of survival and change of ritual practices after their original meaning is lost, and states his anti-idealistic position in interpreting folklore: while some scholars had seen the cult of the dead in Russia as directed to the souls of the dead, Propp insists that such practices were directed to the "real" person as such. The author finally stresses the ambiguity in the cult of the ancestors, which originally included lamentations and sorrow as well as merry making and celebration of vitality, the explanation being that the cult of the dead was part of a general system of beliefs concerning nature, work, and religion, all of which included the cycle of life-death-resurrection as one essential underlying pattern.

The Commemoration of the Dead*

Vladimir Propp

Before beginning a study of Russian festivals, we must observe that while some of them were fixed, that is they fell every year at the same time, others were not. The first ones coincided with the fundamental days of the solar calendar. The holidays of Christmas (the religious Christmas) were celebrated at the time of the winter solstice; the meeting with spring around the time of the spring equinox; the festival of Saint John the Baptist coincided with the summer solstice. One can speak with less certainty of the festivals of the autumn equinox. We shall note immediately that each of these four periods of the year (the two solstices and the two equinoxes) could serve, and in fact did serve, for different peoples and in different epochs, to denote the first day of the new year.

Also the other holidays fell on days that were determined astronomically, but that were not tied to the solstices and to the equinoxes: they depended on the day on which Easter fell. The day of Easter was defined with particular rules and could not be celebrated before March 22 or after April 25 of the old Russian calendar.[1] Fat Week was celebrated seven weeks before Easter, and the holiday of Trinity seven weeks after.

Later on we shall confront the problem of why festivals were tied to specific periods of the calendar. This problem is clarified only if the festivals themselves are examined. The existing relationship is not determined by the Christian religion, but, at the same time, neither is it tied to the solar cult, even if it is defined on the basis of the solar calendar.

In order to better understand the periods of festivals in Russia, it is necessary to keep in mind that in the history of Russia different chronological systems were used, and that at times they coexisted. There was a religious calendar, a secular one, and a folk one, which did not always coincide. In the ancient Rus the new secular year started in May. This date is a clear borrowing: it did not coincide with the agricultural order of the Rus, nor with the habits of the peasants of central and northern Russia. The Church, relying on some Biblical legends, had fixed the beginning of the new year in September. In fact both these dates coincide with fundamental moments of the solar calendar: the spring equinox and the autumn one. In the times of Simeon Gordyj and the metropolitan bishop Feognost, during the council of Moscow of 1348, in which it was discussed on which day the new year should start, it was decided that both the secular year and the religious one should start on September 1.[2] This type of dating lasted until the reign of Peter I. On December 19, 1699, Peter I decreed that the new year should start on January 1. Therefore 1699 lasted in all four months. The Church did not conform to the ordinance of Peter I, because the saints who were commemorated in the months that thereby had disappeared, had remained for that year without their holy day.

Also, among the peasants signs of the more ancient solar calendar did not

*From *Russkie Agrarnje Prazdniki* (Leningrad: Editions of University of Leningrad, 1963), pp. 13–24. Translation by Alessandro Falassi.

disappear. According to the solar calendar, the new year started with the winter solstice. In the old peasant milieu, neither the secular New Year's Day nor the religious one were considered holidays. The true feast day was determined by the day in which the sun, altering its course, changed the point from which it rose. From that moment began an almost uninterrupted chain of ritual festivities.

We certainly cannot expect that the peasants knew with astronomical precision the day of the solstice. They venerated the blessed Spiridion Trimifuntskij, that is the same Spiridion Solonovorot who was celebrated on December 12. According to the Julian calendar it is on this day that the winter solstice occurred. From this day on the duration of daylight began to increase. "Today the sun goes toward Summer and Winter toward frost." Theoretically, on December 12 the New Year's celebrations should have started. However, since the Byzantine Church had fixed the feast of the birth of Christ on December 25, on this very day the folk festivities would start.

The cycle of the folk festivals was started by the "Christmas festivities" (*svjatki*) or by the *"koljada,"* which lasted from Christmas Eve, that is from the evening of December 24 until the baptism of Christ, that is, until January 6. We shall examine some fundamental traits of these festivals, traits that we shall find again in other festivals.

The Christmas celebration began with an official dinner. Upon close examination, this dinner is clearly revealed as a commemorative one. The commemoration of the dead, in different forms, is a constant element of all ritual agrarian festivals. This is why we have decided to begin our research by starting from this custom.

In fact, in many cases it is plainly said that nothing was eaten until the first star appeared, after which people would sit at the table. The official banquet was at the same time a luncheon and a dinner. People ate "fat," that is, salami and pork. While there was apparently no ritual element, if we observe the details, the ritual character of this banquet appears very clear. Many observers relate that one of the dishes that could not be substituted on this day was the *kut'ja*. Sometimes the festival itself was called *kut'ja*. A. Petropavlovskij describes a Bielorussian custom: "During the *koljady* there are three *kut'ja:* the first, the one that precedes Christmas, is lean; the second, the one of New Year's Day, is fat, more or less rich; the third, the one of the Epiphany, is lean."[3] The Bielorussians called the *kut'ja* of New Year's Day "generous" or "rich" since December 31 was called "the generous evening." However, the Russians sometimes call "rich" the *kut'ja* of Christmas Eve.[4]

According to very many accounts, the *kut'ja* was eaten on the eve of Christmas and of the Epiphany. I. P. Sacharov writes: "Even today for the evening banquet people prepare a semolina of cereals, the *kut'ja* of the eve is made of millet and of barley."[5] A. A. Makarenko reports instead, from Siberia, "In the evening people eat cauliflower, *kvas* and *kut'ja*."[6] Sometimes *kut'ja* was not put on the table, but instead in a corner of the entrance way, under the sacred images, together with a sheaf of unground rye. This custom is more common or perhaps simply better recorded in Bielorussia than in the Great Russia. P. V. Shejn reports an annotation made in the governed territory of Smolensk: "The main dish that cannot be substituted in this meal is the *kut'ja*."[7] Among the Ukraines of the governed territory of Saratov, A. P. Minch observed, "On Christmas Eve, the people from Minor Russia prepare a broth and some *kut'ja*; on this day they do not eat anything until sunset; as soon as the star appears they put the *kut'ja* and the broth on the table, light a candle in front of the icons, they kneel and pray to God that He send them a good harvest of wheat, give well-being to the animals and keep them in good health."[8] D. K. Zelenin, in concluding his account of the data from Great Russia, Bielorussia, and the Ukraine which he examined, says that "the ritual dishes of the Christmas festivities of the oriental Slavics indicate, without any possibility of a doubt, that these festivities at one time were dedicated to the cult of the ancestors and that they included some luncheons of commemoration of the dead."[9] It is very well known that *kut'ja* is an indispensable element of the funerary ritual and of the commemorative luncheons. Sometimes, other than on these occasions, it was used for some marriages, for births, and for baptisms. But why is the same *kut'ja* that is eaten on the occasion of weddings and births also used as food to commemorate the dead? As a rule *kut'ja* was prepared using unground grains, most frequently grains of wheat. In cities, where it is usually difficult to find wheat, rice was used. If we suppose that *kut'ja* should be, in truth, prepared with some *seeds*, we will come close to the correct interpretation of this ritual. The grain has the property of maintaining life for a long time, and of multiplying life when it is reproduced. The known continuous circle, seed-plant-seed, witnesses the eternity of life. Men, eating seeds, became participants in this process. The grain or the seed, according to the peasant mentality, corresponds to the egg in the animal world, which has the same surprising capability to conserve, contain, and reproduce life. We shall see later that in fact all peoples have largely used eggs, a sign of immortality, for funerary rites.

With *kut'ja* usually were mixed some berries (wild cherries or, in the cities, raisins). Berries are nothing but seeds surrounded by the pulp of the fruit. Now it is explained why *kut'ja* was used, be it for weddings and births of children, be it for the dead. *Kut'ja* symbolizes the constant element of rebirth of life in spite of death.

Another characteristic of the commemorative banquet consisted in the offering of the bliny, also known as a dish to commemorate the dead. P. S. Efimenko, who had observed in the North the custom of eating bliny for Christmas, supposes that the Slavic people, like other people, commemorated the dead with the bliny and that they imagined that the good souls got up to eat them together with the living.[10] This custom is better established among the Bielorussians than among the Russians; among the latter it already began to fall into disuse at the beginning of the twentieth century. "Since this day was also a day of commemoration of the dead relatives, besides *kut'ja* people cooked cakes and bliny" relates P. V. Shejn from the governed territory of Smolensk.[11]

The question why in commemorative luncheons bliny were used can be answered only by making some suppositions. The reason is not the one indicated by some researchers, according to which bliny, with their round shape, would recall the shape of the sun and would serve then as a magical instrument to make the sun return after winter. The bliny furthermore must have a ritual meaning different from the one of the *kut'ja*, since they are used simultaneously with it, and they are not interchangeable. In all probability, the bliny represent the most ancient way of cooking something made of flour. Before there were ovens, people mixed flour with water, made a liquid paste, and poured it, in small portions, on heated stones. Bliny then, are not a magical food, as the *kut'ja* is; rather they are an ancient food, archaic, a means to be fed to satiety, and which only later acquired a ritual meaning.

In considering the evening ritual banquet at Christmas as a commemorative one, we must keep in mind that people there did not commemorate the dead in general, but their relatives and their dead ancestors.

In Bielorussia the correspondents of P. V. Shejn noticed some other details that erase the last doubts about the true character of this banquet. P. V. Shejn reports that in the governed territory of Grodno, the participants at the banquet drank from a common round bowl and that each one, before drawing it to himself, poured a little of the content on the table. "They also pour the first spoonful of the liquid foods directly on the table for the dead."[12] This custom is without doubt very ancient. Pious Romans maintained that their banquets were attended by their household gods, the Lares and the Penates, the divine representations of the ancestors: to them was given the first bite of food and the first sip of the drinks. Also the dead who had no descendants were remembered at Christmas. It was believed that the souls of these dead would wander the streets, and bliny were put on the windows so that they would eat them. This custom could take another meaning: for instance A. I. Petropavloskij noticed that among the Bielorussians "during the third *kut'ja*, at night [that is on January 5], when the whole family is gathered at the table, the head of the house looks towards the window and invites the 'frost' to come into the house as a guest." "Frost, frost enter to eat the *kut'ja*"; in addition the head of the house begs the frost not to freeze the seeds of buckwheat; otherwise, he threatens, "we shall beat you with the iron whip."[13]

During the Christmas holidays another ritual was observed, which by the nineteenth century had almost disappeared: big bonfires were made, and the dead were called to warm themselves. D. K. Zelenin[14] reproduces a manuscript from 1852 where it is said: "On December 24 in the courtyards fires were burned, because it is believed that the dead parents come to warm themselves and that, thanks to this fire, the wheat will grow gleaming."[15] S. V. Maksimov describes the same custom in this manner: "The ways to commemorate the dead parents are very numerous, and one of them is called 'to warm the parents.'" It is practiced in many places (among others in the governed territories of Tambov and Orlov) and consists of unloading in the courtyard, the first day of the Christmas holidays, a cart of hay which is set on fire, in the blind belief that in the meantime the dead will rise from the graves and come to warm themselves. All the family members during this ritual form a circle and, in the deepest silence, concentrate in prayer. In other places, instead, people circle around these bonfires, as it is done during the *chorovod* of the *radunica*.[16]

In the manuscript of 1852 published by D. K. Zelenin, we are especially interested in the last lines. They show that the rite of warming the ancestors had the purpose of obtaining a good harvest: we will discuss this in more detail after examining analogous rituals that were held in other periods of the year and that supposedly served the same purpose.

Right after the Christmas holidays comes Fat Week. "The Great Fat Week" is famous as the happiest and the most unruly festival of the year. Nevertheless it was also customary during Fat Week to commemorate the dead.

In light of what we have exposed, we can hold that the carnival bliny, like the Christmas bliny, are a commemorative food. Of this speak I. P. Sacharov, I. M. Snegirev, and other researchers. "The characteristic food of Fat Week is constituted by the bliny that," writes Miller, "are, as is known, one of the characteristic elements of commemoration."[17] We have a great number of other accounts. D. K. Zelenin writes:

"Once Fat Week was, as were the Christmas holidays, a feast of commemoration. In favor of this supposition there is without a shadow of a doubt, the use that was made of the usual ritual food: the bliny."[18] In fact, as we shall see, the Carnival is a complex, articulated feast. The commemoration of the dead is only one of its components.

As during the Christmas holidays the first sip of the drinks was dedicated to the ancestors, in Fat Week the first blin was dedicated to them: "In the governed territory of Tambov and in other governed territories the first blin cooked during Fat Week is put in the window for the souls of the parents."[19] In other places the first blin was given to the brotherhood of the beggars to commemorate the dead.[20] "The pious women ate the first blin of Carnival on behalf of the dead."[21]

During Carnival the veneration for the ancestors was expressed also in other forms. It was customary to exchange visits, and to ask forgiveness for all the wrongs committed toward one's own neighbors, on the last day of Carnival before the great fast of Lent began. The younger would kneel before the older, the servants before the masters, and everyone begged forgiveness for the wrongs committed. One asked for forgiveness not only from the living, but also from the dead. "On the day of forgiveness all go to the cemetery and kneel before the ashes of their relatives."[22] We shall report an account by S. V. Maksimov, which is a summary of data collected by himself or sent to him by his correspondents: "The custom of asking for forgiveness from the dead is kept faithfully. The habit of going, the last day of Fat Week, to the cemetery is maintained especially by women. At four in the afternoon they go, in small groups of ten or twelve, to visit the dead and take some bliny. Along the way they try not to talk. Once at the cemetery, each one goes to the family tomb, falls to her knees, and genuflects, hitting her head three times on the ground. Then, with tears in her eyes, she whispers: 'Forgive me (she says the name of the dead one), forget all the evil I have done to you and all the insolent things that I have said to you.' Then, silently, the women put the bliny on the tomb (sometimes also a bottle of vodka) and, silently as they had arrived, they return home."[23]

The commemoration of the dead took place also during the week of the *rusalki*, also called *semik*, that preceded the Feast of the Trinity: "In the old days our ancestors used to go to celebrate the *semik* on the tombs of their parents, and there, after having commemorated the dead, together with their family members they ate, after having divided them, omelettes and eggs fried with milk and flour."[24] These descriptions are typical. They demonstrate to us that the closer spring got, the more explicit became the forms of commemorating the dead. During the Christmas holidays, the commemoration happened in the home, during Fat Week people moved to the cemeteries, and finally the commemoration of the dead continued with the rituals of the Feast of the Trinity. In the north the dead were first of all commemorated in church and later people went to their tombs, where they even held banquets. P. S. Efimenko relates that in the governed territory of Pinezh "the dead are not commemorated only by the priest; they are also commemorated with bliny, fritters, semolina, and *kut'ja*. *Kut'ja* is eaten with the blessing of the priest."[25] The correspondents of P. V. Shejn wrote that in the governed territory of Vladimir, on the day of *semik* "in the morning . . . the dead are commemorated, and in the afternoon and the evening people give themselves up to happiness and sing unrestrained songs of carefree youth."[26] Here we deal with ancient and withered forms of an ancestor cult that once was exceptionally developed. We can get an idea of it by reading the very clear description of it in the

Stoglav (the book of one hundred chapters). In the answer to the twenty-third question is written: "On the Saturday of Trinity, in the villages and in the hamlets, men and women gather in the cemeteries and cry on the tombs with great lamentations. Then jesters and buffoons start performing and also, after crying, start to jump and to dance and to clap their hands and to sing satanic songs; even in the cemeteries impostors and swindlers are present."[27]

It is necessary to remember that the funerals of the dead who, for one reason or another, had not been buried during the year took place on the day of the Trinity. Thus during wars, plagues, famines, the dead in the "houses of the poor," in the "almshouses," and in the "houses of God" were piled in a common ditch, dug in a hovel. This served as a precautionary measure to avoid the spread of epidemics and to protect the cadavers from profanation; furthermore it should not be forgotten that it was objectively hard, in winter, to dig ditches in the frozen ground. During the *semik* these cadavers were sewn into mats, then ditches were dug and they were buried.[28]

The description of the Trinity Saturday that the Stoglav gives is valid equally for the day of the dead (*navij*) and for the *radunica*, that is when the rites of commemoration reached their culminating point. The day of the dead and the *radunica* fell in the week of Saint Thomas. Such was the name of the first week after Easter because, according to the Gospel, it was just in this week that the apostle Thomas expressed some doubts on the real bodily resurrection of Jesus Christ. Christ then allegedly put the fingers of Thomas in his wounds, after which the apostle became a believer. The Monday of this week was called *navij* day, and Tuesday *radunica*. To the difference in names did not correspond, it appears, a difference in substance. In the nineteenth century the *navij* day had almost been forgotten and had become a rarity, while the *radunica* was celebrated in very showy forms. It can be said that in the nineteenth century they had already become only one festivity. The days we have mentioned, that is Monday and Tuesday of the week of Saint Thomas, were only indicative. The commemoration of the dead that took place generally on the day of the *radunica* could, for instance, be done on Easter. In Bielorussia the *radunica* fell on the Thursday of Easter week.[29] The term *navij* in ancient Russian denoted something "pertaining to the dead ones." In ancient Czech, *unaviti* meant "to kill"; in Ukrainian *nava* means "coffin."[30] E. F. Karskij and other researchers report some other analogous terms in Lithuanian and in other languages that leave no doubt about the meaning of this term in Russian. In the Ukraine the Monday of Saint Thomas was called "the tombs," "the coffins," or "the farewell meals."

The etymology of the term *radunica* (*radonica, radanica, radovnica,* etc.) is much less clear. Most linguists relate it to the root *rad* (cheerful, happy). This interpretation is of little help to us since it is not clear what particular reason people had to rejoice. I. P. Kalinskij, for instance, thinks that this term expresses the joy of the dead for being remembered.[31] A. A. Potebnja proposes to relate it to the root *rod* (lineage), but not even this etymology clarifies the meaning that this term had in the daily life of the people.[32]

The customs typical of these days are generally described in a uniform way. The *radunica* was a festivity in which all the people participated. The whole village went to the tombs of their beloved ones. The women raised lamentations on the tombs. These lamentations contained as a theme the life of the dead one. A similar ritual is also performed right after someone's death. The women "crying and sobbing called the souls of the dead, celebrating their virtues."[33] On the tombs were placed foods and drinks: *kut'ja*, bliny, loaves of bread, pies, fritters of ricotta cheese, decorated eggs, wine, beer, *kanun* (a sort of homemade beer). The food was shared with the dead: eggs, bliny, and other dishes were crumbled and left on the tombs. Moreover, on the tombs were poured melted butter, wine, beer; all this was done "to feed the dead." People wished the dead a Happy Easter, believing that they could hear them. Finally eggs were rolled over the tombs.[34] After having performed this rite, they began to eat and drink by themselves and sadness turned into merriment; sometimes also revelry took place. "The *radunica* consisted of a general revelry, accompanied by songs and dances."[35] I. P. Kalinskij writes: "Karamzin is not wrong when he says that our people, following a pagan rite, become crapulous and in the midst of drinking make libations on the tombs of the dead. Consequently, the commemorative meals in honor of our dead parents recall the ancient pagan rite that was held at the beginning of spring or, more generally, the ancient custom of the funerary meals."[36] On the day of the *radunica*, songs were sung and *chorovod* were made. The proverbial saying is known: "On the morning of the *radunica* one ploughs, during the day one cries and in the evening one jumps."[37] E. F. Karskij reports that also in Bielorussia "they prepare a commemorative banquet after which, under the influence of the wine drunk in abundance, they give themselves to indecent amusements."[38] Later, when we treat the farewells to Carnival and other analogous rites, we shall deal with the problem of the sudden passage from crying to merriment and of the quality of the latter.

The *radunica* is an ancient festivity. In the sixty-second sermon of John Boccadorus (fourth century) it is said that, to commemorate the descent of Christ to the underworld, the Church has fixed the period of the commemoration of the dead in the week of Saint Thomas.[39] This festivity however, far from being a religious festival, is clearly of pagan origin. The first mention of the *radunica* is made in 1372 in the Troickij chronicle (*Troickaja letopis'*); later on it is sometimes used as a calendrical date. In the *Stoglav* the *radunica*, like other festivities to which a pagan origin was attributed, was forbidden. The answer to the twenty-fifth question says: "So that in the time of Easter they do not invoke the *radunica* and do not offend each other with insulting talk."[40]

After the *radunica* the rituals of commemoration of the dead ceased. On the day of Saint John the Baptist, for instance, there is no longer any trace of commemorative meals.

In fact, the Church had fixed some other periods in which the dead should have been commemorated, but they had an exclusively religious character. Some "Sundays of the parents" and some days of "universal funerary masses" were established, on which it was proposed to commemorate the dead (the Saturday before the feast of Saint Peter, June 29; the Saturday before the Assumption, August 15; and some others) and that the believers observed. None of these commemorative days established by the Church can be even remotely compared to the festivities of the *radunica* and of the *navij* day; ethnographers and folklorists, in fact, do not report the existence of a rite of any sort in those days. The only exception is the so-called Saturday of Saint Demetrius that was established by Dimitrij Donskoj after the battle of Kulikovo in memory of the fallen in that battle, and that was celebrated on the Saturday between October 18 and October 26, probably because on the twenty-sixth Saint Dimitrij

Solunskij was venerated. On this last day, in all the cemeteries people commemorated their dead, so that I. M. Snegirev could compare it to the *radunica*.[41]

What conclusions can we draw on the basis of the data we have examined? How can one explain the tendency, which reaches its acme at the beginning of spring, to venerate one's ancestors?

The natural affection that people have for their dear ones can explain the tendency to remember their dead from time to time; the lamentations and the shrieks are constant elements in the daily life of the Russian peasants. This is nothing but an outburst of sorrow, a natural desire to venerate the memory of the dead, which has been done since the beginning of the world; it does not pose particular problems of interpretation. The problem consists instead in the fact that these honors took place in specific periods of the solar calendar: they started with the winter solstice and ended approximately with the summer solstice.

The interpretations that have been given cannot satisfy us. I. P. Kalinskij, quoting A. N. Afanas'ev, writes: "For what concerns the reasons for which our ancestors have chosen the beginning of spring to commemorate the dead, it is probable that it was determined by the folk belief that in Spring also the souls of the dead, closed in the underworld, would wake up."[42]

Our data lead us to formulate a different hypothesis. The period between the two solstices is a period of awakening for the forces of Nature which are necessary to agriculture; the cult of the dead is tied to the interests and to the aspirations of the peasants.

The Russian rites do not show clearly in what consisted the tie between these two elements. The Russian rites were by then vestiges of ancient rites. In order to know which conceptions would determine these rites, which was their mental basis and which was their purpose, we must conduct a research among those peoples for whom these conceptions and these rites were not a residual phenomenon, but still living.

The resemblance between the agricultural rites of antiquity and those of modern Europe, Russia included, has long since been noted. This does not mean that one can explain everything with the theory of cultural borrowings; it means that there is a constant tie between forms of work and forms of thought.

Ancient peoples did not understand death as a complete transformation of the being. They believed that the dead continued to live under the ground and that they had over it a greater power than had the peasants who walked over it with the plough. From the bowels of the earth the dead could send a good or a bad harvest: they could oblige the earth to bear fruits or to hold back its strengths. They were transformed into gods of the earth.

Speaking of the souls of the dead, the German historian Rohde writes: "They expect help from them for whatever need, in particular they believe that they, just as the gods of the earth in whose kingdom they have descended, bring blessing and abundance to the fields."[43]

The expression "souls" must be attributed to the idealistic conceptions of the author. Usually not the "souls," but the dead themselves, who were underground in the tombs, were the object of cult. Another historian, Dieterich, expresses himself already with more caution: "The dead persons buried in the earth, spirits or souls as you prefer, favor the growth of the fruits of the earth: to them are raised prayers so that they send these fruits."[44] The words "as you prefer" show that the researcher in this case makes a concession to the leading opinion in the German science, one that he does not, however, share.

The earth and the dead persons who are there are confounded in one entity. "The peasant," writes B. L. Bogaevskij, "just like every individual in antiquity, saw that the earth 'covered' with its surface the plantations and the sowings, that it contained them within itself and that it poured them out of its enormous womb. The earth furthermore . . . contained . . . the tombs of the dead persons who concerned themselves with the plantations and with the sowings."[45] From all this, it appears evident that the ancient Greeks thought that the dead persons, finding themselves under the earth, could influence harvest. These conceptions give life to the peasant rites of spring dedicated to the dead. These beliefs of the Greeks and of the Romans were also present among the old Slavs. This is why the interest for the harvest is tied to the affection for the dead and takes on an ambiguous character. It is necessary to propitiate the dead, to show them one's own love and one's own veneration. In addition, it is necessary to sustain them by giving them something to eat, to drink, and to get warm; it is necessary to feast with them, to leave food on the tombs for them, to make libations with wine, to pour melted butter. But even this is not enough. It is necessary to guarantee them not only life but also immortality. It is necessary to make them share in the life-death-life circle that characterizes Nature and that is indispensable to the peasant. It is necessary that they themselves support this cycle. From this derives, as we have seen, the ritual use of dishes such as *kut'ja* and eggs. To the eggs are tied the most dissimilar conceptions.[46] In the Russian funerary cult only one of these conceptions is developed: the possibility of re-creating, of resurrecting life. The egg, as symbol of resurrection, was consecrated by the Church and therefore is used very often during Easter and immediately thereafter: the *radunica*, during which eggs were minced on the tombs, fell on the first week after Easter. The resurrection of the divinity, the resurrection of Nature and of its strengths, the guardians and bearers of which were believed to be the ancestors, who were underground but not completely dead, all this flows together in a unique body of rites and customs that have a clear agrarian orientation. To this whole belongs also the phenomenon of the sudden passage from crying to merriment which is typical of the *radunica*.

For the day of the summer solstice, that is, the day on which the sun is at its zenith and the earth is in the full bloom of its strengths, people do not turn to the subterranean helpers. Either they have done their duty or else they have not, and people cease to commemorate them until the next solstice, when again they will start to honor the ancestors behind the tables or on the tombs.

Although this ancient meaning of the funerary rites has long been forgotten, they were performed by tradition reinforced by the natural tendency to remember one's own dear ones who have left the world, and to honor them.

NOTES

1. For more precise information on the system of dating Easter, compare S. I. Seleshnikov, *Istorija Kalendarja i ego prestojashchaja reforma* (History of the calendar and its forthcoming reform) (Lenizdat, 1962), pp. 63–66.

2. Compare L. V. Cherepnin, *Russkaja chronologija* (Russian chronology) (Moscow,

1941), p. 27. According to Cherepnin's data, the New Year's Day fixed in September was universally accepted beginning from the year 1492.

3. A. I. Petropavloskij, *"Koljady" i "Kupalo" v Bielorussii* (The Christmas Holidays and the feast of Saint John the Baptist in Bielorussia) in *Etnograficheskoe Obozrenie* (Ethnographic Review) 1908, no. 1–2: 158–65.

4. I. P. Kalinskij, *Cerkovno-narodnyj mesjaceslov na Rusi* (The religious-popular Calendar in the Rus') in *Zapiski Russkogo geograficheskogo obshchestva po otdeleniju etnografii*, Publications of the Russian Scientific Society of Geography—Ethnography Section (St. Petersburg, 1913), 7: 49.

5. I. P. Sacharov, *Skazanija russkogo naroda*, 3d ed. (Volume 1, books 1–4, Moscow, 1841. Volume 2, books 5–8, Moscow, 1849). See vol. 2, book 7, p. 62.

6. A. A. Makarenko, *Sibirskij narodnyj kalendar' v etnograficheskom otnoshenii. Vostochnaja Sibir'. Enisejskaja gubernija.* (The folk calendar of Siberia from an ethnographic viewpoint. Eastern Siberia, gubernatoriat of Enisej) in *Zapiski russkogo geograficheskogo obshchestva po otdeleniju etnografii*, Publications of the Russian Scientific Society of Geography—Ethnography Section (St. Petersburg, 1913) 36: 49.

7. P. V. Shejn, *Materialy dlja izuchenija byta i jazyka russkogo naselenija severozapadnogo kraja* (Data for the study of daily life and of the language of the Russian population of the north-east of the country), 3 vols. (St. Petersburg, 1887–1902), vol. 1, part I, *Bytovaja i semejnaja zhizn' belorusa v obrjadach i pesnjach* (The daily and family life of the Bielorussians in the rites and in the songs) (St. Petersburg, 1877), p. 53.

8. A. P. Minch, *Narodnye obichai, obrjady, sueverija i predrassudki Saratovskoj gubernii, sobrannye v 1861–1888 gg.* (Customs, rites, superstitions and folk prejudices of the gubernatoriat of Saratov, collected in the years 1861–1888) in *"Zapiski Russkogo geograficheskogo obshchestva po otdeleniju etnografii,"* 2d ed. (St. Petersburg, 1889–1980), vol. 19.

9. D. K. Zelenin, *Russische (ostslawische) Volkskunde* (Berlin and Leipzig, 1927), p. 375.

10. P. S. Efimenko, *Materialy po etnografii russkogo naselenija Archangel'skoj gubernii* (Data on the ethnography of the Russian population of the gubernatoriat of Archangel'sk), part 1, *Opisanie vneshnego i vnutrennego byta* (Description of the daily life at the interior and at the exterior) (Moscow, 1877), p. 132; part 2, *Narodnaja solvesnost'* (Folk philology) (Moscow, 1878).

11. Shejn, vol. 1, part 1, p. 53.

12. Ibid., p. 150.

13. Petropavloskij, p. 161.

14. D. K. Zelenin, *Narodnyj obichaj gret' pokoinikov* (The folk habit of warming up the dead) in *"Sbornik Char'kovskogo istoriko-filologicheskogo obshchestva"* (Collection of the historical-philological Char'kov Scientific Society), 18: 256–71.

15. Ibid., p. 256.

16. S. V. Maksimov, *Nechistaja, nevedomaja i Krestnaja sila* (The impure, mysterious and divine force) (St. Petersburg, 1903).

17. V. F. Miller, *Russkaja maslenica i zapadnoevropejskij karnaval* (Moscow, 1884), p. 21.

18. Zelenin, *Russische (ostlawische) Volkskunde*, p. 386.

19. I. M. Snegirev, *Russkie prostonarodnye prazdnikov i suevernye obrjady*, parts 1–4, 2d ed. (Moscow, 1837–1839), p. 120.

20. Sacharov, vol. 2, book 7, p. 72.

21. A. V. Tereshchenko, *Byt russkogo naroda*, 7 vols. (Moscow, 1847–48), 2: 329.

22. E. A. Adveeva, *Zapiski i zamechanija o Sibiri* (Notes and observations on Siberia) (Moscow, 1837), p. 69.

23. Maksimov, pp. 372–73.

24. Sacharov, vol. 2, book 7, p. 84.

25. P. S. Efimenko, *Materialy po etnografii russkogo naselenija Archangel'skoj gubernii*, part 1, p. 137.

26. P. V. Shejn, *Velikorus v svoich pesnjach obrjadach, obychajach skazkach, legendach i td.* (St. Petersburg, 1898), 1: 344.

27. *Stoglav.* 3d ed. (Kazan: Izd. Kazanskoj Duchovnoj akademii, 1912), pp. 89–90.

28. Kalinskij, pp. 207–8; Snegirev, 3d ed., pp. 108, 117–210.

29. E. F. Karskij, *Belorusy*, vol. 3, Ocherki slovesnosti belorusskogo plemeni (Bielorussians, vol. 3. Philological profile of the

Bielorussian population) (Moscow, 1916), p. 159.

30. N. V. Gorjaev, *Sravnitel'nyj etimologicheskij slovar' russkogo jazyka* (Etymological comparative dictionary of the Russian language) (Tbilisi, 1896), p. 224.

31. Kalinskij, p. 202.

32. For more detailed information, compare Zelenin, p. 332.

33. Kalinskij, p. 202; Snegirev, 3d ed., p. 22.

34. Snegirev, p. 48; Makarenko, p. 164.

35. Kalinskij, p. 202; Snegirev, 2d ed., p. 48.

36. Kalinskij, p. 203.

37. For a more detailed description of the *radunica*, compare Maksimov, p. 425 ff.

38. Karskij, 3: 158.

39. Kalinskij, p. 21.

40. *Stoglav*, p. 91.

41. Snegirev, 3d ed., p. 117.

42. Kalinskij, p. 203.

43. E. Rohde, *Psyche* (Tübingen, 1921), pp. 246–47.

44. Dieterich, *Mutter Erde*, 3d ed. (Berlin and Leipzig, 1925), p. 48.

45. B. L. Bogaevskij, *Zemledel 'cheskaja religija Afin* (The agricultural religion of Athens) (Petrograd, 1916) 1: 31.

46. Ju. A. Javorskij, *Omne vivo ex ovo. K istorii poverij i skazanij o jajce* (Introduction to a history of the beliefs and the sayings on the egg) (Kiev, 1909). Includes rich bibliography.

21 / Food for the Holy Ghost: Ritual Exchange in Azorean Festivals

Mari Lyn Salvador

Since Lévi-Strauss's ground-breaking work The Raw and the Cooked, *which sets the conventional beginning of culture at the introduction of cooked food, anthropologists have looked at the social dimension of food and foodways with renewed interest. Food has been recognized as a mode of communication, and the exchange of food as a ritual way of delineating social relationships.*

This essay, fruit of fieldwork conducted over a decade in several visits, discusses the yearly festivities honoring the Holy Ghost on the Island of Terceira, in the archipelago of the Azores, which have maintained strong ties with the Portuguese culture of the mainland and with traditional Catholic religion. The author focuses on the analysis of food rituals, including gathering the ingredients, preparation, display, presentation, exchange, and consumption. Ritual food and food rituals appear as central to Azorean festivities documented since the eleventh century in orally transmitted legends and in historic documents as well. To this day, Azoreans continue to re-enact and repay the original vow made by the saint Queen Isabella (1295–1322) to the Holy Ghost by giving gifts of food as she did. Such contemporary rites of exchange are presented as taking place in both urban and rural environments.

The analysis is placed in spatial, temporal, and social contexts. In each community, members of a lay brotherhood, Irmandade do Divino Espírito Santo, continue to jealously guard the ritual paraphernalia necessary for the performance of the rite, especially the império—the folk building considered to be the house of the Holy Ghost—as well as elaborate flags and banners passed down from generation to generation, and all kitchen utensils necessary to prepare feasts for crowds of several hundred at a time.

The festival includes traditional Roman Catholic rituals such as High Mass, formal processions, presentations of steers to be slaughtered and gifts of edibles, production of large quantities of food, competitive extemporaneous singing, musical, and theatrical performances, dance, and food auctions.

The author points out that the exchange of food expresses both the egalitarian and the hierarchical patterns and principles as they coexist in Azorean social structure. Charity, devotion, cooperation, and competition are central issues in the Azorean festival. Taking a lead from Marcel Mauss's classic study of the Gift, the author shows how food gifts are crucial elements in the festival symbolism and ritual patterns. The patrons of the festival, having received divine favors, fulfill their obligation to reciprocate them by distributing gifts of food to the community. The discussion also shows that the exchanges of food described are of two different kinds. There is a simple reciprocal exchange shown in the funcao, which is an essentially private thanksgiving. There is also the kind that Sahlins defined as "pooling," in which several individuals give to one central figure, who successively will redistribute either to the same individuals or to others. This is shown in the assembly of bread and wine at the Impérios, and the later distribution of them at the bodos, which are public, more formalized events.

Finally, the author argues that aesthetic considerations govern the overall production and presentation of food, and that aesthetics act as the idiom for the transformation of these material goods into the intangible form of social prestige.

Food for the Holy Ghost: Ritual Exchange in Azorean Festivals

Mari Lyn Salvador

Introduction

Food is universally important not only to sustain life and maintain a healthy body but also as a source of sensory pleasure. Claude Lévi-Strauss considers the manipulation of food—passing from raw to cooked—the primary act that symbolizes the founding of culture and points out that the preparation of food is as expressive as it is technical. Human beings cook their food to demonstrate that they are civilized, and they elaborate food elements to mark special occasions.[1]

Raymond Firth describes the cooperative preparation of food as a mechanism that gives concrete expression to the meaning of kin ties, and describes food as a symbolic instrument used to express ideas about social relationships. In a discussion of gift exchange, he states, "The whole intricate system, focused upon food, was a symbolic mode of representation emphasizing some of the basic principles of social structure. . . ."[2] Mary Douglas notes that food is created as a code and states that the messages that it encodes will be found in the pattern of social relationships being expressed. The message is about degrees of hierarchy, inclusion and exclusion, boundaries, and transactions across boundaries.[3] Douglas argues for the interpretation of food as an art form and mentions the fact that the aesthetic elements should be considered as distinct from the nutritional aspects of food. Ortner, in her work with the Sherpas, addresses the issues of the ambiguous meaning of food as vital to health itself and immensely pleasurable, but at the same time inherently dangerous and corrupting.[4] The consumption of especially prepared foods that are distinct from the daily fare serves as a marker of social occasions in many cultures.[5]

Here I analyze the preparation, presentation, exchange, and consumption of ritual food associated with the Holy Ghost festivals in the Azores, Portugal, as an avenue to the understanding of reciprocity, solidarity, charity, cooperation, and competition—concepts that are basic to Azorean folk religion and social organization.

In cultures with rural, agrarian economies, seasonal festivals celebrate the fruits of nature and the fruits of culture. The regeneration of nature is symbolically communicated by food, a sign that can be eaten as well as being ritually prepared, decorated, and symbolically exchanged.

This basic pattern, clearly important in Christianity, is manifested in the sacrament of the Eucharist as the symbolic consumption of the body and blood of Christ.[6] In Portuguese, the integral relationship between food and celebration is expressed in that *festa* means both festival and feast.[7]

Ethnographic Context. The Azores consist of nine islands in the Atlantic off the coast of Portugal, and is an area of considerable seismic activity. Volcanoes and earthquakes plague the islands.[8] The climate is mild and humid, with abundant rainfall producing a rich agricultural system. The economy is based on agriculture, cattle raising, the production of dairy products, and, to a lesser extent, fishing.[9]

Although social stratification and hierarchy certainly exist in the Azores, class differentiation based on material wealth and family power is deemphasized. Ostentatious display and overt conspicuous consumption, except within the ritual context, are likely to be ridiculed. The importance of hard work and frugality is stressed, and collaboration and mutual cooperation are highly valued. Reciprocity, the payment of one good deed for another, a basic underlying concept of Azorean culture, is sanctified by the ritual process.

The islands were uninhabited when they were discovered by the Portuguese in the late 1400s.[10] Colonization began in the mid-fifteenth century, mainly by the Portuguese, although people from Spain, France, and Flanders also migrated to the Azores. People from throughout the south of Portugal, a region of distinct cultural areas, further contributed to the diversity found in the Azores.[11] In 1970 the population was 265,000.[12]

Migration has been an important aspect of Portuguese history. During their period of colonial expansion, the Portuguese reached Africa, Brazil, India, Madeira, and the Cape Verde islands as well.[13] Azoreans have continued the tradition of migration going to Brazil, Canada, and North America primarily, where they settled in Massachusetts, Rhode Island, and California.

Ritual Context. Azoreans have religious celebrations throughout the year following the Catholic liturgical calendar.[14] In addition to the festivities of the Christmas and Easter seasons, there are two important cycles of religious activities. One, in honor of each community's patron saint, occurs during the growing season; the other, in honor of the Holy Ghost, occurs primarily during the eight weeks after Easter with major festivals on Pentecost and Trinity Sunday.

Intense popular devotion to the Holy Ghost, relatively rare in non-Portuguese-speaking Roman Catholic countries, is central to the Azorean religious system. The Holy Ghost, the third person of the Trinity, is part of Catholic theology. Nevertheless, he is considered a separate deity by Azoreans, personified as a powerful but capricious and *vindicativo* (vindictive) male with a decidedly human personality and specific likes and dislikes.

In the Azores the Holy Ghost is symbolized by a silver crown with a dove with outstretched wings on top and a silver scepter. Azoreans have combined the dove, a traditional Roman Catholic symbol of the Holy Ghost, with a Portuguese imperial crown, a symbol of secular authority.

This configuration of religious activities in the Holy Ghost celebrations is specific to the Azores. They include a symbolic coronation of an emperor or emperors, large-scale public distribution of food, the offering of gifts of food to the poor, a communal meal and secular activities such as competitive extemporaneous singing debates, and concerts and traditional Azorean-style street bullfights.

Holy Ghost celebrations have flourished in the Azores since the late fifteenth century. Azoreans have taken these celebrations to Brazil, Canada, Bermuda, and the United States. In contrast, they have almost entirely disappeared in continental Portugal. In the Azores, although individual priests occasionally participate in the ceremonies, Holy Ghost celebrations are only reluctantly sanctioned by the official church. In fact, systematic efforts through the centuries and most recently in the 1950s to eradicate them have been strenuously and successfully resisted in the Azores.[15]

The Legend. The origin of the Holy Ghost celebrations is attributed to a celebration sponsored by the Rainha Santa Isabela, Queen Isabela of Portugal, who reigned between 1295 and 1322.[16] The charter, or rationale, for the event in which food is a central element, is part of Portuguese folk tradition and is illustrated in the following three narratives told over and over again in the Azores.

> Queen Isabel, the wife of King Diniz of Portugal, loved the poor. One day
> in the middle of winter she was going with buns in her cape to give to
> some poor people. Her husband stopped her and asked what she had in
> her cape. She said, "Roses," and he asked, "In the middle of winter?"
> When she opened her cape, the buns had turned to red roses.[17]

This narrative, a type common among the Catholic exempla, illustrates the modesty of the Queen as a benefactor and sets her as an example of charitable behavior.[18] As in many types of Christian folk narratives, bread is the favorite gift of charity. It is a symbol of the body of Christ and recalls the origin of Communion. As the Queen feeds in time of famine, God transforms the bread in the cape to roses in middle of winter. In her act of charity, the Queen repeats the primary gesture of Christ. In memory of Saint Isabela, contemporary Azoreans repeat the ritual and in doing so emulate her as a model for daily and ritual behavior. In the narrative she, like most saints, is placed on an intermediate plane between the human and the divine.

Queen Isabela's role as mediator appears clearly in another narrative told as the sanction for Holy Ghost celebrations.

> Dom Diniz and his son, Dom Pedro, after arguing for many years,
> decided to have a battle on the mainland of Portugal. Both sides brought
> their armies to a certain place, still marked in Portugal today, and
> prepared to fight. Queen Isabela prayed to the Holy Ghost that they
> wouldn't fight and made a promise that she would make a celebration
> each year. She would put a poor person on her throne and crown him with
> her own crown. On the eve of the battle, Dom Diniz gave in, they didn't
> fight, and the celebration began. Later other members of the court began
> to have a celebration to the Holy Ghost on Pentecost Sunday.[19]

Saint Isabela promised to make a celebration each year in return for the miracle from the Holy Ghost. Here the gift is offered after the favor is granted rather than as part of the request. The tradition as carried on in the Azores symbolically reenacts her promise.

The *Promessa*, the promise or sacred vow to perform a specific act in return for a divine favor, is basic to Portuguese religious beliefs. People often give gifts that symbolize the favor they have received. Olive oil and candles, symbols of life, are offered in appreciation or healing. Food, an important gift, is commonly associated with promises to the Holy Ghost. People offer bread and sugar ex-votos made in the shape of the body part that has been cured. Elaborate cakes and liqueurs are also given to support celebrations held in honor of the Holy Ghost.

Queen Isabela, as an ideal benefactor, is symbolized to this day in the Azores by the voluntary self-appointed ritual Emperors or Empresses. After they are crowned they feed the poor and give an elaborate communal meal as payment for favors they have received from the Holy Ghost. In this way contemporary Emperors reenact the promise of the Queen as well as fulfilling their own obligation.

In still another narrative, Queen Isabela promises her jewels in exchange for food and reciprocates the divine gift by feeding the poor and establishing a yearly celebration to honor the Holy Ghost.

> Queen Isabela pleaded with God for help with her starving people, even
> to the point of promising to sell all her jewels, including her crown.
> Sometime after this there suddenly appeared two ships in a Portuguese
> harbor. Neither of the ships had any living person upon it. The only
> contents were cattle on one ship and grain on the other. These ships were
> thought to be a miracle sent from God in answer to Queen Isabela's pleas
> for her starving people. With this supply of cattle and grain, a large meal
> of meat and bread was prepared and a banquet served to the poor. From
> this date forward, an annual banquet for the poor was given in the same
> manner as the first. Queen Isabela continued to offer this yearly ceremony
> as a thanksgiving to God for the peace bestowed within Portugal and for
> the health of the Portuguese people. Queen Isabela gathered twelve poor
> men around a banquet table who were served by royalty as an expression
> of equality.[20]

This narrative dramatizes an idealized solution to a periodic human condition—famine. The Saint/Queen, acting as an intermediary, offers something of her own, her jewels—a sign of royalty—for her subjects, the poor starving people. God accepts the petition, but does not take the offer—her faith and intention are enough, as with Abraham in the Bible. He sends a shipful of cattle and a shipful of grain. Queen Isabela reciprocates, fulfilling her promise by feeding the poor. Food is again a central element. God's gift of food at this desperate time is consumed formally in a ritual meal—an act repeated annually at the beginning of each agricultural cycle. Both main means of subsistence are blessed: grain, for abundance in the fields and cattle, for plentifulness in the stables. The narrative not only gives the rationale for the ritual and makes it clear that it is to be done each year, but also designates the foods to be associated with the Holy Ghost—meat and bread. Wine was added and the ritual communal meal was complete. To make the symbolism more explicit, the Queen picked twelve poor people for the table in the name of the twelve apostles. They are served by royalty as an expression of "equality." Here social statuses of ordinary time are inverted in the sacred time of ritual. In many Azorean communities, twelve of the poorest people of the community are still invited specifically to represent the apostles at a coronation and to be fed and cared for at the communal meal.

Thus the structure of the celebration and its activities, food, and symbolism are defined in a pious story. Although historic documentation of religious rituals prior to 1294 suggests that a configuration of ritual activities similar to the Holy Ghost celebrations described here predates Queen Isabela, it is certainly significant that these narratives are told again and again as a sanction for the ritual, and as the history of the celebration. Further, it is most probable that the confluence of the imperial crown with the dove, the official symbol of the Holy Ghost, can be attributed to the role of Queen Isabela in this ritual.[21]

The Brotherhood. Today the cult of the Holy Ghost is managed by a lay Brotherhood, the Irmandade do Divino Espírito Santo,[22] of which there is a branch in each rural town and in most urban neighborhoods. The Brotherhood is responsible for maintaining the Império, Holy Ghost house, for the administration of its ritual paraphernalia, and for the sponsorship of a Holy Ghost celebration each year.

Brotherhood membership is open to anyone, male or female. Members pay annual dues, participate in ritual activities, and receive a share of the food that is distributed during the Holy Ghost celebration.

Context: Space and Time. Two types of celebration are held in honor of the Holy Ghost, the *bodo* (banquet) and the *função* (function).[23] The *bodo*, a large-scale public festival organized by a committee of Brotherhood members includes a Novena; Mass; a procession and coronation of young children; the distribution of meat, bread, and wine; an auction of gifts given to the Holy Ghost; and an array of secular activities including extemporaneous competitive singing and Azorean-style bullfights.

The *função*, a small-scale ritual performance sponsored by a voluntary Emperor as payment of a promise to the Holy Ghost, is held in a private home. It includes a Novena; Mass; procession and coronation of the Emperor; distribution of food to the poor; offering of gifts to the guests; and a communal meal.

The context for these ritual activities is the Império. These elaborately painted one-room buildings are divided into three parts by the placement of the door and two windows. Impérios, although they are permanent structures, are opened and used only once a year for the festival celebration.

During the celebration, an interior altar is decorated with crepe paper and fresh flowers. When the Coroa (crown) is placed on the altar, the space becomes sacred.

Figure 1. Distribution of Holy Ghost Celebrations

WEEKS	1 2 3 4 5 6 7		8	——July
FUNÇÃO	F F F F F F F		F	
BODO		B	B B B B B B	

People who have promises to pay bring offerings and place them at the altar. By the end of the day, the Império is filled with sugar and bread ex-votos, beeswax candles, olive oil, live chickens, bananas, cakes, and other gifts. These gifts are auctioned to the crowd during the afternoon. Profits from the auction which are used to support the celebrations are not given by the Brotherhood to the church.

Although the Impérios are often located in close proximity to the Catholic church and are described as chapels, the building, the land, and all the ritual paraphernalia are considered to belong to the Holy Ghost and are maintained and managed by the Brotherhood. They could be thought of as a lay counterpart to the Parish since the church does not own the building, nor has the church been able to successfully control the activities therein.[24]

Each rural village and most urban neighborhoods have an Império. There are over forty on the island of Terceira alone. Each Império has a *bodo*, a large public celebration for the Holy Ghost, and rural Impérios have at least eight *funções*. Some Impérios, and thereby the neighborhoods where they exist, are noted for the quality of their celebrations.

The celebrations are run by a committee selected from the Brotherhood members. Considerable rivalry exists between the Impérios, and the committee members co-operate with each other in order to compete with the other Impérios and the memory of past celebrations. Judgments about the success of a celebration are based primarily on aesthetic criteria. The quality of the bread and wine distributed by the rural Impérios is discussed at length and weigh heavily in a positive appraisal of the celebration.

The Altura Do Espírito Santo, Holy Ghost season, falls mainly between Easter and Trinity Sunday with the high point of ritual activities throughout the Azores on Pentecost and Trinity. In most rural communities on the island of Terceira the cycle begins at Easter and a *função* is held each week. The coronations of the *funções* coincide with the *bodos* on Pentecost and Trinity. Urban Impérios have now extended the season by staggering their celebrations from Pentecost through July which enable the Brotherhoods to share the crowns, brocade flags, and other expensive paraphernalia needed for the festival.

The week of the *bodo* is a sacred time marked by excitement and extraordinary events. Firecrackers and rockets announce the beginning and end of important activities and call people to the Império. Flags and elaborate strings of lights decorate the street in front of the Império, transforming it temporarily into a sacred space for religious and social activities. Although the basic components of the celebrations are similar, there are subtle variations in the style of celebrations among the Impérios in urban neighborhoods and between those in the villages. Greater variations exist from island to island.

Ritual activities begin during the week before the coronation. Brotherhood members gather at the Império to visit the Holy Ghost, recite the rosary led by a lay person, and pay their annual dues. After the novena they stroll under the colored lights, visit, listen to Azorean music, buy special foods from street vendors, or bid on bread, candy, and liqueurs at the auction.

Ritual Exchange Events

The ritual exchange of gifts, an essential part of this celebration which centers around the distribution of food, highlights a basic Azorean concern for reciprocity. Brotherhood members pay dues and expect to receive bread and wine in some urban Impérios.

Pezinho. The *pezinho*, a serenade with a parade of decorated cattle, begins the exchange events in those Impérios that distribute meat. During the previous year young animals donated or purchased by the Brotherhood are fattened throughout the year and the meat is distributed. At the end of the week before the coronation, the cattle, decorated with ribbons and flowers and accompanied by the *festa* committee, singers, musicians, and firecracker launchers, are paraded through the neighborhood. The group stops at the Império, the church, and the homes of the *festa* committee and those people who have contributed to the *festa*. While the decorated animals pace, the singers, accompanied by the stringed instruments, create extemporaneous verses to honor the Holy Ghost and the person being serenaded. A committee member provides the initial singer with facts about the contributor, and subsequent singers compete to create more and more beautiful verses elaborating on the theme. These verses give details, often humorous, about the person's life and about his contributions, generally food or labor. The singers thank the family for helping, assure them that the Holy Ghost helps those who help the *festa*, and encourage them to give again next year with verses like the following.

A senhora diga ao seu marido	Lady, please tell your husband
Que o "pezinho" por aqui passou	That the "pezinho" passed here
Que o Divino esta reconhecido	And the Divine is grateful
Da res bela que êle engordou	For his beautiful fat steer.[25]

After the *pezinho* (serenade), the person honored often provides food for the singers and spectators. In some cases wine, soft drinks, and sweet bread may be served outside the house, or the whole group may be invited into the house for elaborate snacks of codfish cakes, potatoes with hot peppers, clams, crab, soft drinks, beer, and wine. As the brass band plays, the group walks on to the next house to continue the serenade.

The *pezinho* provides a conspicuous and prominent indication of those who have helped with the festival. The central theme—the Holy Ghost helps those who have helped with the *festa*, i.e., raising cattle, donating wine or money—reinforces the concept of reciprocity and encourages continued support. The host—the person being honored—uses food as a way of reciprocating and thanking the singers and musicians who themselves are thanking the host in the name of the Holy Ghost.

The presentation of the meat varies considerably. In most urban Impérios young boys deliver a share of raw meat and bread, and sometimes wine, to the houses of the Brotherhood members. The cut and size of the meat depends on the amount a person pays in annual dues or any additional contribution. In most rural areas the meat is laid out on tables in front of the Império for each Brotherhood member to pick up and take home.

The Bodo: Bread and Wine.   Bread and wine, a medium of gift exchanges, are central to Holy Ghost festivals. Pentecost and Trinity Sundays are days of great excitement. *Bodos* are held in rural Impérios throughout the Azores and in some of the urban Impérios as well. The word *bodo* (banquet) is not only used for the large-scale public Holy Ghost festivals but also specifically for one part of the festival—the distribution of bread and wine at the *festa*.

On *festa* Sunday in the urban Impérios sweet bread is distributed after the procession and coronation of young children. The bread, generally purchased at local bakeries, is given out to the children who have participated in the coronation and sometimes to the audience. Throughout the day, as people come to the Império to visit the Holy Ghost and to bring their offerings, they are given a slice of sweet bread. Friends and relatives of committee members also bring gifts of food, fancy cakes, alfinim, and decorated loaves of sweet bread to give in support of the *festa*. All of these gifts are auctioned off, and the money raised is used by the committee to pay for the expenses of the *festa*.

The distribution of gifts is more complex in the rural communities. In the cities the bread is purchased from bakeries but in the rural Impérios an elaborate system for the preparation, presentation, and distribution of bread continued to flourish. In Lages and Vila Nova, for example, several couples are chosen by the *festa* committee to be *mordomos* (stewards). Each couple is responsible for a designated number of loaves of bread—generally between 200 and 400. The *mordomo's* family and friends make about half the required loaves and the rest are produced, ten per family, by other Brotherhood members.

On Saturday all those who have made bread for a particular *mordomo* gather at his or her home for a communal meal of *sopa do espírito santo*, meat cooked with vegetables and broth poured over bread, *carne asada*, baked meat, bread, and wine. In the late afternoon the group loads baskets of bread onto elaborately decorated ox carts and walks in a procession through town, gathering the rest of the bread as they go. The *mordomo* carrying a decorated wooden staff with a silver head, the symbol of his authority, is followed by young girls carrying enormous loaves of decorated sweet bread. As the *mordomo* and his party enter the storehouse of the Império in triumph, the bread is given to the Holy Ghost, counted by the *festa* committee and stored along with barrels and barrels of wine. A table is set with glasses, a pitcher of wine, and the large loaves of sweet bread, and the *mordomo's* staff is installed on the wall behind the table. The *mordomo's* family sits at the table and offers bread and wine to visitors.

On Pentecost and Trinity Sunday the Emperors for the week preside over the ritual activities in the Império, and the *mordomos* interact within the sphere of the *despenca*, the ritual storehouse. On these Sundays the Coronation tends to be grander, often embellished with a larger guest list, additional activities, and a much larger audience. After the coronation of the Emperor the *mordomos* and their assistants distribute hundreds of loaves of sweet bread and wine to everyone there. Many people travel around the entire island stopping at each Império to visit the Holy Ghost, pay their promises, receive bread and wine, and renew their relationships with friends and relatives.

Throughout the afternoon, Brotherhood members come to the Império, pray, leave their offerings, pay their dues, have a glass of wine, and eat sweet bread and meat. Gifts offered to the Holy Ghost or given to the committee are auctioned to raise money to support the *festa*. At the end of the day, names are drawn for those who want to have a *função* the following year to determine who will have the crown and in what order.

Função

The *função* (function), a small-scale celebration sponsored by a voluntary Emperor, represents the payment of a personal promise to the Holy Ghost and involves a series of ritual exchange events. Just as Queen Isabela, through her act of charity, fulfilled her promise to the Holy Ghost, so the Emperor repeats her action, thereby fulfilling his own promise.

The symbolic crown, decorated staffs, and practical items such as pans, dishes, and benches used for the ritual, belong to the Holy Ghost and are administered by the lay Brotherhoods. All of the necessary ritual paraphernalia circulate from family to family in each community in an order established by lot on Pentecost of the prior year.

The event takes place in the home of the Emperor, which becomes the context for ritual activities. A banner of the Holy Ghost with fresh flowers placed in the front of the home marks it as a ritual space and signifies that the Holy Ghost is there. The crown is installed on an altar decorated with crepe-paper flowers, and olive oil and candles are burned at its base. The presence of the crown transforms the domestic, secular space of a private home into the public ritual space of a chapel. During this time anyone may enter the house to worship, and each day of the week people gather to recite the rosary that is led by a lay person.

The main participants in the *função* are: the Emperor, sponsor or host; the *criador*, cattle raiser; the *marchant*, butcher; the *mestra*, ritual specialist and supervisor; and those who help with the cooking. These are the performers, the active participants, and those who generate the gifts. The invited guests, the poor, and the general public are the audience—the passive participants and the recipients of the gifts.

The Emperor and his or her family are responsible for the event. They pay for it, invite the guests, and select and pay for the specialists. The Emperor's family will ultimately either feel the relief and glory of having sponsored a successful *função*— having thereby fulfilled their promise and gained social prestige—or suffer the defeat of failure and have to repeat the event. Although the Emperor's family is responsible for a successful *função*, the result cannot be accomplished alone and depends upon the cooperation and the ability of all specialist helpers.

The *criador* is responsible for raising the steers. He feeds them, cares for them if they become ill, accompanies them in the procession of the steers, and blesses them before they are slaughtered. The *marchant* slaughters and butchers them. He is responsible for dividing the meat, overseeing its presentation to the guests and cooking it for the communal meal. The *mestra,* ritual specialist and cook, advises the Emperor as to proper ritual behavior. She is responsible for the food preparation and orchestration of the people who are helping. She decides on the ingredients and amounts necessary to make the bread and personally oversees the process. She is assisted by the *cantadeira,* the woman who fires the bread oven, and selected female family members and friends of the Emperor.

The *filharmônica* (marching band) provides the music for the *função.* They accompany the crown each time it is moved and play for the coronation and procession. In return they are invited to the communal meal and are often given *rosquilias,* round-shaped sweet bread.

The *convidados* (guests) are invited by the Emperor on the basis of kinship, proximity and previous reciprocal interactions. They are invited to accompany the Emperor in the coronation procession and to share in the communal meal. They are expected to provide some of the raw ingredients for the food and to help with the food preparation. In turn, they can expect to receive portions of raw meat, bread, and wine in quantities directly proportional to their status within the network and to their degree of participation in this particular ritual event.

The poor are an integral part of the process. As Queen Isabela gave to the poor, so must the contemporary voluntary Emperors in order to fulfill not only their obligation but also her promise to continue the celebration.

The general pubic, those who observe the event, provide the essential service of being the audience and are an important part of the evaluation process. Because the *funções* go on for eight weeks in each community, those who may be audience during one particular week may well be the active participants in the *função* in the following week.

Food Preparation. Because this ritual requires the large-scale distribution of food, meat, bread, and wine, the week prior to actual coronation is a time of intense food preparation. These activities can be divided into those that pertain primarily to the production of bread, generally done by the women, and to the preparation of meat, in which men also play a role. During the week before the coronation women from the families of the invited guests bring sugar, butter, and eggs to the home of the Emperor. They spend some time at the altar and help knead bread. Each woman is given a glass of liqueur and a large loaf of sweet bread as she leaves.

Three different types of bread are made using various ingredients and formed into various shapes. (1) *Pão de água,* bread of water, a simple daily bread made of flour, salt, and water, is folded in two shapes. One is folded in the daily fashion and used in the bread soup. The other, *pão dos inocentes,* bread of the innocents, is folded and decorated with a head. It is distributed by the Emperor to young children after the crowning. (2) *Pão de leite,* bread of milk, made with milk and sugar is folded and given with other food to the guests and served with a mid-course at a communal feast. (3) *Massa sovada,* sweet bread, made with milk, sugar, and eggs is shaped into large ovals and may be decorated. It is given to the guests, to those people with special status, to the poor, and is served as a third course of the feast. *Massa* is also made in a circular shape to be given to the members of the marching band.

Meat is important in the *função* and is prepared and presented in much the same way as in the *bodo.* The Emperor either raises the cattle in his own herd or asks a *criador* to raise them. The cattle are decorated and paraded through the community, blessed by the *criador* with the silver scepter of the Holy Ghost and then slaughtered and divided by the butcher. The meat is distributed raw to the guests and to ritual specialists in varying amounts and qualities. The presentation and display of meat varies a great deal from simple baskets held on the handle bars of a bicycle to elaborate processions of young girls carrying decorated platters of meat and baskets of bread winding through the streets delivering it to the homes of the guests.

The Coronation. On Sunday morning, the Emperor, accompanied by the guests, walks in a procession to the church. The procession generally is organized in two parallel lines. People designated as "special," such as the representatives of the *criador* or *mestra*, carry symbolic objects, crown, staffs, batons, banners, and flags and walk between the lines. They are further marked by a person on each side carrying decorated staffs. The procession reads from front to back with the Emperor, the most important person, at the very end. These processions provide a cogent visual delineation of one's personal network and not only make it clear who is and who is not present but also indicate prestige within the network by one's position in the procession and by the carrying of ritual objects. After the Mass, the priest crowns the Emperor with a silver crown. The procession of the crowned Emperor returns to the house in triumph.

Two types of gifts are then distributed by the crowned Emperor. *Pão dos inocentes*, bread of the innocents, is given to the children in the audiences, and *esmolas da mesa*, alms of the table, are given to the poor. First the Emperor kneels, kisses the head of each loaf of bread for the innocents and gives it to the children. He then moves to the tables where *esmolas* have been laid out and gives a bowl of bread covered with broth, cooked meat, cabbage, and cooked blood and two loaves of bread to a previously designated group of poor people.

After the distribution of gifts to the poor, the guests join the Emperor for a communal meal which often includes 200–300 people. All guests walk in the procession and return to the home to eat together. The meal consists of three courses. The first, *sopas*, bread with mint soaked with meat broth, is followed by boiled meat and cabbage served with *pão de leite*. *Alcatra*, meat with bacon, onion, and wine and *massa sovada* are served as a last course. The guests stay and eat together while the poor are given baskets of food to take home. Late in the afternoon the guests accompany the Emperor as he delivers the crown to the home of the Emperor for the following week and the cycle begins again.

Interpretation

The festival shows ritual patterns related to the legend of the Saint/Queen Isabela and expresses central values through the idiom of food. The charitable act of the Queen, in payment for a promise to the Holy Ghost, is repeated yearly by the committee in the *bodo* and by the Emperor in the *função*. The *festa* committee represents the royalty who sponsored the celebrations at the Queen's request. The Emperor at one level represents the Queen herself and at the same time the poor person she honored by placing her crown on his head. The Emperor not only fulfills his own personal promise, but in doing so also fulfills Queen Isabela's promise to continue the cele-

Figure 2

	BODO		FUNÇÃO
	Holy Ghost		Holy Ghost
Brotherhood Members	Queen Isabela	Guests	Emperor
	Poor		Poor

bration. In the *função*, social roles are transformed or reversed. The Emperor, though often a poor person, becomes a benefactor and takes on the idealized behavior of a wealthy, or even royal, person—Queen Isabela.

Gift Exchange and Cultural Values

Reciprocity. Reciprocity, the mutual exchange or payment of one benefit for another, is a basic feature of interpersonal relations in many cultures. The *promessa*, a sacred vow to repay the Holy Ghost, is paid by giving time, labor, and goods to others. The initial favor, the answer to the prayer, descends from the Holy Ghost to the recipient, who then reciprocates by giving laterally to the guests or vertically down to the poor.

Reciprocity is expressed in the *bodo* by various gift exchange events. The continuation of Saint Isabela's promise represents vertical exchange and suggests concern with hierarchy. The original gift—given down from the Holy Ghost—is reciprocated up to the Holy Ghost by giving down to the poor. Most of the other exchange events are horizontal or lateral and reflect aspects of Azorean social organization that stress more equal social relationships. Brotherhood members, for example, pay their dues and expect to receive equal shares of meat. People who give additional money, other gifts, or volunteer their services, expect to receive larger amounts of meat and invitations to communal feasts. In this situation people receive extraordinary gifts because of their contribution, not because of their relative prestige or position in the community. Wealthy or prominent people who do not pay their dues do not receive meat, while a poor person who catches fish for the committee or installs the electric light decorations may well receive additional gifts.

The *função* is a series of reciprocal events. The Emperor, who has received a divine favor, repays it by giving away food and drink and by providing the context for others to repay minor promises. He invites friends, family, and people to whom he is indebted from previous cooperative activities. He can only repay his promise with the help of his network of relatives and friends. All invited guests are expected to bring eggs, sugar, butter, and to help with making bread, and in turn receive bread when they visit the Holy Ghost at the home of the Emperor. Further, the guests give, by their presence, a visual manifestation of support of the Emperor by accompanying him as an imperial court in the procession. They receive gifts of raw meat, bread, and wine, and share in the communal meal.

Specialists are given the same gifts that guests receive, though their portions are bigger and the quality of the gifts is better, generally in proportion to the degree of their participation. The *mestra*, for example, is given larger portions of decorated bread, more meat, pots of cooked leftovers, and an honored position for her representative in the procession. People involved in providing and preparing the meat also receive special favors. The *criador* is given a large cut of meat and a large loaf of decorated bread, and is presented with the tongue and the liver of the animal at the feast. He is also honored by carrying the crown to the church, and walks just in front of the Emperor in the procession. The *marchant* is given a large cut from the top of the thigh, an enormous loaf of decorated bread, a pot of stewed meat, and also an important position in the procession. Members of the *filharmonica*, marching band, without whom no celebration would be complete, are invited to the communal feast and are given large ring-shaped loaves of sweet bread. Here the ritual provides the context for temporary emphasis on extreme hierarchy—an inversion of everyday organizational principles. The Emperor is clearly above all others for the week and is in turn expected to behave as an idealized wealthy person.

Charity. Charity, closely related to reciprocity in this event, further links both the committees and the Emperor to the Queen. The committee provides bread and wine for everyone during the *bodo*. These gifts represent, at a symbolic level, a lay counterpart of the body and blood of Christ in the Sacrament of Communion, the ultimate act of divine charity.

Charity is central to the *funcao*. The payment of the promise must include the distribution of food to the poor and is not complete simply with the coronation and the feast. *Esmolas*, alms for the poor, are distinguished from *ofertas*, those gifts such as bread and meat that are given to the guests. During the week before the coronation, those chosen to receive *esmolas* are notified and given tickets. Only those so invited come to receive them. Here, the *ofertas* can be seen symbolically as being given *laterally* to one's peers while *esmolas* are given *down* to the poor. In this case both communitas and hierarchy are played out by the vertical and horizontal distribution of food.[26]

Cooperation and Competition. Cooperation and competition go hand in hand in this context and must be considered together. Cooperation is essential for the production of a successful festival. A complex series of activities must be properly orchestrated in order to secure a positive evaluation. In the *bodo*, for example, committee members, people of diverse skills, have to cooperate and work together in order to compete with the memory of successful *bodos* from previous years in their own *Império* and with the *bodos* of *Impérios* from other communities.

Even though the *função* is performed as a repayment for a personal promise, the Emperors cannot do it alone. They must rely on the cooperation of family members, friends, and specialists. During the week of the food preparation, cooperative behavior is often ritualized, and idealized social norms are implemented. Cooperation between the volunteers helping with food preparation is essential, and people, although tired and overworked, are expected to get along.

Abundance replaces scarcity; food preparation is done on a large scale by specialists and volunteers rather than by the women of the house. Meals are prepared outside, in a public space, rather than inside the home, and are consumed in a communal rather than private setting. The quantities are larger than those of the daily fare, and special foods are prepared. Meat, seldom a part of the everyday diet, is essential, and dishes which may be part of the daily diet are enriched, enlarged, decorated, and put on display before they are eaten. As in the *bodo,* successful cooperation in the *função* enables families to compete with one another.

Aesthetics and Ritual Evaluation

An important underlying assumption of this system is that the Holy Ghost is considered to be much like a human being with a personality and specific likes and dislikes.[27] He is thought to enjoy and appreciate the beauty and effort expended in his honor. Aesthetics, the concern for beauty or those things that appeal to the senses and give pleasure, is important in the success of the celebration both in terms of honoring the Holy Ghost and thereby fulfilling the promise and in terms of the social prestige and respect that accrues to a person or committee who is responsible for the success.

The configuration of the ritual activities is also very important. How the event is orchestrated can lead to a positive aesthetic judgment that articulates the transformation of goods and services into social prestige and respect.

Marcel Mauss, whose *The Gift* (original 1925) is a classic statement of the social and economic aspects of ritual reciprocity, stressed the importance of going beyond the social and economic aspects of gift exchange to consider its aesthetic side.

> Moreover this institution has an important aesthetic side which we have
> left unstudied. But the dances performed, the songs, the shows, the
> dramatic representations given between camps or partners, the objects
> made, used, decorated, polished, amassed and transmitted with affection,
> reserved with joy, given away in triumph, the feasts in which everyone
> participates—all these—the foods, objects and services, are source of
> aesthetic emotions as well as the emotions aroused by interest.[28]

Aesthetic concerns govern the creation of ephemeral art, the use of ritual paraphernalia, the orchestration of performances, as well as the production of ritual food. Further, aesthetics govern the overall configuration, which ultimately contributes to the successful outcome of the event.

The quality of the food, both for the *bodo* and the *função,* weighs heavily in the positive evaluation of these festivals. Food must be abundant but not excessively so. The wise Emperor graciously reciprocates past gracious acts with food but does not give so much as to overly indebt the recipient. In the Azores, where scarcity can be a reality, extravagant waste would be considered a severe aesthetic mistake that would lead to criticism rather than to a positive response. In the rural towns, where people tend to know one another fairly well, it would be foolhardy to overextend the families' economic resources in order to sponsor a splendid *função*. One should not simply give more and more but rather give better and better or more beautifully.

The meat, bread, and wine should be well prepared and beautifully presented. Steers raised for the Holy Ghost should be fat, beautiful, and well behaved. Gifts of raw meat are carefully cut, and elaborate processions are organized to present it to the homes of the guests.

The bread is particularly important. It is made in the same way as daily bread, except that is is embellished—decorated with flowers or made in larger loaves or decorated shapes. More expensive ingredients make it richer and sweeter than usual. The texture should be fine, the color golden brown. These departures from the norm reflect care and skill taken to make the bread. Large loaves are more difficult to bake properly.

The level of aesthetic criticism is often subtle and sophisticated. Timing is important, for example. Comfort is a sensory perception, and people should not be kept waiting for an unbearably long time.

The quality of interaction between those working together is also a factor. In order to pay the promise, the Holy Ghost must be pleased and his likes and dislikes taken into consideration. The Holy Ghost likes to see people getting along and to see smooth interpersonal relations. "O Espírito Santo nao gosta de ver brigas" ("The Holy Ghost does not like to see arguments") is often used as a rationale to stop heated discussions between people working in the kitchen. Because of the stress on interaction, the *função* acts as a metaphor for idealized interpersonal relations.

Mediocre performances may marginally pay the promise but will not generate prestige. A *função* is rarely judged to be a complete failure; nevertheless, this does occur occasionally. The failure may be noticed by the Emperor himself or the Holy Ghost may manifest his dissatisfaction by sending a sign, generally through dreams, or by spoiling the performance outright. The unsuccessful Emperor must repeat the performance until it is properly carried out. The successful Emperor pays the promise and is able to manifest not only economic but also organizational resources and thereby gain social prestige and respect.

Through the analysis of the exchange of food we see that these rituals provide for the expression of both egalitarian and hierarchical principles both held together in Azorean social organization. Further, by looking at the evaluation of ritual performances we gain insights into the subtle system that generates social prestige and respect.

NOTES

1. Claude Lévi-Strauss, *Structural Anthropology* (New York: Basic Books, 1963), p. 87.

2. Raymond Firth, "Food Symbolism in a Pre-Industrial Society" in *Symbols, Public and Private* (Ithaca: Cornell University Press, 1975), p. 258.

3. Mary Douglas, "Deciphering a Meal" in *Implicit Meanings* (London: Routledge and Kegan Paul, 1975), p. 249–75.

4. Sherry B. Ortner, *Sherpas Through Their Ritual* (Cambridge: Cambridge University Press, 1978).

5. Robert Forster and Orest Ranum, *Food and Drink in History*. Selections from the *Annales, Economies, Sociétés, Civilizations*, vol.

5 (Baltimore: Johns Hopkins University Press, 1979).

6. Carl Jung, "Transformation Symbolism in the Mass" in V. S. de Laszlo, ed., *Psyche and Symbol* (New York: Modern Library, 1958); James Fernandez, "The Mirror of Metaphor in Expressive Culture," *Current Anthropology* 15 (1974): 119–45 (for the Eucharist and basic metaphors of Catholic tradition see pp. 125–29).

7. *The New Appleton Dictionary of the English and Portuguese Languages* (N.Y.: Appleton Century Crofts, 1967).

8. On January 1, 1980, for example, a devastating earthquake did extensive damage to the island of Terceira, where a major part of the research for this article was carried out.

9. For Azorean ethnography see Luis Ribeiro, "Subsídio para um Ensaio sobre a Açorianidade," *Colecção Insulana No. 1* (Angra do Heroismo, Açores, 1964).

10. *Síntese Histórica* (Angra do Heroismo, Acores, Comissão de Planeamento da Região dos Açores, n.d.).

11. Ribeiro.

12. *Demografia* (Angra do Heroismo, Acores: Comissão de Planeamento da Região dos Açores, n.d.).

13. Ibid.

14. Mari Lyn Salvador, *Festas Açoreanas: Portuguese Celebrations in the Azores and California* (Oakland: Oakland Museum, 1981).

15. J. A. Pereira, "Sobre as Festas do Espírito Santo. Censuras e Leis da Autoridade Diocesana desde 1560." *BIHIT* 8: 58–63. Angra do Heroismo.

16. Queen Isabela is always depicted as a queen with a crown and an open cape displaying roses. Armando Carneiro da Silva, *Retratos Gravados de Santa Isabel* Arquivo Coimbrão vols. 19–20 (Coimbra: Litografia Coimbra, 1964). For further information regarding Queen Isabela see Fernando Correira de Lacerada, *Historia da Vida, Morte, Milagres, Canonização e Traslação da Santa Isabel, Sexta Rainha de Portugal*. Occidental.

(Lisbon, 1735); Antonio Maria Ribeiro de Vasconcelos, *Evolução do Culto de Dona Isabel de Aragão Esposa do Rei Lavrador Dom Denis de Portugal (A Rainha Santa)* (Coimbra: Imprensa da Universidade, 1894).

17. This narrative and the two that follow, all common in the Azores and in Azorean communities in California, are versions often typed up, published in the Portuguese newspapers, and given away at the fiestas. This version was collected in 1975.

18. John E. Keller, *Motif Index of Medieval Spanish Exempla* (Knoxville: University of Tennessee Press, 1949).

19. Collected in 1975.

20. Collected in 1975.

21. Rui d'Azevedo, "O Compromisso da Confraria do Espírito Santo de Benavente." Separata da Revista *Lusitana Socia* 6 (1963), União Grafica (Lisbon).

22. For a discussion of the history of the Brotherhood of the Holy Ghost see, P. A. de Azevedo "as Festas Dos Imperadores," *Revista Lusitana* 4 (1895–96): 134–42; L. Bettencourt, *Manual dos Confrarias e Irmandades e Mais Corporações de Piedade e Bineficencia* (Porto: Sorsa Brito e Co., 1894); Braamcamp Freire, "Compromisso de Confraria em 1346," *Archivo Historico Portuguez* 1 (1903): 349–55.

23. For a further discussion of the Holy Ghost celebration see Francisco Carreiro de Costa, "As Festas do Espirito Santo nos Acores," *Insulana 3*, pp. 545–46; Frederico Lopes, "O Espírito Santo ns Ilhas Adjacentes," *Revista da Sociedade Geografica de Lisboa* 20 (1969): 52–59.

24. Pedro Merlim (Angra do Heroismo: Tip Minerva Comercial, 1974).

25. Collected on the island of Terceira in 1976.

26. Victor Turner, *The Ritual Process* (Chicago: Aldine Publishing Company, 1969).

27. For a discussion of a deity with preferences, see Ortner, pp. 85–86.

28. Marcel Mauss, *The Gift* (New York: W. W. Norton and Co., 1967), p. 67.

22 / The Return of the Whale: Nalukataq, the Point Hope Whale Festival

Rosemary Levy Zumwalt

In this article, the fruit of her 1981 season of fieldwork in Alaska, Rosemary Levy Zumwalt discusses the festival held in June by the Eskimos of Point Hope to celebrate the end of a successful whaling season. The whale hunt lasts from mid-April to the end of May, or until the Eskimos have taken their much discussed quota of bowhead whales, which is set annually by the International Whaling Commission.

After briefly sketching the ethnographic background of the North Alaskan Eskimos, the article provides a detailed description of the temporal and spatial frames of reference of the Nalukataq. The time of the festival is particularly significant, falling on the summer solstice, which marks the passage from spring to summer, and a corresponding change from sea to land in the occupations of the Eskimos. The space of the festival consists of two ceremonial grounds at each side of the village, used by the two ceremonial groups into which the village people are divided. Festival space is marked by the umiaks, *the whaling boats that are moved into different positions as the festival activities progress as a sign of its phases. The other space markers are whale bones, arranged in a gigantic arch, or a tripod shape. The article describes the various activities of the three days of the festival: the religious opening services; the informal socializing; the preparation* and sharing of food; the games; the spectacular blanket tossing; the various speeches; and the singing, drumming, and dancing that conclude the festivities in merriment.

The most important element in the festival appears to be the preparation and distribution of the different parts of the whale, which must be shared by all members of the community. The whale meat is shared, first raw, then cooked, then again raw, with an elaborated ceremonialism in which the captain of the successful whaling boat, his wife, and his crew have an especially important role.

The final discussion is rich in interpretive and theoretical leads. The author first provides the natives' interpretation of the festivities from both oral and written sources. In fact, Nalukataq is given in honor of the whale, which is deeply respected, and celebrates the crucial link between the Eskimos and their key source of physical and spiritual nourishment. Second, the festival is related to social structure: Nalukataq represents and reflects the division of labor between men and women in Eskimo culture, and also competition between two ceremonial parts of the village coming together into a unified group at the end of the festival. Taking inspiration from Clifford Geertz, the author views Nalukataq as a self-portrait of the people, presenting themselves in the way they would like to be viewed. The festival, suggests the author, is grounded in what Sherry Ortner describes as "key symbols" and deals with core symbolism of the North Alaskan culture. For instance, the blanket toss is a celebration in the air, a sort of dance representing in jubilant jest the victory over the sea, and possibly also a rite of purification. Symbolic associations are suggested between the captain's wife and the whale, both providers of food to the people. But more important, the festival is related to a traditional conception of hunting and a magic-ritual relationship between hunter and prey. In Western culture, the prey is an antagonist to be killed and carried home as a trophy, but in traditional Eskimo culture the hunt is a magic-ritual operation: the captain is a "hunter of souls" and competes with the animals in magical knowledge. He must have the power to draw the whale to himself. The whale gives itself to the hunter, and the hunter then gives it to the people. That is why the festival stresses the point of making people happy, and people appearing happy: it must be shown to the soul of the whale that the gift is appreciated and that nothing is wasted. After the festival, the skull of the whale, where its soul is located, will be tipped back into the sea, and the hunters will call the whale to come back next year—because the whale never dies, it "just puts on a new parka."

The festival today does not have an explicit myth of reference. But we may be in the presence of what Mircea Eliade called "corruption of myth": a sacred narrative that with time and historical change has lost its textual autonomy and narrative structure, being reduced to the series of ritual practices, beliefs, and cultural symbols that the author presents. The belief in the "return of the whale" that underlies the whole Nalukataq festival may be one of such fallen mythical fragments.

The Return of the Whale:
Nalukataq, the Point Hope Whale Festival

Rosemary Levy Zumwalt

During the second week of June, the Eskimo inhabitants of Point Hope, Alaska, gather to celebrate the success of the whaling season.[1] On the first day of the three-day festival, the crews that have taken at least one whale pull their boats made of bearded sealskin ashore. The time is at hand for the Eskimo to celebrate their continuing relationship with their key source of physical and spiritual nourishment, the whale.

Point Hope is located 125 miles north of the Arctic Circle on a peninsula which juts out into the Chukchi Sea. As Eskimo hunters phrase it, "Our food is in the sea,"[2] and the location of Point Hope yields a bounty to the inhabitants: the bowhead whale (*balaena mysticetus*).

The Eskimos of Point Hope share cultural traits with the other North Alaskan Eskimos. Their lives are a mixture of traditional Eskimo culture and modern Western living. Their language is Inupiaq, a branch of Eskimo spoken along 6,000 miles of coastline between Alaska and Greenland. Most Alaskan Eskimos, save for the very old, also speak fluent English. Inupiaq, however, is definitely the language of tradition; and it is used to conduct all important ceremonies. The North Alaskan Eskimos are Protestant, for the most part Episcopalian, though their formal church services are laced with traditional Eskimo culture. They live in modern prefabricated wooden-frame houses. Yet their worldview is still largely the traditional Eskimo view. They are hunters of the sea and have located their villages along the coastline. Barrow has over 2,000 inhabitants; the other villages range in size from 150 to 450 inhabitants. Point Hope has a population of 464. The total population of the North Alaskan Eskimo is 3,225.[3]

The village of Point Hope is divided into two ceremonial groups, the Ungasiksikaq and the Kaukmuqtuuq. Membership is determined by patrilineal descent, with the women changing to their husband's affiliation.[4] As my host explained to me, "I belong to Kaukmuqtuuq, the same one my father belonged to, and my father's father, and all my forefathers."

Nalukataq, the major celebration of the ceremonial year, occurs just as the sun is moving toward the summer solstice. It is the time of the midnight sun: the sun never goes below the horizon. In August, dark will start to come early. By September, dark will arrive by noon.

At this time, the time of change from spring to summer, the Eskimos of Point Hope are drawing out the last catch from the sea. The *oogruk* (bearded seal) will soon be gone with the final disappearance of the floating masses of sea ice. Then the people will turn to the land: to gather berries, to hunt caribou, and to fish. Nalukataq falls at the point of seasonal change from spring to summer, and of occupational change from sea to land. It celebrates the hunting of the sea, but also anticipates the yield of the land.

The date for Nalukataq is set each year by the captain who has taken the first whale. But the three-day festival always occurs sometime during the first two weeks of June—provided, of course, that at least one whale has been taken. Without a whale, there can be no festival, to the disappointment of the people.

In earlier times, when the sea ice no longer provided leads for hunting the whales, Rainey tells us that the captains determined when it was time to return to shore. "On that day when the sun reached a certain point, all crews raced for shore, each eager to be the first to arrive."[5]

The festival grounds flank the village on the east and west side. The contemporary situation represents a shift in direction: the Nalukataq grounds at the former village site lay to the north and to the south of the village. The *umiaks* (boats) of the successful crews are positioned on the south shore, directly opposite their ceremonial division. In 1981, there had been two successful crews from each division. Thus there were two *umiaks* on the shore opposite the Ungasiksikaq grounds, and two *umiaks* on the shore opposite Kaukmuqtuuq. This situation varies with each whaling season. If, for example, no whale had been taken by the crews of one ceremonial division, then that division would not participate in Nalukataq.

On the shore to the south of the village and directly opposite the festival grounds are the *umiaks*. Each *umiak* is loaded with the whaling equipment; and each is left on the shore until the first day of the festival. The *umiaks* of the unsuccessful whaling crews have no place in the celebration. These are in regular use for *oogruk* hunting or are stored on boat racks. The whaling equipment of the unsuccessful crew is put away for the season.

Thus the first visible sign of Nalukataq is the *umiak* poised on the shore with paddles in the air. These *umiaks* will be present throughout the celebration. Their differing position and treatment will mark the various stages of the festival.

There are other signs of preparation for Nalukataq. Children equipped with large plastic garbage bags pick up cans and litter, cleaning and tidying the village grounds. At the same time, women are busy making new parkas and *mukluks* (skin boots) for their husbands, children, and grandchildren.

The women are also in charge of preparing the ceremonial food. About two weeks before Nalukataq, the successful captains' wives begin the preparation of *mikiaq* (fermented whale meat). The meat is sliced in long thin strips and placed in wooden barrels with the blood of the whale. Care must be taken to ensure that there are no air bubbles to spoil the fermentation process, and all meat must be submerged in the blood. This is the delicacy, the best in whale meat, as my host told me. To the Eskimo, the mark of the well-made *mikiaq* is its tenderness and tangy flavor. In addition, in every household women make batches of Eskimo doughnuts, another food that marks festival time. This is a yeast bread, made with raisins, shaped in a circle or a twisted bar, and fried in oil.

The days before the festival are filled with anticipation: friends and relatives are arriving on regularly scheduled and chartered flights at the Point Hope airstrip. There are no roads connecting Point Hope to the outside world; air transport is the sole means of long-distance travel and the major channel for supplies. People watch the sky to judge the origin of the plane's flight. Relatives come from all over North Alaska, from Barrow, Wainwright, Point Lay, Noorvik; and also from South Alaska, from Anchorage, Fairbanks, and many villages. They travel to Point Hope at great expense to attend Nalukataq.

In 1981 the celebrations opened with services at Saint Thomas Episcopal Church. The announcement was made at the end of the service that the *umiaks* would be pulled up from the shore at 2:00 P.M. At that time groups of villagers made their way to either side of the village, according to their ceremonial affiliation. The members of the whaling crew, intent on pulling the *umiaks* up from the shore, were clustered around them in the distance. The crowd gathered at what is called "the staging area" where the *umiaks* would rest for the first day of the festival.

On the Kaukmuqtuuq side, one *umiak* was hitched to a three-wheel Honda and the other to a pick-up truck. The men flanked it, running alongside, and pushing it on its way. The dust enveloped the two crews as they rushed for the staging area.

Here at the midpoint between the shore and the Nalukataq grounds, the men and the vehicles stopped. Two sleds for the bow and the stern of each *umiak* were propped on the side, covered with caribou skin. The *umiaks* were then placed on the sleds.

The particular arrangement of the *umiaks* appears to be symbolically related to the dichotomy between the land and the sea. The sleds as the traditional mode of land transportation support and lift into the air the successful *umiaks*, the traditional mode of sea transportation. It is sea over land. The wooden frame of the *umiak* is separated by the skins of animals: the caribou skin, from a land animal, drapes the sled; and the *oogruk* skin, from a sea animal, encloses the *umiak* frame.[6] The contrast of the sea and the land, ever-present in Eskimo life, is displayed here at the midpoint between the sea and the festival grounds. The movement of the boats during the festival appears to be a symbolic reversal of the movement of the crews and their boats during hunting.

The paddles, which had been removed from their upright position and stowed for the ride from the shore to the midpoint, were again wedged upright into the body of the *umiak*. The whale harpoon was carefully positioned over the bow. The *umiaks* were loaded with furs, floats, and a wooden chest full of whale equipment. And the flag which was raised when the whale was killed was hoisted on the mast at the bow. One *umiak* flew "the original Point Hope flag," an old, tattered, stained American flag with forty-eight stars. The captain's wife, talking with friends about the flag, said that it had belonged to her husband's father before him.

After the whaling equipment had been carefully placed inside the *umiaks*, with the tarps and the equipment chests positioned on the ground in front of the *umiaks*, the crew members and their wives arranged the festival food on the ground in front of the *umiaks:* barrels of *mikiaq*, trays of Eskimo doughnuts, *muktuk* (whale skin), soda pop, coffee, tea, and chocolate cake. A blessing was offered by the Eskimo Sacristan of St. Thomas Episcopal Church and then everyone rushed for the food. As my host told me, "On this day you have to grab what you can get. The next day you will be served." While one could have a second helping of other things, the *mikiaq* and *muktuk* disappeared immediately. People sat around on the ground, in clusters, talking, eating, and enjoying the celebration. Everyone individually thanked the whale captains; there was a constant recognition of their gift to the people. The festival activities of the first day were finished when the food had been eaten. Families moved off toward home and some whale meat found its way to the tables of Point Hope.

On the second day, early in the morning, the four *umiaks* were pulled further inland to the Nalukataq areas and the preparations were made for the day's celebrations. *Kaqruq* (whale feast) was given by the Ungasiksikaq in the morning at the western festival grounds, and duplicated in the afternoon by the Kaukmuqtuuq at the eastern festival grounds. The whale feast was scheduled to start at eight in the morning. The people gathered, in a trickle at first, and then in groups. They arrived on foot and on three-wheel Hondas. And they chose their places, sitting in an arc which faced the festival area.

The space in the Nalukataq grounds was divided and marked by whale bones. Two large bones formed an arch of approximately fifty feet. They framed the flagpole which on the second and third day of the festival would fly the flags of the successful whaling crews. On the side closer to the village were the remains of whale bones, arranged in neat piles. Here the whaling equipment was placed; it was unloaded from the *umiaks* and piled at the foot of the flagpole. All the equipment was there, even the white canvas tent and the cook stove. On the Ungasiksikaq side, a large welcome sign was hung on the flagpole. This was not duplicated by the Kaukmuqtuuq: the Ungasiksikaq acted as the initial host to the village.

On the other side of the flagpole, the side farther from the village, was the Nalukataq area. This space was bounded by four tripods of whale jawbones. These ostensibly served as supports for the blanket toss which always occurred on the third day. In fact the blanket was not attached to these supports. Yet these four whalebone tripods were significant: they marked ceremonial space. The distribution of all whale meat was carried out from this bounded space; and the blanket toss itself took place within this area.

Significantly the *umiaks* were on their side, directly facing the Nalukataq area. They were empty of equipment which was now at the base of the flagpole. Now they sheltered the whale captains and their wives. In the morning, the whale captains of the Ungasiksikaq sat in the boats or spilled out in front; and in the afternoon, the same seating arrangement was taken by the whale captains of the Kaukmuqtuuq.

After all the whaling equipment had been placed at the foot of the flagpole, the barrels of *mikiaq* and the *ahvrak* (whale flukes) were put in the Nalukataq area; then the members of the successful whale crew sat on the whaling equipment. An elder addressed the crowd; the men gathered around the *ahvrak*; and the people stood. Everyone joined in singing the doxology, and a prayer was offered by a church elder.

The men then returned to their seats on the whale equipment behind the flag, and the women got out the bowls to serve the *mikiaq*. Clearly this was the women's contribution to the whale feast: they were the only ones present in the Nalukataq area at this time. First the women served the successful whalers; next they served the people in the boats; and finally there was a general distribution of *mikiaq* to the crowd.

The manner of serving the *mikiaq* was distinctive. The captains' wives carried it in their hands without the use of a bowl. They ran back and forth to the barrel, all the while surveying the crowd carefully, making sure that everyone was properly served. In the meantime, the crew members' wives were serving the crowd from large containers. Their distribution was less intense, less harried, because they were able to carry a supply of *mikiaq* in the containers and serve a number of people before returning for a refill.

After the *mikiaq* was served, the men went over to the Nalukataq area and began to slice the *ahvrak*. For this, they used long-handled knives, the same ones used for butchering the whale. But before they began slicing, they donned white gloves—this out of respect for the whale. While the slicing continued, the women finished with the distribution of *mikiaq* and began serving the Eskimo ice cream, which is whipped lard mixed with berries. The first serving was passed with the usual admonition, "Old people only!"

All the while the men had been slicing the *ahvrak*, which were now in piles, the white meat framed by the black skin. The captains addressed the crowd, expressing happiness for a successful whaling season. The whale captains and their wives then distributed the *ahvrak*. They stood in the Nalukataq area and, in the Inupiat language, called out the names of the people. They often made joking remarks which were received by the crowd with hearty laughter. Howard Rock reports that the captain, after picking up the *ahvrak*, might call out, "Kakairnok, a highly valued friend, over whose foot I tripped half a year ago and fell into the sea, I give this piece of avahrak (slice of fluke) for his enjoyment."[7] Everyone was included in the distribution—families, relatives, friends. Some calls were for whole villages: Kotzebue, Point Lay, Barrow, Wainwright, Noorvik.[8] And some were even for big cities: Anchorage, Fairbanks, and New York. When New York was called, this was a signal for any outsiders to step forward to receive their *ahvrak*. All persons called approached the Nalukataq area; received the slice of *ahvrak*; thanked the captain or the captain's wife; and then, on returning to their seats, took a bite of the *ahvrak* for good luck.

Sometimes even dead people were included in the ceremony. The whale captain called one man up to receive his *ahvrak* in honor of his father, who had long ago saved the captain from drowning. This suggests the ritual feeding of the dead which was practiced in the ancient village of Tigara. As Rainey reports, the whale captains visited the temporary graves of those who had died during the winter, and gave the dead some pieces of *muktuk* strung on a baleen line.[9]

The slice of *ahvrak* must all be distributed to the people. If any remained, this would be bad luck for the next whaling season. Good fortune in hunting, then, is predicated on generosity to the people. Indeed, the mark of a good whale captain is his generosity. Without this, all the power and wealth will not make him respected. As one whale captain said, "What's the point of catching a whale if I don't just *give away as much of it as I can?* [his emphasis] There's no joy in doing this just for myself, you know. The people are hungry for their whale meat. I don't mind what qalgi they come from, Qaġmaqtuuq or Ungasiksikaaq. When it comes to a whale I catch, we're all one people. Let'em *eat* it!"[10] In fact, according to folk belief, the whale will not come to a crew whose captain is stingy.[11] When all the *ahvrak* had been distributed, the whale feast was over.

The whale feast was repeated in the afternoon by the Kaukmuqtuuq division. Exactly the same procedure was followed as that of the morning on the Ungasiksikaq side. In the evening, after people had rested from the day's feasting, the Kaukmuqtuuq staged a blanket toss and held the Eskimo dance that usually follows the toss. Actually, in 1981, this event occurred on the second day as a special celebration for the whale captain and his wife: they had taken their first whale and they had had their first son. Without the special circumstances, the blanket toss would not be held on the second day, but only on the third day. Finally a whale captain stood to make an announcement to the crowd. His *umiak* skin had to be replaced; he was offering the old skin to the women for *mukluks*. It was stripped and the women cut pieces of the covering with their *ulus* (Eskimo woman's knife).

The stripped *umiak* and the other one were brought to the center of the festival area. They were placed on sleds, again with the caribou skin separating the sled from the boat. The flags were lowered, folded, and placed carefully with the other whaling equipment in front of the flagpoles. All was covered with canvas. For the first time, the *umiaks* faced the village. This new alignment anticipated the final movement of the festival on the following day—a movement which drew people from the periphery to the center of the community.

On the third day, the Nalukataq area was divided into a men's and a women's area. As I was told, "This is the day when the men are served all day by the women." The *umiaks* were placed on their side again, directly in front of the Nalukataq area. This time they faced the sea. This area, farthest inland from the sea, was the men's area. The women's side was parallel to the men's, but closer to the sea. And no man was to be on the women's side. Whereas on the previous two days the whale meat was served raw, on this last day of the festival it was cooked.

The women started their work early, at 5:30 or 6:00 A.M. The oil drum cookstoves were assembled on the tundra in the open air. On a large piece of plywood—the same plywood which had served as a floor for the canvas tent—women cut up the organs of the whale. There lay enormous hearts, tongues, intestines, kidneys. As a captain's wife said about the Eskimos' use of the whale, "We don't waste nothin'!" Pots of boiling whale, caribou stew, duck soup, and moose cooked throughout the morning and early afternoon. At the same time, several women were cooking great quantities of Eskimo doughnuts on portable gas stoves. The doughnuts were served early in the morning with coffee, and were also eaten throughout the day.

At 8:00 A.M. people began to arrive, greeting one another with a friendly handshake and a kiss on the cheek. The men separated from their wives, took their places, and waited to be served. The women who were not involved with the cooking took seats by the windbreak. There was relaxed conversation while people sipped their coffee.

Throughout the morning, people continued to gather at the festival grounds. From 11:00 to 1:00, the greatest quantity of whale meat was distributed. This was carefully collected in plastic bags: some would be eaten during the day; some would be taken home. As one man explained the whale feast, "All day you can get food. If you want some whale heart, you just take it. Put it in a sack and take it home to eat later."

The captains' wives and the crew members' wives were responsible for the cooking and for passing out the food. This involved long hours of preparing the food, cooking it, and serving the people. A captain's wife talked frequently of the last time she and her husband had caught a whale and who among the women had helped her with the cooking. Clearly there was a need for cooperation and support during this period of intensive work. In a real sense, this was ceremonial community service. The captains' wives and the crew members' wives served the members of their ceremonial division; and they served them to surfeit. People vowed throughout the feast to eat no more, but soon a new pot of duck soup appeared, or Eskimo ice cream, or caribou meat. The eating continued. Finally, by midafternoon, the pace slowed. Some people returned home to rest; others stayed at the festival grounds, talking quietly.

Around 4:00, after people had rested, the games started. At this point, the activities at the Kaukmuqtuuq festival grounds had ended. Everyone came to the Ungasiksikaq area. First there was a tug-of-war between the two ceremonial groups. Next the foot races started. The men raced down the spit to the graveyard and back. Then the women raced; and next the children. The winners were awarded monetary prizes of $100, $75, and $50.

Finally, the *nalukataq* (blanket) appeared and people assembled for the toss. Though there had been a blanket toss on the second day, the third day was the most enthusiastic one. Clearly this was the appropriate time for it. The elder men sat inside the *umiaks* with the tambourine drums; their wives sat in front chanting along with their husbands. And the people stood in clusters, or sat on the ground watching the blanket toss. There was a great camaraderie on this the third and final day of Nalukataq. People were tired but pleased and happy. And this was one of the most important purposes of the festival, that it should make the people happy. Certainly the blanket toss achieved this. Everyone took pleasure in it, the participants as well as the spectators.

The blanket used for the toss was a rectangle made from several *oogruk* skins which were sewn together. A rope was laced on the outside of the skin for handholds. The people gathered, side by side, around it. They began a rhythmic snapping of the skin. Soon someone stepped forward to "get in the blanket." An edge of the blanket was lowered, the person took a position in the center. The crowd watched and participated in the *nalukataq* toss with sounds of admiration for those who jumped well, and laughter for those who fell awkwardly, with legs and arms askew. The greatest amusement was derived from those who fell back on the blanket with screams of terror. Occasionally a person performed flips and tuck somersaults in the air. Then the crowd burst into spontaneous applause.[12]

The aesthetics for the *nalukataq* toss called for height, flexibility, grace, and style. The people who were good at the blanket toss literally danced in the air. (*Nalukataq* is sometimes translated as "dancing in the air.")[13] The individual would move the arms in the stylized manner of Eskimo dancing. The head was held erect; the gaze was toward the horizon. And the feet moved in a running style. It was also important to appear calm, in spite of the height of the toss—approximately twenty to thirty feet in the air—and the danger of the event, which was dramatized by the injury of two people.

While the rules for the blanket toss were flexible, still there was structure to the game. Anyone could participate. Usually the person was tossed three or four times, sometimes more. On occasion, a person who was frightened asked to be let off after one toss, and was tossed again for good measure! The successful whale captains and their wives were expected to perform. And everyone watched them with pleasure.[14]

The women who had given birth to sons during the previous year also came up to the blanket to be tossed. But their time on the blanket was special: they tossed gifts to the old people as a way of celebrating the birth of their sons. The gifts of candy, gum, cigarettes, bundles of cloth, and money were held by the young mothers in brown paper sacks. While in the air, the woman tore the sack and the gifts flew through the air. The old women then scrambled after the gifts which had fallen to the ground. As they grabbed for the gifts, they pushed the children back, yelling "Old people only! Hey, you kids, get out of here! Old people only!"

On both the second and the third day, the adults started the toss. After awhile they placed the blanket on the ground, and the children came forward to take up the blanket. When the children were through, the adults were ready to begin again.

When the people tired of the blanket toss, the skin was placed on the ground in front of the *umiaks*. The drumming and chanting were then performed for the Eskimo dancing. People stepped forward onto the blanket, husbands and wives, sometimes men only, or women only, and sometimes just children. The dancing continued until the whale captain from Ungasiksikaq announced that there would be Eskimo dancing in the high school gymnasium at 8:00 P.M.

When the people gathered in the gym, they selected seats in the bleachers, talked, and waited for the dance to begin. In the middle seated on the floor were the prominent whale captains with tambourine drums; behind them, their wives. They began with drum rhythms to "warm up." Finally a man stepped out to the center, faced the drummers, and put on suede gloves with bells over the knuckles but no covering over the fingers. After his dance, another man stepped forward and put on the same gloves. This was the single dancing. It was followed by motion dancing which was done by two or more people. This dancing ended with a whaler's dance in which all the whale captains performed. And finally, in conclusion, there was group dancing. At this point, anyone could step onto the floor to dance.[15]

The Eskimo dance ended at 11:30. The tambourine drums were carefully placed in a wooden box and carried away. The whale captains, crew members, and the wives began bringing in quantities of food. There were apples and oranges for the children, and bowls of raw whale meat and buckets of raw *muktuk* for everyone. After a blessing was offered, the food was distributed to the crowd.

Then some of the men addressed the people. An old man spoke of the importance of hunting to him and added with great sadness, "When you can't hunt, you just hear about it with your ears," which meant that the most vital part of a man's life was over. One of the host captains thanked the people and said, while patting his stomach, that he was happy when he saw that the people had a lot to eat. With a final prayer, people went off in the light of the midnight sun to their homes.

Though the morning of the third day began with the women cooking the whale meat and serving the men, the end of the day, the last moments of the festival, were celebrated with the distribution of raw whale meat. Once again the crew members and their wives were serving the community, as in *kaqruq* (whale feast) of the second day. But there was a difference. In the final hours of the festival, during the Eskimo dance and the distribution of the raw whale meat, the people of the Ungasiksikaq and the Kaukmuqtuuq had come together. They had moved from the festival grounds to inside the village. The whale captains, the crew members, and their wives were for the first time distributing food as a group to the whole community. The movement of the festival had come to rest in the center. And from there the people dispersed to their homes. So the thrust of Nalukataq which on the first day had drawn people from their homes to the staging area, returned the people to their homes.

This movement through space during the three days of the festival first separates the two ceremonial groups and then draws them together. The movement from the sea to the land is begun on the first day of the festival when the *umiaks* move from the shore to the staging area; and it is completed on the second day when the *umiaks* are pulled to the Nalukataq area. This point is midway between the sea on the south of the peninsula and the sea on the north. So, in fact, the events of the second and third day of the festival occur at the point most inland from the sea.

Although the Ungasiksikaq and Kaukmuqtuuq perform parallel and balanced ceremonies, there is a competition between the two. They both distribute ritual food on the second day and host a whale feast on the third day. But the competition emerges on the morning of the second day, when each group tries to be the first to pull the *umiaks* to the festival grounds. And again on the third day, each side endeavors to be the first up and to raise the flags. This competition culminates on the afternoon of the third day, when Kaukmuqtuuq and Ungasiksikaq have a tug-of-war. This competitive show of strength occurs after the Kaukmuqtuuq have terminated activities at their Nalukataq grounds. So both groups come together at the Ungasiksikaq festival grounds, have a final show of competition, and then end the festival as a unified group. They move inside the village, to the gymnasium; together and in the same place they distribute ritual food to the community.

The division of ceremonial space in the Nalukataq grounds is identical for the two groups, and it has important implications for the symbolic meaning of the festival. For the second day, the ceremonial space from which all the whale meat is distributed is farthest removed from the village. It is the area bounded by the four tripods which are made from the jawbones of the whale. The equipment that provides the means for obtaining the whale and for bringing it to the people lies at the foot of the flagpole at the point in the festival grounds which is closer to the village. The whale equipment is the cultural means for procuring nature's gift to the Eskimo people. And these tools lie at the mediating point between the village and the Nalukataq grounds. It is thus the opposition between nature and culture, as well as that of land and sea, which is acted out in this festival.

On the third day, the ceremonial space is divided between the men's area and the women's area. The men sit inside the *umiaks* or cluster around them; they face the Nalukataq grounds. Their area is the farthest point inland. It is also to the north, the direction associated with maleness. The women's area is between the man and the sea, and closer to the south shore. South is the direction associated with the female; it is "from the south that the animals come."[16] Here the women cook the whale meat and serve it to the men. Thus the women's area is a transition point between the sea and the land, the raw and the cooked.

The prestation of ritual food on the second day of the festival also suggests certain symbolic associations for men and women in Eskimo culture. Women were clearly associated with the preparation and the serving of the *mikiaq*. This ceremonial food is made from the blood and the meat of the whale. And in serving it, the captain's wife plunges her hand into the barrel and pulls out a dark red mass of meat, dripping with fermented blood. She runs back and forth with handfuls of this raw meat for the people. This, I suggest, is the symbolic staging of the association between the captain's wife and the whale. In traditional times, this association was explicitly acted out in ritual. When the *umiak* was first launched for the season, the captain's wife lay on the ice where it had been, facing the village. The crew paddled toward her and the harpooner stood in the bow of the *umiak* as if to harpoon her. When she returned home, the captain's wife had to "remain tranquil and act like a sick person so that the harpooned whale would also be quiet and easy to kill."[17]

I suggest that in the serving of the *mikiaq*, the symbolic link between the whale and the captain's wife is in the giving of food, and in the blood of life. The captain's wife gives food to the people just as the whale gives food to the people. They are functional and symbolic equivalents.

The slicing and serving of the *ahvrak* contrasts sharply with the women's serving of the *mikiaq*. While the latter is a soft liquid mass, which in appearance resembles afterbirth, the slices of flukes are pure white, framed with the black of the whale skin. While the women wear rubber gloves which, in the process of serving, become covered with blood, the men wear white gloves which remain spotless. And while the women rush back and forth to the barrels of *mikiaq* in the Nalukataq area, serving the people, the movement is reversed for the distribution of the flukes. The people are called forward, to receive personally their slice of fluke.

The serving of ritual food on the third day of the festival reflects certain basic values in Eskimo culture. The men were provided with a special place in the Nalukataq grounds. The women cooked for them and served them. Thus the women of the

Ungasiksikaq and Kaukmuqtuuq were simultaneously honoring their men for being successful hunters and for providing them with food. And in honoring the men, the women were fulfilling their complementary role. They were preparing the raw meat, cooking it, and serving it. This was a balanced event, taking place at the same time in both festival grounds, with the space divided in the same manner.

And this balance reflected a similar balance in the daily life of the Eskimo. The men hunt; and the women prepare the meat. It is the man's duty to kill the animals; it is a woman's duty to prepare the meat. These spheres of man's life and woman's life are symbolically represented in the festival and explicitly stated by the people in their daily lives. My host told me as he looked to the sea and spread his arms expansively, "I provide the food." And an older Eskimo woman recalled her mother-in-law's advice to her: "If you marry a hunter, you must always attend to the kill. You mustn't put it off. No matter when, you must skin and butcher the seal; or tend to the fish. Otherwise the food will spoil. And you will not be a good wife."

An important symbolic element in the festival is the blanket toss. Nalukataq names the festival and the blanket toss, which is only performed at this time.[18] And I would suggest that this singular performance of "dancing in air" is a significant end to the successful whaling season. Recall, the object of the game is to remain upright, to keep one's balance, to remain in control. It is the individual tossed in jubilant jest by the members of the community. And this spirited play occurs at the center of the festivities with many participants. So the villagers support and toss each other and play on this oogruk skin blanket. But they also replicate in game their life at sea. The individual on the blanket is in danger of possible upset, a situation which certainly exists in the sea hunt. And the people holding the blanket both support and jostle the player on the skin of the oogruk, the same skin which makes the umiak that bears him to sea. Finally, I would suggest that the body of the player hurling through the air marks the individual's celebration of success. It is as if the celebration in the air marks the victory over the sea.

It is also possible to view the blanket toss as a rite of purification by the air. The ones who are believed to have been in the closest contact with the powerful spirit of the whale are precisely those who must be tossed: the whale captains and their wives. Additionally, mothers of new-born boys must be tossed. Possibly this is a way to purify them from the birth process.[19] I might also suggest that Nalukataq, in addition to a rite of purification by the air, functioned as a form of contagious magic. The air purified the bodies of the players; and their good fortune, in the hunt and in birth, was spread to the people surrounding the blanket.

The final moments of the festival bring the people back to their homes. And so Nalukataq ends for another year. But in its ending is its beginning. People are already laying plans for next year's festival. As my host said to me, "There will always be another spring. And maybe this year we'll catch a whale!" Nalukataq then links one year to the next, ties time past to time future.

With ceremony, the Eskimo re-creates the essentials of life that have been his for thousands of years.[20] This rebirth or re-creation is propitiated during sacred time. The Eskimos believe that Nalukataq assures the return of the whales that have come the past season. Indeed, it is because of the ritual and ceremonial treatment of the whales that the spirit of the dead whale is released and reborn in a new whale. To aid in this process of rebirth, the hunters, after butchering the whale, tip the skull of the whale—the place where the whale's soul resides—back into the sea. As the head sinks into the water, they call out, "Come back next year!" And to please the whale, the people dress in new clothes for Nalukataq.[21]

This new whale, in turn, will give itself to the Eskimos who have shown proper respect in the hunt, in carving the carcass, in distributing the meat, and in celebrating the kill. And hopefully, this whale, pleased by the hospitable treatment, will bring other relatives.[22]

A prominent Eskimo hunter remarked, "The old people, before the white people came, believed when you kill a whale, he take his parka off and let you have it. And his spirit went back and join with the group of whales. The spirit of the whale never dies; always lives . . . put on a new parka."[23] A whale captain on Saint Lawrence Island expressed in a similar manner this spiritual connection between himself and the whale: "I tell the people who say that I'm a great hunter that it's just that the whale, he likes me."[24] The whale then gives itself to the hunter; and the hunter gives a portion of the whale to the people. Because of the prestation of sacred food, the festival of Nalukataq, the people are happy. And making people happy is a central theme in Eskimo culture. If people are well fed, then they are happy—they have "plenty of fresh meat," a remark frequently heard when a hunter has brought in a large game animal. Part of ensuring happiness is sharing food, treating people well, and being especially kind to old people, to widows, and to orphans.

This happiness, this harmony among the people, assures them of good hunting. A fifty-four-year-old hunter explained the purpose of the festival in these terms: "After a great deal of thought and considerable discussion with other people, [Iqaaq] said that everybody must be happy at this time so that the same whale could be killed next year."[25] The happiness of the people not only ensures successful hunting, but also brings about the reincarnation of the whale's spirit: Iqaaq had said that the *same* whale would be killed next year.

The whale is a key symbol for the Alaskan Eskimo.[26] It provides the ceremonial focus for the annual cycle, the meat of the festivities both in a literal and metaphorical sense. This culminates in Nalukataq where the villagers gather to honor the whaling captains, and the captains give thanks to the community. But sustaining them all is the whale. And it is for the whale that all this is done. As one Eskimo hunter said, "The whale so big he kill a man easily. He give himself to us. If he don't want to get caught, he don't get caught. He makes himself a gift. That is why we have festivals for the whale."[27]

The whale, then, in a sense chooses the captain. And the captain acts as an intermediary between the whale and the community. Eskimo hunting is laced with ceremonialism, and is framed in a worldview where the good hunter has the power to draw animals to him. This is not the antagonistic hunting of the white culture, where the prey is the enemy, to be conquered, slain, and carried home as a trophy. As Bogoras expresses it, "The chase . . . is not conceived as a natural competition of the hunter and the animal in strength, skill, and cunning. The chase represents far more a competition of man and animal in magical knowledge."[28] And as Chapman remarks, hunters are "really hunting souls" which take on animal forms.[29]

Nalukataq then celebrates this spiritual link between the Eskimo and the whale. And it draws all from the sea to the land. For a brief period of time, Nalukataq celebrates the power of the land (people) over the sea (animals). Nalukataq draws the *umiaks* from the shore, to the midpoint, and finally to the festival grounds. And then the people share the bounty of the hunt, "dance in the air," and pass their happiness onto the whale spirits.

As Arnold Brower, Sr. expresses it: "From way back, from the time I could remember, these people respect that animal. . . . Because the whale is the center of their livelihood, their food, the center of their festivals. The whale is really the center of our life."[30]

NOTES

1. I attended the Nalukataq festival at Point Hope, Alaska, in June 1981, where I was so kindly made welcome by my hosts, John and Molly Iktollik and their family. I wish to acknowledge the generous support given me by the Humanities Research Fund, and the Robert H. Lowie Fellowship, of the University of California, Berkeley.

2. Dorothea Leighton, unpublished biographies from Gambell, Alaska, 1944.

3. Norman A. Chance, *The Eskimo of North Alaska* (Holt, Rinehart, and Winston, 1966), p. 5; *1980 Census of Population and Housing, Advance Reports*, U.S. Department of Commerce, Bureau of Census, March 1981, PHC80-V-3, p. 5.

4. Froelich G. Rainey, *The Whale Hunters of Tigara*, Anthropological Papers of the American Museum of Natural History, vol. 41, part 2 (New York, 1947), p. 242; James Van Stone, *Point Hope, an Eskimo Village in Transition*, American Ethnological Society Monographs (Seattle: University of Washington Press, 1962), p. 101.

5. Rainey, p. 262.

6. I am indebted to Nelson Graburn for noting the association between the skins of the land and sea animals, and the traditional modes of land and sea transportation.

7. Howard Rock, "Season's Over, Now Comes the Great Kaqruq," *Tundra Times*, May 1, 1974.

8. For the ancient custom of calling groups of people by their housegroup name, see Rainey, p. 262.

9. Ibid., pp. 262–63.

10. Tom Lowenstein, *Some Aspects of Sea Ice Subsistence Hunting in Point Hope, Alaska*, North Slope Borough, Coastal Zone Management Plan, 1981, p. 67. For the ancient custom of distributing whale meat and the beliefs

about good fortune, see Robert F. Spencer, *The North Alaskan Eskimo*, Bureau of American Ethnology Bulletin 171, (Washington, D.C.: United States Government Printing Office, 1959), pp. 335–36.

11. For a discussion of the connection between good luck in hunting and generosity, see Lael Morgan, "Point Hope, a Workable Tradition," *And the Land Provides, Alaskan Natives in a Year of Transition* (Garden City, N.Y.: Doubleday, 1974), p. 90; Frederick A. Milan, *The Acculturation of the Contemporary Eskimo of Wainwright, Alaska*, Anthropological Papers of the University of Alaska, vol. 11, no. 2, 1964, p. 41; Lowenstein, p. 64; and Rainey, p. 241.

12. For a similar description of a blanket toss, see Knud Rasmussen, *Across Arctic America* (New York: G. P. Putnam's Sons, 1927), p. 315.

13. Rainey, p. 263.

14. The blanket toss of old was probably a more structured event. For a discussion of the expected order, see Rainey, p. 263; Van Stone, p. 57. Rasmussen mentioned the toss going "on for some hours" (p. 315).

15. For an outstanding discussion, see Thomas F. Johnston, *Eskimo Music by Region: A Comparative Circumpolar Study*, Canadian Ethnology Service, Paper No. 32 (Ottawa: National Museums of Canada, 1976). For a description of Eskimo dancing, see Milan, p. 40. And for a discussion of whaling songs, see Spencer, p. 341.

16. Lowenstein, p. 20. The south wind was female; and the north wind, male. See also Rainey, p. 258.

17. Ibid., p. 259. For further discussion of the identification between the captain's wife and the whale, see Rasmussen, p. 313; and Spencer, p. 338.

18. A blanket toss with the accompanying Eskimo dance is performed on occasion for the few tourists who come to Point Hope. This is a regular tourist attraction in Kotzebue, where the participants are charged to view the toss and to participate in it.

19. For oscillation and the swing as rites of purification by air, see Nicola Turchi, "Attuale rito dell'oscillazione come residuo di un rito di purificazione per mezzo dell'aria," *Lares* 25 (1959): 205–7; Antonino Basile, "L'altalena come gioco rituale," *Folklore della Calabria*, 3 (1963) nos. 3–4: 1–19.

20. See Don E. Dumond, *The Eskimos and Aleuts* (London: Thames and Hudson, 1977), pp. 101, 124, 129, 139–41, for the archaeological evidence of whale hunting among the Eskimos.

21. For a discussion of the soul of the whale, see Rainey, p. 261. The practice of wearing new clothes to please the whale is both ancient and widespread. See Hans Egede, *Description of Greenland*, translated from Danish (London: T. and J. Allman, 1818), p. 102; Spencer, p. 332; Rasmussen, p. 315; and Van Stone, p. 76.

22. For the Siberian Eskimos' treatment of the animal as a guest invited to return, see G. A. Menovshchikov, "Popular Conceptions, Religious Beliefs and Rites of the Asiatic Eskimoes," in *Popular Beliefs and Folklore Tradition in Siberia*, V. Diószegi, ed. (The Hague: Mouton, 1968), p. 439. For a similar belief among the Korvak of Siberia, see Waldemar Jockelson, *The Korvak, Religion and Myths of the Korvak*, Memoirs of the American Museum of Natural History, the Jesup North Pacific Expedition, vol. 10, part 1 (Leiden: E. J. Brill, 1905), p. 66.

23. David Franksen, quoted in *"Umealit: The Whale Hunters,"* *Nova* television series, WGBH Transcripts, Boston, Massachusetts, 1980, p. 19.

24. "Whaling Ban's Threat to a Way of Life," *San Francisco Chronicle*, Oct. 31, 1977.

25. Milan, p. 41.

26. For the theoretical concept of key symbol, see Sherry Ortner, "On Key Symbols," *American Anthropologist* 75 (1973): 1338–46.

27. Zin Kittredge, "The Tradition of the Hunt," *Not Man Apart, Friends of the Earth*, December 1977, p. 2; and Spencer, p. 352.

28. Waldemar Bogoras, "Ideas of Space and Time in the Conception of Primitive Religion," *American Anthropologist* 27 (1925): 207.

29. John W. Chapman, "Tinneh Animism," *American Anthropologist* 23 (1921): 304. For a masterful work on hunting ceremonialism, see A. Irving Hallowell, "Bear Ceremonialism in the Northern Hemisphere," *American Anthropologist* 28 (1926): 2–175.

30. Alan Gussow, ed., "Voices from the Arctic Shore: Inupiat Whaling Captains and Elders Testify," *Not Man Apart, Friends of the Earth*, p. 5.

23 / The Guéré Excision Festival

Elizabeth Tucker

As Arnold van Gennep indicated in his seminal work, some of the most important rituals for a community are the "rites of passage" that mark the progress of community members through the socially prescribed ages and stages. Many festivals include a rite of passage as one of their many component parts; in others, like the one described here, the rite of passage is the explicit reason for the celebration and its most important event.

This article by Elizabeth Tucker is based on her fieldwork among the Guéré of the Ivory Coast, who mark the coming of age of their young people by male circumcision and female excision. Tucker discusses the latter, and the festive celebrations surrounding it. In the preliminary ethnographic notes, the author outlines a profile of the Guéré, a forest people of fiercely independent warriors who resisted equally the French colonial conquest at the beginning of the century and the new policies implemented by the independent government after 1960. Their traditional subsistence economies based on hunting and gathering have resisted the introduction of Western-style agriculture. Their tribal religion, rooted in animism, magic, and sorcery, has resisted both Christianity and Islam. The masks of the forest, the gla, are still ritually used during a wide variety of ceremonies.

The bloan, *the ritual of excision, is presented by the author as based on four phases instead of the classic three suggested by van Gennep (separation, transition, incorporation) as the pattern of the rites of passage. In the first phase, the woman who administers the ritual symbolically "captures" the novices—whether they are willing or not—and makes them march single file, like prisoners, into a special secluded area in the forest. In the second phase she performs the excision there, with the help of some female assistants and the supervision of a powerful female mask, the* nyénongbae-gla.

In the third and most lengthy phase, lasting anywhere from a week to a month, the neophytes remain secluded and receive secret knowledge. In the fourth phase, the girls-turned-women have their final "coming out." They return to the village in new and colorful finery. They wear adult clothes and jewels of copper and gold, and their faces are painted with liquid clay in traditional geometric patterns. A performance of songs and dances follows. The folksongs are either praises of the instructress or pleasantries between men and women. Their lyrics contain references to key cultural symbols such as the panther, the female symbol of bravery. Five different kinds of dances are performed by the instructress, the women serving as her assistants and chaperons, and the newly initiated. Objects carried and displayed by the dancers have symbolic connotations related to dowry, married life, and women's daily chores. The author stresses that in contrast to Turner's general statement (in The Forest of Symbols) that women's economic activities are hardly ritualized, these Guéré ceremonies appear to ritualize women's work and women's chores. The culmination of the festivities is a feast prepared by the female relatives of the young initiates. All members of the community are called to partake in dishes of rice—typical women's food among the Guéré—manioc, yams, a sauce of meat, as well as game killed in the forest—men's food par excellence and the most desirable meat, bringing prowess and power to its eaters. At the end of the excision festival, young men used to choose their brides. The custom is disappearing, and the author reports a legend "explaining" the change with strong metaphors.

Rituals similar to the one described here are still practiced today in a large section of Africa, extending from Egypt, Somalia, and Kenya on the East Coast to Guinea, Gambia, and Senegal on the West Coast. Westerners have been expressing shock and revulsion over what is commonly termed "female circumcision" (more precisely it is either clitoridectomy or infibulation) since the early ethnographers first reported these "savage customs," and more vocally for at least half a century, on the grounds that these practices are degrading, represent sexual oppression of women by men, and cause serious medical problems. But attempts to force Africans to abandon such practices have been so far largely unsuccessful. Female circumcision continues to affect millions of women in spite of the fact that several countries, such as the Sudan and Kenya, have laws prohibiting it.

The reasons for such strong resistance are several. The excision ritual has maintained important social functions such as bringing girls to full womanhood and adulthood, marriageability, and fertility; it asserts female solidarity, power, and status; it gains praise and respect for the initiated females from the community. The ritual may be connected also to other important social patterns, such as polygamy and father-daughter relationships, as Frank Young and Judith Brown indicated in their studies, which the author quotes in her discussion of cross-cultural functions. Circumcision is rooted in a traditional system of beliefs: women who do not undergo it are traditionally believed to die when they give birth, or become sterile, or grow up to be harlots. To *complicate the issue, some African nationalists such as Jomo Kenyatta (who was trained in anthropology in England) have taken up the cause of female circumcision as a way of protesting colonial efforts to manipulate Africans and their traditional culture. As the efforts of several groups, both African and Western, against female circumcision continue, an understanding of the traditional function and meaning of such ritual practices remains an important preliminary to finding ways to bring about change that will be effective but also accepted by the culture bearers. As a Somali midwife observed to a Washington envoy, "There's no quick fix for this. We're trying to change centuries-old attitudes of entire countries."*

The Guéré Excision Festival

Elizabeth Tucker

Among the Guéré of the western Ivory Coast, tradition blends with modernity in most village celebrations. It is not unusual to find a group of young people sitting in a circle, singing and telling stories while they await the evening's main event: an old French movie on television. Transistor radios, available in even the remotest areas, supplement the traditional drum and balaphone music of village gatherings. Even such an elaborate festival as the coming-out of pubescent girls from seclusion after their recovery from the excision operation is not exempt from innovation. The government of the Ivory Coast strongly advocates modern schooling, so excision must be performed during the three school holidays: Christmas, Easter, and the long vacation from July to September.

As a visitor to the Guéré villages of Zagné, Goulaleu, and Mona and as a resident of the town of Guiglo, I attended a number of excision ceremonies and took part in the festivals that marked their culmination. These festivals were conducted by women, on behalf of the young female initiates, but both men and women participated. Along with male circumcision, which took place at the same times of year, excision was a prime occasion for gathering the whole community together. Songs, dances, and a large meal, arranged by the women but enjoyed by everyone, provided a focal point for communal rejoicing. The festivals that I observed took place between 1972 and 1974, when the government's policy of modernization was beginning to limit the popularity of excision; since then, more stringent governmental dictates have imposed further limitations. Nevertheless, the symbolic significance of the festival remains strong in Guéré society.[1]

Estimated to be about 100,000 in the mid-1970s, the Guéré population extends from the eastern extremities of Liberia to the northwestern forests of the Ivory Coast.[2] First and foremost, the Guéré are a forest people. They are known throughout the country as fiercely independent warriors who resist conquest with effective tactics of forest warfare. Although the French military penetration of the Ivory Coast reached Guéré country as early as 1906, it took many years for the occupation to be completed— longer than any other ethnic group's resistance in the new colony.[3] Even when the nation achieved independence from French control in 1960, the Guéré continued their resistance in the form of reluctance to accept new governmental policies. Polygamy and cannibalism, both subject to the new government's disapproval, persisted in Guéré country through the first two decades of independence.

Jean-Baptiste Tegbao Diay, a Guéré priest who received his doctoral degree in theology in 1971, defines the character of his people as "fundamentally anarchist."[4] The need for constant struggle in the forest environment, with difficulties of communication and trade, has contributed to what the experienced ethnographer Alfred Schwartz calls the Guéré "psychosis of war."[5] Their villages are organized in a quasi-military fashion, and even the home is viewed as a stronghold in time of war.

In comparison to other ethnic groups of the Ivory Coast, the Guéré are somewhat deficient in material wealth. Some developers of the newly independent nation decided to avoid Guéré country because of its distance from the capital city of Abidjan; in the mid-1960s, with 13 percent of the national population, less than 5 percent of the nation's investments came to that area.[6] The Guéré rely upon hunting and gathering for their subsistence, in addition to the cultivation of rice, yams, manioc, and other crops. Some coffee and cocoa plantations introduced by the French have succeeded in Guéré country, but many more have not done well for lack of full participation.

The traditional Guéré village has been slow to adapt to change. Any large cluster of patrilineal, matrilocal families that constitutes a village may be told by the government to resettle, for the sake of creating a more viable rural economy. The chiefs of Zagné, Goulaleu, and Mona, suspicious of the political reasons for this resettlement, have tried to maintain the old ties of kinship in new surroundings—and their efforts have been remarkably successful.

Just as the government has encountered resistance in Guéré country, Christians and Mohammedans seeking religious converts have made little progress. There have been few cases of conversion to Christianity, and even fewer of conversion to Islam. The religion that has maintained such stubborn cohesiveness is a propitiatory cult against illness and sorcery. Gnon-Sua, the creator and master of the universe, is integral to Guéré religion but of less daily importance than the preoccupation with sorcery.

On the socio-ritual level, that which most closely concerns the excision festival, Guéré society maintains a fundamental continuity with the past while allowing superficial innovations to slip in. Rituals that involve *gla*, the masks of the forest, are performed in conjunction with war, peacemaking, and judgment, as well as on various occasions for singing and dancing. The forest masks generally represent specific animals, such as the panther, the monkey, and the crocodile; the elephant mask is considered to be the most powerful. Although the masks themselves do not change, the men who wear them can dress in clothing that shows some Western influence. Women are prohibited from any involvement in secret *gla* rituals, other than seeing public performances.

In contrast to the *gla*, the *bloan*—the institution of circumcision and excision—concerns all members of Guéré society. Those who perform the operation, the operation itself, and the surrounding ritual are all known as *bloan*. Male and female initiates are rigorously secluded from each other, as well as from members of the opposite sex, in separate clearings in the forest. Thus, both women and men of mature years know secrets that can never be revealed to the opposite sex. The mysteriousness surrounding these secrets helps to explain the enduring appeal of the *bloan* songs, highlights of both excision and circumcision festivals.

The first phase of excision begins in the village, with the "capture" of potential initiates by the woman who performs the operation. Social class or position is no impediment to being chosen for excision, nor is it a barrier in many other societies studied by anthropologists; male circumcision, on the other hand, may involve such class distinctions.[7] Sometimes the Guéré girl announces that she is ready to be excised; other times, however, she is seized by the *bloan* against her will. Once the candidates have been chosen, they proceed single file toward a clearing in the forest. Victor Turner calls this part of circumcision ritual the "bringing-in."[8] His term is roughly appropriate for this part of Guéré excision, but not specific enough to account for the twofold process: the capture of the girl and her enforced march into the forest, almost in the manner of a prisoner of war.

This emphasis upon forced entry into the forest makes it clear that the two spaces, village and excision clearing, are very different in essence. The village is a place for a variety of activities, many involving free choice, while the seclusion area is a ritually defined space for submission and learning. Without this ritual framing process, the distinction between the two places would be much less explicit.

The second and crucial stage of excision, the operation itself, must be described in order to indicate the meaning of key songs and dances at the festival. The *bloan* and her assistants, some of whom may be the girls' mothers, seize the initiates as they enter the clearing. Each girl's clitoris is excised with a sharp knife. If she does not cry, the girl is deemed courageous and congratulated. In the villages that I visited, serious aftereffects of the operation were said to be rare. In the few cases of serious hemorrhage, the female mask *nyénongbae-gla* had been summoned to stop the flow of blood. Dressed in a simple smock and a skirt of raffia fibers, this woman usually wears a two-horned headdress made of leather, wood, cowrie shells, and small bells in her role as a leader of ritual. She can appear during funerals, help with the sowing of the rice crop, or simply dance before the other women to entertain them—as she does at some excision festivals.

The third and most lengthy phase of excision is the seclusion period, which can be as short as eight days or as long as a month. The *bloan*, having performed the operation, now assumes the role of chief instructress. She has absolute authority over the girls, and is recognized as the judge of all problems between *bloan* assistants and the girls' families. All of the instructresses are strict in maintaining the prohibition of sexual relations during the seclusion period. If any man dares to come too close to the forest clearing where the convalescent girls stay in the daytime, he is punished with the application of red pepper to sensitive parts of his body. Similarly, intruders in the hut where the girls sleep at the edge of the village are quickly apprehended and punished.

The instruction that takes place during the seclusion period is shared with the other villagers at the time of "coming-out," the excision festival. As the girls come out of the forest on the morning of their last day of supervision, their male relatives shoot into the air with guns to announce the beginning of the event. All of the villagers, young and old, male and female, rapidly convene in the central clearing of the settlement to await the girls who have been transformed into young women.

The girls' transformation is immediately visible because of the clothes they wear, badges of their new adult status. Instead of their usual school uniforms of pink or blue cloth, skimpy garments that have no sleeves or ornamentation of any sort, the girls wear several layers of bright-colored cloth that cover their bodies from shoulder to ankle. The elaborate layering of tie-dyed and wax-printed cloths in various colors shows that the girl's family is affluent and eager to present her to the village in proper style. Also symbolic of the girls' entrance to womanhood is the length of the cloths, which shows their allegiance to the home village—one that goes deeper than belonging to a French school.

Still, the social desirability of Western clothes may reveal itself in startling ways. In one village's excision procession, I observed several young girls wearing French brassieres in lurid shades of red, orange, and pink over the cloths covering their breasts. The instructresses who were leading the procession explained that they had recently discovered the brassieres in a neighboring town. They had decided to dress the girls up in these new garments because they were so bright and unusual, the beginning of such a new fashion in the village. In a larger settlement with more Western influence, such a costume would be highly unlikely to be part of an excision procession. Nevertheless, new clothing styles are frequently attractive to the instructresses regardless of their experience.

Ornamentation of the face is another prominent feature of the girls' adornment. At the end of the seclusion period, the women paint their charges' faces with liquid clay. The patterns are always geometrical, nearly always in mirror-image symmetry, but there are many variations from one village to another. One common pattern is a pair of thick parallel lines on the forehead, encircling the cheeks and crossing the chin. Such a pattern identifies its bearer as a member of her home village and an emerging woman, ready for adulthood and marriage.

While every girl can have her face painted with clay, not everyone can afford the luxury of expensive jewelry. Copper earrings and bracelets are relatively costly, but gold ornaments are much more difficult to obtain. Those girls whose families are fortunate enough to own copper or gold jewelry wear it proudly, aware that it contributes a great deal to their status in the group. Even a small pair of copper earrings can be significant, since copper is often a component of the traditional dowry.

As the girls emerge from the forest in their new finery, they march in single file, much as they entered the ritual space. This time, however, there is a significant difference: instead of remaining silent to show their submission, the girls sing some of the songs that their instructresses have taught them during the seclusion period. The songs can be divided into two categories: praise songs in honor of the chief instructress and songs of pleasantry between men and women. Those of the first category are by far the more numerous and appear to have deeper symbolic meaning than the songs of pleasantry.

Certain praise songs are based upon simple, declarative statements of the *bloan*'s power. For example, the song *yao zimuwo* means "you are the one who may command us to do anything"; *manguwo* can be roughly translated as "she is the one who excises; everyone is afraid of her."[9] These short phrases are repeated over and over, sung by several different women to the constantly changing rhythm of the drum. At the end of each song, the final note is held for several seconds before it fades out.

Other more complicated songs tend to focus upon the image of a fierce animal that seizes its prey. One example is *gi we dé won:*

> You have never seen the panther pounce upon her prey.
> You who have not been excised,
> You who have never seen a woman have children,

Come and see the panther-woman pounce upon her prey.

The significance of the panther as a praise-song image can be better understood in light of the animal's broader symbolism. For hunters, the panther (*dji*) is highly prized as an animal whose capture is a proof of courage. The *dji-gla* is recognized by all villagers as one of the most powerful masks, worthy of great respect. Traditionally, the *dji-kou* (panther-skin) is included in the dowry of a bride. According to Tegbao Diay, the *dji-kou* symbolizes bravery, courage, and intrepidity.[10] Thus the description of the chief instructress as a panther-woman shows that she is courageous and powerful, as well as the leader of a ritual that can result in the young initiates' marriage.

Other characteristics of the *bloan* are extolled in different songs. Similes are predominant: her eyes are as red as palm kernels, and her capture of the young girls is like the spring of a panther. Her anger is like the anger of a wild beast; her hand dispenses justice as easily as the shaking of a cow's tail. She is like the hawk, and those who have never been excised flee from her like small birds from a hawk circling in the air. Each of these similes makes it clear that she is a woman to be feared, but also to be respected and honored.

In the festival dances as well as in the songs, the panther-woman is a dominant figure. Although the initiates have spent many hours learning dances from their instructresses, they refrain from dancing most of the time after the procession reaches the village center. Each girl may be called forth for a brief demonstration of dancing steps, but the main focus of attention is on the *bloan* and her assistants. Dressed in ordinary, dark-colored clothes, the *bloan* wears a high headdress made of dark brown hawk feathers. These feathers bring to mind the circling hawk of the praise song, and the panther skin that is worn over her shoulders reminds the onlookers of her power and courage. Both male and female onlookers remain silent during the dances, out of respect for the *bloan* and the excision ritual.

One of the most impressive dances is performed by the *bloan* alone, with no musical accompaniment but the beating of a small drum. In one hand she holds a white hen, and in the other the small, sharp knife used to perform the excision operation. As one initiate beats the drum, she circles around the group: first slowly, then faster, searching for her prey, demanding "Where is it? Where is it?" and making stabbing motions toward the hen with her knife. Although the dance is strikingly violent and threatening, the girls show no sign of fear; they are too well trained to react to such a performance with anything but simple acceptance.

Four other types of dances are performed by the women who serve as assistants and chaperons. One of them dances with a white plate in each hand, waving the plates back and forth in a swooping motion as she circles around the group. Her gestures are more fluid than those of the *bloan*, and certainly less threatening. The plates chosen for this dance are usually made of china and imported from Europe; thus, some superficial modern influence is evident. The second dance involves much the same motions, this time with two raffia shakers; one of the chief's wives is often chosen as the performer. The bell dance is somewhat different in form: one of the assistants runs back and forth, ringing a small bell in time to the drum playing and singing. Finally, another assistant performs with no props but strongly expressive gestures: pointing to the *bloan*, beckoning to the girls, embracing everyone in the group, and shaking hands.

The objects used in the dances of the *bloan* and her assistants are not without symbolic significance. The white hen represents the "marriage chicken," presented by the young man's family to the parents of the prospective bride; after the chicken is eaten, the marriage becomes official.[11] Small bells are traditionally included in the bride's dowry, as are plates of some durable material. Copper plates are most desirable, but china or enamel substitutes are necessary in these days of costly precious metals.

Like the dancers, each of the initiates carries a symbolic object: a small stick that resembles the larger sticks of women's festival dances. In these dances, called *banti*, the women move their sticks up and down as if they were pounding rice or boiled yams. One of the excision songs that tends to be sung most often is *doho zimwe*, which states "Come with your pestle; we are going to pound some rice." Thus, the girls' duties as preparers of food are strongly emphasized in their coming-out. This emphasis contrasts sharply with the focus discerned by Turner in his study of Ndembu ritual: "Women's economic activity, which is, when all is said and done, essential to the existence of the community, is hardly ritualized at all, while that of men is steeped with ritual."[12] No such custom prohibits Guéré women from demonstrating their economic status, a highly important attribute of the excision festival.

The culmination of many hours of singing and dancing is a lavish feast prepared by the female relatives of the young initiates.[13] As the sun begins to set, the cooks and their assistants invite everyone in the village to partake of the feast. They carry out large wooden or enamel bowls filled with rice, manioc, and yams. *Foutou*, made of boiled yams or manioc pounded to a smooth texture and rolled into a ball, is one favorite dish. Even more important is an abundance of rice, which the Guéré regard as a prime symbol of comfort and affluence. If a family eats rice every day, it is considered fortunate by the village standard of living. A family that cannot usually afford rice will make a special effort to buy some for a daughter's coming-out, as this food shows the family's generosity and position in the community. A girl whose family serves high-status food is traditionally eligible for a good marriage, if the right man appears.

Beyond its implications of status, rice is known as women's food among the Guéré. Women harvest the rice, if it is grown near their own village; they serve rice on many ceremonial occasions, including the seclusion period of excision. The *bloan* and her assistants feed rice to the girls with their hands, so that the girls need do nothing for themselves. As initiates, waiting for the moment of "rebirth" into womanhood, the girls must remain in a state of passive receptivity like that of very small children. Their entrance into young womanhood makes it appropriate for them to eat rice again at the banquet, but to consume it without the help of their instructresses.

Another significant food served at the banquet is meat, mixed with palm oil and tomato to form a large bowl of sauce. Although beef and mutton are easily obtainable from nearby markets, the most desirable meat is monkey, bush-rat, or other game killed in the forest. The Guéré believe that forest game brings prowess to the hunters that kill it and power to all the people who consume it. At the opposite extreme from rice, with all of its feminine connotations, forest game represents the masculine values of bravery, conquest, and perseverance in the hunt. The inclusion of forest game in the excision feast can be considered a symbolic bringing-together of the male and the female, as well as a bestowal of power upon all who take part in the meal.

At the end of the feast, all the women in the village help to clear away the dishes and remaining food. Each of the initiates goes home to her mother's house, bringing along the new clothes and jewelry that she has received. Although she has now officially reached womanhood, the initiate's return to normal life involves almost no change in daily activities. She continues to help her mother with food preparation and other household chores, but from now on the other villagers view her with greater respect. Some of the boys and younger girls may tease her for details about the seclusion period, but the initiate knows that the *bloan*'s edict of secrecy must never be broken.

Although it was once traditional for young men to choose their brides from among the initiates at the end of the festival, such choices are quite rare today. One of my young female informants explained the change with a story which, she said, is sometimes told at excision festivals:

> A girl became affianced to a black fish in the pool beside her house.
> Whenever she wanted to see it, she summoned it by a special song: "I
> will give you a collar of ivory." Her mother, curious about her daughter's
> activities, stayed home from the fields one day, hid, and watched the girl
> summon the fish. Afterward, she returned and sang the secret song; when
> the fish appeared, she cut off its head and served it to her daughter to
> eat. When the girl learned what had happened, she waited until her
> mother had left, cut off her little brother Guei's head, and prepared it to
> serve to her mother. The mother was horrified to learn what it was that
> she had eaten, but it was too late. Since then, young people have been
> allowed to choose their own partners without interference.[14]

This explanation, typical of the many graphic Guéré legends, does not mention the fact that young people in the Ivory Coast today are often tempted to free themselves of traditional restraints. Boys and girls who attend school and prepare themselves for modern jobs cannot marry when they reach puberty; their choices are broader than those of village-bound adolescents. Nevertheless, the excision festival remains highly significant for them as a dramatic entrance into adulthood.

The tenacity of this Guéré festival, despite changing marriage customs, shows its close comparability to other African celebrations for female initiates. During the years of Kenyan government described by Jomo Kenyatta, excision was such an important mark of sexual maturity that it persisted despite stringent opposition.[15] The Masai belief that an unexcised woman risks dying in childbirth and losing her child is illustrative of the great import of the ceremony. Similar to this fear is the Mandingo concern with infertility: a woman who has not undergone excision may never be able to bear children.[16] While these worries stem from real dangers, they reinforce Turner's contention that initiation ritual constitutes an ontological transformation.[17] After the excision festival, the young woman is eligible for safe and productive years of child-bearing; without initiation, she is not truly a woman and so may forfeit all the benefits of adult female status.

Concerning this major change in status, cross-cultural studies have shown close parallels. Frank Young suggests that the main purpose of the female initiation ceremony is to teach the girl about her role as a woman and to inform other women of her changing position in the community. As the unit of women's solidarity becomes smaller, the ceremonies become less elaborate.[18] Judith Brown similarly observes that the most elaborate rites are found in societies where women make a notable contribution to subsistence activities. Initiation rites such as excision, in which the girls are subjected to extreme pain, occur in societies where a conflict of sex identity arises from certain conditions in childhood and infancy.[19] Brown's statistical survey does not include the Guéré, but the applicability of this approach calls for closer examination of the connections between such factors as polygamy, father-daughter relationships, and excision in Guéré society.

With all of its symbolic and social ramifications, the Guéré excision festival is an event that succeeds very well in drawing the whole village together. It is proof of the strong solidarity of Guéré women, the rich symbolic association of the culture, and the continuing need for traditional celebrations in changing times.

NOTES

1. The significance of excision in other African societies is discussed in such studies as Jomo Kenyatta, *Facing Mount Kenya* (London, 1938); Bohumil Holas, *Les Sénoufo* (Paris, 1957); and Otto Raum, *Chaga Childhood* (London, 1940). For information about female initiation in another region of the Ivory Coast, see M. A. de Salverte-Marmier, "Le 'Do': Société Initiatique Féminine, Fonctions Sociale et Economique," *Etudes Régionales de Bouaké* 9 (1964): 39–49. For folklore, and folksongs in particular, related to female circumcision, see Elizabeth Hasthorpe, "Girls' Circumcision Songs Among the Pokot of East Africa," M.A. thesis in folkore, U.C. Berkeley, 1977.*

2. *Area Handbook for Ivory Coast*, ed. T. D. Roberts et al., 2d ed. (Washington, D.C., 1973), p. 67.

3. Alfred Schwartz, "Traditions et Changements dans la Société Guéré," O.R.S.T.O.M. (Paris, 1971), p. 16. See also René Viard, *Les Guéré: Peuple de la Forêt* (Paris, 1934).

4. Jean-Baptiste Tegbao Diay, "Christianisme et Integration Culturelle en Afrique Noire (Pays Guéré Côte d'Ivoire)," Doctor of Theology dissertation, University of Fribourg, Switzerland, 1971, p. 51.

5. Schwartz, p. 28.

6. Ibid., p. 16.

7. "Circumcision," *Encyclopedia of Reli-*

gion and Ethics, ed. James Hastings (New York, Scribner's, 1951), 3: 668.

8. Victor Turner, *The Forest of Symbols* (Ithaca, New York, 1967), p. 93.

9. Most of these songs came from the village of Zagné. They were translated by young men of the village.

10. Tegbao Diay, p. 70.

11. Alfred Schwartz, "Ziombli: L'Organisation Social d'un Village Guéré-Nidrou (Côte d'Ivoire)," O.R.S.T.O.M. (Paris, 1965), p. 107.

12. Turner, p. 8.

13. For comparable descriptions of initiation feasts, see "Feasting," *Encyclopedia of Religion and Ethics*, 5: 801–3.

14. Told in the town of Guiglo on January 6, 1973.

15. Kenyatta.

16. "Circumcision," p. 669.

17. Turner, p. 102.

18. Frank W. Young, *Initiation Ceremonies: A Cross-Cultural Survey in Status Dramatization* (New York, 1965).

19. Judith Brown, "A Cross-Cultural Study of Female Initiation Rites," *American Anthropologist* 65 (1963): 837–53. See also Bruno Bettelheim, *Symbolic Wounds* (New York, 1954) and Leo Frobenius, *Beschneidung und Reifezeremonien bei Naturvölkern: Studien zur Kulturkunde* (Stuttgart, 1933).

*For the recent debate on circumcision, excision, and infibulation, see for instance Fran P. Hosken, *The Hosken Report: Genital and Sexual Mutilation of Females* (Lexington, Mass.: Women's International Network News, 1979); Awa Thiam, *La Parole aux Negresses* (Paris: Denöel-Gonthier, 1978).

24 / The Dragon-Boat Festival

Wolfram Eberhard

The different rites that form a festival may be related not only to myth but also to other narrative genres, such as legend or folktale, or to folk custom and belief of daily life. One such elaborate pattern of correspondences between narratives, rites, customs, and beliefs, all revolving around a festival and its history, is reconstructed, condensed, and discursively exposed in this article by a leading Sinologist.

Wolfram Eberhard discusses the celebrations of the Fifth of the Fifth—the fifth day of the Chinese fifth month—known as the Dragon-Boat festival. This was one of the great festivals in Chinese tradition, and the only one limited to the area south of the Yangtse River.

The article starts by describing the festival in its most recent form: the festive crowd showing its holiday costumes, having picnics on the shore, dinners on the boats, and tea parties under the bamboo awnings, all to the sound of folksongs and opera tunes. The central part of the festival is the parade of the enormous dragon-shaped boats, painted in red—the color of the number five, and symbol of heat, summer, and fire. In the boat are rowers, flag-wavers, and musicians. The festival culminates in a dangerous competition between crews, very often resulting in the capsizing of boats and drowning of crew members.

286

The author then reports and discusses the legend from the third century B.C. which contains the alleged origin and the implicit rationale of the festival. The protagonist of the legend, Ch'ü Yüan, his suicide in the river, and the characters of his poetry lead the author to the Tai, a native group settled in the South before the advent of Chinese civilization, and to their spring and summer festivals, which were centered on a human sacrifice, and meant to secure agricultural fertility. The victim was a stranger, for some time one of the Chinese settlers, secured by head-hunting. Pieces of his body were distributed and buried in the fields. As the Chinese established themselves in South China, head-hunting was replaced by a sham fight of two groups, trying to wade through the river. The inevitable death of one or more contestants was considered a sort of sacrifice to the river, and the ritual battle as a selection of the victim through ordeal. The winners celebrated the victory with a sex orgy in the nearby woods. This was considered the early form of the Dragon-Boat festival. The dangerous boat races later replaced the wading and fighting through the water as the ordeal; conviviality replaced the orgies.

The author also reviews evidence of other ritual forms of human sacrifice to the river, reporting a modern Buddhist narrative centered on a great man-eating river snake. The narratives of Ch'ü Yüan's suicide, of the river snake, and later the impersonal ordeals of the dangerous games all seem to the author attempts to rationalize and symbolically depict the custom of human sacrifice to the river.

The author then examines similar narratives related to other festivals held at rivers in different parts of China: in the Canton region there is the legend of Chin-hua fu-jen, a girl drowned during the spring festival who then became a goddess; in the Shanghai region the protagonist is a girl who committed suicide when her father drowned during the spring festival. The author then discusses ceremonial variants from several groups, ranging from the Tibetans at the western border of China, who detest water, to the Yao tribes, who instead indulge in bathing and swimming.

In southwestern China, people dive into a pond to find an object at the bottom, which will indicate whether they will have a son or a daughter. In many parts of South China the ceremony consists instead in a ceremonial bath. The author then focuses on a narrative from Taiwan, dating from the third century B.C.; its central motif is a magic bath in iris broth, taken on the day of the Dragon-Boat festival.

The motif is the lead-in to another set of beliefs and customs practiced on that date, such as bathing in an orchid broth, drinking wine seasoned with iris, or the hanging on doors of iris or artemisia branches bound with five silk threads of five different colors.

Some of the festive customs carry their consequences into daily life: special plants collected on the festival day are kept as preventives for all diseases for the whole year, sometimes bound into the shape of charms; a special water ritually collected on the Fifth of the Fifth is used as a remedy against all kinds of disease—a narrative from the Fukien province explains its origin and value.

Customs and beliefs relative to the festival are finally reviewed to show, as the author had anticipated at the beginning, that the fifth month of the year—and the festival day itself—are believed to engender many dangers. Even if the Dragon-Boat is one of the three big "lucky festivals" or "festivals of the living," in the middle of its *light and vibrant new life there lies the hidden threat of death and decay, in accordance with Chinese philosophy and its eternal dualism of yin and yang, each carrying within itself the sign of its opposite.*

The Dragon-Boat Festival*

Wolfram Eberhard

Introduction

The old Chinese calendar was based primarily upon the phases of the moon, so that many festivals were celebrated on the day of full moon (the fourteenth or fifteenth day of each month), so that the night was light and festivities could go on until late at night.

There are, however, a few exceptions, and the "Dragon-Boat festival" is one of them. The reason for this seems to be that it was a festival which had to be celebrated during the heat of the day. Though it falls on the fifth day of the fifth month, it is basically a solstice festival (June 21 in our calendar), because the old calendar began the New Year on the day of the second new moon day after the winter solstice (twenty-first day of December in our calendar), i.e., between January 22 and February 18, so that the fifth day of the fifth month is close to June 21. The festival has also another important aspect: it is the only great Chinese festival that is limited to South China, i.e., roughly speaking, the area south of the Yangtse River. In the north, people celebrate a totally different festival, which, however, has a similar symbolic meaning.

The Boat Race

Spring is over; summer has begun, and tormenting heat alternates with torrents of rain. A white layer of mould covers the shoes one put into the corner only yesterday; gray spots of moisture stain the walls; luxuriant vegetation covers the garden overnight. Life in crowded cities with their narrow streets becomes almost unbearable. It is hard to find refreshing sleep during the night, for the temperature remains unchanged and no cool breeze enters the room. People avoid motion and work as little as they can; they doze during the heat of the day and do what is urgently necessary and unavoidable in the early morning or late evening. Or they try to escape to the mountains or the lakes.

It is not just the physical effect of the heat and moisture that weighs heavily upon men; there is something indefinable and undescribable that oppresses the heart of everyone. Is it a feeling of helplessness against the powers of nature, a feeling of being surrounded, of being encircled by enemies hidden in the dark shadows of the excessively vital vegetation? Or is it the knowledge that this wild growth inevitably initiates the decay which fall and winter will bring? Chinese philosophy, with its eternal dualism of *yin*, the female force, and *yang*, the male force, fighting, united though they are, perpetually against each other, has always stressed the idea that too

---

*Reprinted from Wolfram Eberhard, *Chinese Festivals* (New York: Henry Schuman, 1952), pp. 69–89. Revised by the author.

great strength, too much power, in itself bears the roots of decay and reversal. Darkness is hidden behind excessive light, and death behind vibrant life. It is the thought of death and darkness that overshadows this period of the year, the fifth month of the Chinese calendar, corresponding to our late June and early July, the time of the summer solstice and the longest day of the year.

We should expect a festival on this day, the twenty-first day of June, as we find it in Europe of yesteryear, where big fires lighted up the night and boys and girls, hand in hand, leaped over the flames and were thus purified from all contagious influences of nature; where burning wheels rolled down the hills, symbolizing the rolling sun, whose power inevitably would diminish from this day on.

There is indeed a festival in China on this day, but the ordinary citizen is hardly even aware of it. In earlier times it was, contrary to Western custom, forbidden to light any big fire or the iron-smelting furnaces on this day. For every Chinese, this was only logical; how can one attempt to strengthen the already overstrong power of the fire, the heat? For the same reason one was not permitted to start a fire in times of drought. There was an official sacrifice made by representatives of the government on the day of the solstice. But this was not the ordinary citizen's business. He did not participate, and he did not regard this day as a festive one.

His day was the "Fifth of the Fifth," the fifth day of the fifth month, the second of the three big "lucky festivals," or "festivals of the living." But unlike the first of these, the New Year's festival, wherein every detail is permeated with the idea of a new beginning, of new, untainted life, here an element of fear or horror is hidden in every ceremony, even the gayest and most colorful. Man is on the defensive against dangerous enemies, overwhelming dark powers. He knows that these enemies will find their victims. So the only thing he can do is divert their attacks from himself to some object, a scapegoat, in his midst.

We should perhaps add that this festival of the "Double Fifth" is a "southern" festival; its roots are in South China and here it is most celebrated, whereas in North China the day is marked by only a few ceremonies.

When the great day arrives, crowds in the coastal provinces of Central and South China hire boats or go to the shore of the nearest river or lake, dressed in their best holiday costumes. Sounds of folk songs or melodies from famous operas, sung or played on the Chinese flute, echo over the hazy surface of the romantic "West Lake" in Hangchow or the mouth of the West River in Canton. A barely perceptible breeze keeps the small boats in constant movement. They float around without aim or direction while the celebrants eat their dinner, talk, or admire the neighbor's boat or his daughter's new dress.

The crowds on the shore are perhaps still gayer. They move around from one shed of straw mats to another, or sit under one of the bamboo awnings and drink tea. They wait. A tension is in the air, comparable to that which we feel before a big race begins.

And suddenly the parade of the dragon boats has begun. These boats are different from all common boats; they are big—up to a hundred feet in length—and so narrow that two members of the crew have difficulty sitting side by side. The body of the boat is shaped like a dragon, and the high prow shows the beast's fierce mouth and its dangerous fangs; the sides are gaily painted and gilded, with red the prominent color because it is the color of the number five, the male number, the symbol of heat, summer, and fire. The crew consists not only of rowers but also of men waving flags and playing cymbals or beating gongs. And so the parade of the dragon boats is accompanied by a deafening noise, exciting the crew and the onlookers alike.

The boats are manned by different guilds or clubs or any two crews from the same village with a hereditary or traditional enmity toward each other, such as exists between the crews of Oxford and Cambridge during the races on the Thames. What a tremendous increase in prestige for the crew that wins the contest this day! And what an exciting as well as aesthetic sight—the slim, shining boats shooting through the water! The motions of the crew are coordinated and rhythmic to the utmost; a single slip of one of the rowers will cause the boat to capsize, and this not only means losing the contest but may be fatal to the crew.

The evening following the race brings another highlight of the festival, as the boats, decorated with colorful lanterns, parade on the river. Slowly they pass the crowds, emerging from the still, lukewarm, dark waters like fairies, and disappearing again in the phosphorescent gleam of the summer night.

And yet, this pageant that one could see until only a short time ago was but a poor relic of incomparably greater pageantry and ceremony of a hundred years ago. Then the boats were often manned by more than fifty men. The leader of each crew was dressed in white and had a big white banner in his right hand, with which he waved and signaled the movements of the rowers. The left sleeve of his dress was especially long, almost touching the ground, and his signaling was accompanied by the rhythmic motion of the sleeve, such as to give the impression of an elegant ceremonial dance. In other regions, the leaders were dressed like generals in the Chinese theater, with real weapons rather than the usual wooden swords.

What was the reason for the oft-repeated orders of the government against this festival? Was it the well-known contempt of the Chinese for sports and everything else which has to do with physical activity? Or was it because sometimes these "generals" behaved like real generals, killing an innocent victim and fixing his head on the prow of the boat? Admittedly this happened, but it cannot be the only reason for the proscription. The race was dangerous. Boats might capsize, and not every Chinese is a good swimmer; when an accident happened, somehow nobody came to the rescue of the unfortunate victims.

But there is a reason which goes much deeper; when reading the reports on the boat race one has the feeling that the "accidents" were not always accidental, but rather something that was predetermined: at least one of the boats had to capsize, and at least one man had to die. It was a kind of ordeal—some god expected a victim and selected one from among the rowers. This was also the reason nobody came to the rescue of the crew; one should not interfere with the will of the god. Let him, alone, select his victims. Otherwise he might take the would-be rescuer as a substitute.

If we ask what the people themselves say about the festival and how it came to be, we are told a touchingly beautiful story.

The third century B.C. was the period of the "warring states," the age of incessant, heroic struggles among the great feudal lords for supremacy. Most of the feudal kingdoms had already disappeared; only seven were left, and Ch'u, in the South, in the modern provinces of Hupei and Hunan, was one of the mightiest of the seven. This was a somewhat barbarian kingdom, and the "true" Chinese despised it, but it had an elegant, luxurious court, the center of politics as well as of refinement. Ch'ü

Yüan, member of one of the highest native families, was minister and councilor to the king of Ch'u. He was also a court poet of great fame. He was deeply concerned with the fate of his country and tried to influence the king to do his best for his country. His advice was not accepted; he had to leave. He departed, wandering restlessly about in deep despair and growing melancholy. Thus he reached the river. He saw the endless stream of water flowing toward the great Yangtse, to the ocean. Here he composed one of his most beautiful poems, a summary of his life and activity, ideals and achievements, a farewell to the world, his country, and his king. Then he threw himself into the water. People in his country pitied him and threw rice into the water as a sacrifice to the dead, because a soul which gets no offerings will suffer all the vexations of starvation. But the soul of Ch'ü Yüan appeared to a group of fishermen, telling them that he was still starving because a huge dragon had taken away the rice they had offered him. They should wrap the rice in small pieces of silk and bind the packages with silk threads of five different colors. This they did, and appeased the soul of the loyal minister of Ch'u. The rice cakes still exist today, wrapped not in silk but in leaves. Everyone likes these rice cakes, and the sacrifice to Ch'ü Yüan is now forgotten. But the fishermen's boats still start out to offer the sacrifice. Such is the origin of the Dragon-Boat festival.

Ch'ü Yüan is undoubtedly a historical figure, and the poem he wrote supposedly just before his suicide, one of the "Elegies of Ch'u," is one of the most beautiful of classical Chinese poetry. This much is fact; the rest is just a tale.

A folklorist does not dismiss a tale; his interest begins where the historian stops. Ch'ü Yüan's family is well known to us as a family of Hunan province. And we know that at the time of the kingdom of Ch'u there was a very sparse settling of Chinese in this province, all the rest being natives, belonging to different cultural groups. The Yao lived in the hills and cultivated the slopes with their primitive slash-and-burn technique. The Tai, however, preferred the valleys and plains near the rivers and lakes, and built rectangular rice fields which they irrigated by a complicated system of canals. It is more than likely that Ch'ü Yüan's family originally belonged to one of these native groups before it adopted Chinese manners and civilization. We know that the style of the "Elegies of Ch'u" is typical of the native groups; it was used in sacrificial texts which were sung during festivals to the accompaniment of drums. Some of the "Elegies" are obviously copies or imitations of sacrificial or ceremonial songs.

The Tai had their spring and summer festivals in connection with the growth of the rice. Rice meant life and death to them and thus their first thought was to secure growth and strength for the rice. The idea of fertility was the center of their primitive world concept, and for them fertility was life—in plants, in animals, and in man. To secure fertility of the fields one had to give strength and vigor. Since man was the strongest creature of the universe, a human sacrifice would be the best one could give. We know that the Tai tribes in South China sacrificed men in a time when such a practice was unheard of in any other part of China. The way to acquire the victim was always the same; it was the method still used by wild tribes in the Indonesian world: head-hunting. (Ancient China, a thousand years earlier than the time we talk of here, knew human sacrifices, it is true. But, so far as we know, these sacrifices had quite a different character and never took the form of head-hunting.) The preferred victim was a stranger, because then no retaliation from relatives or his tribe was possible. So the Chinese settlers in South China were the chosen victims for a time. Further, because a man with a beard seemed to the Tai to be a stronger man, the Chinese scholars, who were always proud to wear beards, even small ones, were in greatest danger. There are many reports of such unfortunate scholars who, traveling through the hills and mountains of the South, were caught by the natives in ambush and taken to their villages. Here they were treated quite well for a time, until the day of the festival. They were not only given good food but, so that their physical strength and fertility might not suffer, were also provided with a maiden. Love affairs between the ill-fated scholar and the native girl were not uncommon; thus the lovers sometimes escaped and continued to live together in China. But most of the captives were sacrificed. The body was distributed among the villagers, who brought the parts to their fields to be interred, thus ensuring fertility. The one who got the bearded head was the most fortunate of all and displayed the trophy on a stick in his field.

There was a fatalism about the ceremony that kept the celebrants from feeling any guilt: the victim was sent to them by a deity; it was a kind of selection by ordeal whereby the natives were simply fulfilling the destiny of that man. This idea of an ordeal is very common among Tai tribes and their relatives. It is the central theme of their justice: a man under accusation could prove his innocence or guilt by putting his hand into boiling oil or by throwing himself in front of an elephant to see whether he received harm and, consequently, whether he deserved punishment.

When, with the growing influence of Chinese civilization in these parts of South China, head-hunting became impracticable, another form of ordeal became popular— a sham fight between two groups. We know of such battles between two villages, where the two groups throw stones at each other until one man on one side is hit and killed. And there are other ceremonies at the border of a river. Two groups stand on either side and sing and dance. Then they try to wade through the river. The contest often ends with the death of one or several contestants, whereas the others celebrate the victory, and the whole ceremony ends with a sex orgy in the adjoining woods. It is believed that this was the original form of our Dragon-Boat festival, the boats being added later, in the coastal sections of Central and South China, replacing the original custom of wading through the water.

Ch'ü Yüan's death in the river Yüan was, the story tells us, a voluntary act, but— in a way—it was also a sacrifice to the river. This is quite obvious from further study. There is an interesting parallel to this story reported from Central China. We know that sacrifices to the large rivers were quite common in those parts—not only during a flood, when the tormented population knew of no way to stop the power and wrath of the waters but to sacrifice a victim, usually a child, into the gap in the walls which protect the banks of the river, but also as an annual ceremony. Interestingly enough, Chinese literature does not mention this as a regularly occurring custom, but refers to it only in relation to a governor who is said to have abolished the cruel ceremony. The text we have was written in pre-Christian times, and the event supposedly took place some hundred years before it was written. But modern folklore preserves the same motif, now in Buddhist terms. The story of the old text says that in a certain region the sorcerers each year gave a young, beautiful girl in marriage to the god of the river. The girl, dressed in the finest wedding dress, was first solemnly given to the god, then seated on a raft made of light material and grasses. She floated down the river until the raft with its victim went down in the rapids, still in sight of the priests and the populace. There came a newly appointed governor to the place, who, disapproving of the custom, found a good means to end the cruel spectacle forever. He sent the sorcerers into the water first, to inform the river god about the approach of his "bride." When the men, naturally, did not return from their mission, the governor convinced the population that the sacrifice of the girl was unnecessary.

In its modern, Buddhist form, the tale which is told in connection with the feast of the mid-summer is as follows:

> In some place, I do not remember where, there was a lotus pond. Every year, in June and July, the lotus flowers opened, as big as the head of a man. There was something very remarkable about them; the flowers rose from the waters during the night and disappeared again in the early morning. Nobody could explain this. Moreover, when one put something on the blossom, it also disappeared in the water.
>
> Now, there was a monk who knew this and also knew the hidden reason. He told the villagers, "This lotus flower is connected with the Western Paradise; it is a lotus seat, just like the seat on which the Buddhas of the Past, the Present, and the Future used to sit. If a person of high virtue sits on this flower, he will come into Buddha's Western Paradise." Within a few days, men and women in the town had heard of this message, and many persons of sixty years of age came, sat on the flowers, and were transported to the Western Paradise.
>
> This continued for a couple of years. Many, many old men and women had reached the Western Paradise by way of the lotus flower. One day, the mother of the local officer celebrated her sixtieth birthday. She, too, had heard of the story and intended to depart for the Western Paradise. She said to her son, "Dear son, I am just like all other women. They all ascend to Paradise. Now, I, too, am sixty years of age and should not wait any longer. I am determined to leave tomorrow. I hope that you live an honest life and prepare yourself for the life in the other world. I will be able to see you from Paradise and this will be a consolation for you."
>
> When the official heard these words, he was thunderstruck. His mother's maidservant told him the whole story about the lotus pond. But when he heard it, he said, "Dear mother, how can you believe in such a story? Try to forget about it. I want to have you here, in this world, for a few more years and I will not allow you to leave." But his mother became quite angry and said, "You pretend to be a district official but you do not even know how to treat your own mother. Every son, daughter, and wife is glad to know of a way their parents can enter the Western Paradise, but you want to prevent my going. Are you devoid of any love?"
>
> Thereupon the son could only answer, "Forgive me, mother, forgive me. I will bring a good meal for you now and prepare everything you might need for the trip to the Paradise, so that you can go." But before he had finished his words, she interrupted him, "I do not need anything. In the Western Paradise I am in Buddha's country, and there is no need to eat or drink. The only things I would like to have are a walking stick and some incense. But have a sedan chair prepared so that I can start early

tomorrow, before the sun rises." This the official promised to do, and then he went back to his office.

He thought about the whole affair; he thought and thought, until he had a plan. He asked his servants and employees to go and collect as many bags of lime as they could get, and he had all of them transported to the shore of the pond. Two full shiploads arrived at the pond during the night. A large lotus flower had just opened, rising a few feet above the water level. Now he asked his servants to pour one bag of lime after the other into the flower. And the flower opened and closed, after having devoured bagful after bagful, until all the lime had reached the Western Paradise.

Next morning, the official with his sons and wives and many others accompanied his mother to the pond to enter the Paradise. But when they reached the place where the lotus pond was, a crowd approached them, saying, "The lotus pond has become a big river, a great snake." The river—the snake itself—was cut by the servants of the official. They cut for three days and nights, and found three bushels of buttons, buttons from the dresses of those old men and women who had thought of entering Paradise. The lime was still smoking and burning in the stomach of the animal. Now people knew that the lotus flower was nothing more than the tongue of a formidable snake. . . .

Sixty years is the great cycle of the Chinese chronology, and life should conform to that cycle; a person should not live more than one cycle. The river or pond should have its victims in summertime, the time of the great festival. The primitive motif of love and death of the older tale has disappeared and given way to the belief in Buddha's Paradise. Nowadays the snake-shaped river god has not changed but gets his victims by ordeal in an impersonal manner which is typical of all the characteristics of the mid-summer festival.

That the tale of Ch'ü Yüan, the unhappy poet and statesman, is only one attempt to rationalize an age-honored custom of human sacrifice can be seen not only from this fairy tale but from many other reports which tell of religious beliefs of the same type. There is the story of "Chin-hua fu-jen," a goddess in the Canton region. She was formerly a girl who was drowned during the spring festival along the river and became a goddess with a local cult when the population found that her body had a miraculous fragrance and that she was more beautiful than during her lifetime. Since that time she has been the protectress of the festival of the fifth day of the fifth month. In the region south of Shanghai, she is a girl who committed suicide when her father was drowned during the ceremonies of the spring festival. Her supernatural character was recognized by the people when her body drifted upstream and was found many days later in perfect condition, beautifully fragrant.

The motivation for the festival at the river is different in southwestern China. Here, people dive into a pond and try to find an object at the bottom. If one finds a stone, he will have a son; if it is a piece of a clay vessel, he will have a daughter. As in all the other tales, the idea of fertility is here expressed quite clearly. Love, sex orgies, sex ceremonies, and death go together, among the South Chinese natives and their descendants as well as in many other parts of the world.

Another custom belonging to the festival, and in a way a substitute for the community fertility ceremony at the water, is the ceremonial bath which is taken in many parts of South China on this festival day. The attitude of different ethnic groups toward the bath is very interesting and instructive. In the Far East we find all possible variations of this theme, from that of the Tibetans on the Western border of China, who detest water and never have any contact with it, to that of the water-fanatic Yao tribes, who indulge in bathing and swimming as do their distant relatives, the Japanese. The Chinese in general are not too fond of water, it must be admitted, and, for them as well as for the Tai, water is a magic power. Many tales express this idea. There are the Amazons of the South who live without men and become pregnant by taking a bath in a river. They bear children of both sexes, but in the course of the first three months all boys die, and the girls grow to become the next generation of Amazons. Perhaps the most beautiful expression of this idea in connection with our festival is to be found in an especially appealing folk tale recently collected among the Chinese on Formosa:

> When Emperor Shih-huang-ti (246–210 B.C.) started to build the famous Chinese wall, he mobilized the youth of the country to go to the North to help with its construction.
>
> There was a young scholar, named Han Chi-lang, who was so delicate that he was not capable of physical work. Moreover, he was an only son, living alone with his old mother. How could he possibly leave home and be conscripted? The only way out was for him to run away, hiding during the day, traveling at night, in order to escape the conscription officers.
>
> Now on the day of the dragon-boat festival, he missed the road and found himself in the garden of a rich family. Happily enough, there was a tall tree in the garden, so he climbed it and concealed himself in the branches.
>
> It is our custom to prepare a broth of iris plants, and men and women take a bath in the broth this festival day. Thus, the young daughter of the family went into the garden, under the tree, to take her bath in a huge jar. The man in the tree could see her and look at her bare young body. Suddenly she observed the onlooker's reflection in the water of her bath. She was frightened. Meng-chiang was a well educated girl of good manner, and, without knowing who he might be, she took an oath that she would marry this man because he had seen her in the bath. She expressed her wish to Han Chi-lang and, as he was willing to take her, a formal wedding was celebrated immediately.
>
> The rich family prepared a magnificent meal and invited all the relatives from near and far. Unfortunately, they forgot to invite the local police officer, and this man, who now knew Han Chi-lang's secret, denounced him at the provincial court. Han was caught and had to leave his young bride on the third day of their marriage. He died under the hardships of the construction for which he was conscripted. They buried his body within the foundations of the Great Wall.
>
> Meng-chiang did not know of his sad fate, and as a faithful and devoted wife she started for the great journey toward the North to take him warm clothes for the wintertime.

When, after a thousand hardships, she finally arrived at the Great Wall, and heard from the other workers that her husband had already succumbed to the hardships of the labor, she could not even find his bones.

Meng-chiang was in despair; she wept and wept so long that her tears undermined the Great Wall and it collapsed in its full length of eight hundred miles. Innumerable skeletons were exposed, but poor Meng-chiang did not know which was her husband's. Then, all of a sudden, an old man approached and told her, "Bite into your fingers and let the blood drip on the bones. If any bone turns red, it belongs to your husband." And so she did and finally recovered those of her beloved.

And as she tearfully began her homeward journey, her tears moistened the bones, which became covered with skin and flesh, and it looked as if the dead were soon to be resurrected. Again the old man appeared, saying, "See how difficult and tiresome this is for you. Wouldn't it be much more comfortable to put the bones into a bag and carry it on your back?" She did so, but when she later opened the bag the flesh and skin on the bones were dried and dead again. She became furious and refused in her anger with the old man to allow him to leave the place where she finally buried her husband. People say that the figure of the god of earth at the tomb is this old man.

This tale of the loving wife is known everywhere in Central China, and its motif of the magic bath reminds us of another set of beliefs in connection with the festival. Instead of bathing in iris broth, one can take a bath in an orchid broth, or one can drink wine seasoned with iris. It is just as efficient to hang artemisia or iris branches, bound together with silk threads in five colors on the hinges of the door. This is another manifestation of the custom of averting bad spirits and magic influences by a powerful remedy. But the people have a different explanation for this usage. It is said that, when bandits threatened a village, a mother fled with her young son at her hand and her small daughter-in-law on her back. The bandits caught her and, when they heard that this woman had tried to save not only her own boy but also her three-year-old daughter-in-law, they were touched by so much love and told her to return to the village and to mark her house with iris and artemisia branches. When the bandits later entered the village, they did not harm her house or the surrounding neighborhood. This is the reason every family today puts these flowers on the hinges of the door on the day of the Dragon-Boat festival.

This tale does not give a very satisfactory explanation of the custom. We do not blame the storyteller, but satisfy ourselves with the fact that the main motif which is ever the same—love and death—is present. Our attention is drawn to a parallel custom, that of binding colored silk around the arms as a charm against war, bad ghosts, or pestilence, or to achieve long life, or simply as a sign that the womenfolk are busy with rearing silkworms as the men are busy working in the fields.

Some people collected the above-mentioned plants and others on the festive day and kept them as preventives for all kinds of diseases, or bound them in the form of small figures to be used as charms. There is indeed a great variety of these customs and beliefs. One amusing tale which was collected in Fukien province is quite instructive:

The family Kuo in Ch'üan-chou had the custom of exposing on the fifth day of the fifth month the old paintings the family possessed, so that everybody could see them. The guests were feted with a dinner and all kinds of attractions and, in addition, the family brought out a cup of water which is secured by grinding an old and holy stone. This water is partaken of by the visitors, because it is a very valuable drug. If one grinds the stone at noon on the Fifth of the Fifth, the water which remains is a remedy against all manner of disease. Therefore everybody wants some of it. The stone, however, is a stone from the god of thunder, and the pictures which are exhibited together with the water represent wind, clouds, rain, and thunder.

After the feast the pictures are stored away and the stone is wrapped. All this comes from Tung Po-hua, whose story is as follows: Tung, the saint, loved his parents very much, and, as his mother liked to eat pork liver, he went to the market every day quite early and bought her some. A young boy of the Kuo family, who loved his parents just as much, did the same, as his father loved pork liver. So both boys met every morning in the meat store. And, as young Mr. Kuo had a liquor shop besides holding a job as district officer, Tung came to the shop every day and took a drink. Whenever he had no money, he put his drink on his account, until the small shop went bankrupt due to the never-paying guest. Tung, when he heard of it, was very sorry and advised Kuo to fill the empty barrels with tangerine oil. He would certainly get much money later, he told Kuo, who did as he was told, because he believed in Tung's words. That year there was a great pestilence in Ch'ün-chou. No medicine except tangerine oil could help. Now Kuo could sell his oil and thus he became quite rich.

Tung soon left Kuo and traveled among the immortals. One day an immortal gave him a thunderstone and told him, "If you want to return home, just go toward the east and you will find the way. The stone is to be your traveling money. If you have need of any, just cry 'I am selling thunderclaps,' and, if anybody wants to buy a thunderclap, write a word into his hand and ask him to close the hand. When he opens his hand again, he will hear a tremendous thunderclap." The immortal disappeared and Tung did as he had been told. He walked by day and slept by night, traveling eastward, passing many big cities and small towns, and whenever he needed money he did as the immortal had told him. Many people loved to buy thunderclaps, and so he easily kept himself in traveling funds.

A few months later he arrived in Ch'üan-chou and saw his mother again and also his old friend Kuo. Tung sold his thunderclaps from time to time. Now, one day, a man who had to participate in a meeting with the district official had bought some thunderclaps, and, when he and his friends opened their hands during the meeting, tremendous thunderpeals were heard. The audience was amused and bought more thunderclaps, making more noise. The official was bewildered when he heard the thunder roaring while there was sunshine and blue sky, and when he saw people laughing he sent a few servants to make inquiry. He heard that

Tung sold thunderclaps and put him in prison, accusing him of sorcery and troublemaking.

Happily enough, Tung's friend Kuo had to judge the case. One day, when the official was out of hearing, Tung said to Kuo, "The official will soon have an accident. Please do not accompany him when he leaves his house." Kuo said, "How can I avoid that?" Thereupon Tung gave him a pill to protect him, insisting that his friend swallow it before his eyes.

As soon as Kuo had swallowed the pill he became ill, and the illness became worse every day.

Soon, when bandits appeared in the district, the official took over the command of the local army; he was soon defeated and killed because his troops were too weak. Kuo had been so ill that he could not take part in the expedition and thus was saved.

Now, Tung gave him the thunderstone and the pictures of wind, thunder, rain, and clouds which he had painted during his stay in the prison, where he died soon afterward. This is the reason Kuo's descendants exhibit the pictures and the stone every Fifth of the Fifth.

In some parts of China, the charms used are specifically called the "charms against the five kinds of thunder." And we know that thunder is a symbol of fertility rather than a sign of danger. The number five is one of those classificatory numbers the Chinese love so much.

Perhaps Tung's stone was sulphur. In many parts of China powdered sulphur is drunk with wine as protection against illness, and children's faces are smeared with sulphur powder. Sulphur, a stone which can produce fire, is regarded and respected as a strong medicine which kills animals and ghosts.

All these charms protect people against imminent dangers. But this is not enough. The day of the festival itself engenders many dangers, as indeed, does the whole fifth month. An official, for example, who is appointed during this month will never be promoted again. Climbing onto the roof should be avoided during the fifth month, although in parts of China, where flat roofs are common, one sometimes has to go up to smooth the earth on top of the house, especially after a rain. If one were to go to the roof, he would perchance see his own soul—for during this month man changes his soul as a snake changes its skin—and then would become ill. One should not cover the roof, moreover, lest he become bald. Beds and mattresses must not be exposed to the sunshine, because the children of the household would then be exposed to the blood of a magic owl and would soon die. To prevent this danger, children drink an owl broth, which is recommended by many experts.

Children born on the day of the festival should not be allowed to live, for they invariably kill their parents as the owls do. Such children will, after their deaths, never decay. This is a belief still voiced in some parts of the country.

Bibliography

All the material used for the preparation of this essay comes from original Chinese sources which are used in my book *The Local Cultures of South and East China* (Leiden: E. J. Brill, 1968), pp. 170 ff. A description of the festival as it was celebrated in Hong Kong is in V. R. Burkhardt, *Chinese Creeds and Customs* (Hong Kong, 1953), vol. 1, pp. 26–29 and some further data are to be found in J. J. M. deGroot, *Les fêtes célébrées à Emouy* (Paris, 1886), p. 320, and H. Doré, *Recherches sur les superstitions en Chine* (Shanghai, 1911), vol. 4, p. 431 and vol. 9, p. 642.

An early Chinese painting, supposedly by Wang Chen-p'eng, fourteenth century, is in the Boston Museum of Fine Arts, no. 12.899 and published by O. Sirén, *Peintures Chininoises dans les Collections Americaines*, plate 18; another picture, also from the thirteenth century, is in the Chinese journal *Ku-kung*, 3d ed., 1932, no. 15. A study of related interest is Lawrence A. Schneider, *A Madman of Ch'u: The Chinese Myth of Loyalty and Dissent* (Berkeley and Los Angeles: University of California Press, 1980).

25 / The Saba Gêdê Festival in Trunyan, Bali

James Danandjaja

Hinduism has commonly been considered the religious and philosophical basis for passive resistance to Western colonialism and ideology in India and Asia. But what happened when Hinduism itself was introduced into older religious and cultural systems?

This article by Indonesian-born, Berkeley-trained anthropologist James Danandjaja gives an example of the "tactful manner" in which Balinese culture has undergone the process of acculturation, by using what the author terms "the passive resistance way" against the Hindu and other "great civilizations" as they have landed on the island. The article focuses on the Saba Gêdê, the great festival held in Trunyan, on eastern Bali, applying a basically ethnographic approach to data collected during fieldwork. The festival commemorates the anniversary of the Trunyanese patron, the native high god Ratu Sakti Pancêring Jagat, who has maintained his important place in the Trunyanese pantheon even after the diffusion of Hinduism on the island. There are two such festivals, celebrated alternately every year: the Kapat Lanang (male fourth full moon) staged by the virgin boys' society, and the Kapat Wadon (female fourth full moon) staged by the virgin girls' society. The author focuses only on the former, its elaborate preparations, and its main events, which also constitute for the virgin boys a rite of passage into adulthood.

The preparations for the festival show the close relationship, correspondences, and communications between the gods' world and the people's world in Trunyan. For instance, as the people prepare for the festival, the gods are also believed to have a three-day meeting to plan the festival; the results of their meeting will be communicated to the villagers by a woman in trance. The visit of the Trunyanese to nearby towns and villages to offer blessed rice is considered penance to make up for the wrong done by one of their gods. Furthermore, the Trunyanese gods play an active part in the symbolic exchanges of gifts, food, visits, and hospitality between the Trunyanese and their neighbors. When the virgin boys journey in search of special banana leaves for their ceremonial costume, hospitality and gifts offered to them will be reciprocated by the blessing of their patron god. The food gathered will be redistributed, blessed, and served at the banquet to the crowd, who will attend the festival.

The article then focuses on the ten days of the festival, and the activities of each are punctiliously described. The first seven days are dedicated to the parading, slaughtering, and offering of the animals presented to the gods, patrons of the underworld and the lake, and to the patron god. The meat of the main victim is distributed to villagers. Flowers, coconut fronds, palm wine, and the victims' blood are also offered. Other ceremonies concern the purification of festive paraphernalia, of the villagers, of the players in the sacred drama, and of the village from lurking devils. The temple is decorated, and bamboo rods and a sacred ferris wheel are erected and decorated. Sacred dances begin on the sixth day: first, a dance in warrior style, then a dance and game, and, last, the mating dance of a wild rooster and a wild hen. Gods are solemnly carried to visit the sacred banyan tree and the edge of the lake.

The highlight of the festival takes place on the eighth day, and is repeated on the following day. It is a pantomime called Bêtara Bêturuk, allegedly very ancient and unique to the Trunyan alone. In the first part, the gods dash wildly about, armed with whips and whipping anyone within reach. While most spectators flee, some choose to be whipped so that their sicknesses can be driven away or a god's grace can be obtained. Finally, the gods are subdued, sprinkled with holy water, fanned, and cooled off. The pantomime is then repeated with the gods armed with bamboo rods.

The climax of the Bêtara Bêturuk is the sacred pantomime played at dusk. The myth of the first meeting of the Trunyanese high god and his future royal consort and his raping her is ritually dramatized. Then the naked gods, followed by the virgin boys and the spectators, rush into the waters of the lake. The gods, it is believed, will then send a fertility-bringing rain, soon after or even during the final banquet and the other closing ceremonies of the festival, marking the return to daily life.

In conclusion, the author states that the Trunyanese have assimilated some foreign cultural traits from Hinduism, garbing in Hinduism their native gods, but essentially maintaining their native religion based on ancestor worship, fertility cults, and animism. The patron god is, after all, son of a Javanese king and his consort is a Bali-born daughter of a goddess exiled in Bali. The sacred pantomime is part of the festival but has its own separate function and magic identity. It enhances the fertility of the people, livestock, and plants. Thus it is part of the native fertility cult and belief system.

The festival shows gratitude to the patron god for his patronage against natural and supernatural dangers, and provides the Trunyanese the means to restate their identity.

The Saba Gêdê Festival in Trunyan, Bali

James Danandjaja

Trunyan is a village located on the east shore of Lake Batur, a crater lake, in the district of Kintamani, regency of Bangli, on the Island of Bali. The Trunyanese form a conservative peasant society, called by other Balinese the Bali Aga (Mountain Balinese) or Bali Mula (Original Balinese). Their culture is a mixture of pre-Hindu tradition, elements from the Han of Northern China, as well as Javanized Hindu-Balinese tradition. These diverse cultural elements are apparent in the festival of Saba Gêdê, the Great Festival, held on the fourth full moon of the Balinese calendar (Purnama ing Kapat). The festival, also called Purnama ing Kapat, occurs sometime between October and November.[1]

An examination of the festival of Saba Gêdê will illustrate how the Trunyanese, as an ethnic minority in Indonesia, have managed to select certain cultural elements from the great civilizations while maintaining their own cultural tradition. The Trunyanese have not been passive recipients of dominant cultural elements. Rather they have chosen aspects of the dominant cultures that mesh with their own cultural values; and they have ignored or actively resisted those elements which are not compatible. This has been done in a tactful manner, which I call "the passive resistant way."[2]

At present, the Trunyanese follow a version of Balinese Hinduism which can be called the Hindu Trunyanese religion. This is part of the Hindu Dharma religion, one of the religions officially recognized by the Indonesian government. While the religion of the Trunyanese may be considered Hinduism, still it is only a version of it. It is animistic in nature and includes the worship of spirits, ancestors, and supernatural powers. Hinduism in Trunyan, to quote Stutterheim's view, "is not a copy of what India presented to Indonesia, but a new mantle for the old national soul."[3]

Though the Trunyanese religious liturgy is, without doubt, Balinese Hindu, it is not directed toward the worship of the Hindu gods, such as Shiva, Vishnu, or Brahma. The Trunyanese worship their own native gods: the patron god, Ratu Sakti Pancêring, his first wife, Ratu Ayu Pingit Dalam Dasar (the goddess of Lake Batur), the patron god's ministers, and his children. Due to the influence of the Hindu Dharma religious movement, some of the educated Trunyanese are now familiar with Sang Hyang Widhi, the Almighty God. But they also believe that their patron god, Ratu Sakti Pancêring Jagat, is the manifestation of this Almighty God. Some of them even believe that Shiva, Vishnu, and Brahma are the sons of their patron god, Ratu Sakti Pancêring Jagat.

Because of the attempts for centuries to Hindu–ize Trunyan, the people are reluctant to tell strangers that Hindu gods are not the principal gods worshipped inside their main temple.[4] The Indian gods in the main temple are considered the lesser gods; and their permanent abodes (*pêlinggih*) were built in the least holy front courtyard of the Trunyanese main temple, the Bali Désa Pancêring Jagat Bali temple. These lesser gods are Bêtara Gangga and Bêtara Indra, Bêtara Sri and Bêtara Rambut Sadana. Although the permanent abodes of the latter two gods are located in the holiest part of the main temple (the *Pênaleman*), they are nothing but the subordinates of the patron god and his consort.

Before tourists came to Trunyan, the village's limited fame was due to an article written in 1933 by Walter Spies, a German artist, describing a festival unique to Trunyan, the Saba Gêdê festival.[5] Since Saba Gêdê is held on the fourth full moon of the Balinese calendar, it also goes by the calendrical name of Purnama ing Kapat.

There are two kinds of Saba Gêdê (Purnama ing Kapat) festivals: the male or Kapat Langang, and the female or Kapat Wadon. These two festivals are held on alternate years. The Kapat Lanang precedes the Kapat Wadon, and this order must always be followed. Thus if the Kapat Lanang festival is cancelled due to unpropitious circumstances (such as the birth of twins, especially of opposite sex which is believed to cause a state of impurity or *sêbêl*), the following year Kapat Wadon will not occur, but rather Kapat Lanang.[6] Though both festivals are supervised by the traditional village council, they are conducted by two different associations: the Kapat Lanang is organized by the *têruna*, or unmarried boys' association, and the Kapat Wadon is organized by the *dêbunga*, or unmarried girls' association.

The temple is decorated distinctively for the two Saba Gêdê festivals. For the Kapat Lanang, the villagers erect a sacred wooden ferris wheel in front of the main temple gate. For the Kapat Wadon, many colorful pagoda-like structures made from rice cakes are set in the front courtyard of the main temple.

Additionally, the two festivals are concerned with different themes. In the Kapat Lanang festival, the *têruna* (unmarried boys' association) performs a sacred pantomime called Ilèn-Ilèn Bêtara or just Bêtara Bêrutuk. The myth of the first meeting of the Trunyanese high god, Ratu Sakti Pancêring Jagat, and his future consort, Ratu Ayu Pingit Dalam Dasar, is ritually dramatized. For Kapat Wadon, the wives of the members of the traditional village council weave a long piece of white cloth. This is dyed orange by the *dêbunga* or unmarried girls' association. This long cloth (*wastra*) is then used to clothe the huge ancient stone statue of the patron god. The members of the *dêbunga* are forbidden to have sexual intercourse during the twelve days prior to the dyeing ceremony. If a girl does not observe this proscription, her behavior will be known: the result of her dyeing will be uneven and of a poor quality. She will be discharged from the *dêbunga* association. Thus the Kapat Wadon is a kind of virginity test ceremony.[7]

The preparation of the 1976 Saba Gêdê started from the second full moon of the Hindu Balinese calendar.[8] At this time, the *têruna* (unmarried boys' association) carried the Trunyanese gods and goddesses on wooden palanquins down the megalithic stone steps to Paruman Hill on the outside of the ancient Batur crater. On this hill, it is believed that the gods have a three-day meeting to plan the coming Great Festival. The results of the meeting are then conveyed to the villagers by a woman who goes into a trance.

Since all proceeded propitiously, the following month on the third full moon, the members of the unmarried boys' association went to the ghost cave (*Song Rêrindi*) to gather white clay. This would be used to make the face and body powder for the patron god's statue and for the actors in the sacred pantomime Bêtara Bêrutuk. To make the powder, the young unmarried boys mixed the clay with other materials, such as saffron, rice flour, and perfumed oil.

On the same day, the married villagers began their preparations for a journey to the neighboring towns and villages to do the *murub*, a kind of bartering of a begging nature. Before leaving Trunyan, the participants went first to the village council to obtain a kind of offering of uncooked rice, *malang pênglantih*, which had been blessed.

This was strewn on potatoes, garlic, shallots, red beans, and other agricultural products, which would subsequently be bartered. *Murub* is considered to be degrading. Yet the Trunyanese must do it as a punishment for the wrong done by their patron god's minister, Pasêk Trunyan, who stole a gamelan and gave it to his master, instead of to the rightful owner, his master's brother. For this he was cursed by the patron god's father, King Dalam Solo.[9]

The Trunyanese believe that the rice offering exerts influence over the people of the lowlands, and that this results in a more generous exchange of rice products from the fertile lowland valleys. The rice thus obtained is used to feed the hundreds of visitors from the neighboring villages who attend the Kapat Lanang festival to pay homage to the Trunyanese patron god, as their ancestors had done for centuries.

Fifteen days later, on the third dark moon (Tilêm Kêtêlu), all the members of the *têruna* association gathered in the main village of Trunyan. From here, they journeyed in search of dry banana leaves which would be used as costumes by the actors in the sacred pantomime of Bêtara Bêrutuk. For the trip, the boys have to bring their own food. Their hosts will provide them with no food, save for the bananas that grow in their gardens. Still the people of the host villages welcome the Trunyanese; and, it is believed, through extending welcome they will receive the blessing of the Trunyanese patron god.

The twenty-one actors in the sacred pantomime of Bêtara Bêrutuk will each need ninety-nine leaves. These leaves must be of a certain kind, *biu kukun*, those that have dried on the tree. These dry leaves are procured from villages of a long-standing relationship with Trunyan, the subvillages of Songan, named Pinggan and Blandingan. First the young boys go to Pinggan. And if they are unable to gather a sufficient quantity of leaves, or if something unfortunate makes the village impure (such as the birth of twins), then they must fetch the leaves from Blandingan. If they are unable to gather leaves in the latter village, they must journey to the village of Bayung Gêdê which lies in the southern part of the subdistrict of Kintamani. After they have gathered the requisite number of leaves, they return to Trunyan and store the leaves in the Bèlagung Maspait pavilion, which is located in the outer courtyard of the main temple, Ratu Sakti Pancêring Jagat Bali.

Ten days prior to the Kapat Lanang festival, the virgin boys build a temporary shed of bamboo and grass. This shed (*pêkêmit*), to be used as the boys' dormitory during the festival, is built on the lefthand side of the permanent abode of the patron god, which is located in the innermost part of the temple courtyard. The first task which they will have to perform while staying in this shed will be to clean the ancient and holy *bêrutuk* masks. These masks, which they will wear during the performances on the last two days of the festival, are believed to come directly from heaven. For this reason, they are not called *tapêl* (mask), but *druwé* (holy object that came from heaven) Bêrutuk. The identities of the masks, save for that of the patron god and his first wife, are no longer known.

The Kapat Lanang festival which I observed in 1976, formally fell on October 8. But the festival really began three days prior, on October 5, and ended seven days after the fourth full moon, on October 14. On the first day of the festival, there was the Nyêjêp ceremony, also known as Tabuh Rah. This ceremony was conducted in front of the permanent abodes of the goddesses Ratu Ayu Manik Surat Mêpura Kaoh and Ratu Ayu Manik Surat Mêpura Kangin. The important part of this ceremony involved the pouring of chicken or duck blood on the earth around the goddesses' dwellings. This blood libation was intended for the god, Ratu Gêdé Dalam Dasar, who is lord of the underworld and the lake. This god is also the firstborn of the Trunyanese patron god and his first wife, the goddess Ratu Ayu Pingit Dalam Dasar. After the Nyêjêp ceremony, the villagers are allowed to slaughter the animal which will be used for the offerings to the gods in the festival.

On the second day of the festival (October 6), the *mêkala-kalan* ceremony was conducted at the front gate of the main temple. This ceremony has the function of purifying the villagers and all the ceremonial paraphernalia, the palanquins, umbrellas, and all the symbols of the gods and goddesses. For this ritual purification, the virgin boys used a concoction of violet-colored sugarcane juice which was mixed with honey and aromatic lemon (*C. hystrix*). This mixture was prepared during the third full moon in the Ngêjêroan Keramasan ceremony when the face and body powder for the patron god and the Bêrutuk performers was made. Along with the ritual powder, this purifying liquid had been stored in the pagoda abode of the patron god. After the ritual articles were cleansed, the liquid was drunk by the workers; it is believed to have magical powers for healing any kind of illness or disease. Next a duckling was sacrificed and the villagers were allowed to enter the main temple through its main gate. The rest of the ceremony, starting at 5:00 P.M., lasted about an hour.

The activities of the third day (October 7) began about 2:00 in the afternoon and lasted for an hour. Pêkidêh was a religious procession of the sacrificial animals—a young black water buffalo whose horns had just grown, a pig, a goat, chickens, and ducks—around the inner courtyard of the main temple. The animals were decorated with colorful cloth, little mirrors, and flowers.

On the fourth night, which fell exactly on the fourth full moon of the Hindu Balinese calendar, the sky glowed with the mystical radiance of the full moon. The members of the village council woke early in the morning to sacrifice the water buffalo in the Bah Kêbo ceremony. The head, the forelimbs, the bones, and the hide would be reconstructed as a whole animal and given as the *bantên ayu* offering to the patron god. The flesh would be distributed to the villagers.

After the offerings were arranged in front of the permanent abode of the patron god (*méru*), the virgin boys gathered all the gods' symbols from the main temple and from extended family temples, placed them on palanquins, and bore them to the inner court of the main temple. All of the other gods' ritual belongings were placed in the pavilion-like altar which was located in front of the high god's permanent abode. The gods' symbols would remain in the two pavilion altars for two days so that the gods could make obeisance to their king.

Other important ceremonies were executed on the fourth day (October 8). The patron god's statue was smeared with the body and face powder which had been prepared on the third full moon. Also on this day the decorated bamboo rods (*pênjor*) were erected in the three most important places in the main temple: in front of the patron god's permanent abode in the innermost courtyard (*méru*); in front of the altar, *sanggar agung*, in the outer courtyard of the main temple; and at the front of the main temple's entrance.

The sacred ferris wheel was erected in front of the main gate to the temple. The ferris wheel (*jantra*) could only be ridden by virgin boys. For the *dêbunga*, or virgin girls, a plain small bamboo swing was erected. The ferris wheel and the bamboo swing offer a symbolic contrast between the male and the female. While the ferris wheel is more than four meters tall, the bamboo swing is only one and one-half meters in height. And while the ferris wheel is sacred, the bamboo swing is profane. The former is carefully dismantled a month after the festival and stored for the next Kapat Lanang; and the latter is thrown away and a new one is made for the next festival. To illustrate the sacred nature of the ferris wheel, we should note that a special ceremony must be enacted on the fourth dark moon: an adult pig must be sacrificed to the ferris wheel.

On the fifth day (October 9), there is only a small ceremony consisting of an offering of flowers along with carved young coconut fronds.

The Ngigêl Gayung Ngaji Bêtèn, held on the sixth day (October 10), was a sacred dance with a wine libation offered to the god who was the firstborn of the patron god and his first wife Ratu Ayu Dalam Dasar. This god, Ratu Gêdé Dalam Dasar, is the god of the earth and the lake. The members of the traditional village council performed the water scoop dance (Ngigêl Gayung) in the baris or warrior-style movement. They were accompanied by the mystical tone of the sacred iron xylophone, sêlunding. Each dancer carried a small metal water scoop filled with palm wine; and while dancing would pour out some drops of the wine. The dance consisted of three parts. In the first part, the sixteen members of the traditional village council from the saing class danced under the leadership of the moiety leaders, the bau mucuk. For the second part, two members of the traditional village council from the saing nêm class performed. And for the third part, four people danced; two from the bau mucuk, one from bau merapat, and one from the saing nêm class.

On the seventh day of the festival (October 11), the mêncêngkrama ceremony (also known as mêgama) was performed. All of the belongings of the gods and goddesses which had been displayed on the pavilion altars in front of the méru were moved to a stone dais under the great sacred banyan tree. Here the members of the traditional village council performed the Ngigêl Gayung dance and played the adu tingkih game as entertainment for the gods and goddesses. To play the game, two candle nuts, encased in hard shells, are dashed together until one breaks.

The gods were also entertained by the mating dance of a wild rooster and a wild hen. This dance was enacted by the moiety leaders of the traditional village council. Each wore on his head a copper statue of either the wild rooster or the wild hen; and each was protected by a ceremonial umbrella held by a virgin boy. The sacred dance ended when the other virgin boys in the arena engulfed the dancers, lifted them high on their shoulders, and carried them to the dais where the gods were supposed to sit. Then the copper chickens were returned to their palanquin, and the gods were carried in a procession to the edge of the lake in the Danu Kuning area. Here, it was believed, the gods could purify the village and its contents with the holy water taken from the lake. The day ceremony ended when the gods were returned to the two pavilion-like altars in front of the high god's permanent abode (méru).

On the eighth day of the festival (October 12), the first Bêtara Bêrutuk pantomime was enacted. Early in the morning, virgin boys began sweeping and burning all the trash found in the inner courtyard of the temple. Here the first act of the drama would be staged. Others were repairing their ten-meter-long whips used in the pantomime. And still others were spreading the sugar palm mats on the ground for the ceremonial meal which would be eaten by the players before the pantomime began. During the meal, the boys separated into two groups. One group sat in a row facing the hill (*kaja*); these were the members of the male moiety. The other group sat in a row parallel to the former, but they faced the lake (*kalod*); these were the members of the female moiety. The ceremonial meal of steamed rice, baked chicken, and pork was set in two rows in front of each group.

After the meal, the players went into the shed to don their Bêtara Bêrutuk costumes. The boys had to take off all their clothes, and then put on the loin cloth made of batik sarongs. The members of the traditional village council assisted the boys in arranging their costumes, which consisted of a skirt and coat of dried banana leaves.

In costume, the actors of the high god and his consort, and his prime minister, entered the *méru* to ask for the blessing of the patron god. The rest of the players went to the permanent abode of the goddess to pray that all would be well, and to receive the blessing of the village priest, Mangku Madias. After this was done, the boys went back to their temporary shed to don the sacred masks.

Around 11:30 A.M. the sacred pantomime commenced. One by one, the players were ushered into the outer part of the inner courtyard of the main temple. First came the patron god, followed by his consort, and then the other characters. The patron god and his consort stood apart from the other characters, and on their heads they wore a pair of bamboo flowers that resembled horns.

In an instant, the atmosphere in the temple was electrified. As soon as the gods were released by their ushers, they dashed wildly about, whipping everyone in their path. They ran in small dainty steps, and occasionally lifted their skirts to show a buttock. Most of the spectators fled. If caught they would be whipped mercilessly, and released only when they said, "*Nawêgan nunas ampun*" ("I beg for your forgiveness").

Yet not everybody avoided the bêrutuk's whip. Some were looking forward to the thrashing. The husband of a barren wife could bring fertility to the union through a whipping. People who were ill also chose to be whipped so that their sickness would be driven away for good. These people who desired a whipping would taunt the players, trying to guess their identities. When this was done, the players became furious and violent. Some of them even went into a fit of trance and had to be subdued by the other virgin boys who were not taking part in the pantomime that day. After being sprinkled with holy water and fanned with bamboo leaf sheets by the *pêngopét* (the boys who were to fan the players when they got hot), the angry gods grew tranquil.

Another fit of violence was brought on if someone was standing, instead of squatting, in front of the permanent abode of the patron god, or that of his consort. The boy who acted the role of the patron god became so violent that he could only be subdued by six people. And he would become tranquil only when his present and beloved consort, Ratu Ayu Pingit Dalam Dasar, was brought to him.

The Bêtara Bêrutuks were very nice to young children. If a child approached them, they would give him a dried banana leaf from their costumes. The leaves were used by the Trunyanese as protection from evil and a source of good luck. Should an adult want a dried banana leaf, he would have to steal it from the players.

Throughout the sacred pantomime, there was a procession of villagers, mostly women, who carried beautiful pagoda-like offerings on their heads. These they bore to the innermost court of the temple, to the permanent abode of the patron god and his consort. The people in this procession came from Trunyan and from other villages, from Kêdisan, Buahan, Abang, Songan Mètrê, Candi Kuning (Bêdugul), and Pêngotan.

The sacred pantomime is marked by the absence of gamelan music. Instead there is the laughing and the shrieking of the spectators. Precisely at 3:30 P.M. the *pêngopèt* (the boys charged with the care of the dancers) and the members of the traditional village council captured all the Bêrutuk players, took them to the shade of the vast banyan tree, and cooled them with fans. All the whips were wrested from them, and they were given long bamboo poles with stinging nettle tips.

Each player, accompanied by two members of the traditional village council, was led through the gate of the outer temple courtyard. The atmosphere, at that time, was extremely intense and exploded when the players passed through the gate of the inner temple courtyard and stampeded toward the gate of the outer courtyard of the temple. The players were followed closely by all the spectators, and the pounding of their feet sounded like thunder. When they reached the outer courtyard gate of the temple, the players grew calm again. In *baris*, or warrior dance steps, they entered the temple.

Then the patron god prayed on the Bèlagung Maspait pavilion; while his brother-in-law, the minister of religious affairs (Ratu Sakti Mêduwe Gama Ujung Sari), prayed on the Bèlagung Tilêm pavilion. The two gods prayed in a sitting position, legs folded in front; they faced the hills (*kaja*) which were located behind their main village. Before paying tribute with their hands together on their heads, they dipped their fingers in an earthenware bowl full of coconut oil. The oil was used to purify themselves and the other players from the evil demons who lurked in their village. From this moment, the players were freed from demonic possession; and in the second act of the pantomime, no one would fall into a trance.

Following this rite of purification, the two gods joined the other players in paying homage to the other gods whose symbols were gathered in the Sêmangèn Têruna pavilion. After the prayers were offered, the Bêrutuk players began anew to chase the spectators. This time they used their bamboo rods tipped with stinging nettles. Shrieks and laughter filled the air.

At 4 P.M. all the Bêrutuk players—save for the high god, his consort, and his minister of religious affairs—were disarmed of their bamboo rods, and forced to sit in a row in front of the Balé Maspait pavilion. Their costumes had been untied so that they could be easily stripped from the players' bodies at the appropriate time. Their masks were removed, and their faces, especially around their eyes, were covered with grey volcanic dust.

The spectators gathered in the outer courtyard of the temple and were safe now from the fierce players, who by this time had become very meek. Only two could be seen walking the courtyard as keepers of the peace. At this moment, the gods were believed to be in the midst of them, to see the climax of the holy drama, where the first meeting and the mating game ended with the patron god raping his future consort. For this scene, the spectators were asked to squat as a gesture of full respect.

This last act, called the *mêtambak*, is more a game than a dance. The two gods faced each other, but were separated as if by an invisible line drawn from the decorated bamboo pole (*pênjor*) to the lake. The goddess, standing on the north side, tried to cross the invisible line; but did not do so for fear of being caught by the god on the other side.[10] At times, in an attempt to cross the line, the goddess moved to the side in a classical ballet step, *bâtement couru*. Followed closely by the god, she would suddenly give up her attempt and squat. Her movement was immediately mirrored by the patron god. And in this squatting position, they rubbed noses, the way Trunyanese kiss each other. Their bodies trembled terribly. Suddenly, she stood up, and tried again to cross the line. Again she was thwarted for her suitor was ready to clasp her in his arms.

For this last act, the two players had already stripped off their banana-leaf skirts. And without these encumbrances, they had more freedom of movement. They were garbed only in their banana-leaf coats, which had been untied. To keep them on, the players had to hold them with their hands, as if they were wings. The image created by their movements in this act gave the impression of two chickens in a mating dance.

Around 5 P.M. the tension gradually increased. The spectators in the outer courtyard of the temple were asked to clear a space between the inner courtyard gate and the main gate that led to the lake. As dusk fell and dark clouds began to gather over the crater, the movement of the players became more intense, which made the audience stand. The act abruptly ended. Without warning the goddess made a dash across the line and was caught by the watchful god in a lustful embrace of both arms and one leg. For a brief moment, they stood there majestically on their discarded banana-leaf coats, their naked bodies gleaming with sweat.

Through the act of copulation, the god and goddess brought fertility to the village, to the people, to the livestock, and to the plants. To ensure this fertility, the villagers were prepared to catch the goddess when she escaped the patron god. A failure to capture the goddess not only resulted in the absence of fertility for the village, but for the two boys as well: they would never be allowed to marry, and would become old bachelors (*têruna tua*).

As abruptly as the love act occurred, so also did it end. The naked god and goddess rushed to the lake and leapt into the cold water. The virgin boys ran after them into the lake, stripping off their loin cloths but keeping their masks propped on the top of their heads. And finally the spectators followed in a wild stampede that shook the village ground. Some people remained behind to collect the costumes and to store them in the innermost court of the main temple for the performance on the following day.

After cleaning themselves, the players were given fresh clothing by their relatives who stood at the lake's edge. The boys then placed their masks in huge bamboo baskets, and sat down to a ceremonial meal. Since this was the first performance, the boys had to remain in their shed for one more night. While the boys were isolated in this temporary shelter, the girls were having a good time in the front courtyard of the main temple. They watched the performances of the folk drama, *arja*, the *baris* dance, and *topèng*.[11] According to local belief, there would be a shower after the *mêtambak* scene. The sky was cloudy and there was a drizzle during the night, but it did not rain.

On the ninth day of the festival (October 13), the virgin boys rose early to prepare for the second performance of the Bêtara Bêrutuk pantomime. This performance was identical to the first, except that there were more actors, nineteen instead of eleven. Arrangements were made so that boys who had not performed the first day got a turn the second day.

On this day, the spectators had doubled in number. City dignitaries and people from other villages were attending. To entertain them, the Trunyanese provided a banquet. At the end of the performance, after discarding their banana leaves at the edge of the lake, and bathing in the cool waters of Lake Batur, the virgin boys were released from their restrictions. They could join in the feast, which lasted until early in the morning.

On the tenth day of the festival, the members of the traditional village council performed the closing ceremony, the *nyinêp*. All the belongings of the gods, except those of Ida Ayu Maospait, were removed from the Semangen Têruna pavilion and returned to their permanent abodes. The symbols of the goddess Ida Ayu Maospait, which were two sets of iron xylophones (*sêlunding*), would be returned to their permanent abode after they were used in the ceremony. The members of the traditional village council danced to the music of the iron xylophones around the sacred ferris wheel. Then the ferris wheel was dismantled and stored in the Bèlagung Patêmon pavilion of the main temple. This ceremony, Mantèning Ayunan, occurred on the fourth dark moon and marked the end of the Kapat Lanang festival.

The result of cultural contact on Trunyan has been what Robert Redfield defined as adaptation.[12] The Trunyanese have assimilated some foreign cultural elements and have worked them into their culture in a meaningful way. To achieve this end, they have even clothed their native gods in the garb of the dominant culture. They have been successful due to their passive resistance attitude and to geographical isolation. Thus, even though the Trunyanese profess Hinduism, they still retain their cultural identity. And they must still be identified as Bali Aga, and not as Bali Hindu or Indian. The Hindu proselytizers have only succeeded in changing the garb of the Trunyanese folk religion. They have not changed the Trunyanese themselves, who still profess their forefathers' religion which is based on ancestor worship, fertility cult, and animism.

The Saba Gêdé festival commemorates the anniversary of the Trunyanese patron god, and is part of their native belief system. This yearly festival honors the first meeting of their patron god—who is believed to be the son of the Javanese king Dalâm Solo—and his consort—who is believed to be the daughter of a goddess who was temporarily exiled in Trunyan thousands of years ago.[13] This is all dramatized in the Bêtara Bêrutuk pantomime.

At this point, we should differentiate between the function of the festival itself and the function of the sacred pantomime. The latter, though part of the festival, has a separate function of its own. The sacred pantomime magically ensures fertility to the village and all within it. This is necessary due to the unpredictable nature of the god who is in charge of the fertility of the Batur area. At times, he postpones the rain, even though the dry season should have passed.

The Saba Gêdé festival itself has at least two functions. Through staging this festival, the Trunyanese can give thanks to their patron god for his protection against the evil powers of the supernatural world and the unfriendly forces of the natural elements, such as the potential eruption of the Agung and Batur volcanoes. And the second function provides for the revitalization of the Trunyanese Bali Aga identity.

NOTES

1. The author had the opportunity of viewing the Kapat Lanang, a portion of the Saba Gêdê festival, in October 1976. This study is based on the observations made at that time.

2. For a more detailed discussion see James Danandjaja, *Kebundayaan Petani Desa Trunyan di Bali* (Jakarta: P. T. Pustaka Jaya, 1980), p. 60; and idem, "The Trunyanese, the People Who Descended from the Sky," in *Dynamics of Indonesian History*, ed. Haryati Soebadio and Carine A. du Marchie Sarvaas (Amsterdam, New York, Oxford: North-Holland Publishing Company, 1978), pp. 41–60. We should note that the Hindu influence on the Trunyanese culture calls into question the classification of R. Goris, who says the Trunyanese are "non Hindu Balinese," and J. L. Swellengrebel, who says they are "non-Javanized Hindu Balinese." See R. Goris, "The Position of the Blacksmiths," p. 379; and J. L. Swellengrebel, "Introduction," p. 31, both in *Bali: Studies in Life, Thought, and Ritual*, ed. W. F. Wertheim (The Hague, Bandoeng: Royal Tropical Institute, 1960).

3. W. F. Stutterheim, *Indian Influence in the Lands of the Pacific* (Weltevreden, Koninklijke Bataviaasch Genootschap van Kunsten en Wetenschappen: G. Kolf and Co., n.d.), p. 7.

4. Ironically, the Hindu proselytizers who become the Hindu priests in Trunyan end up serving the Trunyanese native gods.

5. Walter Spies, "Das Grosse Fest im Dorfe Trunyan (Insel Bali)," in *Tijdschrift voor Indische Taal-, Land en Volkendunde*, 73, pp. 220–48, with additional notes by R. Goris, pp. 249–56. Walter Spies observed the Kapat Lanang festival.

6. According to Covarrubias, among the Bali Hindu the birth of twins, especially of the opposite sex, is considered to be a state of impurity (*sêbêl*). It is believed that the twins have already committed incest while in their mother's womb. See Miguel Covarrubias, *Island of Bali* (New York: Alfred A. Knopf, 1937), p. 126. Furthermore, according to Jane Belo, in bearing twins of the opposite sex, a Balinese of the lowest caste commits a double offense to the gods. Besides incest, they as a human being have emulated animals by having more than one offspring at the same time. See Jane Belo, "A Study of Customs Pertaining to Twins in Bali," in *Tijdschrift voor Indische Taal-, Land-, en Volkenkunde* 75: 483–549.

7. For a detailed description of Kapat Wadon, see James Danandjaja, *Kebudayaan Petani Desa Trunyan di Bali*, pp. 385–86.

8. Like other Balinese, the Trunyanese use two kinds of calendars simultaneously. The Hindu Balinese calendar consists of twelve solar-lunar months, running from the new moon (*tilêm*) to the full moon (*purnama*). The Javanese-Balinese calendar consists of thirty weeks, of seven days each. For a further study of these calendars, see R. Goris, "Holidays and Holy Days," in *Bali: Life, Thought, and Ritual*, pp. 115–29.

9. The legend relates how Pasêk Trunyan embezzled the gamelan which was supposed to be given to his master's brother, the King of Tampak Siring. Instead Pasêk Trunyan gave it to his master, Ratu Sakti Pancêring Jagat. And for this he was cursed by his master's father, Dalam Solo, who was the King of Java. And as a result of this curse, Pasêk Trunyan could have no descendants. Since the King of Trunyan was involved in this scandal, his descendants, the present-day Trunyanese, must perform this degrading *murub* once a year.

10. Elsewhere in Indonesia this kind of children's game can also be found. In Jakarta, it is called the *galasin*; while in Central and East Java, it is called the *gobak sodor*.

11. For a more detailed description of these Balinese folk dramas and dances, see Beryl de Zoete and Walter Spies, *Dance and Drama in Bali* (Kuala Lumpur: Oxford University Press, 1973), pp. 196–205 (*Arja* drama); pp. 165–74 (*Baris* dance); and pp. 178–95 (*Topèng* drama).

12. Robert Redfield, Ralph Linton, and Melville J. Herskovits, "Memorandum on the Study of Acculturation," *American Anthropologist* 38 (1936): 152.

13. For a more detailed description of this legend, see Danandjaja, "The Trunyanese," pp. 40–42.